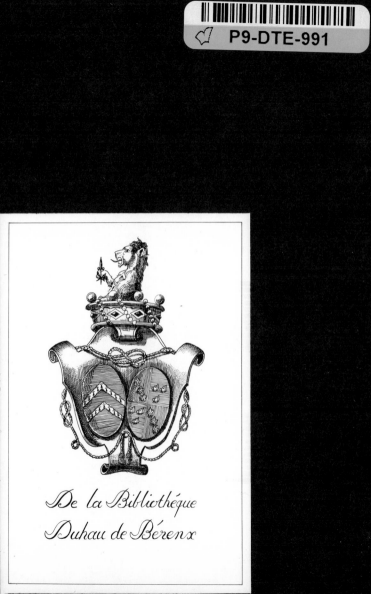

De la Bibliothèque
Duhau de Bérenx

Pour Francis
Très affectueusement
M
Juin 2009

The Empress of Farewells

Also by Prince Michael of Greece:

Crown Jewels of Europe
Louis XIV: The Other Side of the Sun
Sultana
Living with Ghosts: Eleven Extraordinary Tales

PRINCE MICHAEL OF GREECE

The Empress of Farewells

The Story of Charlotte, Empress of Mexico

Translated from the French by Vincent Aurora

Atlantic Monthly Press
New York

Originally published in French under the title *L'Impératrice des Adieux*
by Éditions Plon, Paris.

Published simultaneously in Canada
Printed in the United States of America

FIRST EDITION

Library of Congress Cataloging-in-Publication Data
Michael, Prince of Greece, 1939–
    [Impératrice des adieux. English]
    The Empress of Farewells : the story of Charlotte, Empress of Mexico /
Prince Michael of Greece ; translated from the French by Vincent Aurora.
        p. cm.
    ISBN 0-87113-836-0
    1. Maximilian, Emperor of Mexico, 1832–1867.   2. Empresses—Mexico—
Biography.   3. Emperors—Mexico—Biography.   4. Mexico—History—
European intervention, 1861–1867.
    I. Title.

F1233.M45 M5313 2002
972.07'092—dc21
[B]   2001055966

Atlantic Monthly Press
841 Broadway
New York, NY 10003

02 03 04 05   10 9 8 7 6 5 4 3 2 1

From M. to M.,
and for Patrick, the inspiration.

The Empress of Farewells

1

Although it was August, it was pouring rain, and though the family had gathered for the "joyful wedding," the wails were heartbreaking. The father, mother, four sons, and three daughters were so closely knit that they still could not accept the idea that one of them was leaving to get married. Nonetheless, they were forced to resign themselves to the inevitable.

This was not an ordinary family. Indeed, it was the First Family of Europe. The Orleans belonged to the House of France. The father was king of the French, Louis-Philippe. Strangely enough, considering his lineage, he got along beautifully with his wife Marie-Amelie, to whom he had always remained faithful.

❊   ❊   ❊

The revolution that had brought him to power two years earlier had made waves throughout Europe, and had thrown the king of Holland's states into chaos. Belgium had seceded from them to declare independence, and for this reason, Belgium is to some degree the child of France, if not of Louis-Philippe. But England had been fiercely opposed to one of his sons assuming the crown in Brussels. In the end, it was England's candidate, Leopold of Saxe-Coburg, who was permitted to become king of the Belgians, provided he marry one of Louis-Philippe's daughters. Reasons of state imposed this marriage.

It was the summer of 1832. Louis-Philippe had decided that the ceremony would take place in the Château de Compiègne. He and his family had arrived the day before, their eyes already red, and already it was raining. Marie-Amelie had managed to enjoy herself somewhat by visiting the castle from basement to rafters, counting its five hundred beds herself. Louis-Philippe, whose cheapness was legendary, had ordered no restorations, despite the grandeur of the event. The suites would have to do, even if they were run-down and smelled slightly of mold.

That afternoon, Louis-Philippe went down to the courtyard to welcome his future son-in-law, Leopold of Saxe-Coburg, first king of the Belgians, who had made everyone wait for hours when his procession fell behind schedule. Now, finally, he was introduced to his fiancée, Louise. The girl, twenty years old, cast a frightened glance at the imposing forty-year-old, whose cold expression and starchy manners made him look even older than his years. He spoke French slowly, with a thick German accent. His eyes were piercing, his hair sparse and combed over onto his forehead, and his beardless chin was nearly square. The uniform he wore only accentuated his stiffness. Impassively, almost indifferently, he observed the young woman who was soon to become his wife. Of the three princesses of Orleans, she was the one who most resembled her mother, which is to say she was no beauty. Still, less bony than Marie-Amelie, she had so much gentleness in her expression, so much grace in her bearing, that she might have passed for seductive.

The conversation, already awkward, quickly became moribund. Louis-Philippe had the brilliant idea to bring the Belgian king into his private office. Louise's brothers and sisters finally exhaled, making no effort to hide how boring they found their future brother-in-law. Tears flowed anew. But they were forced to put on brave faces, for the "joy" had been organized: a review of the national guard with a great assembly arranged by the country folk in festive costumes, a large feast where the public would be admitted to watch its princes make merry. The receptions for delegations came in quick succession. During one of them, Louis-Philippe, overwhelmed with fatigue, admitted that he was making the greatest sacrifice of his life by giving his daughter to the Belgian king. Immediately realizing his faux pas, he corrected himself: "But she will be happy."

Finally the dreaded wedding day arrived, the ninth of August, 1832, whose phases Marie-Amelie described. At 7:30, she prayed with Louise: "With all my soul, I beg Almighty God to shed His heavenly blessings on that dear child."

At a decisive meeting between Louise and Louis-Philippe, even though they were only hours away from the ceremony, the King asked his daughter one last time if she was truly resolved to marry Leopold. If Louise preferred to change her mind, he said, so be it. He, Louis-Philippe, would take the blame, and one of Louise's sisters would be offered to Leopold in her place. After a pause, she answered that she sincerely found the marriage "reasonable," that all the relatives and friends she trusted had told her it was right, and her mind was made up.

The dressing hour arrived: Louise was wrapped in a sumptuous gown of English lace, adorned with a necklace, earrings, and a diamond medallion that had been given to her by her fiancé. A lace veil was placed upon her head, held fast by diamond clips, and topped with a wreath of orange blossoms.

It was 8:30 in the evening. Everyone had gathered in the King's large office. The fiancés were standing between Louis-Philippe and Marie-Amelie. Louise looked pale and woefully sad. Luckily, the ceremony was short, followed by a Protestant service, for though he was king of a Catholic country, Leopold had remained faithful to the Lutheranism of his childhood.

Now, Louise needed to be left alone with her husband. After supervising her while she said her prayers, Marie-Amelie undressed her daughter and tucked her in. Then, with the usual roundabout phrases, she explained to her what she should expect. Louise cried a great deal and did not want her mother to leave. Finally she fell asleep from faintness, and Marie-Amelie went into the next room to wait for Louis-Philippe to come to bed. Then she retired, exhausted in mind and body.

The next morning, the earliest risers were shocked to see the groom jogging as usual in the park. It was still raining, and on top of everything else, cholera was raging in Compiègne. As if to prove their point, the cavalry came trumpeting in to take their regiment's flag: their colonel had died of the epidemic during the night.

The bride and groom's departure, a few days later, marked the true rupture between Louise and her family. After a great many prayers, blessings, and entreaties, the parents, brothers, and sisters accompanied Louise and Leopold to their coach, and they watched as the treasure and angel of their lives disappeared. Afterward, the king and Marie-Amelie locked themselves in the king's office and cried together.

❈   ❈   ❈

The people of Compiègne could not stop complaining about their sovereign's stinginess. The "great feast" had left them hungry. They had hoped for glittering galas, processions, fireworks, balls whose magical splendor they could have seen through the castle's windows. No, the princes had preferred to keep their joy to themselves, sharing nothing with their good subjects. But those subjects would have been stunned to see the state the First Family was in. Marie-Amelie was softly weeping on Louis-Philippe's shoulder. Princess Marie, closest to Louise, sobbed inconsolably as she repeated how unhappy she was, while even the youngest, Toto, the duke of Montpensier, was struck by his family's sadness and began to cry.

Left alone with Leopold, Louise had no other solace except to pour out in letters to her mother all her longing for the family that she had left behind, and that her husband could never replace. No matter how hard she tried, she could not feel love for him. Friendship, yes, but not love. Even this friendship could not compete with the love she felt for her parents. She admitted it: she had not loved him before she had married him, and she did not love him any more now. If she could have done it over again, she would have remained a spinster, as she had accepted she would become before Leopold's proposal. The worst part was, she hated sex. Could she be frigid, or was it Leopold's fault? How could she judge, since she "knew" no other man? "I am as indifferent to his caresses as I am to his familiarity," she wrote. "I bear it, I let him do what he wants, but I find it more revolting than pleasurable. If he wanted to love me as my brothers and sisters love me, and if he let me love him in the same way, I would be perfectly happy. There are things that still chill and upset me as much as they did the first day. I cannot perform what I would call the animal part of my new situation—it sickens and disgusts me. I think that he notices it, because he often says, 'Doesn't my little wife love me anymore?' I reassure him, but only half-heartedly." If she had to sum up her feelings toward Leopold in a nutshell, it would be with the word "indifference." But she had no other choice than to resign herself to the inevitable: she had been married before God and she was queen.

As soon as she had arrived in Brussels, she'd had to begin her new "career" with barely a moment to adapt to the new situation. Of course, her education had prepared her to become an accomplished princess, but until now, she had performed her duties only with her family. Now she was alone. Shyness paralyzed her, and meeting so many strangers at once, at such a quick pace, was becoming torture. In her own words, she was dying of shame; she felt so ill at ease that she almost fell out of her coach during the official visit to Louvain. Every formal dinner she had to preside over turned into a nightmare.

Louise's first moments were difficult because she felt unsupported. Though Leopold did everything he could to smooth things out for her, the cold man did not know how to show the tenderness that Louise expected, and more importantly, there was another matter, something a woman feels instinctively through the silence and the lies: he loved another, or rather, he had loved another who was now dead but whom he continued to worship beyond the grave.

Leopold, born at the very beginning of the French Revolution, belonged to the lesser branch of the ancient house of Saxe. As the eighth and last child of a sovereign who had reigned over a minuscule duchy, he was part of that herd of countless Germanic princelings who lacked wealth or an apparent future. He was barely sixteen years old when Germany had first been shaken, and then toppled, by the French invasion under Napoleon. He had seen his home, his father's duchy, under occupation. His father had died from the sight of it. Since his elder brother was busy elsewhere,

Leopold had had no choice but to take control of the duchy's foundering affairs. He decided therefore to plead his realm's case before Napoleon's court. There he won over Empress Josephine and her daughter, Queen Hortense; Napoleon himself noticed him, repeating even during his exile at Saint Helena that the young prince was the most handsome soldier he had ever seen, and insisting that he enroll in his army. But Leopold had felt the winds changing direction. He remembered that one of his sisters had married the brother of the tsar, and that another had married the brother of the tsarina dowager. Russia welcomed him with open arms and gave him a command. He fought against the French with courage and intelligence — he was a warrior down to his soul and a magnificent officer.

He entered Paris with the allies, waltzed at the Congress of Vienna, and visited London with the victors. It was then that an unexpected opportunity presented itself. The king of England, George IV, had only one daughter, Princess Charlotte of Wales, who was destined to inherit the crown. She had come to an age at which she herself, her father, the government, and everyone else was looking for a husband for her. Leopold's ambitious heart skipped a beat. He undertook the task of seducing the princess — but to no avail, for she was secretly in love with a handsome Prussian prince who had preferred to slip away. George IV wanted his daughter to marry the son of the king of Holland, a more prestigious suitor than was Leopold. Since Charlotte refused to listen to reason, she soon found herself nearly imprisoned by the ladies-in-waiting on her father's payroll. Her captivity weighed on her so greatly that she came to regard Leopold as a way out. She did not love him, but the marriage would at least bring her freedom. She announced her decision to her father, who shouted his refusal at her in no uncertain terms. Leopold was not a good enough alliance. The Dutchman, for his part, had grown tired of waiting for Charlotte, and had married a Russian grand duchess. In his irritation, George IV permitted Charlotte to be wed to Leopold. Of course, who should have been invited to the wedding but George IV's great friends, the Orleans, who, since the Hundred Days of Napoleon's return to power, had returned to their Twickenham residence. They all rushed to the wedding — Louis-Philippe, Marie-Amelie, and their children, including the young girl, Louise.

Slowly but surely, Leopold's heart supplanted his ambition. He sincerely loved Charlotte; he understood her. Charlotte had been a miserable only child of parents who loathed each other with a passion, and who had savagely separated, leaving Charlotte with a hidden, wounded sensitivity under her curt, even vulgar appearance. Leopold was able to soften and calm her personality, and Charlotte, in gratitude, loved him for it. A few months after their marriage, Charlotte discovered she was pregnant. For her, for Leopold, and for their future subjects, it was an immense joy. Charlotte would declare to any and all she met that when she succeeded her father, she would not settle on Leopold's becoming a prince consort: she would make him a king. And if the nation refused her this, she would just have to retire with him to a cozy country cottage. . . .

When she went into labor, it was long and very difficult. Charlotte gave birth to a boy stillborn from exhaustion. His mother was just as badly off. Several hours later, she died suddenly, in the space of a breath. All of England was heartbroken for their beloved princess, but for George IV, who saw his throne now heirless, it was a tragedy. For Leopold, it was the end of everything. Charlotte's death returned him to his former obscurity.

A few years later, luck seemed to smile upon him once again. A newly independent Greece was seeking a king for itself. Leopold managed to remind the British government of his existence, and they encouraged his candidacy. The throne of Greece was offered to him, and he rushed to accept. But, ever prudent, he placed conditions on his acceptance, and when these were rejected, he withdrew his name.

Another opportunity arose with the arrival of the independence of Belgium. Once again, his candidacy was forwarded, and this time his conditions were accepted. The union between this cold, calculating German and the seething Belgians worked immediately. Leopold sought a wife in haste to give Belgium a dynasty. He chose Louise. But he could not forget Charlotte, and not one day passed that he did not mourn her. He had brought to Brussels with him her portrait that she had given him, and each time he looked at it, he was torn by powerful emotions. Louise may have been jealous of the dead woman, but she had the tact finally to accept her, and even hung another portrait of Charlotte in her suite, an act that won over her husband's friendship.

"Mother, I am happy . . . I love my husband, but above all, I esteem him deeply. Each day adds to my admiration and affection, to the bond of our thoughts and feelings," Louise wrote home. Decidedly, her tone had changed. Leopold and she possessed so many fine qualities that mutual respect, friendship, and trust had at last been able to unite them.

Their first child was a son, ensuring the future of the dynasty. Leopold was crazed with joy, and Louise was happy with her husband's happiness. They named the boy Louis-Philippe, in honor of his grandfather, and the baby seemed to have inherited his grandfather's legendary good health. Everything was going beautifully for the new family when suddenly, ten months later, the baby died inexplicably. After this tragedy, a second child was born, another son, who was named Leopold after his father. Then a third son, Philippe. Louise hoped that the success of two healthy children would put an end to her conjugal duties and pregnancies, but

Leopold was starved for descendants, and she found herself pregnant again, and exhaustingly so.

Near the due date, Queen Marie-Amelie arrived from Paris, accompanied by her favorite lady-in-waiting, the countess of Hulste, Louise's childhood friend. The labor was long and hard. The child, a daughter, was born on the seventh of June, 1840, at one o'clock in the morning. The birth of the royal princess was followed by all the usual pomp: the firing of cannons, lights in windows, delegations, speeches, compliments, and flowers.

The Belgians' happiness was touching. Everyone was overjoyed—except the father. In his mania to insure the dynasty, he had wanted three sons. He was so disappointed that without waiting a week, he ran off to his beloved Ardennes mountains to pout, leaving baby, mother, and grandmother behind.

Meanwhile, in an attempt to appease him, Louise gave the baby the name of his first wife: the little princess would be called Charlotte, after the late princess of Wales. Louise was worried about Leopold's disappointment. Marie-Amelie reassured her with her wisdom, predicting that his fit of anger would not last. The grandmother was right, and in a few years, Charlotte had become her father's favorite. Simply put, she was ravishing: beautiful cheeks, big dark eyes, a delicate nose, a tiny pink mouth, and long black hair. Her eyes were already shining with intelligence and boldness.

Leopold was proud of his daughter's beauty, but he raised her the hard way, as he did his sons: horsehair mattress, wake-up at dawn to a glass of cod liver oil. As soon as she was old enough, Charlotte began classes with a number of professors. Out of respect for his wife, Leopold put Louise in charge of their children's education: catechism both began and topped off long days spent in a succession of classes. There would be no treats: all sweets were forbidden to the children. From Paris arrived whole boxes of toys sent by the grandparents, but the children were given no time to enjoy them. Yet Charlotte did get her share of the delicacies Marie-Amelie sent Louise: grapes from Fontainebleau, tangerines from Malta, figs from Naples, plum preserves, coffee- and vanilla-flavored cashews, Bonnet candies to ward off coughs, Terrier fruit pastry, jams from Tours, lozenges from Vichy. These packages sent from the Tuileries, feverishly ripped open, these letters unsealed with news to be told and retold, comprised Charlotte's greatest entertainment.

When she had first arrived in Brussels, after her marriage, Queen Louise had found her new home to be a sturdy palace, well situated on a hill, but glacially cold, and she had slowly gone about making it more livable. She had set herself up in an office on the second floor, with two windows opening out onto the park, which, though rather small, had been planted with beautiful trees. She'd lined the walls of her office with red wallpaper and portraits of her family, and she let her daughter stay there with her longer than the boys.

While Charlotte played with dolls, Queen Louise lost herself in the classics. Her great passion was serial novels, such as *The Last of the Mohicans,* and she devoured Alexandre Dumas and Eugène Sue. Or, abandoning her books, sometimes she painted. Like all the members of her family, she had a true talent for it. She had taken lessons from Redouté, the rose portraitist; Charlotte watched in awe as beneath her mother's brush appeared blue and yellow pansies, to which she would add a drop of dew. There was no music, for Queen Louise, like all the Orleans, detested it. Though she had met Rossini and Liszt at her parents' house, and though she had received Paganini and Johann Strauss at her own palace, concerts and especially opera bored her to death. This was in glaring opposition to her husband, who, as a good German, lived for music.

On weekends, the entire family went to Laeken Castle, just outside Brussels. Everyone loved it, especially the children, who could run around and frolic in the vast, terraced park. There remained, however, the risk of unpleasant encounters, as the first letter from Charlotte to her father showed: "Dear Father, I have a favor to ask of you. I would very much like for you to lock up the big swan that is so tiresome. I don't go out into the park anymore because it scares me. You are so good and you love your little Charlotte so much that of course, you won't refuse what she asks you."

For vacations, Leopold took his family to Ostende, where swimming in the sea was just coming into fashion. The rather modest royal villa was barely built when word arrived of the visit of their illustrious niece, Queen Victoria of England. When Victoria had assumed the throne at eighteen, her uncle Leopold had been the one she had turned to for advice. She had listened to his suggestions on marriage when, determined to push his own family's interests, Leopold had let slip that his brother's son Albert would make an ideal husband. It was love at first sight, and Victoria had married her first cousin, to the immense satisfaction of her uncle.

The British royal couple had arrived at Ostende on their yacht amid great pomp, escorted by warships. Charlotte had been tingling with excitement. She had stared with curiosity at that little wisp of a woman twenty years her senior, her first cousin, but also a powerful queen. Victoria had brought dolls for the child, and Charlotte immediately got down to work writing a thank-you card in her best English, for the gifted girl spoke English as well as French and German, and later she would learn Italian and Spanish.

Queen Victoria was indeed someone great, but Louis-Philippe was someone greater still. The British court looked provincial in comparison to the court of France, and Queen Louise, who was still close with her family and visited them frequently, brought Charlotte along to see her grandparents, but also to meet her uncles and aunts—all young, beautiful, and brilliant. Aunt Marie, closest to her sister Louise, was the most beautiful; Aunt Clementine, the youngest, was by far the most intelligent. As for the uncles—Nemours, Aumale, Joinville, and Montpensier—they were ardent soldiers, ladies' men who knew how to show interest, even too much interest, in a pretty girl. Nor did they refuse the bawdy joke from time to time, for the Orleans always loved to laugh.

Brussels was a quiet and calm town, so much so that it sometimes seemed deserted, whereas Paris was noisy, overpopulated, and feverish. Aware that he still had to consolidate his recent position, King Leopold sought to maintain a certain decorum, but Belgium could afford only a limited court; Louis-Philippe, on the other hand, despite his frugality and democratic airs, was surrounded by a magnificent court. Though the old complained that after Napoleon's court and that of the Restoration, Louis-Philippe's was a wet blanket, to Charlotte it seemed a dazzling universe. Dashing lieutenants, smiling ladies-in-waiting, innumerable servants wearing the blue and red of the Orleans' livery all crisscrossed the enormous Tuileries palace. It was a string of immense, gilded salons, enormous suites spread out with fabulous collections of paintings, objets d'art, and books that the Orleans, incomparable art patrons that they were, had amassed for generations.

At this court, Charlotte discovered to her great joy that she would be treated as an adult. She attended plays by Molière that actors from the Comédie Française came to perform at the palace. She was even brought to the theater. One day, she had been seated at a window to watch the military review taking place in the gardens, and immediately she felt an attraction for uniforms—and for the French uniform in particular.

Another pleasure was castle-hopping. At Neuilly Castle, true home of the Orleans, uncles, aunts, and cousins played every kind of sport. At the palace of Saint-Cloud, just outside Paris, a beautiful setting in the middle of a vast, fairy-tale park, life was a little more formal. But the family discarded this formality at Eu Castle in Normandy, where the order was more patriarchal, and where everyone swam in the sea and took long walks through forests brimming with game. Yet even with these innumerable diversions and the stimulating company, Charlotte did not forget her father for an instant: "Despite all the fun, I would like to leave, because a month is a long time to go without seeing you . . . I'm sad to be at Saint-Cloud without you, even though I like being here with Grand-father and Grandmother," she wrote.

No matter how much Grandfather Louis-Philippe professed his simplicity, at heart he was a lord, a prince, and a worthy successor to his ancestors, who themselves had been the envy of Europe. Ever talkative, he loved to tell his life story, which was a whirlwind of adventures. Born under Louis XV, he remembered Louis XVI, Marie Antoinette, the court of Versailles: an entire world lost forever. As a leftist general, he had rubbed elbows with the great names of the revolution — Marat, Robespierre, Danton — whom he spoke of as if he had just seen them the day before, as if he were not among the last living witnesses of that terrifying era. He told how, when forced into exile, he had led excursions to Lapland, where he had impregnated a minister's daughter; how he had traveled to the United States, to Cuba. He mentioned his meeting with George Washington and his visit to New Orleans, named in honor of his great-grandfather, the regent.

As a child, he had been raised to adapt to any circumstance, and this allowed him to laugh at the squalor he was subjected to when he wandered as a penniless traveler. Marie-Amelie smiled when he spoke of his engagement to her, and of her introduction into the royal family of Naples, considered the most conservative in all of Europe. But he always ended up returning to the story of the revolution of 1830, which had propelled him to the throne. He had asked for nothing, sought nothing, expected nothing. When Charles X fled with his family, and Louis-Philippe, the duke of Orleans, was approached to succeed him, his first reaction had been to send an emissary to the legitimate heir, the young duke of Bordeaux. But the Bourbons had refused, and the only reason Louis-Philippe had accepted the throne was to save the monarchy—he would not budge an inch from that answer.

Charlotte was too young to understand everything. The descriptions of his travels were fascinating, but the names of the characters meant nothing to her. Yet she felt the listeners' wonderment and concentrated on what she did not grasp. Though he appeared a smiling grandfather, Louis-Philippe actually remained rather indifferent to children, and perhaps, more generally, to all mankind.

It was Grandmother Marie-Amelie who dispensed the real love and warmth. She was in love with her descendants, the little Orleans, and the little Wurtenbergs—Marie's sons—but she had a special place in her heart for the Belgians, as if she could already foresee their future. When she was still a baby, Charlotte had grown inseparably attached to Marie-Amelie. Grandmother created consensus, a quality her husband lacked. Charlotte overheard certain judgments that her father King Leopold let slip about his father-in-law: "Father is truly incorrigible." She also noticed her mother's shrugs and silences. In his trust for his wife, Leopold told Louise of his most serious concern: the mistakes into which Louis-Philippe's intrigues and blindness were leading him.

In this month of February 1848, Leopold was particularly worried, because he saw the danger hanging over his father-in-law's throne, and he knew that Louis-Philippe was unaware of it. Leopold himself had sent trusted messengers to warn him, but Louis-Philippe would have none of it. "Tell my son-in-law that everything is fine, and that I'm sturdy in the saddle," he said. On February twenty-third, Leopold sent one of his right-hand men off to Paris to observe the events he thought to be imminent. Two days later, the Belgian public works minister, Brother Orban, threw a sumptuous ball in Brussels that all of society rushed to attend. It was at the end of a polka that the bombshell struck: revolution had broken out in Paris, and the royal family had run away. They had disappeared.

Leopold had received information several hours earlier from his agent, who had furnished many details. Leopold confided these details to Queen Louise, and in their anxiety, the parents paid no attention to Charlotte, who was sitting nearby and did not miss a word of what they said: the left had organized a ridiculous banquet campaign, and Louis-Philippe's government had outlawed it. The conflict degenerated. Suddenly a riot broke out, the national guard refused to take up arms to defend the throne, and the rioters tore down the fences around the Tuileries. Louis-Philippe, surprised and grown old, did not know what to do. Marie-Amelie begged him to hold on, but the ministers, and even the one son present, the duke of Montpensier, urged him to abdicate. Louis-Philippe sat down at his desk and slowly, deliberately, scratched out a few lines, leaving the throne to his grandson, the count of Paris. Outside, the shouts and gunshots were growing nearer. They had to flee. The exit from the Tuileries was blocked. The old king and his wife trudged across the entire length of the garden. They did not find a coach until they reached the Place de la Concorde, whereupon they left for an unknown destination.

Leopold gave his opinion without ambiguity: "Father should never have abdicated. One must never abdicate, under any circumstance." Little Charlotte listened, and without completely understanding what was going on, she agreed with her father. She would never forget the lesson. The idea that her grandfather and grandmother—who had been so radiant in their palace, surrounded by a respectful court anxious to grant their every wish—should now be transformed into fugitives hunted by the police revolted her. The commoners had invaded and pillaged the Tuileries, tearing the paintings, smashing the objets d'art, shattering the glass, throwing furniture out the windows. As for Neuilly Castle, it had been burned to the ground; nothing remained of Charlotte's enchanted kingdom. She experienced the destruction of those beloved places much as a rape.

Louise trembled for her family, for her brothers and sisters, for her nieces and nephews, but especially for her parents, whose fate was still uncertain. Day after day, she sank into an ever deeper depression that infected Charlotte as well. France had shown its true colors during the revolution, and now it wanted to catch its runaway king again to inflict horrendous punishment. Images from a none-too-distant past haunted Queen Louise. She sent out for news in every direction, all in vain. Louis-Philippe and Marie-Amelie had quite simply disappeared into thin air. Louise could not eat, could not sleep—she was growing ever thinner, ever paler.

Finally a courier brought a tiny letter: "For Louise," it read. The queen of the Belgians recognized her mother's handwriting: "Newhaven, March third, 1848, 1:30. Dear angel of my heart, after nine days of an agony I will tell you of later, I arrive here with your venerable and unhappy father, and I bless God for saving that precious treasure for me. He is well. I am half dead, and I know nothing else about my children. May God protect you and yours, whom I kiss tenderly, and save you from similar misfortune."

Once they had escaped from Paris, Louis-Philippe and Marie-Amelie had made their way in stages toward Normandy. Nearly caught and recognized, they had had to take refuge wherever they could, never knowing what the next hour might bring. They had wanted to board a ship at Le Tréport, but a storm had spoiled their plans. They were just about to be caught when the vice-consul of England had appeared. He had offered them a steamship, which they had boarded, and after several hours, they were in England again.

At the same time, Louise had learned that, many adventures later, the rest of her family was safely out of France. With some hesitation, Queen Victoria had let herself be won over by pity, and had offered the fugitives Claremont Castle, the very same castle that Leopold had occupied when he was married to the princess of Wales, the same one in which she had died in labor. The sad memory matched the sad situation. Nevertheless, Louise said, at least her parents were out of danger.

To make a bad situation even worse, the revolution that had begun in Paris was now spreading throughout Europe. Outrageous rumors were in the air: the French were about to invade Belgium and banish the monarchy. Belgium shuddered, grew uneasy. How would Belgium—this country and this throne, both so new—withstand the storm? Berlin with all of Germany, Naples with all of Italy, were aflame. Even the most solid throne of all was shaken to its foundations: the prince of Metternich, the very symbol of stability, the patriarch of European politics, the permanent chancellor who held his master the emperor of Austria's domains in an iron fist, had been chased out by riots, and while the empire fell to pieces, he had chosen to take refuge . . . in Belgium. Leopold's prudence and the Belgians' common sense had brought this miracle about: almost alone in Europe, Belgium was holding out.

The emotion and anguish hit Queen Louise very hard. The year 1850 had begun very badly, and Marie-Amelie, wallowing in sad thoughts, was worried for her daughter: "Dear child," she wrote, "you must look after your health. At thirty-eight, you simply cannot let sickness develop, it is your sacred duty." She advised tests, she asked for daily reports, she suggested therapeutic treatment. Louise replied that there was no way she would take the waters: "I'll take anything anyone wants here, but I will not leave."

Indeed, Louise did take "anything anyone wants": poultices that burned her back, vials that opened wounds. The best remedy would have been Leopold, but he shied away. Everything annoyed him, and she had the impression that she was to blame. They had ceased all physical contact, so much so that Louise asked herself if he had ever truly been attracted to her. She feared she had grown ugly, prematurely aged. Fleeing her and the children, Leopold isolated himself in the Ciergnon domain he had created in the Ardennes. Louise was too proud, too noble, to complain, though she admitted that if Leopold could find a little more time to spend with her, she might feel better. Charlotte, on the other hand, could not hide how much she missed her father. She wrote him a letter: "I want you to come back soon. I am so sad not to see you . . . I am sad you left, and would like to come see you in the Ardennes. Dear Daddy, will you let me come?" But Daddy would not allow it. Daddy was becoming grumpy: he even forbade his wife to leave for a water-town for the cure Marie-Amelie had again suggested. He trusted only British doctors, so those were the only doctors they consulted.

Louise crossed the English Channel. Her mother was terrified when she saw her: so thin, gray, and weak. Louise believed she was suffering from asthma because she lost her breath when she climbed stairs. The British doctors diagnosed the problem as a simple gastritis and prescribed soothing powders. Unfortunately, Louise could not spend much time with her family, and Marie-Amelie watched in misery as she set off again.

Louise had just returned to Belgium when Charlotte was struck with whooping cough. To quarantine her, Louise brought her to Tervuren Castle, a large, square, colonnaded building, several decades old, built at the top of a wooded hill, not far from Brussels. Instead of improving, Charlotte's condition worsened. A gastric inflammation appeared and her fever increased. Louise spent sleepless nights at her daughter's bedside, all the more upset because Charlotte remained remarkably calm and reasonable. She took all the medicines prescribed to her without protest. She did not cry, she did not moan, but her eyes stared fixedly at a mother slowly sinking into despair.

The young girl was brought back to Laeken Castle. Immediately she began to feel better. She was loaded up with herb-based remedies, and soon enough, she was back on her feet. Louise, on the other hand, emerged from the ordeal exhausted.

The news Marie-Amelie sent her from Claremont further undermined Louise's health: her father Louis-Philippe was growing weaker, his system was deteriorating. At the end of July, he attended the first communion of his grandson and heir, the count of Paris: it was a ceremony he had truly wanted to see, and it gave him back some strength. He seemed twenty years younger. But the improvement did not last. Marie-Amelie knew that all hope was lost. Now she worried for her old husband's eternal soul. For his entire life, he had believed in neither God nor devil, and if he had observed religious practices, it had been purely out of social obligation. Would he die without last rites? Not expecting much, Marie-Amelie proposed summoning a priest. Louis-Philippe understood: "I see it's time for me to go." Not only did he receive the priest, but he confessed and accepted the final sacrament.

On August twenty-sixth, 1850, at eight o'clock in the morning, Louis-Philippe died gently, without suffering, his hand held by the woman with whom he had remained through thick and thin for forty-one years. His gentle end could not console Queen Louise, however, who deeply mourned her beloved father. She was distraught over the loss of a guide, of a loving support, just at the moment when she needed him most.

Louise's condition worsened to the point that, at the end of August, Leopold brought her to Ostende, an incomprehensible decision. Queen Victoria was outraged: why had Leopold always forbidden Louise to leave for a spa when her health had been better and when traveling had been easier, only to drag her out on an uncomfortable trip now? And why Ostende, when just a week earlier, he had refused to bring Louise there to meet Queen Victoria, who had recently arrived for a visit? Uncle Leopold answered Victoria's concerns by saying that while it was true that Louise's intestinal problems were getting worse, she was very courageous, and in any case, she did not realize how bad her condition was. Victoria was shocked that Leopold, under these circumstances, should be taking Louise from the comforts of the capital to a vacation site scarcely equipped to deal with her needs. Leopold protested: Ostende was only four hours away from Brussels, and he wanted to take Louise out to the sea, where the fresh air would do her good.

In reality, Leopold's stubborn insistence on traveling to Ostende could be summed up in a single name: Arcadie, one of the eleven children of an officer from Namur and a woman from Gent. She was not yet eighteen years old when she met King Leopold. Was it at a ball, at a concert, at the opera? One look had been enough to make Leopold fall desperately in love with Arcadie. But it was unthinkable for a minor to be the king's official mistress: she needed to be married off immediately. For this purpose, Leopold had found Frederic Meyer, an employee of his court, and a widower originally from Coburg. The wedding was performed in haste, and the husband expedited far from Brussels. Leopold and Arcadie could at last be together. He was fifty-five, she thirty-six years his junior. Soon the birth of little George would crown this illicit passion.

Unlike her fellow Belgians, Arcadie was not discreet. The Belgians did not appreciate the little palace the king had built for her on Royal Street, right next to his home, nor did they appreciate the many servants in livery, and the overly sumptuous clothes. Arcadie paraded around every day in her magnificent green coach lined with black cushions, aching to be seen. Did Queen Louise know of the existence of her rival? Whatever the truth, she said nothing, but it was inconceivable that in the palace, as in any court, there had not been a single soul good enough to tell her what was happening. Louise was sick, she was suffering physically as well as emotionally, and now she learned that her husband was cheating on her with a woman who put herself on display in the streets of the capital. The tension between Louise and Leopold became heavy and tedious. Was it because all of Brussels knew he had a declared mistress making an utter spectacle of herself that prompted Leopold to whisk Louise off to Ostende? It was one logical explanation.

Nothing but the sentry boxes distinguished the royal villa in Ostende from the others, but that was the sort of modesty that Louise liked so well. She had never enjoyed pomp or decorum, and her illness made her hate these things now. A garden connected the villa to another building with a small suite, where Louise occupied a bedroom on the third floor. From her big mahogany bed, she could see the gray- and white-capped sea. She was so weak that she could no longer climb the stairs, and had to be hoisted up in a wicker basket like a cripple. She coughed; she had a bout with dysentery. She was treated with ass's milk, with rhubarb and iron syrup, with leeches, poultices, quinine, and cod liver oil, but still her strength diminished. The doctors were called to examine her thoroughly, and indeed they did find problems: an endemic diarrhea, an edematous swelling of the lower left limb, a failing liver, a wheezy and dry cough, menstruation that had ceased for several months, abundant perspiration. Half of them believed it was consumption; the other half disagreed. In their ignorance, they could not recognize that Louise was dying of advanced tuberculosis. The weather did not help the situation. It was the beginning of October, and the cold had come early for the season. It was raining, the wind was blowing—it had been madness to bring a consumptive to a wet and stormy seaside. Louise's condition worsened to the point that rumors began to circulate in the capital, and soon throughout the entire country. Ever modest, Louise did not suspect the depth of her popularity. But the Belgians knew their sovereign's good nature. No matter how shyly she remained in the background, they knew she was compassionate, generous, the perfect wife and mother. So when they learned of her condition, they hurried to the churches. All of Belgium was in prayer and candles covered every altar.

At the same time, indignation at the mistress was growing. Arcadie was booed in the streets, and one night, stones shattered the windows of her house. The most intimate of Leopold's counselors came to hate her, and openly said that they would like to "kick her in the backside." Leopold could not understand their resentment. Had he not conscientiously fulfilled his duties? For nearly twenty years, he had worked day and night for the good of his country. He had always shown himself to be an attentive husband, and in this time of crisis, he was spending almost all of his time at Ostende, at Louise's bedside. So why did they hold Arcadie against him?

At the palace, tension was rising every day. It was Arcadie who made the first move. On the eighth of October, she wrote a letter to her royal lover to announce that she was leaving for Germany. It was useless to answer or protest, she added. It was high time, since at Ostende, Queen Louise was dying.

Apprised of the situation, Marie-Amelie took the night boat to Ostende with her sons, daughters, and granddaughters. Leopold invented chores to escape the scene. The suffering this good woman had undergone with such resignation and patience made the situation unbearable for him. His counselors did not mince words: they told him in no uncertain terms that his place was at Louise's side. She did not seem to realize the seriousness of her condition, and in any case, she had always hidden her feelings. But a sentence the countess of Hulste inadvertently blurted out let her know that she was at death's door. She demanded last rites, which Father Guelle, Queen Marie-Amelie's confessor, hastened to administer to her. Still Louise was not at peace. She was thinking about all those she was going to leave behind, about her children, and especially about Charlotte. Hours passed as death slowly overtook her. Louise forgot her own suffering to worry about theirs. She was sorry to cause her family so much pain, and apologized for making them wait so long.

A terrifying storm had risen over the North Sea, the wind wailed in the chimneys, rain beat savagely against the windows, and murmured prayers surrounded the dying woman's bed. Her mother, Marie-Amelie, was holding her in her arms, whispering "my angel, my angel." Louise still had the strength to say "Mama" before she fell back, dead. At the foot of the bed, Leopold sobbed with all his soul. "Her death is as blessed as her life," he mumbled. This man, usually so in control, was now overwhelmed—for in his own way, he had sincerely loved Louise.

All of Belgium went into mourning. Ships sailed at half-mast. Belfries and even trains were covered in black crêpe paper. At ten years of age, Charlotte had lost an attentive and firm mother with an endlessly giving heart, who had surrounded her since birth with love and warmth. Now she found herself alone with an old, icy, and inaccessible father who was often absent, and whom she suspected with her child's instinct had made her mother's life miserable and had hastened her death. And yet, she had always favored her father, probably because she had more in common with that strong and introverted man.

2

On her deathbed, Queen Louise had entrusted Charlotte to her best childhood friend, the countess of Hulste, intimately close to the Orleans, and bound to them by generations of devotion.

The countess of Hulste was an intelligent woman, with a moral strictness able to withstand any test. Her responsibility toward the child perhaps made her accentuate her severity at the expense of her tenderness. She was a dutiful woman who wanted to inculcate that very quality in her ward. She chose Charlotte's entourage, for despite her youth, Charlotte already had her own home, with a senior mistress and ladies-in-waiting. Her tutors taught her Latin, mathematics, geography, history, literature, calligraphy, diction, and eloquence. She practiced horsemanship and swimming reli-

giously. Everyone who met her was impressed by her precocious-
ness, her intelligence, and the keenness of her mind. Charlotte's
religious instruction, which had so worried Queen Louise, was
entrusted to Father Deschamps of the Redemptionist order, a
sermonist of the highest quality. Charlotte was inflamed with a
burning piety that manifested itself in strange ways: "With His
overflowing arms," she wrote, "the Holy Spirit poured His precious
gifts into my heart and flooded it with His light. On that blessed
day that my eyes were opened, that my feet already sunken into
the path to perdition were gently nudged onto the path of righteous-
ness, my mind clouded by the shadows of warmth and of ignorance
saw the heavenly light that cast away the veil enshrouding it. Ah, if
ever I have the misfortune of drifting away from the one who gave
me such abundance, I will no longer be worthy of mercy, for I have
been much more favored than so many others who still moan
under the yoke of the demon and yet who do not recognize their
unhappiness."

These convoluted words from the mouth of a precocious little
girl put others ill at ease. For a child of her age, what could the path
to perdition and the shadows of warmth and of ignorance be? But
Charlotte persisted: "The only thing I want is the one thing I cannot
have—my mind must be poorly formed. I can't overcome my laziness. I fall so easily, I make resolutions only to forget them later. If I
don't watch myself constantly, I can't even recognize myself. No
matter what efforts I make, I have great trouble changing, and sometimes I truly feel so tired when I try to do better. It's terrible to be
discouraged so often. At times, it's like a fever, a delirium that over-
whelms me. And when it passes, I have no idea how it could have
come over me; I think that it is the demon coming to torture me."

What was the "demon" doing with a little girl whom everyone
found well behaved, responsible, and studious? Her words betrayed
some sort of feeling of guilt that neither her guardian, nor her tu-

tors, nor her spiritual director—all humane and balanced individuals—could have imparted to her. They guessed that Charlotte was
setting standards too high for herself, and that she was blaming
herself too harshly for not attaining them. These extremes, this
unconscious desire to see herself as guilty, this pride over striving
for perfection, were strange in a child, troubling and inexplicable.

As a little girl, Charlotte had always been reserved. But her
mother's death had turned her even further inward. She spoke little,
but when she did, she used the silence to think. She reflected, she
got worked up, she tore herself apart. Her mind was seething and
no one noticed.

No one except perhaps for her grandmother, Marie-Amelie.
Charlotte stayed with her in Claremont for a few weeks each year.
At Ostende, when she boarded the ship, her governess, a lady-in-
waiting, and of course her maids accompanied her. Landing at
Dover, she took the express train to Waterloo Station, where she
jumped onto a bus for Echer. At the station, coaches discreetly
decorated with the Orleans' coat of arms were waiting for her. She
crossed the countryside, passed through the high gate and then
through the sumptuous park, whose perfectly maintained lawns ran
down to a large fountain where swans frolicked. In the prairies,
cows, goats, and sheep grazed amid copses of tall trees. She arrived
at the white castle; the coach stopped before the colonnade. Charlotte entered the vestibule paved with marble, where one of her
grandmother's ladies-in-waiting welcomed her. Several foot servants in Orleans livery escorted her into the ground-floor office.
The bookshelves along its walls were overhung with familiar portraits: her own father, Leopold I, and his first wife, Princess Charlotte of Wales, once owners of the castle; King George IV, Charlotte
of Wales' father; but also, closer to the girl, a bust of her grandfather, Louis-Philippe. She registered the scene in a glance. One
aunt was playing a ballad on a Boulle piano, another was scratch-

ing out a letter on a large, silver writing case, and uncles sunken into a red leather couch were reading newspapers or leafing through books on the round table. The cousins were watching images projected by a magic lantern. When she came in, everyone rushed to coddle and kiss her: Uncle and Aunt Joinville, Uncle Nemours, and Uncle Aumale, and the cousins, Ninette, Gaston, Condé, Guise, and her favorite, Cousin Chiquita, Uncle Joinville's daughter.

Informed of her arrival, Marie-Amelie summoned her to her bedroom. Charlotte ran up the staircase four steps at a time, and when she entered the room, Marie-Amelie rose to kiss her. She was tall, thin, and majestic, dressed simply, almost without jewels. She squeezed her granddaughter against her bosom, then sat back down in the big armchair where she spent part of the day, and picked up her tapestry. Charlotte responded to the stream of questions while looking around at the familiar decor, the iron bed worthy of a convent, the big black prie-dieu in the Gothic style, the mass of souvenirs, family photos and etchings that she knew by heart but that never failed to interest her.

Charlotte soon fell into the rhythm of Claremont. Following Marie-Amelie's lead, she woke up early, around 7:30. She attended daily mass with the family before Marie-Amelie disappeared to write her correspondence or do the books. In the afternoon, Marie-Amelie either received visits or read in Charlotte's company; she also took her along on walks in the park or on rides in the countryside. After dinner, Charlotte played with her cousins while her aunts and uncles chatted or played whist.

Meals were simple, compared to those at the Brussels palace. At dinner, there were only two dishes, one of red meat, the other of poultry, with potatoes or green vegetables, followed by a dessert. Sometimes there was game, or pastries brought from France, but these were served mainly for guests. Marie-Amelie took care of everything herself—even household expenditures, as she had when she reigned at the Tuileries—as well as the alms she distributed so generously; her guests' well-being; and finally, gifts. Charlotte always found a beautiful book bound in leather and marked with her monogram waiting in her room for her, or a sewing box, or a precious toiletry kit Marie-Amelie herself had chosen.

Marie-Amelie was the true granddaughter of the glorious empress Maria Theresa. Her mother had been Marie-Caroline of Austria, the scandalous and ruthless queen of Naples. She often thought of her father, who spoke only the Neapolitan dialect, and who would go down to the market to sell the fish he caught, arguing with the fishmongers. She had known Nelson and the garish Lady Hamilton. She had crossed countries at war, she had lived through revolutions, and these dangers had only strengthened her serenity. Confronted with the loose morals of the dying days of the eighteenth century, which lasted until well after the revolution, she had reacted by armoring herself in a steely morality. Her dignity always silenced the smallest criticism. This noble woman was also gentle, humane, and compassionate. Far from being weak, she knew full well what she wanted; she had always been of invaluable help to her husband from behind the scenes.

After Louis-Philippe's death, she became the head of the family. She had to silence her own sorrow in order to keep her children together and take care of the grandchildren. Among the latter, Charlotte was by far her favorite, because she was the daughter of Louise whom Marie-Amelie had adored, but also because she was now orphaned of her mother. She favored Charlotte mostly by devoting more time to her. The other children were somewhat jealous, particularly Cousin Chiquita, who endlessly reminded the family that Charlotte's father was still a reigning king, while theirs belonged to a dethroned dynasty. Chiquita was especially annoyed by Charlotte's pretentiousness and bent low to her in clownish curtseys, calling her "Madame Princess Charlotte." This would always make Charlotte blush with anger and squeeze her fists.

Marie-Amelie observed everything, but she did not intervene. It was not Charlotte's pretentiousness that worried her, but rather the way she remained closed, alternating between an adult's seriousness and weird moods and bouts of melancholy. Marie-Amelie tried to make her talk, but the child refused to open up. She spoke, but she did not say anything. Marie-Amelie could not manage to get inside her heart and soul, but the lucid woman understood that the child was not at all like the others, and that her mother's death was not the only factor to blame.

For her part, Charlotte adored her grandmother, but she did not want to be analyzed, even by her. She loved her mother's family, to whom so many memories of true intimacy bound her, but the style, tone, and mentality of the Orleans were things she could not share. She was deeply attached to them, but she was closer in character to her father Leopold. From him she had inherited the taste for power, ambition, and a headstrong will, and also the distance she knew to keep between herself and others. It hurt her to see him so rarely, but Louise's death had finally allowed the king of the Belgians to indulge his taste for isolation. Most often, he communicated with Charlotte and her brothers through letters, and saw them as little as possible. As might have been foreseen, Arcadie was back, and a second illegitimate son, Arthur, had been born. This time though, Arcadie had become more discreet; she had been given a home no less sumptuous but much less central than the palace on Rue Royale, and the garish green coach most often remained in the stable.

To get to see her father, Charlotte participated as often as possible in official ceremonies at his side, despite her young age. Aware that she was taking her mother's place, she oversaw charitable works and visited institutions. She enjoyed this; as a teenager,

Charlotte had developed a pronounced liking for official pomp. By instinct, she knew the right gesture to make, the right word to say in public. Her heredity had made her into the perfect little queen.

Of her two brothers, Charlotte by far preferred the younger, the one closer to her in age: the count of Flanders, "good fat Philippe," always jolly, outgoing, affectionate, and kind, a nice boy who remained in the background. Charlotte shared ambition, stunning intelligence, pride, and also the strange mood swings with her elder brother Leopold, duke of Brabant and the heir to the throne, but she did not much like his sarcasm and cynicism. She held against him the fact that he was always bored, and she feared his violent temper. Like Charlotte, Leopold was so introverted that for a long time he was thought retarded, first by his father. His genius had just been starting to show when his father the king decided to marry the awkward teenager off, and chose for him Archduchess Marie-Henriette of Austria. "I was greatly surprised when I learned of his choice," the fiancé Leopold admitted, "but I have accepted his supreme desires. She is of average height, a little chubby. Not too pretty, but not ugly either." Marie-Henriette was an accomplished athlete. Leopold hated sports. Marie-Henriette was outgoing. Leopold was just the opposite.

In the beginning, Charlotte gave her new sister-in-law a warm welcome, but soon she began to criticize her, never to stop again. How could Marie-Henriette like opera? How could Marie-Henriette be so materialistic? How could Marie-Henriette like charades so much? And the way she dressed, she looked like a circus performer! She had no dignity, and knew nothing of manners. "Fat Marie never gets tired, Leo," Charlotte told her brother, "I think she could have written just once to dear Dad, who has been so good to her—that's not very polite. He is surprised not to have received a letter from her. I also went through a lot of trouble to write her in German, it's not easy. That was nine days ago, and I don't know whether the

letter got to her, because I haven't had a response." This snippy tone
suited to a harsh governess in fact belonged to a fifteen-year-old.
What did she think gave her the right to criticize her sister-in-law?
Where did this bitterness come from? Jealousy could not be the
reason, for Marie-Henriette was far from pretty, while Charlotte
dazzled people with her beauty.

Charlotte had always been a stunning child, but now the big,
dark eyes ringed with long lashes, the tiny pink mouth, the alabas-
ter skin, the mass of black hair, and the perfect bone structure made
for an enchanting appearance. The grace of her face took attention
away from her overly accentuated jaw, the sign of a headstrong will.
She stood up very straight, which hid the slight defect of her short
neck. Despite her youth, she was already a lady. Her perfect manners were matched by a pride that made her stare down those
around her in an almost provocative, and thus attractive, way. Her
father, who had always been proud of her, discovered that his child
had become a woman. He declared her the most beautiful princess
in Europe—which meant, in royal code, that she was ripe for marriage, and that King Leopold had decided to look into the matter
immediately.

Just then, at the end of May 1856, Ferdinand Maximilian of
Habsburg—archduke of Austria, brother of the reigning emperor
Francis-Joseph, and admiral of the Imperial Fleet—came for a visit.
He was completing a special mission to the court of Napoleon III,
who had recommended that he pass through Belgium out of deference to King Leopold I, but also perhaps to see Charlotte, who, at
twenty-four, was now in the marriage race. Maximilian arrived at
Ostende in a yacht lent to him by Napoleon III. He was made to
visit many Belgian cities before being set up in Brussels. The first
night, there was a banquet in his honor, and the next day, a more
intimate luncheon. But most importantly, he was granted the exceptional privilege of private conversations on politics with Leopold I,

considered by all to be the mentor of Europe. This did not impress Maximilian at all.

Leopold's conversations seemed to him to be little more than interminable repetitions of articles he had read in the newspaper. The old king promised him another conversation, and Maximilian yawned with boredom at the prospect. "Every word he said confirmed what a windbag he is," Maximilian said later. "He went on with banality after banality on 'good Austria,' with the endless refrain of how much others should learn from him. . . . In accordance with my principle that I should act onto others the way that they act onto me, I responded to the king's aphorisms with aphorisms of my own. I thought myself all the more in the right to do this in that everything said to him is immediately gossiped elsewhere."

Yet the hospitality offered him suited him well, especially after Napoleon III's court, which was ruled by a "nouveau riche etiquette," whereas at Brussels, "the court is well set up, though the palaces are all in sorry state. . . . But there is everywhere a certain dignity, a feeling of proper company, the traditional forms of a court, so much so that in comparison with Paris, here I had the wonderful feeling of being among equals," he told his brother the emperor.

To his relief, Maximilian came to prefer Brussels to Paris, which lacked the "national stamp" of a decent king. He was won over by admiration for Belgium, all of which appeared graceful and blossoming—its land, its cities, its commerce and industry. This, as Maximilian sincerely recognized, was thanks to the meticulous work of King Leopold.

But the young man wondered whether that prosperity and the monarchy would outlive its old sovereign, so he turned his gaze toward the heir, Leopold of Brabant. Leopold tried hard to woo him, burying him in so many compliments with his "mind-numbing politeness" that Maximilian took them for flattery motivated solely by Leopold's hope for strengthening ties with Austria, in order to benefit from that great empire's protection.

But Maximilian was wrong. The Belgian heir, a few years his junior, conceived an unconditional and almost delirious admiration for the archduke. To judge from Leopold's words, Maximilian had the most open of minds, and a beautiful and generous intelligence, because he was aware of humanity's suffering. With this keen awareness, he grasped everything going on around him. His entire being exuded dignity, and one could tell immediately that he belonged to a noble race. He was perfectly sure of his duty, and of the constraints it imposed. Everyone he met was shocked by his bearing and radiance. Unfortunately, Leopold noticed, the archduke's health was poor, for not one day passed that he did not suffer from headaches, stomachaches, toothaches, and especially, pains in the liver. The normally cynical and sarcastic Leopold smothered Maximilian with overwhelming praise in his journal. It was a marked exception to his usual rule, and an inexplicable exception, at that.

Charlotte could have borrowed these compliments word for word and then magnified them — from the first glance, she had been seduced by the young Austrian, so fine and delicate, so blond with honest blue eyes. He had a weak chin, but no one could see it under the beard he had let grow. Maximilian obviously possessed a great heart, a rich and faithful soul, and he was a poet, a romantic who loved nature, animals, and flowers. He was profoundly sincere and loyal, fun and pleasant, very witty. This almost feminine side of Maximilian's personality corresponded to the masculine side of Charlotte's. In a word, she had fallen in love.

In his letters to his brother, Maximilian wrote pages about King Leopold, about the duke of Brabant, but not a word on Charlotte. He left several days later without even seeming to have noticed her.

Meanwhile, another suitor presented himself, with just as many qualities recommending him. He was a direct nephew of Leopold, which in the king's eyes spoke in his favor, and he occupied a throne: he was Pedro V, the king of Portugal. Leopold I did not dare push this candidate in person, so he did it by letter. To judge by what he wrote to Charlotte, Pedro V had a good and faithful character, and one could trust him implicitly; he was young, of course, but the future would make a shining example of him. Portugal was a charming country, completely safe for a royal family, despite its little revolutions. And the highest position of importance Charlotte would hold there could not of course be neglected: what was comparable to the status of queen?

Leopold left the choice up to his daughter. She needed not answer right away, but she would have to decide sooner than later. His vote was seconded by his niece, Queen Victoria, who could not resist sticking her nose into everything, especially when it came to matters of family marriages. For Victoria, there was no hesitating: between the two candidates, Pedro won hands down. He was the more distinguished, he had everything to satisfy the most demanding of hearts, he was lovable, and Charlotte would make a peerless queen. As for happiness, Victoria assured Charlotte that she would surely find it with a man of Pedro's status, rather than with any of the innumerable archdukes. Yet she knew that Maximilian had made a very favorable impression on Charlotte, so she went on the attack, hoping that Charlotte had not yet made up her mind. If Charlotte decided in favor of Maximilian, Victoria told her, she would find herself ensconced in Austrian society, so backbiting, mediocre, and morally ambiguous. Victoria would not hesitate to give any of her own daughters to Portugal, if Charlotte wanted her opinion. . . .

But Charlotte did not want it. She wanted nothing to do with crowns like the one Pedro V had to offer. They were heavy burdens, and, if blinded by the false glitter of the diadem, she might give in to foolish considerations she would regret later. In any case, the Portuguese king did not much please her. When he had been on a visit to Belgium, he had acted almost vulgarly with her — if you want to be liked, she remarked, you should act in a different way. In the end, she accepted the comments of her old governess, the countess of Hulste, who assured her that Portugal was a country peopled by orangutans, that it was devoid of resources, and that the priests there were complete fools bounded on all sides by their limited intelligence. In Portugal, Charlotte would be walled in, an outcast isolated by the natives' total incomprehension.

Now that Pedro V was out of the picture, Maximilian came back in force. Leopold had already sent an Austrian nephew off to Vienna to discreetly suggest to the archduke that he might ask for Charlotte's hand. Maximilian began to consider her in retrospect. "She is short, I am tall, which is as it should be. She is dark-haired, I am blond, which is also good. She is very intelligent, which is a little tiresome, but I'm sure I'll get over it," he remarked, which was surely not an admission of wild passion. He also wondered whether King Leopold's maneuverings stemmed purely from his political aims or if Charlotte really felt something for him. Old Leopold responded to this question with a masterpiece: "My dear and gracious sir takes me, I believe, for a great diplomat whose every step tends toward a political end. This is not, however, the case, and in May, without any political designs, you won over all my trust and good-will. I also noticed that my daughter shared this opinion, though it was my duty to proceed with caution. Now I can announce to you that my daughter consents to the marriage, and that I approve of her choice with pleasure." Maximilian was thus accepted. Queen Victoria, whom Maximilian had had the prudence to go see, forgot the Portuguese, and from then on, swore only by him. He had simply to appear for the queen and her husband the prince consort to fall in love with him, as her letters show. He was so charming, so intelligent, so natural and likable, but above all, he possessed a supreme virtue: he was so English in his feelings and tastes, and so anxious for better relations between Austria and England. Perhaps he was not completely handsome, since he had that somewhat fleshy mouth and especially that weak chin, but beyond that, he was pleasant to look at. Victoria was glad for Leopold that Charlotte would have such a good husband.

Maximilian wrote ceremoniously to his fiancée: "Madam, the gracious response of His Majesty your august father has rendered me profoundly joyful, and permits me to address your Royal Highness directly, and to express my most cordial and heartfelt gratitude for the consent you have been willing to grant my request, a consent which insures my life's happiness. I have pined after such happiness since the first moment I was able to appreciate the nobility of soul and of heart possessed by the most lovable and august of fiancées." He was dying to go to Charlotte, he said, but duties were detaining him at Trieste, where the Austrian fleet he commanded was docked.

In a second, less solemn letter, he switched from "Madam" and "Your Royal Highness" to "gentle cousin." He sent her his portrait and announced that all of Austria rejoiced to have her as archduchess, since the reputation of her rare virtues had already spread to the most distant villages in the empire. Charlotte could no longer contain her excitement, and thanked God day and night. Not only did her fiancé possess every good quality—which she tirelessly enumerated—but she also felt that her heart and Maximilian's beat as one. They understood each other better and better, they had the same outlook, the same feelings on marriage. As for her future in-laws, the Habsburgs, they were blessed with the most fortunate combination of charms and virtues one could ever imagine. Truly, Maximilian was the most wondrous of men. In evidence of this, her brother Leopold, normally so filled with mockery for everyone, had told Charlotte that no matter how much he scrutinized him, he could

find no fault with Maximilian, a man superior in every way. Char-
lotte was surprised, not by Leopold's legitimate admiration for
Maximilian, but rather by Maximilian's friendship with her brother.
What could Maximilian have seen in the ever dislikable Leopold?
Whatever that may have been, she was glad she would soon be
seeing Maximilian again, since Leopold had invited him to spend
Christmas with them to give Charlotte a chance to become better
acquainted with her beloved.

Maximilian's birth, twenty-four years earlier, had been linked
to a tragedy. His mother, Sophie, a Bavarian princess, had been
raised at the rather calm court of Munich. When still very young,
she had been married off to Archduke Franz Karl, son and brother
to emperors. Uprooted from Germany and new to the Viennese
court, Sophie had been snubbed by the beautiful but harsh family,
and by the stiff and suffocating court. As for her husband, he was
worthless. She found only one person to care for, a very handsome
young man, very sad, very romantic, whose destiny was unlike any
other. He was the only son of Emperor Napoleon and Archduchess Marie-Louise: the "Little Eagle," Napoleon II, Austrianized
despite himself. He and Sophie soon discovered they shared interests and personal qualities. His sorry fate moved the young woman;
likewise, he was sad to see her beauty barely blossomed, and imprisoned like him by Vienna's gilded cage. She did not hide her
affection for him, and they spent hours together. Then he began to
cough and to spit up blood. He had caught consumption, which
would in the end bring them even closer together.

Sophie set Little Eagle up in her winter garden, where he
played with the young woman's firstborn, little Francis-Joseph. In
the spring of 1832, the young man's condition worsened, and she
became pregnant for the second time. He did not understand the
seriousness of his illness and spoke of long vacations in sunny countries. Not daring to ask him to see a priest, she proposed that they

take communion together, side by side, so they could pray for his sickness to be cured and for her baby to be born smoothly. On the appointed July morning, Little Eagle saw that his dear Sophie was not coming. He was surprised, until he was told that she was in labor. The ensuing coughing fits gave him no rest; each one wore him out a little more. As the end approached, he was informed that Sophie had given birth to a boy, who would be named Ferdinand Maximilian. Little Eagle heard the cannon salute and the bells ringing to celebrate the joyful event. Meanwhile, instead of feeling happy with the rest of the country, Sophie could not stop crying, and as the baby was given his provisional baptism, her only topic of conversation with the Bishop was the Little Eagle, who, several suites away, was dying, accompanied only by his mother, Marie-Louise, Napoleon's widow, and his uncle, Archduke Franz Karl, Sophie's husband. He died without seeing his beloved friend, and the painful task of informing Sophie fell to her husband.

The shock was so great that she fainted and remained unconscious for several hours. Extraordinarily, her milk dried up, which provoked a violent fever. She arrived at death's door, but somehow survived, and several weeks later was strong enough to appear in public. No one recognized her. The ravishing and cheerful young woman had turned into a matron, prematurely aged and severe, thin, bossy, and strict. Gossips immediately began to spread the word that Maximilian was in fact the Little Eagle's son, an empty rumor, since Napoleon's son probably died a virgin. For the rest of her life, however, Sophie would show a marked preference for her little Maximilian, born at the very moment that her dear friend had been dying. She showered him with her attention, surrounded him with her concern, and protected him almost to the point of smothering him.

Maximilian had been sixteen years old when he had passed his first big test. Following the revolution that chased out Louis-

Philippe in 1848, the empire's provinces had risen up one after the other. Agitation had washed over Vienna, where protests occurred every day, each time more out of control. The imperial family had left the capital and withdrawn to Schönbrunn, the immense castle just outside Vienna, where the protestors soon followed them, shaking the beautiful rococo gates more violently each day. The imperial family then took refuge in loyal Tyrol, at Innsbruck, despite the determined opposition of Sophie, who had tried in vain to put an end to their flight. Young Maximilian had lived through these nerve-racking days; he had heard the arguments between his parents; he had felt his mother's rage. Events had taken a turn for the worse, and the reigning emperor, Maximilian's half-senile uncle, had been forced to abdicate. Because he had no children, the crown had fallen to his younger brother, Franz Karl, Sophie's husband. But Sophie had not thought her husband was up to the job, so she had refused the crown for him, and thus for herself, forcing him to leave it to their eldest son, Francis-Joseph. Since it was impossible to crown him in Vienna, which was still in the insurgents' hands, the ceremony had taken place at Olmutz, in Moravia, at the archbishop's palace. The service had been quick, and Maximilian had attended it. But the rise to the throne of a young man full of promise had not been enough to calm the revolutionaries — half the empire had seceded, the other half had been shaken by horrifying jolts, and yet already the wheels had begun to turn again. Able but ruthless generals had put a stop to the revolts, at the price of thousands of deaths. They had massacred Hungarians, Italians, and Poles, but order was restored.

During these trying times, Maximilian had shown the greatest devotion and loyalty toward his elder brother. He had been anxious to serve him, even to sacrifice himself for him — he had awaited but a nod to do anything the other might ask. But Francis-Joseph had merely sent Maximilian back to his fleet, to which he would appoint him admiral.

Several years later, there had been a new test. Francis-Joseph had been walking along the ramparts of Vienna when a Hungarian revolutionary suddenly appeared and stabbed him. He had lost a lot of blood, and his life was in danger. His heir, Maximilian, had been summoned. Nearly fainting from anguish, Sophie had written an almost hysterical letter to Maximilian, begging him to return immediately. Francis-Joseph was violently opposed to this. Maximilian had arrived as quickly as possible, only to be received icily by Francis-Joseph: "Who gave you permission to leave your post?"

After this assassination attempt, the young emperor became even more popular than he had ever been before, and he had even less use for Maximilian. He mistrusted his heir, and moreover, he was jealous of him, since their mother openly favored him — sufficient reasons to get him out of the way. So, like sailors everywhere, Maximilian had decided to travel. His assignments brought him to the Middle East, to Greece, to Italy and Spain, and finally to Portugal. As custom dictated, he stopped to pay his respects to the local royal family, and went to a villa outside Lisbon to call on the empress dowager of Brazil.

There he met her daughter, the stunning Maria Amelia of Bragance. She was the perfect balance between the most startling innocence and all the graceful sensuality she had inherited from her great-grandmother, Empress Josephine.

Before he met Maria Amelia, Maximilian had had a tryst or two, notably with the Countess von Linden, but nothing of consequence. With Maria Amelia, it was completely different. He fell head over heels in love with her. It was mutual: they declared their love for each other and secretly became engaged. Maria Amelia's mother, empress of Brazil, said that she was overjoyed. Maximilian's family stuck up their noses a bit, for the fiancée's Beauharnais lineage was none too sparkling, though she was the daughter of an emperor. The engagement was announced, and Maximilian could not wait to see Maria Amelia again. Unfortunately, tuberculosis struck the young woman, and she was sent to spend the winter in Madeira, where the climate was considered healthy. She grew sicker and died. She was twenty-two years old. Maximilian was heartbroken.

These events had taken place only three years before Maximilian's arrangement with Charlotte, and not a single day passed that he did not think of Maria Amelia. It was with her memory in his heart that he got engaged to another.

Maximilian arrived at the Brussels train station on December 22, 1856, at four o'clock in the afternoon. His friend and heir to the throne, Leopold, Duke of Brabant, and Leopold's younger brother, the count of Flanders, met him in dress uniform, flanked by the military authorities and rows of soldiers. There were great crowds in the street to watch the procession pass by, escorted by a squadron of cavalry. King Leopold was awaiting his future son-in-law at the bottom of the steps of the royal palace. First he brought him to his suite, then to the Blue Salon, where Charlotte was waiting with her sister-in-law, Marie-Henriette, wife of the duke of Brabant.

Two days later, on Christmas Eve, Maximilian spent the day with the family at Laeken, and there he drew his friend Leopold aside to ask him about Charlotte's tastes. But above all, he asked very precise questions about Charlotte's fortune.

Maximilian had brought along his private secretary, Baron de Pont, who endlessly cornered the viscount de Conway, treasurer of the civil list and King Leopold's right-hand man, in long discussions. Without beating around the bush, de Pont demanded enormous sums of money. Young Leopold remembered having heard that Max was extremely grasping. Not only was he getting the prettiest princess in Europe plus three million francs, but now he wanted more! Leopold found the Austrian's demands exorbitant, and refused to add another penny to the dowry already agreed upon. So Maximilian, with the aid of his secretary, tried a little blackmail. What would be said in Belgium, in Austria, if they were to find out how petty and penny-pinching the king was toward his beloved daughter, refusing to let go of even a little of his immense fortune? Leopold gave in and raised the dowry. Maximilian was ecstatic: "I am proud to have managed to force that old skinflint to separate from a little piece of what he holds most dear in the world."

Later, at a luncheon at Laeken, young Leopold tried to ensnare his future brother-in-law. "How long have you considered marrying my sister?" he asked.

"Ever since I saw her for the first time, last May."

"That is nice of you to say, but hardly close to the truth."

Maximilian stared agape, then mumbled, "It is true. A few months ago, I was at Trieste, I felt alone and abandoned. So I resolved to get married, and once this resolution was made, I told my confessor again that I was seriously thinking about marrying Charlotte."

"Are you sure she was the one you were considering? You told me a long time ago that you wanted to get married."

"I have felt the need to marry since I was fourteen years old."

"You have forgotten the number of times you told me you wanted a rich princess, and that, failing that, you would even marry a countess, provided she was rich."

Nonetheless, the festivities in honor of the fiancé went on. He was brought to visit the port of Anvers, and at the Royal Theatre, he was given a performance of an opera by Verdi, *Les Vêpres Siciliennes*. His arrival coincided with the twenty-fifth anniversary of Belgian independence, which was to be celebrated with a ball attended by 1,400 guests. Charlotte was radiant. Everyone rushed to praise her beauty, her elegance, her white chiffon dress festooned with green ribbons and garlands of blossoms. In her first official appearance as a fiancée, she did not leave Maximilian's side, especially seeing as she had received permission to waltz with him. Maximilian commented on the party with these words: "The aristocracy there rubbed elbows with its tailors and cobblers, or with English shopkeepers who have retired to Brussels to save money, and perhaps others simply to get an invitation for themselves and their families."

At every family meal, Maximilian singled out young Leopold in his attack on the Orleans. He brashly declared his hatred for Louis-Philippe; he forbade Charlotte to bring her grandfather's portrait with her to Austria. Indignant, but trying to avoid arguments, Leopold told Maximilian that he found him unfair. Maximilian went further, accusing Louis-Philippe of having left for exile with an immense fortune. Leopold fought back: "That is a terrible accusation, and it is odious to say he was greedy. Today, you should mourn the late king for his generosity. Instead of getting three million from my sister, you would be getting five, if it hadn't been for the revolution of 1848 and the openhandedness of a family you're trying to depict as self-interested, working only for themselves, and according to you, the epitome of selfishness."

Then Maximilian laid into Leopold's uncle, the duke of Montpensier, and accused him of having lost his composure during the 1848 revolution. Leopold responded in kind, reminding his future brother-in-law that his own uncle, Archduke Albert, had lost his composure just as much during the same revolution.

Maximilian stubbornly declared that under no circumstances would Charlotte's Orleans uncles be invited to the wedding, because they were the sons of a usurper, or so they were considered by the Viennese court, and he kindly asked young Leopold to announce this decision to his father. Leopold replied, "I can only carry out the errands that I understand. I cannot believe that someone would dream of limiting the rights of my father the king to invite to his own home whomever he likes."

"You are so intractable. Well then, the marriage will take place in Vienna."

The argument settled down. Leopold took advantage of the silence to ask Maximilian about his future. He had heard that a good position was being dangled before his eyes: what was it? He got his answer easily. Francis-Joseph had promised to name Maximilian the governor general of Lombardy-Venetia (at the time still Austrian provinces), a difficult but prestigious position. But Leopold should not breathe a word of it, Max cautioned; no one knew yet, and if Leopold were to repeat this secret to anyone, it would be a catastrophe.

Maximilian switched into a fairly good analysis of his future brother-in-law's personality. But no one likes to hear such things — the portrait of Maximilian that Leopold painted in return thus differed distinctly from the one he had painted the year before. First of all, Leopold began, Maximilian could not pass in front of a mirror without looking at himself and adjusting his clothing. He was a distinguished boy, graced with a deep intelligence. Though lively and animated, his character was capable of self-restraint. In conversation, he exaggerated and waxed lyrical in order to create scenes. He seemed to attach a great importance to his castles and to the few Austrian ships he commanded. He said he was able to destroy the people he spoke to with a simple gesture or a well-placed word. He liked to put on offensive and tyrannical airs, and he bragged that he had "corrected" the bad habits of the people of Trieste. He had a passion for etiquette. In a word, he was affable, capable, brave, and had a good heart, but he was sometimes a blowhard and a little too in love with the trappings of glory. He

was certainly broad-minded and very generous, but never had
Leopold seen such rapacity and desire for riches.

Leopold was convinced that Max wanted this marriage only
for money: he and the Austrians thought they had stumbled across
a diamond mine the day he had been promised Charlotte's hand.
But now they had found out that they had only struck gold, and
they were sorry for it.

Maximilian also had a taste for silly tricks, which Leopold
hated. He pushed, he pinched, he jostled his friends, he spun them
like tops. One day, he treated Leopold that way as they were leaving the table, and Leopold showed his displeasure. Immediately
acting meek and almost feminine, Maximilian placed his hand on
Leopold's arm and said, through his smile, "You're furious with me,
but I'm one of your best friends, don't you think so?"

"Oh yes, I know you love us, but I think that you love our
money just as much, and that your desire to get a piece of it has a
lot to do with why you're here. You are generous, very generous,
but greedy beyond belief."

"If I like money, you're the one I learned that little fault from."

More kindly, the fiancé complained that he was given no privacy with Charlotte. Leopold I, who belonged to the old genera-
tion, remained pitiless on proprieties. The fiancés were allowed to
dispense with their titles when they spoke together, but they could
not address each other in the familiar, or remain alone, or kiss. But
when at last Maximilian had to leave, Charlotte could not help
herself and threw herself into his arms. King Leopold scolded her
so sharply that she burst into tears.

Young Leopold concluded that Maximilian's visit was not a
smashing success. His aloofness and overbearing behavior had
worked against his favor. Moreover, since he had not gotten everything he wanted, he had left worried and sad. Leopold came to pine
after the previous suitors. The king of Portugal had not worked out

because he had proven dislikable in Brussels, but there had been others. The king of Naples and the grand duke of Tuscany had made tantalizing offers. But instead of those glorious candidates, it would be Maximilian, Leopold told himself, over and over, with ever-dwindling enthusiasm.

But Charlotte did not regret her decision for a moment. She tirelessly told her old governess, the countess of Hulste, how charming Maximilian was. She was so happy in his company. She found him even more handsome, and morally, he left nothing to be desired, which for her was everything. Despite King Leopold, they had often managed to find some privacy and chat. She was confirmed in her good impression of him, and he had even managed to increase her esteem for his character. He had proven gentle and attentive. On Christmas, he had given her a bracelet containing a lock of his hair, earrings, and a diamond brooch. They had strolled in the icy Laeken park and spoken of their plans, especially the castle that Maximilian was having built for himself at Miramar, near Trieste, which inflamed Charlotte's desires.

The castle would overlook the sea. There would be a terrace decorated with a fountain, a Moorish gazebo, a winter garden with a large cage for exotic birds, and finally, a chapel for daily mass, worked in such a way that the servants would be able to follow along from a nearby vestibule.

Did Charlotte find out that Maximilian only wanted her dowry? It is doubtful, as she never let a single comment slip out by accident. She may have been listening, but she did not want to hear. She had chosen Maximilian because he was a paragon, and a paragon he remained, despite everything she might have learned about him. Unlike her brother Leopold, she made no corrections to the image she had of Maximilian, because already her prodigious stubbornness was at work, to see only what she wanted to see and as she wanted to see it.

Yet at the same time, she was not mistaken, for Maximilian's feelings for her had evolved. Love had taken over affection, coating his self-interest, as could be seen in the letter he wrote her moments after his train had pulled out of Brussels: "Dear Charlotte, on this very day of my sad departure from Brussels, I want to write you, my darling fiancée, to express to you once again the sorrow I feel at our separation and all the gratitude for your goodness and sincere love. The days I was able to spend in your company, dear Charlotte, vanished too quickly. Yet they will ever remain the happiest of my young life. In the present, they make up the joyful promise of a future full of delight, of noble sentiments, and, God willing, of unshakable serenity."

On February 26, 1857, Francis-Joseph named his brother governor general of Lombardy-Venetia. Since the Renaissance, Lombardy had never stopped being occupied, passing from hand to hand, exploited and pillaged. As for Venetia, Bonaparte was the reason she had lost her independence. These two former Italian states, now reduced to simple provinces, had been grouped together and ceded to Austria at the Congress of Vienna. For years, they had suffered a petty tyranny, bureaucratic, but in the end bearable. Then, in the ever-growing winds of war, the situation had deteriorated. Underground forces were working to chase the Austrians out and unite Italy. Revolts were multiplying, each time followed by massacres, snuffing them out one after the other.

Several months earlier, Francis-Joseph and Empress Elisabeth had conducted an official visit that had ended in a series of snubs. At a gala at La Scala, instead of coming to pay their respects to their Austrian sovereign, the women of the aristocracy had sent their servants dressed up in the family jewels. During a performance of *Nabucco* (the opera Verdi had composed with political aims), when it had come time for the chorus to sing the famous prisoners' song, the singers turned to the imperial box and sang the stanzas demanding liberty as they stared at the emperor and empress of Austria. All this meant that under the pretext of giving his brother a prestigious position, Francis-Joseph was in fact offering him a poisoned gift.

Maximilian told none of this to Charlotte. In his letters, he described the wealth of Milan, the splendor of the palace, the luxury of the Monza royal villa. He boasted of the support his brother showed him. He depicted social issues such as the Italian high life and the theater. Finally he told his future wife that she should not forget to learn Italian, for one was helpless without it in Italy.

Another letter spoke of jewels, in which royalty is always extremely interested. He was happy to find out that as part of her dowry, Charlotte would bring four exquisite necklaces, one of diamonds, another of topaz, another of delicate pearls, and the last of emeralds. Maximilian's brother the emperor had chosen a large diadem to go with the diamond necklace, as well as a beautiful pearl brooch. Maximilian's parents would offer a sapphire necklace, extremely beautiful and precious. He himself would give her a diadem that he was to have sculpted, as he and Charlotte had decided together. The Belgian royal family had chosen to offer her a necklace made up of thirty-four enormous diamonds. A full set of large amethysts would be her grandmother Marie-Amelie's gift. To that set, she would add a few baubles: twenty-three necklaces, thirty-four bracelets, fifty-two brooches, eleven rings, medallions, and pocket watches.

Before he officially assumed his post, Maximilian took as much advantage as he could of his dear Miramar, the castle he had not yet finished but already loved. He was in despair at having to leave his safe haven, and would have preferred staying there in humble conditions to all the vainglories that awaited him. Before he left, he went to visit the work site one final time with a few friends, lingering in the garden as the sea murmured and the gentle spring breeze caressed his face.

Finally, on April fourth, Maximilian made his official entrance into Venice, and was coldly received by the Venetians. On the nineteenth, it was Milan's turn to welcome him, in beautiful weather that he described to Charlotte. The reception remained quite solemn, but given the circumstances, Maximilian considered himself satisfied. The streets and balconies overflowed with people saluting them with reverence and courtesy. The *corso* was splendidly decorated, and for once, the aristocracy arrived in force at the palace, so much so that the procession seemed endless, and Maximilian was forced to shake more than five hundred hands. He got down to work immediately. He attacked all the problems at once—financial, fiscal, judicial, and municipal. He looked into the canals, the education system, the draining of swamps, the restoration of monuments, and urban planning. His obvious kindness and charm soon made him popular.

He commissioned artists to paint magnificent watercolors of the interiors of the palaces of Venice and Milan, which would soon be Charlotte's residences. He entrusted them to Court Counselor Gaggern, who was being sent to Brussels to finalize the marriage contract. But Gaggern went about finalizing it in quite a strange way: instead of bringing watercolors to the king of the Belgians, he brought him more demands. Leopold grumbled: he would make efforts, but he would not make them alone. Let the emperor of Austria make an effort too for his brother. At last, they reached an agreement: to the dowry already established, one hundred thousand florins were to be added, as well as a gold and silver vase, and an annual stipend of twenty thousand florins to be paid by the Belgians. From the Austrian side, Maximilian would receive one hundred thousand florins, and thirty thousand florins more as a wedding gift. In his shame for the demands he had been charged with transmitting, Gaggern apologized to King Leopold for having to keep pushing for more. The old sovereign understood and reassured Gaggern. He said he had understood Maximilian perfectly well, and wanted to spare him the sad experiences he himself lived through in the course of his two marriages: Louis-Philippe had promised him a dowry that he had received only in part and very late; and his first father-in-law had given him as a dowry all the debts his daughter the princess of Wales had accumulated, explaining to him that if he paid them off for his fiancée, he would make the best of impressions on her. Leopold I concluded: "It was true, but that impression was, and remained, extremely disagreeable."

3

The summer of 1857 was approaching, and with it, the marriage. In the beginning of July, King Leopold took Charlotte and her brother Philippe, count of Flanders, to the court of England. The Channel was choppy as they crossed it, but as soon as they arrived in London, Charlotte forgot her seasickness. She was happy to see her British relations again. "Good cousin" Victoria and her husband Albert, then Bertie, Vicky, and Fritz Wilhelm — or in other terms, the prince of Wales, Princess Victoria, eldest daughter of the Queen, and the prince and heir to the throne of Prussia; and finally Princess Beatrice. Parties, spectacles, and fun were mixed into the family gatherings. Charlotte saw Charles Dickens direct the presentation of *The Frozen Deep*, and act in it wonderfully. At Count Bernsdorf's ball, there were so many people that "we were squeezed in like sardines, which is exactly what happens, so I have heard, at many of London's salons." The only thing missing in this whirlwind of delights was good weather, because "it rains endlessly *in the most provoking way* every time we are in an open carriage."

Of course, they went to visit the Orleans at Claremont, though "dear Papa is not coming along because of his bad chronic cough." Charlotte's grandmother Marie-Amelie was in the best of health. Poor Uncle Joinville was limping. As for the duchess of Montpensier, born the Infanta of Spain, she never went out without her jewels, and wore no less than three sashes of foreign honors. Her daughters, however, found favor in Charlotte's eyes: "The little Spanish girls are gems, the prettiest children I know."

Barely had Charlotte returned to Brussels when her wedding festivities began in earnest. Her brother Leopold wrote of them in his diary, with words dipped in vinegar. The ritual began with a time-honored ceremony: the official request for Charlotte's hand presented by the ambassador extraordinaire of the Austrian Empire. This was Count Archinto, a former Milanese lord, and a hunchbacked buffoon with dyed hair and an enormous nose. He was sarcastic, intelligent, extremely rich, and rather nasty. Leopold remarked that he ate uncouthly, and spread tobacco in his green beans to flavor them up. His conversation was bizarre: he asked Leopold how many boys the queen of England had produced. He affirmed that the best peaches were called "Venus' nipples," and the best prunes "nun's thighs." But the intelligent man also gave Leopold a clear picture of the Italian situation.

On July twenty-first, Count Archinto and his entourage took two six-horse court coaches surrounded by footmen to the royal palace, where the royal family, the court, and the ministers were awaiting them in full dress. He presented the letters accrediting him as the ambassador extraordinaire, and he offered a short speech to which King Leopold responded, graciously according his daughter's hand in marriage to the House of Austria. Charlotte said nothing. She limited herself to a prolonged and formal curtsy that signified her acquiescence. It was her first official step into her new life, and her family was as moved by it as she was.

As the days went on, the guests began to arrive; first Queen Marie-Amelie; then her daughter, Aunt Clementine, the only Orleans allowed to come to the wedding because of Clementine's marriage to a Saxe-Coburg, Uncle August; then the brother of Emperor Francis-Joseph, sent to represent him; Charles-Louis with his wife, the archduchess Marguerite; the reigning duke of Saxe-Coburg; scandalous Uncle Ernest; and other less important relatives.

On this the twenty-third of July 1857, at five-thirty, the fiancé, Archduke Maximilian, arrived with great pomp at North Station. He rode to the palace to salute his future father-in-law and to introduce him to the Italian ladies and gentlemen who would make up his daughter's household. Because of a misunderstanding, King Leopold happened at that moment to be at Laeken. Livid at what appeared to him to be an insult, Maximilian declared that since the Italian ladies had made the trip for nothing, he was going to dismiss them, and that he himself would not go to Laeken at all that day. His face showed his emotions strongly enough that young Leopold took him by the arm and pushed him into the next room to try to calm him down. Maximilian let himself be swayed, and returned to the main salon more serenely. Officially, they decided to say that Charlotte was a little under the weather, and they would postpone the Italian ladies' presentation for a later time.

Shortly afterward, young Leopold again found the fiancé furious and falling victim to an attack of bile. Maximilian told him that the Italian gentlemen had strongly urged him not to go to Laeken, since the king of the Belgians' attitude was nothing but a thinly disguised slap in the face. Young Leopold managed to convince him to go, but Maximilian only whined, cursed, and complained throughout the journey. When he arrived, he was so cold-natured and displayed his bad mood so openly that the entire assembly was left indignant. He pushed away the hand that Leopold I held out to him, and barely responded to his welcoming compliments, so much so that the king turned his back on Maximilian in outrage. Young Leopold, blaming himself for the misunderstanding, went back and forth between Maximilian and his father, trying to reconcile them. Maximilian answered only with violent reproaches. The luncheon went on in embarrassment and sadness. King Leopold made no effort to hide what he thought of his future son-in-law. Never had anyone shown him so much disrespect, and he bewailed the fate in store for his daughter.

Luckily, peace was seemingly restored the next day, and the fiancés had a few moments to see each other in private. They strolled through Laeken park, under the lime trees, listening to the birds sing and watching the rabbits hop in the meadow. They stopped on a little rustic bridge and contemplated their reflections among the water lilies. Like all the lovers in the world, they carved their interlaced initials, C and M, into the bark of an old beech tree. Charlotte bent over to pick some wild strawberries and gave a taste of them to her fiancé.

Still, Maximilian and young Leopold fought over everything. When they inspected the bridal trousseau, Maximilian seemed anxious only to point out what was missing, which made Leopold furious: "As he plunders my father, it seems like such fun to him that he brazenly grabs at anything he covets." To complete his future brother-in-law's already loaded portrait, he added: "My dear cousin reigns supreme wherever he goes. His witty frankness and rare abundance of speech have as always something pompous and bombastic about them. He needs a court, movement, balls, and pleasure. Without all that bustle, life for him is empty. Thus Laeken and our solitude seem horrifying to him. Our family evenings he finds a long torture, and with all his energy, he can barely muster the strength to stifle the yawns that come over him."

A dispute arose over decorations. Maximilian refused to give the Golden Fleece to the count of Flanders, since he considered it too important for a younger brother. He also opposed awarding the honor of an Austrian order to two members of the Belgian court who had dared resist him during the dowry negotiations.

But there were also moments of truce, as when the archduke and the heir to the Belgian throne talked about women, a topic Leopold would later find himself greatly interested in. For the moment, it was Maximilian who could not stop talking about them, which to Leopold seemed natural for a young man "who has a little blood in his veins." Though Maximilian talked a lot, he did not appear to have acted upon the things he said, and as confidence led to confidence, he came to tell a bewildered Leopold that he had never had a mistress. Leopold commented that Maximilian seemed a little too informed on women not to have had some acquaintance with them. In fact, Leopold was convinced that Maximilian, so passionate and headstrong, was as incapable of self-control as he had found him to be, and could not possibly have maintained a perfect abstinence so long. But Maximilian swore to it: he was a virgin.

On the eve of the marriage, Maximilian went with the whole family to the Laeken church to visit Queen Louise's grave. Young Leopold felt melancholy for his sister, but faith was supporting her, God was guiding her and helping her overcome the huge changes in her life. When he had cried for their upcoming separation, she had been the one to console him, for Charlotte, wrapped up in the idea of her duty and of the Almighty, showed no emotion. Leopold was sure that in no one ever again would such peacefulness be found, such loftiness of sentiment, such strength of will.

On July twenty-seventh, the very day of the wedding, Leopold had to leave at dawn for Anvers to pick up the prince consort of

England, cousin Albert, who was disembarking at seven o'clock from the magnificent British royal yacht. Once back with his guest, he found the royal palace filled both with flowers and with students from the military school who would be acting as bodyguards. When Charlotte arrived from Laeken, he barely had time to kiss her in her rush to get dressed. But someone had forgotten the jewels she was supposed to wear, so the ceremony was going to begin late. It was not until 10:45 that all the guests gathered in the Blue Salon: married couples and royalty around the big table, the court and magistrates a little further back. The *burgermeister* of Brussels quickly performed the civil ceremony, and then everyone marched in procession to the palace chapel, where the archbishop of Malines was officiating. After a quick mass without music, a *Te Deum* without a choir, it was finally time for congratulations. Leopold went up to kiss his sister and was dazzled by her beauty. She was wearing a silver and white gown, and over her hair, a long lace veil from Malines, held up by orange blossoms interspersed with diamonds. Still more diamonds glinted at her ears and around her neck, and on her wrist she wore a bracelet containing a miniature portrait of her grandmother, Queen Marie-Amelie. Holding Maximilian's arm, she stood at the palace balcony and received an ovation from the immense crowd covering the square.

Next, there was a parade of magistrates who had come to present their wishes for a happy marriage, and at last, they returned to the Blue Salon, where the family separated until the grand luncheon that would take place at one-thirty.

"Superstitious people," Leopold curiously remarked, "would have noticed that it did not rain during the day, that the bouquet fell out of Charlotte's belt, that her chair was knocked over during the mass, and that finally, in the morning, my cross of Saint Stephen was shattered. All day, there is an 85 degree heat unbearable to Belgians." Yet the Belgians held nothing back in celebration of the event. In the Grand-Place, thousands of them had come together in an enormous and raucous feast, and the entire country was overjoyed.

Leopold, who gladly used off-color language, spoke of the wedding night: "Grandmother had spoken a few words to Charlotte about the duties of marriage and of the natural operation of that act. Apparently, she was not overly frightened by the prospect. That night, Max tried the operation, they went to bed together. From what her husband says, Charlotte remained quite reasonable. Everything went well. Charlotte was just very surprised and kept saying, 'How astonishing it is, how astonished I am.' Needless to say, they slept very poorly and warmed each other up nicely."

This was neither the fear of a virgin about to be sacrificed, nor the lustfulness of a woman discovering her sensuality. The next morning, when Leopold saw the young couple almost as they were getting out of bed, he thought Charlotte looked "tired but resigned." Tired perhaps—all the better for her! But resigned? Resigned to what?

Performing his duty, young Leopold strolled with his guests: he took Archduke Charles-Louis through the crowded streets to see the fountain of Mannekin-Pis. He maintained a decent relationship with Maximilian's younger brother, though they had little affection for each other. Nor did he care for the Italian entourage Maximilian had brought with him. The gentlemen were very stiff and standoffish with the Belgians: they would leave hated by everyone they met. As for the Italian ladies, they were neither pretty nor pleasant.

In his diary, Leopold failed to mention three people whose names figured on the magnificently penned list of noteworthy guests, and who were destined to play an important role: a certain Schertzenlechner, Maximilian's butler; the count of Bombelles, his quartermaster; and Madame Kuhacsevich, whose husband was part of the fiancé's entourage.

July thirtieth was the date set for Maximilian and Charlotte's departure. After breakfast, the dreaded moment arrived. Leopold found this departure so much more painful than the others, even cruel and hurtful. For once, Maximilian's behavior moved young Leopold. He had seen him proud, haughty, and domineering, but when it came time to leave, Maximilian began to cry, along with all of Charlotte's relatives. He cried from seeing his in-laws heartbroken at losing her. During the miserable last hour, a weeping Charlotte passed from King Leopold's arms to her grandmother Queen Marie-Amelie's to her brother's. Young Leopold had not cried so much since his mother's death. The honeymoon had a decidedly mournful beginning. The sadness was so great that no one had the heart to see Maximilian and Charlotte off to their coach, so the young couple left alone.

A special train carried them off into the night. First they stopped at Bonn, before visiting the German cities. At Regensburg, they boarded a cruiser that brought them toward Vienna along the Danube. In the empire's lands, in every riverside village, the people had erected arches of triumph, and they shouted cheers from their barges at the boat that was easily recognizable by the Austrian and Belgian flags draped across it. Charlotte met her mother-in-law, Archduchess Sophie, when she came aboard during their stop at Linz.

At Vienna, court coaches brought them to the Austrian sovereigns' summer residence, Schönbrunn Castle. The young couple's coach passed between two columns decorated with trophies before it crossed the vast terrain between the commons to the impressive rococo residence. Charlotte walked through endless series of white and gold salons, and from a window, she discovered the park, which, from tree-covered walkways to flowerbeds, from paths to copses, ascended all the way up to the distant colonnaded pavilion of the gazebo. Although she was used to Buckingham Palace and Windsor, Charlotte had never seen such elegant grandeur, such harmonious majesty.

Her brother-in-law, Emperor Francis-Joseph, raised her very graciously from her curtsy, but Charlotte had eyes only for his wife, Empress Elisabeth, called Sissi, and considered the greatest beauty of her time. Charlotte greeted her father-in-law, Sophie's husband, overshadowed by his wife to the point of nonexistence, next Maximilian's second brother, Archduke Charles-Louis, and then she met the young last child, Archduke Louis-Victor. Behind them, a forest of archdukes and archduchesses, cousins, nephews, and uncles were anxious to be seen. She had been allotted Little Eagle's suite, and she breathed in its romantic memory.

Her confidences overflowed with enthusiasm. She found her mother-in-law as kindhearted as she was motherly. The emperor and empress's welcome overwhelmed her. The others vied with each other to show her kindness, and Charlotte concluded: "I already feel like a full-blooded archduchess, because I love them all, and from the very first day, I felt completely at home with them." A snap judgment, it would seem, since Maximilian and Charlotte had spent only one night at Schönbrunn.

Was Empress Elisabeth's welcome really so "charming"? She had just lost her first child, little Sophie, and had only set aside her mourning for a few hours. Shy and reserved, the woman was not particularly affectionate. She hated her mother-in-law, the "kindhearted and motherly" archduchess Sophie, who hated her a hundred times over in return—this fearsome dragon was so kind toward Charlotte only to spite Elisabeth. Charlotte saw none of this, or refused to see it, and the train quickly whisked her off toward Trieste.

Charlotte discovered the Adriatic, a sea so different from the North Sea, in wonderment, as well as a sky so deep blue that it made her forget the gray skies of Belgium. She breathed in the warm air, the golden light. But above all, she discovered her husband's enchanted domain, for Maximilian was most anxious to show her Miramar. It was a rocky peak in the middle of a craggy coast. Pines, cypresses, tamarisks, mastics, and palm trees covered it, all cut through with small paths bordered by fragrant flowers. From the castle to the construction site, the estate hugged the entire gulf of Trieste, and on the other side, on the coastal cliffs, Duino Castle rose on a stony outcrop. Since the construction was by no means finished, the young couple would live in the Castelleto, a small neo-Gothic villa built a little farther back from the coast to house them until the castle was complete. The four rooms on each of the first and second floors were loaded with souvenirs that Maximilian had brought back from his travels in the Middle East, particularly treasures plundered from the tombs of the pharaohs. From the windows of their small bedroom, Charlotte saw only pines, the sky, the sea—and immediately, between her and the Mediterranean, it was love at first sight. But Charlotte was not given the chance to linger: Maximilian needed to take up his post as governor general of Lombardy-Venetia, and he could hardly wait to present his wife to his subjects.

On September sixth, 1857, they made their formal entrance into Milan, after leaving the train at Monzo, already dressed in court clothing: the men in uniform, the women in diadems and gowns with trains. Over his Austrian Navy uniform, Maximilian had hung the Golden Fleece around his neck, and the wide sash of the order of Saint Stephen crossed his chest. Charlotte was dressed in silken, cherry-red crinoline petticoats covered with luxurious lace, and she had sprinkled roses and diamonds in her hair. At the city outskirts, they traded their traveling wagon for six-horse court coaches. At the city's eastern gate, which they reached at four o'clock, an honor pavilion had been set up, where the Austrian garrison awaited them together with the podesta, Count Sebregondi, who delivered a welcome speech on behalf of the municipality. Then they rode in parade down the *corso* to the sound of gun salutes and military orchestras singing the imperial anthem and *La Brabançonne*. At the royal palace, situated next to the cathedral, Baron de Burger, the emperor's lieutenant, greeted them and led them to the second floor, to the immense and radiant Hall of Caryatids, the most beautiful in the palace, where rows of crystal chandeliers hung from the ceiling. Charlotte was introduced to all the aristocracy's representatives, the members of the court, the magistrates, and the city's main dignitaries. She spoke to all of them in nearly perfect Italian, which elicited murmurs of approval. While piling politeness upon politeness, she still did not fail to catalogue who was who, who of the rebellious aristocracy had come and who had not. She tried to detect who among all those Austrian dignitaries had power and who did not, who would be a friend and who a foe. Charlotte was particularly interested in Count Gyulai, commander in chief of the Austrian armies in Lombardy-Venetia. She knew that he was a powerful man, as well as Emperor Francis-Joseph's protégé. Would he get along with Maximilian? Would he allow him to act as he saw fit? At that moment, Count Gyulai led Maximilian back downstairs to the square in front of the palace for a military review organized in his honor. Charlotte went out onto the balcony. The crowds cheered her, as they had cheered her all along her route. She watched the sparkling uniforms, the soldiers on display, flags snapping in the air. She was intoxicated by the bright colors, by the rhythms. She took possession of her realm.

❊ ❊ ❊

At the royal palace, Charlotte's suite was sumptuous. She had never seen more grandiose décor, for in all truth, nothing could compete with Italian palaces. Even Schönbrunn, which she had left such a short time before, could not compare with this prodigious collection of marbles, gilded bronzes, extravagant stuccos, brocades, frescoes in which entire scenes of Mount Olympus meandered, paintings by the masters, sculptures, and enormous and ornately gilded furniture. Nevertheless, the palace, crammed in between the famous cathedral and the old city, was a little suffocating, all the more so for its lack of a garden. So Charlotte moved to her country home, the Monza Villa Reale. As far as villas went, it was an enormous building, much less luxurious than the city palace, but sparkling with tactful décor and all the grace of the last days of the eighteenth century. Most importantly, it was surrounded by a gigantic English park with lakes, centuries-old trees, and endless lawns. Charlotte was excited to discover the flora of southern Europe, especially the big magnolias with their sweet-smelling blossoms.

It wasn't long before she invited her relatives to come visit. Her favorite brother, "fat Philippe," count of Flanders, hurried to see it, and sent back a detailed report to their elder brother, Leopold, duke of Brabant. At Monza, he said, breakfast was at nine, lunch at one, dinner at the court at seven. They did not wear uniforms, but short trousers. The household was well equipped, everything was in order, the service was perfect, the meals were quickly and diligently served, and even ordinary livery was rich without being overdone. The food was good, though it could not compare with the cuisine at the Palace of Brussels. According to the count of Flanders, the stables were the most meticulous thing there. He was forced to admit that the coaches and horses outshone anything to be found at the Belgian court. On the other hand, he did not like

the butlers saluting to the ground, or the Swiss guarding the salons'
doors, superb without a doubt, but obtrusive for privacy. As for
the Villa Reale, Philippe found it large and beautiful. It even reminded him a bit of Laeken, and he stood in awe at the size of the
park, three hundred hectares enclosed within walls. Every day,
anywhere from twenty to thirty guests came to lunch to the music
of a chamber orchestra. The evening receptions were grander. As
their position dictated, Maximilian and Charlotte had chamberlains
and majordomos at their command, ladies-in-waiting, Dalmatian
guards in picturesque uniforms, and pages: a truly royal court.

Charlotte loved everyone, especially Countess Lutzow, her
favorite lady-in-waiting, a charming and ever cheerful personality,
and the great mistress of the court, Princess Auersberg, so full of
wit and compassion, with whom it was a pleasure to chat. As for
the great lord of Charlotte's court, Count Cittadella, he was the
consummate gallant, a well of knowledge, and a wonderful father.
Charlotte admitted that she loved the social life, the receptions,
seeing people, surrounding herself with new and interesting acquaintances. Perhaps later she would prefer a more quiet existence,
but for the moment, she confided, the court's swirl enchanted her.

With the pleasures, Charlotte also accepted the obligations.
She had been raised to fulfill the duties of her rank; she had been
trained in them from a very young age, and thus she carried them
out to perfection. She visited orphanages and charitable institutions
on a daily basis. She inaugurated, she inspected, she got herself seen,
she presided, she distributed alms. Serious beyond her years, fully
aware of her elevated but trying position, she "worked" a great deal
and she did it well, managing to make herself popular during her
tours of her realm — not least, during the unforgettable journey of
Easter 1858, when she discovered Venice.

On an immense gilded boat, she and Maximilian went up the
Grand Canal, he in a uniform spangled with medals, she in a white

moiré dress. Over her shoulders, she had thrown a very long and very heavy red velvet coat embroidered with gold, worthy of the one worn by the doge's wife—two pages held up its train. In her hair, she wore a high diadem of diamonds that sparkled in the sun. There, as well, the crowds enthusiastically welcomed the young, beautiful, glittering couple. Maximilian and Charlotte went through the magnificent halls of the doge's palace. Stopping at the top of a splendid marble staircase, each step of which had played a role in history, Maximilian was overcome with a wave of pride. He felt that he was the first and foremost; he felt every inch the sovereign. He even compared himself to the Sun King. Charlotte shared his pride, and even liked the official visits and pompous parades which others considered tiresome chores.

She and Maximilian did not stay in the doge's palace, but across from it, in the royal palace adjoining the famous Marciana library. The rooms had been decorated in the delicate Pompeian style by Eugène de Beauharnais, the former viceroy of Italy. Charlotte was given a vast bedroom with an alcove, the entrance of which was set off by two gilded columns. Her windows afforded an incomparable view of the Grand Canal, the Dogana, the Salute, and the Giudecca. She never tired of the endless movement back and forth of boats and ships of every type and tonnage.

It was at Venice that she discovered in herself a profound taste for tourism. Nothing gave her greater pleasure than to visit the churches, palaces, and museums, of which she kept a careful count. She fell in love with the gondolas, and, like Maximilian, could not get enough of the narrow and silent canals. Venice stirred her, as it did everyone. But in this idyllic setting, two elements left a discordant note: when it rained, the city looked sinister; and the condition of the monuments was deplorable—marvelous productions of the Renaissance were left to crumble into dust. "We'll have to fix that," Maximilian and Charlotte decided.

By tradition, Venice was home to exiles, some of whom happened to be distantly related to Charlotte. Thus she received the
duchess of Berri, her mother's first cousin, "the ugliest creature the
green Earth has ever seen," and her daughter, formerly Mademoi-
selle d'Artois, now duchess of Parma, "full of wit, but extremely
chubby."

Charlotte told whomever would listen that she was insanely
happy. Max was perfect, so excellent, pious, and tender. She was
swept away by a joy that did not allow her to miss her former life,
for her new married life was enough to feed her mind as well as her
heart. There was not a shadow to be found in the rosy picture. Of
course, she knew that life in this world was not a bed of roses, but
the years then sliding by would forever remain a sweet and cherished memory of perfect pleasure. With each passing day, she loved
and respected Max a little more. Her husband, supreme in every
way, was the epitome of love, but also of duty and energy. Simply
put, everyone adored him, but no one as much as Charlotte.

Nonetheless, several less joyous details stood out in this idyllic picture.
A few months after the wedding, Charlotte was thought to be pregnant, and her family discreetly began to celebrate. But Charlotte
was not expecting. The months passed, and still no pregnancy. A
young married princess who was not pregnant was nearly inconceivable in the logic of royalty, and yet, that was precisely
Charlotte's situation. She grew sick over it. Nothing was known of
the nature of her pain, but from Brussels, King Leopold sent letter
after worried letter to ask for news.

It happened that Charlotte admitted to moments of loneliness.
Always on the road, called from one city to the next by his duties,
Maximilian sometimes spent several consecutive nights on his yacht,
leaving Charlotte alone at the palace. He traveled for one or two

days without bringing his wife along. And why did he not bring her? That was what Charlotte's family wondered, and as they begin to mumble that perhaps there was some trouble between the two. Charlotte denied it fiercely.

It must be said that Maximilian spared no effort in taking charge of all branches of government—agriculture, industry, the arts, urban design, education—each time going into the most meticulous detail, creating a thousand projects and a hundred construction sites at once. Under his watchful eye, the country was transformed in leaps and bounds. The young archduke at once proved to be a remarkable administrator. Yet did he win his people over to his cause? Did he make the Austrian occupation bearable to them? Nothing was less sure. The aristocracy remained aloof, the intellectual circles even more so, and the middle class did not come willingly to the palace. The Italians liked Maximilian, and they admired Charlotte, but they wanted nothing to do with the Austrians.

The bomb exploded not in Milan, but in Paris. On January 14, 1858, an Italian patriot in a state of romantic exaltation threw an explosive device at Napoleon III's coach as he left the opera. The emperor of France was unhurt, the assassin, Orsini, was arrested, and his trial became a grandstand for denouncing the Austrian occupation of Lombardy-Venetia. Orsini had wanted to kill Napoleon III because he had been doing nothing to liberate Italy, despite his repeated promises. Orsini's lawyer, Jules Favre, spoke publicly against the intolerable Austrian occupation, and before he met the guillotine, Orsini wrote a letter repeating that he was offering his life as a sacrifice for the Italian nation yet to be born. This letter, reproduced in hundreds of thousands of copies, made its way secretly to Lombardy-Venetia, and Maximilian's citizens could not get enough of it. The underground forces that were just barely visible beneath Italy's emancipation—the same ones found behind most revolutions—turned Orsini's assassination attempt into a call for a new wave of anti-Austrian activity.

In this context, the anniversary of the 1848 revolution raised tension even further. In Lombardy-Venetia, everyone expected trouble. Maximilian and Charlotte courageously strolled through the streets without an escort, as if there were no problem; they passed in front of cafés without listening to the catcalls; they appeared at the opera without noticing that the noblewomen were wearing mourning clothes for Orsini. Nor did the agitation simmer down. At the Venice Theater, the Venetians booed the Austrian flag. Students at the famous Padua University demonstrated against the occupation.

Francis-Joseph immediately sent his brother a long letter. He had also felt the impact of Orsini's assassination attempt, and he feared that Napoleon was wavering. Meanwhile, recent incidents were unacceptable to him. He called the Venetians "Turks" and upbraided Maximilian for not having sent in troops against the miserable students. "Send in the troops"—the emperor of Austria had only these words on his lips and in his letters. He sent Maximilian a new secret code to tighten the security of their communiqués. He suggested that his brother consolidate the police for greater efficiency. His instructions were clear: if it moves, beat it down, which were welcome words for Count Gyulai, the commander in chief of Austrian forces. Francis-Joseph also supported the traditional method, which had been honed to perfect efficiency under Metternich's system, of repressing enough to keep things under control, and then repressing more.

Maximilian was firmly opposed to this solution. They should caress the Italians, he believed, not oppress them, and win them over by gentleness and tolerance. Time was on their side. Provided they kept their composure, he was sure he could persuade and tame the

Italians in the long run. Francis-Joseph was not at all convinced. The reports that Count Gyulai sent persuaded him that Maximilian was wrong; the gentle solution would do nothing but encourage the nationalists. Maximilian took the initiative and went to Vienna with Charlotte to defend his point of view, but to no avail. Francis-Joseph would not budge. On the contrary, his mistrust of his brother and his brother's liberalism only grew. In wanting to win the Italians over he wondered, could Maximilian have been nursing some secret and dangerous ambition? The malcontents would only be too happy to encourage Maximilian along on this slippery slope, even to the point of naming him their leader. It was only a small step from suspecting this to fully considering the archduke a subversive element.

While Maximilian was in discussions with Francis-Joseph, Charlotte went sightseeing through Vienna, and wrote what she saw in letters to her brother Philippe. She visited Hofburg, the Belvedere, and also the private collections of Prince Schwartzenberg and Countess Harach. She attended the military review given in honor of the official visit of the grand duke of Saxe-Weimar, and was stunned by the beauty of the spectacle, by the ancient imperial livery dating back to Charles V, and by the horses bearing the colors of each of the empire's provinces. On her birthday, her in-laws' kindness deeply moved her: Francis-Joseph had come especially from his Laxenburg retreat to congratulate her, Empress Elisabeth gave her a beautiful bracelet as a gift, and everyone seemed to want to outdo everyone else with gifts and best wishes. Afterward, Charlotte left for Schönbrunn with her mother-in-law, Archduchess Sophie, whom she liked a great deal. Meanwhile, Max had gone to and come back from Italy, where, as she put it to her brother, his subjects had showered him with such expressions of affection that he returned dazzled. Everything was going well, but Charlotte dreamed of returning as soon as possible to Milan and Venice, for she had fallen completely in love with Italy. Did she realize that the tension was growing dramatically between Maximilian and Francis-Joseph? Perhaps she did not want to admit it, but whatever the case may have been, the reassuring and impulsive tone of her letters contrasted markedly with the hard reality that was facing her husband.

Once she returned to Italy, in the middle of the summer, in a realm swirling with so many underground currents, her principal concern seemed to be with celebrating with all due pomp the long-awaited birth of the empire's heir, Archduke Rudolph, son of the imperial couple. She described in detail the *Te Deum* at the Milan cathedral, where she had gone with her entire court in a procession of gala coaches. The Venetian patriarch had officiated according to the Ambrosian rite as the army shot off an artillery salute. Afterward, at a grand reception in the Hall of Caryatids, the congratulatory speeches were given. Max had responded with a speech of his own that had elicited impassioned applause, and which so moved the audience that some broke into tears. Maximilian had appeared with Charlotte on the balcony overlooking the square filled with people to propose a toast to the little royal and imperial child. The applause had been thunderous. "It was magnificent," Charlotte summed up.

As often in those days, it was hardly strange that there were both anti-Austrian demonstrations and heartfelt applause for Maximilian and Charlotte at the same time.

For his part, Maximilian felt the danger growing. He had begun to fear an explosion of nationalism as much as the Austrians did. Hoping to increase efficiency, he asked Francis-Joseph for permission to consolidate the civil authority he already possessed with the military authority held by Count Gyulai. Francis-Joseph refused in no uncertain terms, commanding Maximilian to get along with Gyulai, which was a roundabout way of forcing his brother to follow the hard line championed by the commander in chief—and, if he disagreed, to keep his reservations to himself. Quite simply, Francis-Joseph expected Maximilian to ignore his convictions and submit entirely to his rival's views. Maximilian wrote his mother a letter soaked in despair: "If I did not have a sacred duty, I would already have left this country of suffering where I must live through the double humiliation of representing an inactive and unimaginative government and one that any intelligent person would have difficulty defending. With a true sense of shame, I went to Milan recently, and the feeling weighed down on me and humiliated me all the more because of the kindness with which they received us personally, as if we were respectable individuals outside of the government. This private kindness, so dismissive of my authority, showed me the true extent of my own powerlessness. It also showed me how poorly the government has acted in contrast to the goodwill of the masses . . . there is only one voice throughout the country—the voice of indignation and disapproval—and I am alone and helpless before it. I am not afraid, for that is not the Habsburg way, but I am ashamed and I keep my mouth shut. If it continues this way, I will soon consider sending Charlotte to her father in Brussels. I have no intention of letting her be sacrificed for weakness and confusion. Young women without experience have no business being in the middle of danger. We live in a state of utter chaos, and only the air of calm I put on despite my twenty-six years of age is managing to keep everything together, however temporarily. Everyone around me has lost heart and is panicking, and sometimes I wonder whether my conscience only allows me to follow the orders coming from Vienna blindly." A healthy and honorable reaction, though in reality, there was nothing else he could do other than obey the orders coming from Vienna—that is to say, from his brother.

Charlotte categorically refused to flee to Brussels, and insisted on staying at Maximilian's side. She went back and forth between Venice and Milan, and continued strolling through the streets without an escort or police protection, where people greeted her with respect, almost with affection. But at the beginning of the new year, she was booed for the first time in the streets of Venice. The next day, on January 3, 1859, without consulting her, Maximilian sent her off to Trieste, to the Lazarovitch villa where he had lived before their marriage. The boat crossing was excellent, she told her father, and during it, she had given pieces of bread to seagulls that were nearly tame. She awaited the visits of a great number of her in-laws, who had announced their arrival. It would be a "true caravan of archdukes." As for Max, he had an inflammation of the gums, but otherwise he was very well, she told her father.

But her husband missed her desperately. As soon as she left, he began writing her letters every second day in ways that betrayed his vital need to communicate with her. Since she had been gone, he wrote, the palace, but especially his heart, had been sad and empty. Alone and abandoned, his only reason for living was work, and the only distractions were the arrival of a magician or the discovery of an enormous eagle's carcass. Maximilian lived a peaceful and monk-like existence, which he regretted sometimes to set aside—such as when he needed to go to La Scala to show his face, lest the rumor spread that he had secretly left Milan like a coward. There he found the theater more crowded than ever, and thought Rossini's opera *Semiramis* was wonderful. Nonetheless, with each passing day, he missed Charlotte more.

At the end of January, he declared that he was satisfied with the state of mind in Milan and Venice. The people expressed their peaceful and positive political attachment to him. Even his enemy Gyulai seemed to be calming down. Perhaps all the agitation was but a brief storm that would move off without causing too much damage. Life went on. In his letters to Charlotte, he laughed at the comedy going on at the court of Turin. Napoleon III's first cousin, Prince Napoleon, whom everyone called Plonplon, had gone to Turin in order to marry King Victor-Emmanuel's daughter, Princess Clotilda. Only she wanted nothing to do with him, and rightly so, because everyone thought Plonplon was a brute. In anger, her father had dismissed all her ladies-in-waiting, and Minister Cavour, the dogged champion of Italian unity, was doing everything he could to make her change her mind. With all his soul, Maximilian hoped to see Plonplon finally snubbed. But it was a hope that did not come to fruition, for Plonplon did indeed marry Clotilda, which set the poor girl up for a life of sorrow. But now the alliance between Piedmont and France was sealed. From then on, Victor-Emmanuel and Cavour could go ahead with their plans to chase out the Austrians: the French and their might were behind them.

In his discouragement, Maximilian turned again to his mother, rather than to his wife: "Here I am in exile, and as lonely as a hermit in this vast Milan palace. All around me the carnival swirls, but within me, there is only the silence of Lent. . . . I am the prophet whom others laugh at, who has to taste the misery he foretold word for word to deaf ears, and on whom others now want to exact revenge, as if I had caused the disaster by false meekness or sickly sweet kindness. . . . Despite the irony I was expecting, despite the slander, I remain steadfast at my post. Though in the midst of danger, I will not turn back. Two reasons hold me here: the duty not to leave the post entrusted to me at a moment of hardship, and the duty to prevent any missteps due to fear and nervousness."

In any case, uncertainty ate away at him, and he woke up every morning wondering how the day would end. In his letters to Charlotte, he watered down the situation; two days after writing that almost desperate letter to his mother, he wrote another to his wife to assure her that Milan was calm as usual and that the population was as docile as last winter, but that it was so long, so endlessly long, this separation from Charlotte, "my life."

Two days later, on January 28, 1859, he once again wrote to Charlotte in joy for the birth of the first child of two of their close cousins and dear friends. The eldest daughter of Queen Victoria and her husband, the crown prince of Prussia, had just had a son, the future Kaiser William II. Maximilian added in an aside to Charlotte: "Now we have to follow Frederick-William and Vicky's example. It must be a special joy to have children." Then why did they not have any? This sentence of Maximilian's was peculiar, written while his kingdom was collapsing around him, and while he pined away for his wife, whom he had sent so far away of his own accord. "We should have children"—did that mean they had stopped doing what it takes to have them?

Meanwhile, events were speeding up. In Paris, Napoleon III gave a speech before chambers that set everyone thinking. In Maximilian's opinion, the French emperor would have liked to move back toward peace, but had stopped short of excluding the possibility of war. Be that as it may, Maximilian wanted Charlotte to leave Trieste and put in an appearance at Venice, which would make the best of impressions and would pacify the people while bringing them closer to him. He went so far as to specify in the postscript of one letter what jewelry he suggested she bring for the visit: nothing but pearls, or otherwise coral, malachite, and other semiprecious stones. To prove that all was well, and that all would be well, Maximilian held a ball in Milan. He thought constantly of the guest list, which promised to gather all the elegant men and women together that Lombardy had to offer. The following day, he was finally able to join Charlotte again for a few weeks of happiness and intimacy amid the storm. Then again they parted, with even more sadness than the first time. Charlotte returned to Trieste, he to Monza, which soon became unbearable to him, as the beauty of the site only increased his melancholy. The landscape yielded total silence. The blue sky pained him when he thought of how happy he would be if Charlotte were there with him. Life in the splendid Villa Reale had been sad and lonely ever since its star had gone across the sea, he repeated in a letter on April 18.

Everyone who had kept up his spirits—his entourage and his friends—all had left him. The palace was becoming empty as furniture, paintings, decorations, and other expensive objects were sent off for safekeeping in Trieste. In everyone's opinion, war was inevitable. Faced with this danger, Francis-Joseph decided to follow Maximilian's old suggestion and unite civil power with military power. The person in charge, however, would not be his brother, but Count Gyulai, Maximilian's rival. There was no room left for Maximilian. Francis-Joseph announced his decision, which was nothing short of a barely disguised dismissal, peppered with compliments and thanks for his administration, flattery that even to the most naïve of ears seemed to lack conviction. For prudence's sake, he sent a handwritten order to Count Gyulai, granting him full powers in case hostilities should erupt. Finally rid of his brother, Francis-Joseph sent the king of Piedmont, Victor-Emmanuel, an ultimatum only two days later—demanding that he disarm immediately.

The only thing left for Maximilian to do was vacate the premises. His last hours at Monza were marked by a profound sadness. A terrible hot wind from Africa blew endlessly, setting everyone on edge. His trip was long and tedious, the weather abominable, and the troubles many. His special convoy came across sixty-six trains

loaded with soldiers heading for the capital of Lombardy. A torrential rain had begun to pour, and the second special train bearing courtiers and baggage got stuck in the flood.

His arrival in Venice contrasted sadly with his previous en-
trances, so official and joyful. Maximilian did not want to stay in
the royal palace; instead, he went aboard his beloved yacht, the
Fantasy. That is where he wrote his official resignation. As he explained to Charlotte, he went about writing the letter serene in the
knowledge that during his mandate he had never once committed
an injustice or given in to weakness, nor had he ever acted against
his principles and conscience. He had tried to serve his emperor
and his country, and if for now that must remain unrecognized, he
had no doubt but that the future would one day judge him more
fairly. God knew his intentions, and that was enough for him.

His only consolation was found in the sadness that his departure left behind him. The Italians had crowded aboard the yacht to
express their loyalty to him. Another satisfaction had been the joyful, even exultant welcome given to him by the naval squadron of
which he was now ordered to take charge. For it had not been
enough for Francis-Joseph simply to fire him: he had given him
"as compensation" a few old boats that even now remained under
the command of a general who was hierarchically his inferior. If he
had wanted to humiliate his younger brother, he could not have
done a better job. But Maximilian was not unhappy to return to
the navy where he had spent so many happy years, and where he
would have the chance to fight for his country.

The chance to fight came immediately, for war against Piedmont
and France had been declared. Maximilian was worried about Charlotte. In the event that the French navy would threaten Trieste, he
planned for her and the treasures to be moved to Innsbruck.

A revolution broke out in Florence. The grand duke and his
family fled to Ferrara. A state of siege was declared at Venice. At

Trieste, French ships were seen approaching, certainly come to bomb the city. Charlotte decided to leave for Laybach, but it turned out to be a false alarm—the ships had not been French at all, but English, and therefore neutral; Charlotte had left for no reason. Gently, Maximilian upbraided her for her overreaction, telling her she should have telegraphed him first for his opinion, and that by running away she could only have made the worst of impressions on the Triestians. Because she was protected by the English and by the neutrality declared in the Adriatic, it was better for her to return to Trieste as soon as possible.

Charlotte arrived back at the Lazarovitch villa to find the park transfigured by spring, which gave her a sense of serenity otherwise hard to come by in those troubled times. Max's departure and his mission at sea had deeply saddened her. She hoped only that he would not have to risk his life in naval battles. In the meantime, as she told her brother, the change of scenery had done her a world of good. The sea air, the lightened responsibilities, and the newfound rest restored her health, which up until then had been undermined by worry.

As for the war, it was going well. The news Charlotte received of the Austrian armies was excellent. All the people in the monarchy had enthusiastically taken their emperor's side, and were willing to share the expense of the operations. Never had there been such a surge of royalist and patriotic spirit. The extreme danger had also offered one advantage: it had stirred up deep feelings. Charlotte was truly happy to find out that the empire had never been more secure, with nothing to revive the horrible memories of the 1848 revolution. In Italy itself, the situation was favorable. The army was the best the empire had ever had, beaming with excellent morale, and even the Italian regiments were begging to be allowed to fight rather than to be held back. In short, she looked forward to the future with optimism.

Between patrols, Maximilian was sightseeing. He told Charlotte at length that when he had come ashore in Dalmatia, he had discovered a wonderful place with an abandoned house of which only the foundations remained, with a terraced garden, paths that lead to a vine-covered walkway, and an unbelievable view of the sea, the yellow and golden rocks, the domes in the historic city of Ragusa, and the many islands and distant mountains. They could plant palm trees there, any plant found in the south, he said; they could buy the place and name it Villa Carlotta.

But then, there was the war. When Maximilian was still in Venice, French ships had been spotted, but they quickly turned around and sailed off. Maximilian had immediately returned to his private affairs. He summoned a garden designer, and with him, planned out the garden at Miramar down to the smallest details, happy to be aboard his yacht, and happy to be engaged in his favorite pastime.

Several days later, the French returned. Taking advantage of the darkness of the night, they had tried to land at the Lido. The navy had found them out, and sounded the alarm. In seconds, everyone had sprung into action. A few cannon blasts had sufficed to chase them away. Maximilian patrolled the lagoon. He went to the church of Pellestrina and prayed for everyone he loved, when suddenly the misery of being separated from his beloved Charlotte overwhelmed him.

As it continued, the war turned foul. It seemed that there had been a large battle near Magenta, and that the Austrian forces had been defeated. And the fault lay with Gyulai: his cruelty and incompetence had aroused universal indignation and disgusted everyone.

Two days later, on June 9, 1859, Maximilian sent Charlotte a new batch of bad news. Milan, dear Milan, the object of all his prayers, had fallen into French hands. His sorrow was so great that he felt like crying, especially when he thought of all the people who had been sacrificed and abandoned by the Austrian government. He cried for that sad and magnificent land, for Lombardy, which would otherwise have been blessed by God. What was happening to Austria?

Charlotte's optimism was crushed in one fell swoop. The news "gave her bile," as she told her brother Philippe. She felt alone, ill, but above all, far from Max, who was still detained near Venice. Like a lion in a cage, he could do nothing, given his troops' inferiority in numbers. Moved to despair by his powerlessness, Maximilian could only think about returning to Charlotte. This was impossible for the moment, since he could not abandon his squadron without destroying all their courage and morale, just when the French could attack them. Charlotte became embittered: "We are still paying the price for the huge mistakes made at the beginning of this campaign, which made us lose so many fine soldiers, and no one has any idea how our army is fighting at all, especially when they always find themselves faced with an enemy superior in numbers, a fact which, in itself, gives a hint of the quality of leadership."

She was still staying at the Lazarovitch villa, and already the paintings, furniture, and artwork had been moved to Miramar, which was standing ready to receive its new landlords. When would they be able to enjoy it? Far from getting closer to Trieste, Maximilian was summoned to the Austrian headquarters in Verona. There he found Emperor Francis-Joseph, and behind closed doors, face-to-face, the two brothers were able to have "a good, long conversation." Maximilian finally got the satisfaction of telling his older brother everything that had been weighing on his mind; his brother welcomed him with kindness, and treated him with frankness and sincerity.

From Verona, Francis-Joseph and his brother traveled to Villafranca, where the troops were gathering for the upcoming battle. They lived together in a little house that was clean but "poorly furbished." Ironically, Maximilian found etchings of the Ostende port hung on the wall of his small bedroom. He had nothing to do but watch regiments head off toward the front. The days passed in monotony. One such afternoon, Maximilian dined with the generals and the emperor, and then they spent the evening with the princes from Tuscany and Modena, their cousins dethroned by the revolution—company that was nothing if not disheartening.

A few days later, the battle of Solferino took place. Maximilian told Charlotte that the fighting had lasted from four o'clock in the morning until nightfall. He suspected that both sides had suffered considerable losses. The Austrian armies had had to retreat. The headquarters had remained in Villafranca, but he and the emperor had gone back to Verona. Seeing so many wounded was a terrible, sickening thing for Maximilian, and the spectacle of the retreat had been a humiliation he would never forget. "What is happening to Austria?" he repeated over and over.

The final chapter was not long in coming. Late one evening, Maximilian saw a coach arrive bearing Napoleon's coat of arms. General Fleury, the emperor of the French's emissary, presented a letter proposing an armistice. Francis-Joseph received him kindly and wrote an acceptance for Fleury to take back. Thus it was armistice, and soon peace—the end of this horrible war. Nothing further detained Maximilian at Verona; he joyfully boarded his yacht and set course directly for Miramar. He apologized for not going to meet Charlotte at Trieste, but his shame was too great for him to be seen in public. "What is happening to Austria, and what will happen to her now?"

❈   ❈   ❈

Francis-Joseph had had to give up Lombardy, the first step toward Italian unification. Just for a little added humiliation, Napoleon had forced him to give it to him only to turn around and offer it to Victor-Emmanuel, in the hope of getting in exchange the Savoy he so coveted. Which left Venice. Napoleon III had learned that Maximilian was very well liked there, and that, if his advice had been heeded, the Austrians might never have fallen so low. He knew that Charlotte had also enjoyed great popularity there. Therefore, by sheer kindness, he suggested that the Austrian emperor create a Kingdom of Venetia and name Maximilian and Charlotte its sovereigns. Francis-Joseph nearly choked with indignation. "I feel that great changes are needed there," he answered Napoleon III. "I will carry them out under *my* scepter, and Venice will be not only happy, but satisfied." No crown for Maximilian and Charlotte.

Nonetheless, a magnificent homage was offered to Maximilian by one whose sincerity could not be doubted — the architect of the Italian unification, Count Cavour: "Do you know who was our greatest enemy in Lombardy, the one we most feared and the one whose progress we followed day by day? Archduke Maximilian, young, active, diligent, who gave himself over body and soul to the task of winning over the Milanese, and who was about to succeed. His perseverance, his way of acting, his fair and liberal spirit had already seduced quite a few supporters away from us. Never had the Lombard provinces been so prosperous and well administered. Thank God, the Viennese government intervened, and as always, did not miss the chance to act stupidly, an impolitic move, mortal for Austria, but most advantageous for Piedmont. Emperor Francis-Joseph recalled his brother. I breathed at last upon hearing this news: now Lombardy could never escape us."

4

Finally reunited with Charlotte, Maximilian shut himself away with her in Miramar's Castelleto and refused to see anyone. They lived "like hermits." Since Charlotte's optimism had made her view Max's situation in a very rosy way, their fall had been all the harder and the truth all the crueler. The only good thing was that she was back together with Max, and just seeing him again, just being with him, allowed her to forget the rest. Yet she found her beloved in a terrible condition. Worn-out and crushed, he bore the weight of shame on his shoulders, and though he had been in no way responsible for it, he felt the empire's defeat as if it were his own.

Charlotte's brothers were saddened by the situation. Not only had Max been ousted from his position as viceroy, but the defeat had also robbed him of his functions in the navy. He had no position anymore, nothing to do, practically no future, and he was not yet thirty years old. If only Charlotte had married the king of Portugal, Philippe sighed. But Charlotte fought back: with Max, she had a lot more than the crown of Portugal. Times were hard, yes, the present and future were gloomy, but Portugal might very well have gone through the same difficulties. "It is not a throne that makes happiness," she insisted. Who said Max would not have a brilliant future? "He is too striking not to leave his mark on the destiny of the world," Charlotte argued, citing the example of "dear Father," King Leopold, who had lost a position of eminence when the princess of Wales died, only to find another when he had become king of the Belgians. The same fate might well await Max, who resembled Father so much in the qualities they shared. "Maybe they are just unfeasible hopes, but why should I not dream?"

Less encouraging to her dreams, however, was the family reunion at Ischl in Tyrol. The imperial villa, vacation home of the Habsburgs, was a large white house with porticoes and terraces shaded by striped cloth awnings. A magnificent garden filled with fountains and blooming bushes surrounded it, and the view stretched out on all sides to the forest-covered Alps, their summits forever buried in snow. In summertime, it was almost hot, and light clothing was a must. The men left at four in the morning to hunt chamois in the mountains, dressed in short leather breeches and caps decorated with brushes. The women woke up later and dressed in cotton crinoline, escaping the sun and heat by taking walks in the shade of lime trees or chatting beneath climbing vines.

The meeting had taken place at the behest of Archduchess Sophie, who was determined to repair her sons' misunderstanding. Despite the arguments that had driven a wedge between them, Francis-Joseph and Maximilian were glad to see each other; in the relaxed vacation atmosphere, far from the hardships they had both endured, it wasn't long before they rediscovered their intimacy.

If they had been alone, everything would have been fine, but the wives were there as well. Brought up in the mountains of Bavaria, Empress Elisabeth might indeed have won the first prize for beauty, but she still remained a provincial. Charlotte willfully repeated the fact that her sister-in-law was only a duchess *in* Bavaria, meaning she belonged to a poor and obscure branch of the illustrious house, and that she was not a duchess *of* Bavaria, which would have meant that she was a member of the royal, and thus chic, branch. What was more, Elisabeth butchered French. Charlotte, on the other hand, was a daughter and granddaughter of kings. By her mother, she belonged to the House of France. Her upbringing and social position had given her an international culture. She was an intellectual who liked to show off the different facets of her wit, so much so that Elisabeth could not help grumbling against "that pretentious little Coburg." The nickname "little Belgian goose" even began to circulate, which hardly did much to improve relations between the two women. In fact, neither could bear the other or even tolerate being in the same room together. Archduchess Sophie was sorry for it, but since she hated Elisabeth and was herself far from possessed of a pleasant character, no one expected harmony to come from her. The wives made the atmosphere so disagreeable that Charlotte and Max were both thrilled when the "vacation" was over.

They returned with relief to the Lazarovitch villa, their principal residence in Trieste until Miramar was completed. The bland house stood on a cliff overhanging the sea. Max had decorated its interior with the most careful taste: the walls were hung with brightly colored velvet or damask and innumerable family portraits, Habsburg and Coburg, but just a few Orleans. The furniture was either light and graceful or extremely heavy, and everywhere there were clocks, vases, knickknacks, books, landscapes, watercolors, treasures taken from the Milan palace, and souvenirs Maximilian had brought back from his travels. The home was comfortable and welcoming, but it seemed tiny compared to the palaces of Lombardy. They saw few people, simply because there were few people to see. Maximilian and Charlotte found themselves alone together, for the first time since their wedding, and moreover, alone in a tight space. Even when the war had still been going strong, Max had already been thinking and worrying about Miramar. Now that peace had been restored, and with it idleness, he devoted all his time, energy, and money to building his castle. He took Charlotte on countless cruises. Now that it had been decommissioned, they used the *Fantasy* for excursions up and down the Dalmatian coast.

One day, across from Ragusa, they came upon paradise on Earth: a little island covered with lush and fragrant plant life. The waves of the Mediterranean gently kissed its small beaches, and there was even a minuscule saltwater lake. When he had sailed home en route from the Crusades, Richard the Lion-Hearted had been shipwrecked there, and a monastery had been built, which was now abandoned and falling into ruin. Charlotte and Maximilian immediately fell in love with Lacroma, as they discovered it was called. Maximilian was in such debt for Miramar that Charlotte had to buy the little island with her own money. The monastery was quickly restored, and they were soon able to set themselves up in it, to their immense happiness. Charlotte went horseback riding and swimming, painted watercolors, read, and strolled. Maximilian wrote pamphlets on the state of the empire. He also rediscovered his teenage talent for poetry. "Oh Max, if only we could always be as happy as we are today," Charlotte whispered to him one night when the moon and the air, the sea and the scents mixed headily.

Charlotte was wonderfully happy . . . but no one had had the courage to tell her the legend of Lacroma, her little island paradise. When the last Benedictine monk had been chased out of the little monastery, he had laid a curse of violent death on any usurper blasphemous enough to live there.

Roaming between the Lazarovitch villa, Miramar's Castelleto, and Lacroma, Charlotte lived in a dream world, especially since she was still madly in love with Max, and felt she was learning something new and wonderful about him every day. She came to admire him more and more, and she was ecstatic to hear around her only unanimous praise for her beloved. She was proudly aware that she made him completely happy.

Charlotte proclaimed her happiness in each letter she sent to her family and friends, but they had only her word to take on it. In the same way, Maximilian's happiness existed only because she affirmed it. Yet this man, who had grown used to exertion, needed activity. Idleness weighed on him: he reacted more slowly, and apathy was spreading within him. So they decided to go far away, to Brazil. Charlotte was thrilled at the idea. They prepared the *Fantasy* for their voyage—it was a fine, large ship, with two big wheels, two tilted smokestacks toward the stern, two masts, a particularly tapered prow, and at the stern, cabins with large windows that opened onto the sea.

They set out in the beginning of November. The weather was horrid; as Charlotte told it, the elements were at war with each other, it rained, and the wind blew with gale force. The superstitious would have seen it as a bad omen. Luckily the weather improved when the *Fantasy* passed to the south of Italy, hugging the coasts of Andalusia and northern Africa. During layovers, they did some sightseeing; in her letters, Charlotte described in detail the places, plants, climate, colors, people, and village festivals she saw.

They began to cross the Atlantic. The first stop was Madeira — a strange choice, since that was where Maximilian's first fiancée, Maria Amelia of Bragance, had died. He had spent her last winter with her there. Seeing the site again, he was stricken with endless melancholy. "Much to my sadness, I see the valley of Machicot and beautiful Santa Cruz again, where just seven years ago we had such tender moments — seven years filled with joy and sorrow, so fertile in pain and bitter disillusionment. True to my word, I am coming back to seek on the waves of the Atlantic the peace that tottering Europe can no longer give my worried soul. But a deep melancholy sweeps over me when I compare the two times. Seven years ago, I was just waking to life; I was walking happily toward the future. Today, I already feel tired; my shoulders are no longer free and light, they are bent under the burden of a cruel past." For days on end, he wallowed in gloomy memories. He went several times to visit the hospital founded by the empress of Brazil, the house where his beloved had died, the church where he had attended Sunday mass with her. "It is here that on February 4, 1853, the empress of Brazil's only daughter, a fully accomplished woman, died of lung disease. She left this imperfect world like a pure angel of light to return to heaven, her true home."

The weather also worked against them. The storm caught up with Charlotte and Maximilian in Madeira. It rained endlessly. Huge waves broke against the cliffs, sending up clouds of foam with ter-rifying roars. A small schooner almost sank — the ten crewmen aboard were saved only by a miracle. The tall ships had had to leave the harbor, which was no longer safe. A Spanish three-master disembarked all her passengers, and everyone feared she would be run aground.

❖   ❖   ❖

Two days later, Charlotte's perspective changed completely: Madeira
had become charming. She had seen the most beautiful, lush vegetation, a mix of tropical and northern plants. Everywhere they
went there were sugarcane fields, banana trees, cacti, orange trees,
and a slew of trees from the New World—"too many to list"—but
oak and chestnut forests grew thick on the mountains. There was
only one thing wrong: certain tropical fruits tasted disgusting, and
others, like guava, stank horrendously. Charlotte tirelessly described the magnificent landscapes and her inspiring strolls. They
reached the end of 1859 bathed in the wonderment of the island.

Then, out of the blue, Charlotte's family found out that Max
had left for Brazil, leaving Charlotte at Madeira, even though she
had been meant to go with him. In a letter to her father, she told
how she had accompanied him to the Canary Islands, where she
had been annoyed not to be able to go ashore because of violent
wind. A rowboat had brought Max to land, and, according to Charlotte, he had immediately boarded the *Elisabeth,* a cruise liner sailing to Brazil. Saddened not to have been able to see Tenerife because
of the clouds, Charlotte had returned to Madeira on the very day
fine weather returned. She was enjoying the tropical winter among
flowers and birds. It remained light until late in the afternoon, but
the twilight barely lasted a few minutes. She could not wait to have
news of her family, but mail took an eternity because of the ineffi-
cient Portuguese administration.

Christmas arrived, and she decorated a tree with what she had
on hand: oranges and bananas. "Though Max's absence made the
evening a little less enjoyable than usual, I am having a very good
time," she wrote. Two days later, she invited the local authorities
to dinner—the bishop who only spoke Portuguese, the civil governor, the military commander "who looks like some sort of hippo-
potamus," as well as a former minister of foreign affairs, decorated

with the wide Belgian sash of the order of Leopold. She also undertook a long expedition to the center of the island, which forced her to spend the night in the Austrian consul's villa. She wrote not one word on the reasons that led her not to go with her husband to Brazil. Officially, it was announced that she was ill and ordered to remain in bed, but nowhere in her letters did she ever mention an illness.

From Cape Verde, on January 1, 1860, Maximilian wrote Charlotte a letter that she did not receive until several weeks later:

"My dear and beloved Charlotte, I hope that now and in the years to come, God will send you only the best. For if you are happy, your happiness will reflect back on me. You are everything to me. . . . Our parting at Tenerife caused me more sorrow than you can or do imagine. When I saw you leaving, I felt so desperately sad . . . and I think back with longing on our happy days at Madeira and its flowery villa.

"If I didn't have my sailor's duties, and if I weren't ashamed before God, I would have come back to Funchal, back to you, a long time ago."

Despite his fine words, Charlotte remained alone in the middle of winter on an Atlantic island while her husband was sightseeing in Brazil. She offered no news of him, no explanation for his actions. In Brussels, her father and brothers were more and more curious, if not worried. They sent her letter after letter, which took an eternity to get to her, and which remained unanswered.

At the end of February, Charlotte finally received news from Max:

"My dear, best angel, as chance would have it, a steamship is about to leave for Europe, and I will take the opportunity to send you these few lines I'll scribble down quickly, my dear, adored angel. I have been traveling through Brazil for about twenty days now. That said, we did the right thing when we decided together in the end that you shouldn't come along, even if the trip was divine on a sea as calm as a lake. This country is no place for women, and you would have made such a long trip for nothing. Except in the filthy and boring cities and villages, no decent woman can live here. This country rules out traveling for women. Only a man able to withstand great hardships can feel at home in Brazil. . . . Soon I will return to Bahia, and then I will fly with the wings of love toward Madeira, toward you, my life."

At last, that was the explanation: Charlotte had agreed not to make the long crossing of the Atlantic because she suffered from seasickness. And Maximilian was glad for the decision, though it had cost him so much pain, for after seeing the conditions in Brazil he knew Charlotte could never have kept up with him on his wanderings—wanderings during which he could only think of the moment he would finally see "his life," his Charlotte, again. Maximilian was sincere, but had he convinced Charlotte? In any case, now that she had gotten news from him, she could send it along to her family.

In the beginning of March, she once again wrote to her brother Philippe. If her family had not heard from her in such a long time, the fault lay with the awful Portuguese postal system, she said. She could do nothing about it. Moreover, she did not understand why her family was so surprised that she did not accompany Max to Brazil. Anything more about it and she would start to get angry with them: "You ask me where I am and what has become of me; my dear, I never said that I had to leave Madeira. So I don't understand why you are so worked up about it. You mustn't listen to the gossip in the papers. If we had had to leave here in December, don't you think I would have mentioned it to you? It is true that we once thought of going to Brazil together, but that only remained a possibility, and that's why we didn't mention it. When the logistics turned out to be too difficult, we dropped the idea. As for Max, I think he will be coming back soon, and I recently learned that he has been to Bahia, and thus that, all alone, he has completed the trip that we were supposed to take together. You can tell that to dear Father. As for the rest, it might be better not to speak of it, because I don't know how much Max would like that, before the end of his expedition. I think I should be getting more letters from Max by the steamship that will be coming from Lisbon. I don't know what else to tell you from here: the weather turned bad a few days ago, but before that, we had some beautiful days."

It is difficult to draw a conclusion from this obviously embarrassed, if not dishonest, writing. In subsequent letters, her vision of Madeira had changed: no more flowers, no more birds, no more tropical vegetation. She described the unemployment, the poverty of a people living in cabins no better than doghouses.

On March 5, 1860, Max was back from Brazil and made his reappearance at Madeira. A mandatory quarantine forced him to remain aboard for five days before coming ashore. He and Charlotte could only see each other from separate boats, which "was very funny." There was not another word on this reunion to resolve three months of separation. A week later, they set off again for Europe. Charlotte admitted to Philippe that she missed Madeira, to which she had grown attached. She did not mention Max, but described in detail a layover in Tétouan, a Spanish colony in Morocco, and her reunion with her cousin, Gaston d'Orleans, the count of Eu, and an officer in the Spanish army. Far from calming her family's curiosity and concerns, Charlotte's omissions and confusing explanations only increased them. Philippe, in particular, bombarded her with questions and criticisms: Why would she not have announced that Max was leaving for Brazil? Why would she have remained alone in Madeira? Why would she have sent no word?

Charlotte admitted to her brother that she sometimes dreaded her family's letters, because she could no longer bear their questions. Maximilian and she had returned to their heaven on Earth in Lacroma, but still her family did not understand. Nor did any of their descendants—for even today, the mystery remains complete. Why had Maximilian abandoned Charlotte for three months, with no other explanation than fear for her seasickness? Charlotte said nothing.

To top it all off, no sooner had they returned home when Maximilian left her again to go to Vienna alone. Once again, there was no explanation for the separation.

His stay in the empire's capital and his meetings with his family inspired Maximilian to make the bleakest of observations on the situation. Everywhere, in all levels of the administration, there was corruption, graft, fraud, incompetence, and paralysis. The people complained and the imperial government did not listen. Maximilian came to compare the situation to that of France under Louis XVI on the eve of the Revolution. He admitted that his pessimism may have been unfounded, but he felt it necessary to put his affairs in order—which meant he sent a secretary to Brussels to meet secretly with his father-in-law, King Leopold, and ask him to pretend to acquire his properties at Miramar and Lacroma, so that, in case of an emergency, he would be able to hold onto them. Maximilian returned to his home on the shores of the Adriatic embittered and disappointed, but Charlotte welcomed him back light and carefree. In her letter to Philippe, she expressed her joy at seeing her husband again. As soon as he arrived, she took him on a "charming trip" to the mouth of the Cataro, surrounded by beautiful landscapes. And so they resumed their peaceful and, to judge from what she wrote, enjoyable life together.

Charlotte used the same words to describe the situation to her old governess, the countess of Hulste. Charlotte told her over and over that she had the consolation and satisfaction of having made "the one to whom God united me" so perfectly happy. Certainly, the life Max and Charlotte were leading was not the one she had foreseen—they had no honors, no court, and no responsibilities any longer—but she thanked God for it, since in the times they were living, it was better to stay away from the world, and the less you had, the less you had to lose. Nonetheless, despite their present situation, she was sure that Maximilian would have a brilliant future: "For he was made for that and gifted by Providence with everything that makes a nation happy, and it seems to me an impossibility that all those gifts should go forever buried and hidden after only three years of being allowed to shine."

Charlotte's elder brother, Leopold, duke of Brabant, stopped off at his sister and brother-in-law's home during the layover of a cruise he took in May 1860. What he saw there painted a much more realistic portrait of the couple's situation. After they received him with open arms, the couple "smothered" him with embarrassing niceties he felt he did not deserve: "I feel so sorry for my poor sister, falling from the grandeur of Milan and Venice into that little house, a collection of past glories, and really just a storage place for furniture. My brother-in-law has put on some weight, and his sideburns are much too long, his teeth are worse, and to put it quite simply, the poor boy, who by the way is now quite bald, has not improved with age."

Yet much to his admiration, the couple seemed to be coping. They bore their misfortune with nobility, and did not complain, despite the cruelty of their situation. Their little court was as sad as the city of Trieste. The war had ruined the port, and there were almost no ships anymore, since most of the merchants had gone bankrupt. Almost all the big names that had surrounded Maximilian and Charlotte when they had ruled were long gone. Leopold found only the old, faithful Countess Lutzoff.

Their life seemed to Leopold to be no fun whatsoever. One afternoon, they took a coach ride, during the course of which it was obligatory to wax poetic over the view of the sea or of the mountains still covered with snow. They dined at seven o'clock in tuxedos or short trousers to "passable food." But it was Charlotte's fate that most obsessed Leopold. "My poor sister, the brilliant queen of Venice and Milan where she thought herself loved, forced to flee in haste to Trieste, after having had to make several trips to evacuate her jewels herself, then to go into exile at Madeira so as not to be close to the beautiful realm they had lost. How sad it is, how unfair. But about all that, my sister does not breathe a word. I find her unchanged, and as she was at Brussels, a little languid in her mindset, in her voice and eyes, though she is in the best of health."

Of course, the couple took Leopold to see Miramar Castle, which was still under construction. He found the site and the building splendid. It was a great deal of fun to build and decorate castles, he thought, though one needed to know when to pick one's moments. He was horrified to see Maximilian not only throwing all his money into Miramar, but going into debt for it besides.

His sister took him to the Castelleto for a few days. The view was magnificent, but the house was truly tiny. "Poor people, poor Austria, poor Europe," Leopold concluded. His clear-sightedness shook the optimism Charlotte had been faking. A few weeks after he left, she had only one idea in her head: to leave everything behind and run to Brussels to be with her family in the beloved place of her childhood. "To see Belgium, if only for a day, would do me a world of good," she wrote to her brother Philippe, "because you can't stay away from those you love for such a long time without suffering." Yet she feared she would not be able to bring Max along with her, because the political situation was growing tense again. Italy had erupted. Garibaldi pushed, and behind him Cavour, and all the small conservative monarchies crumbled one after the other.

With sieges and landings, battles and bizarre shifts of fortune, Italy was making great strides toward unification. It was possible that in their momentum, the Italian nationalists might attack Austrian Venice or even Trieste. Charlotte lived through the same worries, the same uncertainties as she had the year before. As reality tore through the idyllic scene she had painted for herself, she reacted in her usual way: she said nothing, admitted nothing, and what she felt came out not in what she said, but in what she did not say. Gone were the enthusiastic descriptions of excursions through wondrous countryside, the lyric hymns to her delicious existence in sun-warmed tranquility, the paragraphs overflowing with love for Max.

In a sense, the circumstances alone could explain why there was a crisis in the household. Yet when they were apart, Charlotte's letters to her husband showed how much she was still in love with him, and Maximilian's letters also bore the mark of his unchanging passion for "the beloved angel": "For me, your letters are rays of sunshine in my monotonous life. I am so sad not to be with you that tears are coming to my eyes." For their third anniversary, he wrote her a letter burning with love. Even though he no longer had the excuse of official duties, however, he still left often and distanced himself from her. Of course, the political situation might explain a certain bitterness in him that came out in what he told her, but already one could sense something deeper and more personal than that. But this difficult period of their relationship remained obscured in the silence in which they both cloaked it.

During Christmas of 1860, Maximilian and Charlotte finally realized their dream of moving into Miramar Castle. Since the workers were still busy on the second floor, the couple moved in to the first floor only. In ecstasy, Charlotte described to the countess of Hulste the beautiful apartments, warm in the winter, cool in the summer, filled with the murmurs of the sea. In accordance with royal tradition of the time, the gardens had been opened to the public. Natives of Trieste and foreigners alike rushed to see the new attraction. Their opinion was unanimous: Maximilian had created a masterpiece.

Actually, the castle was odd, to say the least, especially in that it was composed of fairly kitschy elements, but as a whole, and even today, it has maintained an extraordinary romanticism due in part to its position perched above the sea. Terraces and vine-covered walkways surrounded it, inviting visitors to stroll. A sumptuous park of shade and boughs, flowers and sweet-smelling paths, rose all the way up to the mountains. Next to the castle, a miniature port was dug out and given a tiny pier, at the end of which a granite Sphinx, brought back by Maximilian from one of his trips, crouched, scanning the Adriatic with its blind eyes. The castle's interior was a mixture of styles, though it retained a certain unity, if only by its opulence. There was the heavy somberness of different eras: German Renaissance, Tudor, neo-Gothic, Victorian, and Napoleon III; there were thick doors torn from monasteries, overly ornate nineteenth-century furniture, and a few examples of fine ebony work from centuries past, not to mention the many opulent tapestries and delicately toned silks next to masses of gold leaf, bronzes, marbles busts, the unavoidable family portraits, and contemporary landscapes. Knick-knacks, exotic souvenirs, and books were piled high next to some old paintings. As the creator of the castle, Maximilian had a taste that was decidedly questionable, but instantly recognizable and personal. After his first attempt at decoration in the Lazarovitch villa at Trieste, he found his true expression in setting up Miramar, which would forever remain his signature piece — so much so that the hordes of tourists today that tread the castle's inlaid parquet floors have still not managed to crush the atmosphere of the place. Heavy yet welcoming, busy but somehow pleasant, the ghosts of the tragic couple can still be felt within it.

Barely had they moved in when Maximilian had to leave Charlotte again, this time under orders. His brother Francis-Joseph was sending Max as his representative to the funeral of King Frederick-William IV of Prussia. To help him in this task, Max took along his best friend, Bombelles, whose father was Maximilian and Francis-Joseph's tutor. Bombelles had been raised with the young archdukes, but his age and personality brought him closer to Maximilian, whose side he had almost never left.

Returning from the king's funeral in Berlin, Maximilian decided to pass through Vienna. During the trip, an accident occurred that could very well have proven deadly: "I lived through the greatest fear of my life. The royal compartment I was in with Bombelles and the servants overheated and caught fire on one side. Everything began to burn, the flames were licking the car, and the fire could only be seen from the inside—from the outside, it was invisible. No matter how loudly we shouted, no one heard us, and we were absolutely sure that we were about to lose our lives. The train was speeding up. The flames were becoming more and more threatening, and the acrid smoke was beginning to choke us. We were staring death in the face. That was when clever Bombelles had a brilliant idea. Despite the train's speed, despite the frost and ice outside, he managed to climb out the window and onto the roof. He found a cable that went all the way to the engine and pulled twice on it, which set off a whistle and thus the alarm. The train stopped and we were saved, but just in the nick of time."

Maximilian's gratitude toward Bombelles for saving his life only strengthened the friendship between the two men.

Once back at Miramar, Maximilian spent his evenings more and more without Charlotte, and instead with Bombelles and the officers of the Austrian garrison he had invited over. They drank a lot, smoked big cigars, told bawdy stories, and enjoyed themselves. Another person who was beginning to take on importance was also at these parties: Schertzenlechner was Maximilian's head bedroom butler and everyone hated the vulgar drunkard except Maximilian. Not only did Maximilian make Schertzenlechner his drinking partner, but he also named him chancellor, an extravagant promotion, considering the imperial house's usual stiffness regarding ranks and titles. For a servant to sit at his royal and imperial highness's table, he must possess truly extraordinary qualities—but which ones?

Charlotte grinned and silently bore the fact that her husband had abandoned her for his friends. She moped but did not protest, even though her imperious temperament normally made her speak her mind to anyone annoying her, beginning with her brothers. There was none of that with Maximilian. She refused to bother her husband, even over the smallest matter.

When he had been in Vienna during a family gathering, Max had happened to describe Madeira to his sister-in-law Empress Elisabeth as such a beautiful place that she had decided to go see it for herself. At the time, she was suffering from one of her usual neuroses, refusing to see anyone in the single-minded obsession of isolating herself as far away from others as possible. Everyone tried to talk her out of going to Madeira—the court, the government, and especially her husband, Francis-Joseph. If she must have a retreat, they said, why could she not pick an isolated corner of the empire, as if there were not enough of them? These objections only strengthened the empress's determination, and in the end, everyone gave in— though they warned her that no Austrian ship would be able to carry her to the middle of the Atlantic. Refusing to be stopped, she wrote to her friend Queen Victoria, who immediately put her yacht, the *Victoria and Albert,* at Elisabeth's disposal. Thus, the empress went to spend the five winter months at Madeira. Francis-Joseph was furious with Maximilian for putting the thought into Elisabeth's head.

As soon as the empress left her winter retreat, the emperor, still madly in love with her, ran to meet her at Miramar. He boarded the *Fantasy* with Maximilian, and together they sailed off to rendezvous with the *Victoria and Albert,* while Charlotte waited on the castle's dock. The painter Dell'Acqua immortalized the scene in a painting that still hangs in a Miramar salon: the emperor's rowboat has just pulled up against the dock, which ends with the Sphinx. The sailors hold their oars at attention, as Maximilian in his navy uniform helps his brother ashore. A few steps further up, the empress and the archduchess greet each other, surrounded by richly bedecked officers and even more decorated servants. Elisabeth is wearing a type of dark green and black tartan, while Charlotte has chosen bright colors: a large white shawl over pink crinoline.

The two sisters-in-law seemed to overflow with cordiality, and yet barely had the two brothers set off for the city when Elisabeth deliberately turned her back on Charlotte. That "little Belgian goose" truly annoyed her. Even worse, Elisabeth refused to put a leash on the huge sheepdog she had brought back from Madeira, and what was bound to happen did: the beast pounced on the little toy dog Queen Victoria had given Charlotte, and finished it off in one bite. Charlotte was disconsolate, but Elisabeth did not deign to apologize. In fact, she went so far as to express her surprise for all to hear that so much was being made of so little, and that in any case, she had always hated little dogs. Charlotte reacted intelligently: poor Elisabeth, in her condition, already so fragile, had truly begun to require help. Charlotte told her brothers over and over how worried she was for her sister-in-law. In other words, she told them the woman was insane.

Soon, much to Charlotte's relief, the imperial couple left for Vienna, but it did not take long for Max to follow them. Elisabeth was planning to set off again, not for Madeira this time, but for the island of Corfu, where her white villa, the Achileon, had been built, and she had decided that Maximilian would be the one to escort her there. Francis-Joseph squeezed out his permission through clenched teeth; once again, Elisabeth had forced his hand.

Charlotte was bitterly disappointed. She had not noticed that love had sprung up between her husband and her sister-in-law. And yet the signs were everywhere: Elisabeth hated Charlotte, Maximilian had a certain grudge toward Francis-Joseph, just as Elisabeth did, though for other, older reasons. Elisabeth and Maximilian were alike, two romantics, in love with poetry and flights of the spirit, souls that soared over the pragmatism of Francis-Joseph on the one side and of Charlotte on the other. With her grandiose tendency to do whatever she pleased without taking anyone else into consideration, Elisabeth must not have hesitated a second to go after her brother-in-law, and Max must have been enchanted by her siren song. Elisabeth was not overly interested in physical love, and in any case, carnal desires between a brother and sister-in-law would have been a bit excessive. In that way, Max could feel an impossible love for her, the same love he had felt, and still felt, for a dead woman, his first fiancée, Maria Amelia of Bragance. Love without obstacles, like the one he had had with his wife Charlotte, attracted him less than the intense feelings buried in the dark recesses of the soul, feelings unable to become physical, and inflaming the imagination alone.

So few details on the affair between the empress and the arch-duke have come down to us that it must not have lasted very long — just long enough to exasperate everyone. Francis-Joseph was furious with his brother. Rumor had it that he had sent him a rage-filled letter and was considering punishing him. The relation-ship between the two brothers was extremely tense.

Charlotte had always hoped for a new post for Maximilian, but after what had happened, nothing more was to be expected from

Francis-Joseph. Charlotte and Max had lost their harmony, and now they were in the process of losing their future.

The situation had not changed when, in the beginning of October 1861, an important visitor was announced at Miramar: Count Rechberg, minister of foreign affairs for the Austrian empire. His visit, he wrote, was to remain secret. He arrived at the Trieste station in a special train, and unmarked coaches brought the minister and his men to the castle where his hosts were awaiting him, as curious as they were impatient. He quickly described the purpose of his visit: would Maximilian and Charlotte agree to ascend the throne of an empire yet to be formed—the empire of Mexico?

Empire, emperor, empress, throne, crown . . . the words resounded like triumphant fanfare in Maximilian and Charlotte's ears. But how had this come about? Around forty years earlier, Mexico, until then a Spanish colony, had gained its independence, and had not found its balance since. The coups d'état and *pronunciamentos* had come in quick succession, two hundred and fifty in all. For a short time, Mexico had even given itself an empire, which was soon destroyed with the assassination of Emperor Iturbide. In this state of anarchy, the coffers were forever empty, and Mexico had had to borrow from other countries, only to renege on its loans. Instability and debt had become the two pillars of the country.

Amid this endemic chaos, an extraordinary person had come to the fore in the last few years: Benito Juárez, who had been born fifty-four years earlier in a peasant's shack somewhere in the hills surrounding the city of Oaxaca. A Zapotec Indian, he had spent his childhood in the most abject poverty, but his intelligence had led him to great academic success. As a lawyer, he had embarked on a political career and had quickly risen through the ranks, beating out rivals and superiors, to become the leading figure in the

Mexican political scene. Filled with hatred for the Church, he had nationalized the clergy's property and instituted civil marriages. Since he hated foreigners just as much, he was determined to stop them from spreading their influence in Mexico and prevent them from recouping their loans. Many Mexicans had, of course, been violently opposed to this radical leftist Indian, who had swept them aside with a brush of his hand. Descended for the most part from important and wealthy families, these particular citizens had once held important posts in their country, but had since been living in exile for years.

Among them was the former ambassador José Hidalgo, who had gone on vacation two years before in Biarritz. One day, he took a stroll that led him out of the city, and he had to try to hitch a ride home. A coach came at him with great speed and he waved for it to stop. As the coachman continued along his way, the woman he was driving noticed the gesticulating man and had the sudden impression that she recognized his face. After a few seconds, she realized it was Hidalgo, and she ordered the coachman to come to a halt. The woman was Napoleon III's wife, Empress Eugenie. She was also spending her vacation in Biarritz, a town whose popularity she herself had launched. She had once met Hidalgo in Spain, for they were both related to important Castilian families.

They exchanged news and spoke of the past as the coach drove on, and Hidalgo went off on a diatribe about Mexico, a country that needed to be restored, a people who needed to be saved. First, he said, the evil Indian Juárez had to be gotten rid of so that, with France's help, they could found a great Christian empire to educate the Mexicans in the shadow of the Cross and bring them prosperity in the shadow of France. Eugenie's Catholic and Spanish blood boiled immediately. Mexico would be her cause.

The next day, she had invited Hidalgo aboard her imperial yacht, and as Napoleon III steered, Hidalgo repeated to him the same things he had told the empress the day before. After his wife's lecture on the subject, the emperor was as enthused by the plan as she was.

To build an empire, however, one needs an emperor, so Eugenie, Napoleon III, Hidalgo, and other Mexican exiles had set about looking for a decent candidate to the throne. Among the names they had pulled out of their hats, Maximilian's had appeared, but it had not made the short list.

Meanwhile, at Miramar, Countess Lutzoff had had a brilliant idea. She was one of the former ladies-in-waiting from Maximilian and Charlotte's court in Milan who had followed them in their disgrace, and the entire family loved her for her kindness and loyalty. Devoted and brave, she had almost become part of the furniture, so used were they to seeing her that they barely paid attention to her anymore. She, on the other hand, observed her masters carefully, and had not failed to notice the disenchantment, disappointment, and frustration eating away at Maximilian and Charlotte. She had a son-in-law, José Maria Gutierrez d'Estrada, a former minister of foreign affairs, also important in the Mexican exile community. She had written him to say that if anyone were looking for an emperor for Mexico, Archduke Maximilian would be perfect for the job. The son-in-law had swallowed the bait and asked for details on Maximilian, on Charlotte, and on their situation and state of mind. Kind Countess Lutzoff had answered with wisdom and finesse. Thus convinced that Maximilian was the ideal candidate, her son-in-law had managed to convince the other exiled Mexicans with his overblown and wordy rhetoric, and they in turn had spoken with Napoleon III and Eugenie. Immediately, Maximilian was the name on everyone's lips.

But there was a catch: the consensus was that the United States would never accept the creation of a Mexican empire led by a European prince. Indeed, decades earlier, the United States had established the Monroe Doctrine, which definitively set aside Latin America as the private domain of its own, Latin America's great neighbor to the north, which would brook no rival. But the United States had become embroiled in the Civil War. Pushed to the breaking point by the demands and pressures placed on it by the North, the South had seceded from the Union. In retaliation, the North had sent its armies to call the South to order once and for all, and for the moment the United States became unable to apply its Monroe Doctrine in Mexico. As for the South, it would surely support the creation of a Mexican empire. In Europe, anyone truly interested in the foundation of the empire declared himself pro-South, especially since Washington, D.C.'s repeated acts of insolence had only swelled the ranks of the North's enemies. Napoleon III, Queen Victoria, and her uncle King Leopold were among this group, and they dreamed of supplying military aid to the South — even if Marie-Amelie's young grandchildren, Charlotte's nephews, the count of Paris and the duke of Chartres, had become so carried away by youthful exuberance that they had gone to fight for the North. It was the South that had to win, as it was the South that would accept the existence of a Mexican empire. There could not have been a better moment: an empire there would be, and Maximilian would be its emperor.

Since Maximilian was a prince of the House of Austria, they asked the head of the House, his brother the emperor, for permission, who in turn sent his minister of foreign affairs to transmit the proposal.

Maximilian and Charlotte's first reaction was to bombard the minister with questions about the Emperor's position on the project, since they were sure he must have been against it. Of course Francis-Joseph would have been ecstatic to get rid of his younger brother by sending him to the other side of the Atlantic, but the thought of seeing Max raised to the same imperial rank as himself had to have irked him immensely. Moreover, he had almost refused to consider the proposal at all when his mother, Archduchess Sophie, had argued violently with him, saying that he had always been a bad brother, and threatening to leave the court if he opposed the Mexican project, a departure that would have caused all sorts of gossip and scandal. Francis-Joseph had finally bowed to their wishes, all the more since the pearl of his empire, Hungary, was acting up once again, going so far as to demand some autonomy—there had also been talk of creating an independent kingdom there that would eventually have been offered to Maximilian. All these rumors, even if they were empty, had been enough to make Francis-Joseph tremble. The further away Maximilian was, the better it would be. Therefore, though expressing some reservations, he had not declared his opposition to his younger brother's acceptance of the crown of Mexico.

Charlotte had already known of Mexico, thanks to a first-rate eyewitness: her uncle Francis d'Orleans, prince of Joinville. In fact, this had not been Mexico's first default on debt. Under Louis-Philippe, long before Benito Juárez had come onto the scene, the same situation had arisen, and a fleet had been sent to coerce Mexico into reason. The admiral, prince of Joinville, had participated in the expedition, first taking over the fort at San Juan de Ulua that protected Veracruz, then landing on Mexican soil. Not only had this joyful adventurer told his stories in the most vivacious way, but he had also painted beautiful watercolors depicting scenes from his life. His tales and paintings had stoked Charlotte's imagination when she was a little girl.

To respond to the still unofficial offer of the Mexican crown, Charlotte turned to her family, and most of all to her father, whose wisdom and prudence she respected, seeking the most lucid advice from him. First of all, she wrote, they had to find out the real reasons why France had created this empire and offered it to them, since she doubted it was out of pure kindness. She was right to be wary, but in her innocence, she was far from knowing the full truth of the matter, in which the highest ideals were mixed with the most pedestrian concerns. Benito Juárez's predecessor to the leadership of Mexico had taken out a private loan of sixty-five million, at six percent interest, from a Swiss banker in Mexico, a man by the name of Jecker. Knowing Mexico and its risks, Jecker had sought out a heavyweight ally and found one in the duke of Morny, Napoleon III's illegitimate half-brother, to whom he had offered thirty percent of the profits in exchange for his help in getting reimbursed by Mexico. The goateed emperor's strategies had been a mixture of convoluted politics and grandiose, high-flown ideas. But for the seductive Morny, a true political genius, it had always been a question of business and money. The banker Jecker had aimed true: just like Eugenie, but for totally different reasons, Morny had used his access to the emperor and made Mexico his cause. Not only would they force the Mexicans to pay back their loan (thirty percent of which would find its way into his account), but with a Mexican empire under France's wing, there would also be an open door to rich markets and unimaginable profits.

Having no idea of these dealings, Charlotte hesitated. England did not seem overly warm to the project, which was a great handicap. In any case, the couple would have to ask questions before they accepted, and above all, find out what the Mexicans themselves thought of the proposal. Once that was done, the idea was still enticing. Mexico was one of the "richest countries on the globe." Of course, it was on the other side of the Earth, and its population was not homogenous, but its endless anarchy paved the way to power for anyone brave enough to seize it. The country had never been governed well, but if it were, it would gain considerable importance, and perhaps even win back some of the provinces it had lost to the United States. "The idea is not without its appeal," Charlotte wrote. "To found a dynasty and work for the good of a people are huge tasks. They have their difficulties, but also their rewards when the job succeeds. And isn't it the path that dear Father marked out with his example?"

"Dear Father" was very confused. He would love to see his son-in-law, and especially his daughter, fitted with imperial crowns; besides, great adventures, like creating an empire, had always sparked his imagination. But in that particular project, there were so many unknowns, so many unsure factors, obstacles, and stumbling blocks, that he had to remain noncommittal: "Keep your options open but don't refuse."

Maximilian reacted differently. He began by locking himself in his room to sleep on his thoughts. "I will always be ready, at anytime in my life, to make the harshest sacrifices for Austria and for the prestige of my house. In the present situation, the sacrifice would be all the greater in that it would require my wife and me to leave Europe and its standard of living," he wrote. He was fully aware that his family had lost some of its radiance and power. Take the Coburgs, for instance, he said: they had risen from nothing to snatch up thrones one after the other, spreading their influence more widely every day, while his own family had lost its land piece by piece. The desire to win back some of his family's former glory made him consider the Mexican proposal carefully.

To learn more about the Mexicans' opinion, he decided to send a secret emissary to Gutierrez—and whom did he choose but Schertzenlechner. Rumor had it that the former butler was so ignorant he did not even know where Mexico was. Gutierrez d'Estrada immediately came to the same unfavorable conclusion about him, but he did give him the requested information nonetheless. Mexico had only one hope: to see Maximilian come as soon as possible and don the crown. Let the archduke rest assured, he would be welcomed in triumph. As if that were not enough, Maximilian had entrusted the former butler with a letter for Pope Pius IX, and sent him to the most solemn court in Europe—the Vatican. Schertzenlechner was received by Cardinal Antonelli, the haughty secretary of state, who wondered what could possibly have come over the archduke to have himself represented by such a low-class peasant. Pius IX answered the archduke in the most ingratiating way, encouraging him in his mission, and congratulating him on having been chosen. In a word, the pope hoped that once Maximilian became emperor of Mexico, he would return the property stolen by the Zapotec Indian back to the clergy.

Understanding that Schertzenlechner was not the ideal intermediary, Gutierrez wanted to meet Maximilian as soon as possible to persuade him to accept the crown. With persistence, he managed to have himself invited to Miramar, where he arrived in time for Christmas. His mother-in-law, the kind Countess Lutzoff, had already done the groundwork, explaining to him in letter after letter the type of man he would be dealing with and how he should act. Subtly guided by her, he painted a beautiful picture of almost endless opportunity for Maximilian and Charlotte. His way with words broke down their hesitations, and convinced them.

With his head full of the wonderful images distilled by Gutierrez, Maximilian set out for Venice. His brother, Francis-Joseph, who was visiting the still-Austrian city "betrothed of the Adriatic," had invited him there. Maximilian accepted the invitation with trepidation, for he had many favors to ask, and beneath the seeming warmth of family ties seethed the tension and almost fear that Max felt toward his elder brother, his master, the sovereign who was suspicious and envious of him. The two brothers met in the magnificent Pompeian halls of the royal palace, where Maximilian had stayed during the time of his kingship. Far from their wives and the friction those two caused, the brothers soon discovered their old intimacy.

Encouraged by this, Maximilian began by asking for money. Francis-Joseph agreed to a loan, to be put together by the Rothschilds with French and English capital, and as a sign of good faith, he added two hundred thousand Austrian guldens for Maximilian's initial expenses. Maximilian could not have hoped for more. He also needed military support; Francis-Joseph responded with a promise to recruit some Austrian volunteers, who would be placed under Maximilian's direct command. Francis-Joseph's generosity astonished his brother. The bad blood of the past seemed to be gone. Maximilian had rediscovered the brother he used to know, the one he had so loved.

Once these questions were settled, they got down to work on Maximilian's future imperial household—the titles that needed to be created, the decorations that needed to be bestowed. They talked it over at length, with the innate interest and professionalism that royalty always applied to such esoteric subjects. The two brothers then parted the best friends in the world.

Back at Miramar, Maximilian received another Mexican diplomat in exile: Almonte, a former ambassador and a general to boot, like so many of his countrymen. Almonte brought a letter from Napoleon promising money, soldiers, and anything else Maximilian might need. Almonte threw in some flattery of his own, saying that all of Mexico was awaiting its emperor. Empress Eugenie started writing directly to Charlotte in the same tone: "We hope that the moment is near when the hopes of the Mexicans and of all civilized countries will come true." She was happy just at the thought of what a godsend Maximilian and Charlotte would be for the populations thus far abandoned to despair.

All the flattery turned Charlotte's head. The plan was becoming "quite a beautiful thing," as she told her brother Leopold. It was certain that Maximilian had all the skills necessary to govern a great empire, and restoring order and civilization would be a task worthy of him. Once Maximilian was emperor of Mexico, the sun would never again set on the Habsburg empire. "This year will decide whether or not you will become the brother-in-law of an emperor," she wrote. When all was said and done, Charlotte liked the idea of founding "a new dynasty"—this was a natural, almost banal sentence almost lost in the letter, and yet it was strange. In order to found a dynasty, one would need children . . . and Charlotte was still not pregnant.

5

At the same time, massive squadrons were sailing toward Mexico. In his predecessors' coffers, Benito Juárez had discovered a war chest that had been meant to pay back some of the immense debt incurred by Mexico to world powers, but he had decided instead to use the gold to start cleaning up the country. He had gotten the vote passed by the Mexican congress to stop repayment of debts. Without warning Maximilian and Charlotte, Mexico's three largest creditors — France, England, and Spain — had signed a convention on October 31, 1861, to force Mexico to pay. They had immediately dispatched warships to back up their demands, with as many cannonballs as would be necessary. The three squadrons arrived in the waters off Veracruz. But Juárez had had the city evacuated, leaving nothing behind him but yellow fever—and there was no need to start bombing, since the yellow fever microbe was impervious to cannons. Once they landed, therefore, the allies had no idea what to do. Juárez let them stew for a while, then sent them a few delegates. To avoid remaining in Veracruz's swamps, the allies had set themselves up in a much healthier locality called La Soledad (Solitude).

By the allies' calculations, the debt came out to a total of two hundred fifty million gold francs. Even the creditors themselves found the sum a little outrageous. The Mexican government persuaded the allies that by exaggerating their demands, they would only exacerbate the anarchy, and squander any chance of ever seeing a penny of their money again. In return for their cooperation, Mexico offered to try to work something out—Benito Juárez would be ready to make an effort. As a guarantee of his good faith, he would hand a few cities over to them, on the condition that they not interfere with the sovereignty or borders of Mexico as a whole. The allies accepted Juárez's offer without hesitation, and got it in writing in a document called the Soledad Convention.

Now they could discuss money, or, in other words, the sum to be reimbursed.

Meanwhile, everyone had become good friends. Not only did the allies respect Mexican sovereignty, but they also accepted Juárez, since after all it was with his delegates that they were dealing. The Soledad Convention was an implicit recognition of Juárez's regime, and as soon as he was told of it, that was exactly how Napoleon III understood it. His curses proved the extent of his rage: goodbye Mexican empire, goodbye Emperor Maximilian! By getting in touch with Juárez, his own people had torn his dream to pieces.

Napoleon III's first reaction was to fire the expedition's commander and replace him with another general, backed up by four thousand men, under orders to advance and conquer, to chase Juárez out, and to put Maximilian on the throne.

The new commander, General Lorencez, sailed across the Atlantic at top speed and arrived at La Soledad with his emperor's bloody and warlike declarations still ringing in his ears. He found the Englishmen and the Spaniards talking calmly with Juárez's representatives about nothing other than peace. How could France's allies have had the gall to meet with brigands, representing the arch brigand, Juárez? The Englishman and the Spaniard replied that they had come to Mexico to have the money owed them paid back, and that this was exactly what they were doing. But Lorencez objected—what about the Christian faith, he said, what about civilization, progress, the prosperity that the empire would have insured for Mexico? The Englishman and the Spaniard shrugged their shoulders. Their instructions were clear and precise: money and nothing but money. Who cared about the empire? The argument began to escalate.

Back in Mexico after his meeting with Maximilian, Almonte was working at a fever pitch. They must push on to Mexico City, topple the godless Indian, and install Maximilian on the throne, he shouted in front of Juárez's representatives. The Englishman and the Spaniard grew angry. Would Lorencez have Almonte be silent! Lorencez refused, and the break between them was complete. The Englishman and the Spaniard, thrilled with this pretext, slammed the door, went back aboard their ships, and raised anchor for Europe. A total catastrophe.

Not at all—it was a triumph, Eugenie assured Charlotte. "Thank God we have no more allies!" She explained that as long as the British and Spanish were in Mexico dealing with Juárez, not a single native would have come out in support of the empire; but now that they had gone, Mexicans were freed of their inhibitions.

Now they could finally express their true desires. And their desires had a name: Maximilian.

All of a sudden, angry voices were heard in opposition to the Mexican project. The ambassadors stationed in Washington sent warning after warning. Though he was busy with the Civil War, the American secretary of state, William H. Seward, declared that the creation of an empire in Mexico, headed by a foreign prince, would be an affront to the United States. The Austrian minister of foreign affairs, Count Rechberg—the one who had come to offer Maximilian the imperial crown—warned Maximilian not to feel bound by his promises to Napoleon III. Queen Victoria and the prince consort advised Uncle Leopold to proceed with extreme care. But the most authoritative warning came from General Prim, who had been in command of the Spanish squadron sent to Veracruz, and who was just back from Mexico. He wrote Napoleon III a long letter in which he stated that, with all due respect, there was no real feeling in favor of a monarchy in Mexico, that Iturbide's brief empire had left neither a nobility nor a moral example behind it, and that, above all, Mexico's close proximity to the United States and "the constant vituperations its republicans inveigh against the institution of a monarchy" had aroused a feeling of hatred in Mexico for the monarchy, and had created a republican strain "that will be difficult to destroy."

Charlotte had other things to do than listen to these gloomy thoughts. Her father King Leopold had fallen sick, and was in grave danger. After a painful operation for bladder stones, he now had a serious illness of the lungs. As soon as she had heard the news, Charlotte had jumped onto a train and traveled day and night to Brussels, only to have access to Laeken, where her father was staying, denied. She learned from her brothers that even they had not seen him since he had been bedridden. She waited a few days without any sign that she would be allowed to visit him, until it became clear that there was nothing for her to do but announce her departure. It was only then that King Leopold agreed to see her, but only in a manner appropriate to the dictates of protocol. He got up and dressed, and even had his makeup applied before he saw her, as he would have done for any of his subjects. He proved so cold and distant that the minister of the interior felt pity for Charlotte: "The poor girl traveled so quickly and so far and only saw her father that one time. Oh, kings!"

Fortunately for Charlotte, good news was awaiting her at Miramar. As Empress Eugenie had told her, now that the French were rid of their allies, they were free to act as they saw fit in Mexico, and were already reaping the benefits. Seven thousand soldiers were marching double-time toward the Mexican capital. The cities they encountered along the way were surrendering so quickly that soon they would be in Puebla, the big town halfway between Veracruz and Mexico City. On June 7, 1862, Eugenie wrote Charlotte in triumph: "The news is excellent; General Lorencez says that the country is under his control. Generals and cities defect to us every day . . . my next letter will probably give the news of our arrival in Mexico City. . . ."

One week later, on the fifteenth of June, the "next letter" arrived, announcing a crushing defeat for the French. General Lorencez had arrived at Puebla, an efficiently fortified town, defended by thousands of Mexicans ready for anything, and above all, by the nearly impregnable fort of Guadalupe. To make a good impression on Napoleon III, Lorencez had rushed things along. Without preparation, without a reconnaissance of the terrain, and without a battle plan, he had ordered an assault. The fighting was fierce and bloody. The French were resoundingly beaten, and Lorencez had no choice but to call for a retreat. A small horde of mestizos and Indians, poorly trained, barely equipped, had defeated the most powerful army in the world.

A shout of joy went out across Mexico, where even today this surprise victory is celebrated each year on the Cinco de Mayo. The Mexicans' cheers were matched by Napoleon III's howls of rage. Lorencez was nothing but an idiot, and like an idiot he had made a long series of mistakes. Exit Lorencez. A new commander, General Forey, was dispatched with twenty-eight thousand men and two adjuncts, General Douay and General Bazaine. Under this panoply of men, Napoleon III declared, it would be the height of incompetence if France were unable to "pacify" Mexico.

Meanwhile, the Greeks were chasing out their own king. Thirty years beforehand, upon obtaining their independence, they had sought out a sovereign and found him in the person of Otto I, a Bavarian prince. After Otto I's three decades of loyal service, interspersed with attempts to establish an absolute monarchy, he had been thanked with a small revolution. Since then, the Greeks had been trying to replace him. Several candidates had already bowed out when the Greeks came across the name Maximilian.

The British government had been ecstatic. To see the throne go to the first cousin of Queen Victoria, and to the daughter of such an Anglophile as Leopold I, would mean anglicizing Greece. Lord Palmerston, grand master of British foreign policy, begged King Leopold to present the offer to his children, with the full and heartfelt backing of Queen Victoria. Leopold hesitated. Still, the throne of Greece was better than a throne that did not even exist—like that of Mexico, an even more unstable country with an even more volatile population. Furthermore, Athens was closer to Brussels than was Mexico City, and King Leopold liked that closeness. He sent his opinion to Maximilian, who immediately flared up. How dare they make him such a humiliating proposal? "I would be the last to accept a crown already turned down by a half-dozen princes," he declared.

Charlotte was more diplomatic. To accept the throne of Greece, she said, she would have to convert to the Orthodox religion, and thus renounce Catholicism, which would be unthinkable.

At the end of winter, 1863, beyond the Mexican affair, Charlotte's only concern was to marry off "Fat Philippe." It had become her obsession, and she wrote him long letter after long letter, ten pages or more at a time. Staying at her desk for hours, she covered the paper with her delicate and slanted handwriting, so elegant and clear; it was her little vice, as she herself recognized: "Here I am writing volumes again. It's a bad habit that just today I have decided to do away with." In each letter, she went over her little brother's possible candidates. Her favorite would be their first cousin, Chiquita, Prince Joinville's daughter (who in her childhood had found Charlotte such a snob), but Philippe would have none of it. He seemed to favor the crown princess of Brazil. For Philippe, it would be an incomparable marriage, but he would have to leave Belgium forever. When Charlotte brought this up, mentioning the time that she left Belgium, she had a moment of tenderness that was an homage to her native country: "When I left all of you, it felt as if my heart had been taken from me. When I came back for the first time in four years, and when I got off at Brussels station, I thought I would fall over backward. And yet I am perfectly happy, and enjoy all the good fortune anyone could have on this Earth. I even have more happiness every day."

She went on and on about her conjugal bliss, comparing herself to her English cousins: "Things that last never begin with too much passion, and so it goes with good marriages. Vicky and Fritz were wild about each other before they got married, while I was completely calm, and today Max and I are so much happier than Vicky is with Fritz . . ." Six years after her marriage had taken place, Charlotte contradicted everything she had proclaimed up till then, and let slip that love was not the only reason she had married — that her decision had been thoroughly thought out.

In Mexico, the war was heating up. General Forey, who had replaced the incompetent Lorencez, had only one goal: to please his sovereign, Napoleon III, and to that end, to take Puebla. This time, the French had thirty-seven thousand men and one hundred seventy-six cannons ready to attack the town. Despite everyone's expectations, the siege lasted so long that Napoleon nearly lost his patience, but in the end, the town surrendered. From there it was only a quick march to Mexico City, and one that was soon glorified by an act of heroism. In the little town of Camarón, sixty-four soldiers from the Foreign Legion held out for nine hours against two thousand Mexicans, and the name Camarón thus entered into legend.

Juárez, however, realized he had lost the game, and fled north from the capital with whatever troops he had left — and, of course, with the wealth of the country's treasury. General Forey entered the capital together with his adjunct, Bazaine, and matters were dealt with quickly.

The French command picked out thirty-five Mexican notables and baptized the Mexican junta, which in turn pulled out of its hat an assembly of two hundred fifteen representatives, all chosen for their obedience to France. The first act of this puppet parliament was to vote for the establishment of a monarchy, which it then offered to Maximilian. A delegation of the most illustrious Mexicans was to leave immediately for Europe in order to meet with the emperor-elect.

Mexico finally seemed within Maximilian and Charlotte's reach. They had begun to learn their future empire's language, and it was in the purest Castilian that Maximilian wrote to Charlotte: "*Mi querido ángel,* my beloved angel"; "*Mi más que querida Carlotta,* my more than beloved Charlotte"; "*Señora de mi corazón,* lady of my heart"; and other phrases of love.

They were again apart, because Maximilian had left for yet another trip on the *Fantasy.* He laughingly described the Hungarian dinner cooked by Schertzenlechner who, unlike Charlotte, had been brought along. The menu was "so national that it gave some of us savage stomachaches. Others left the table still hungry but disgusted, and everyone but the Hungarians sang a hymn of praise to the insulted cook. . . ." In short, everyone had had a great time during those cruises away from Charlotte.

In the beginning of 1864, Maximilian and Charlotte decided to find out what to expect in Mexico, since the reality of their distant empire seemed to elude any attempt at analysis and understanding. They called Mr. Bourdillon, the special correspondent for the *Times* in Mexico, to Miramar. Without hesitation, this man told them that all Mexicans were lazy, liars, and thieves. But he said that the country's riches, its mines and land, were practically inexhaustible. And how much money! Money was "the Mexicans' god—they'll do anything for a peso." Above all, he told Maximilian and Charlotte not to trust the politicians, all of whom were crooked. The country had no clue what "democracy" meant, and if they wanted to keep it, the French army would have to stay there as long as it took. The only solution for Mexico was a monarchy, and Mexico's only hope was Maximilian and Charlotte.

Though they were a bit taken aback by the straightforward manner of the analysis, they retained only the last part of it, which corroborated the reports sent by General Almonte, who had gone to Mexico with General Forey, and who was working feverishly for Maximilian, bombarding him with letters addressed to "Sire" and "His Majesty."

For his part, Napoleon III had certain ulterior motives. Indeed, he did order his troops to move on to Mexico City, to chase Juárez out, and to get things ready for Maximilian, but he found that everything had been going a bit too quickly. He did not think that the junta, the parliament that his generals had thought up, seemed very real. As he himself wavered, he hoped to see a massive rally of support among the Mexicans for Maximilian.

Meanwhile, Francis-Joseph summoned Maximilian to Vienna to rediscuss the Mexican project. Charlotte refused to let him leave alone, and thus they found themselves together in the gloomy suites of Hofburg, the Austrian imperial palace. The huge rooms decorated in deep red damask looked out through tiny windows on gray courtyards. The dark wooden furniture was organized gracelessly, and on the walls, uninspired religious and contemporary paintings alternated with portraits of Habsburgs long dead. Maximilian and Charlotte paid the décor no mind, for they were worried about what awaited them. No one advised them openly to refuse the Mexican throne, but warnings seemed to abound: in the speech given by Count Rechberg, the minister of foreign affairs; in the reports of the Austrian ambassadors; and in the agreement of the imperial family. The most categorical was Maximilian's mother, Archduchess

Sophie, who in the beginning had been ecstatic to see her favorite son assume the crown. Since then, her realism had made her change her mind: "The project is too dangerous. You must refuse."

"The situation is far from being less favorable now than it was in the beginning," Charlotte objected; "everything seems instead to be heading for a worthy and happy outcome."

"But look at what happened to my nephew, King Otto of Greece," Sophie responded. "The powers had guaranteed him a throne, but all they did was send an English destroyer to pick him up when the Greeks chased him out. You, on the other hand, won't even have a destroyer to bring you back home once the Mexicans have rebelled against you."

"I beg of you, my aunt, don't sadden us by persisting in a belief contrary to our own, although of course, nothing will change Maximilian's decision once he has made up his mind," Charlotte answered.

Archduchess Sophie, who had always openly supported Charlotte against Elisabeth, now wondered whether she had made a mistake. She tried to make her son and daughter-in-law see that, in Mexico, they would always remain foreigners. Charlotte fought back: "There can be no question of foreign influences or conquests as long as Mexico remains a part of Austrian dynastic possessions." There was no use in continuing the futile conversation. Archduchess Sophie was convinced that nothing would persuade Charlotte to change her decision, and she trembled.

Another old woman was trembling just as much, and for the same reason: Queen Marie-Amelie was stoutly opposed to the Mexican project, and was supported in this by all her descendants, the Orleans. She wrote to her granddaughter, advising her to abandon the project, implying that in the illusion of Mexico, she saw only the vanity of a throne. Charlotte grew angry. "I am the last person who wants a throne. If you remember, I could have had one when I was seventeen years old, and I refused it. If we refused Mexico's throne when we feel we can accomplish a great task, we would be trampling on our conscience and shirking our responsibility toward God."

Marie-Amelie was upset by this stubbornness—all she had wanted was a better future for her granddaughter. "But," her granddaughter replied, "Mexico is such a beautiful country." Marie-Amelie did not give up: what would happen if, after he accepted, Maximilian found himself chased out of Mexico? He would have nothing left. "Yes, he would," Charlotte objected, "he would still have the succession to the Austrian throne, because rumors notwithstanding, he has not given up one ounce of his hereditary rights."

We will succeed, Charlotte endlessly repeated. We will succeed, Maximilian answered her. He started off his foreign policy by warming relations with the American Confederacy and establishing a good rapport with General James Williams, the Confederacy's representative in Europe. He wrote the Confederate president to promise the tightest of alliances: "The South's cause and the Mexican cause are one." These schemes acted to provoke public opinion in the North, which now flared up against Maximilian. As senators gave firebrand speeches in Congress, newspapers, magazines, pamphlets, and conferences whipped up fervor against him.

As for England, King Leopold was convinced that he had been able to "push" the British Cabinet in the right direction. After all, Lord Palmerston remarked to Queen Victoria, this empire might not be such a bad thing. It would allow England to have decent trade relations with Mexico, which would open the door to wonderful business for England. Victoria, for her part, felt a deep affection for Maximilian and Charlotte, the latter of whom reminded her so much of the angelic Queen Louise by her good judgment and common sense. Of course, the Mexican project had its dangers, but Max had had enough of his sweet idleness, and he wanted a job. Victoria was sure that it was Max's idea to go to Mexico; Charlotte was merely happy to follow him wherever he went.

In the midst of the storm that the Mexican project continued to stir up, Charlotte's rock of stability remained her father, Leopold I: "If anything could increase my feelings of love for you, the veneration and gratitude that I have felt for you for as long as I have been in this world, it would surely be your dear letter which touched the depths of my soul. Many years ago, I once had the joy to receive from Mother the same written testimony that never once in my life had I given her a moment of pain. I was ten years old then, and these words from such a mother as she have always remained one of the deepest satisfactions of my life. Now, dear Father, you are the one who, with words so warm that I will never forget them, deigns to give me your approval and tell me that you have always been happy with me. I cannot tell you the profound joy that this highest of all praises I could receive on Earth has given me, the peacefulness that it spreads on my entire past, and the confidence it inspires in me in the rest of my existence. My greatest desire has always been to be worthy of your affection, the value of which I have always known, to satisfy you, to contribute to your happiness, and to honor you in the world ever since I left you . . ." She wrote page after page in this tone of love, sincerity, and lyricism. Despite the almost insulting coldness with which he had treated her when she had gone to visit him during his illness, she felt that, despite the distance his depression forced him to maintain, he loved her— not only that he loved her, but that he esteemed her. For Charlotte, only her father counted. Never had she written her husband in the same tone. Compared with Maximilian, the graceful charmer and daydreaming poet, Leopold was the type of man who, in all his authority and superiority, attracted Charlotte, perhaps even because of his reserve. Leopold was the one from whom she awaited the final word on her questions, and Leopold was the one she decided on her own to go see in Brussels.

Once there, for several days, Charlotte discussed the arguments for and against the Mexican project one-on-one with her father. It was an endless conversation that seemed to lead nowhere, but that nonetheless ended in this dialogue:

"Dear Father, should I go now with Maximilian to Mexico?"

"My daughter, it is your duty."

Enraptured, Charlotte telegraphed Maximilian: "So happy — everything is for the best."

The delegation sent to formally offer Maximilian the throne landed in Europe. Once they crossed the Continent, the Mexicans got off the train in Trieste, and, on October 3, 1864, the coaches brought them to Miramar. Maximilian's aides hastened to welcome them and lead them up the marble stairs, into the great vestibule, and, from there, into Maximilian and Charlotte's bedroom, from which the big twin beds had been removed. The Mexicans looked around at the walls covered by blue-gray damasks decorated with arabesques, at the inlays of dark wood against a light wood background, at the well-sculpted ceilings. The view through the two large windows stretched out toward Venice over the sea and the Adriatic coast.

The Mexicans were wearing tails and all their insignia. Among them were old acquaintances, including Gutierrez d'Estrada and Hidalgo. Charlotte had not been invited; the meeting would remain among men.

Because of his slenderness, Maximilian looked much taller than his actual height. The dark blue uniform and gold buttons of the navy became him. Around his neck, at the end of a red ribbon, shone the gem of the Golden Fleece. With his smile and warm welcome, he seemed courteous, affable, and kind.

Gutierrez d'Estrada was the one to speak. He came forward and read his speech from the sheets of paper he held in his hand. The representatives of the people had unanimously voted to reestablish the monarchy, and to offer the crown to Archduke Maximilian, he said. The Mexicans therefore asked him to accept the crown. Just as the contents of this speech were known in advance, so had Maximilian's response been laboriously worked over in many exchanges and discussions. Maximilian did not, in a word, refuse, but before he accepted, he put forth the condition that the Mexican people should first be allowed to freely express their opinion on the matter. In effect, he demanded a sort of "universal suffrage" — a catchword of the nineteenth century, the motto of intellectuals and liberals, the banner of demand and protest, the sugarcoated pill administered by enlightened princes. No universal suffrage, no acceptance of the crown, Maximilian said.

It might have been expected that the Mexicans would be skeptical. How could they have possibly organized free elections in a country half occupied by foreign troops, half wracked by anarchy? Yet they accepted Maximilian's decision, understanding that he, with Charlotte, had made his decision.

Everything that had happened thus far was the work of Providence, Charlotte affirmed to her former governess, the countess of Hulste — Providence that had manifested itself so clearly to her for two years that she could not possibly doubt its involvement. They had therefore to follow Providence, though naturally also following the course laid out by human prudence. Charlotte compared her and Maximilian's decision to a true calling sent directly from heaven by her mother Queen Louise, for she felt that that angel had never once stopped encouraging her down this path. "For two years, everything has been weighed, reweighed, and finally been found to be worth undertaking." Such was Charlotte's answer to a stern letter from the countess of Hulste accusing her of seeking after the Mexican adventure only to satiate her contemptible ambition.

King Leopold, to whom Charlotte had complained of the remark, now also wrote to the ex-governess:

"Charlotte, ambitious? You must be dreaming, Countess. All she wants is to have a useful and active life, to put her talents to the best of her ability. . . . Between us, life at Miramar was really quite boring. As the second in the line of succession, Max has all the disadvantages of his position without the financial means to improve it. Charlotte had not gotten carried away by the Mexican offer; on the contrary, she was well aware of its dangers. The one who is really enthusiastic is Max." Leopold I shared Queen Victoria's conviction that Max was the one who was pushing to accept the deal, whereas everyone else seemed to think it was Charlotte.

Mexico had not yet gotten around to universal suffrage, but it was on its way toward it, thanks to the somewhat rough French pacification. General Forey had been replaced because he had begun taking himself for a conqueror, and what Napoleon wanted was a liberator. Forey's former adjunct, General Bazaine, had been put in his place. He had fifty thousand men at his disposal, and he knew what to do with them. The "pacification" thus continued, which meant that the supporters of Benito Juárez were hunted down without mercy. One by one, towns and provinces surrendered, Juárez's partisans melted away like snow; even his closest friends abandoned him and advised him to resign since his chances were gone.

This news thrilled the Mexicans who were stuck at Miramar trying to convince Maximilian to leave for Mexico as soon as possible. But Charlotte distrusted them: "They have a right to be impatient, but underneath it all, there is a certain propensity toward scheming in them that bothers and even disgusts me sometimes, though in other respects they are good people." Thus Charlotte refused their invitation to leave on the first ship. "Without the vote, or money, or any sort of guarantee," she wrote to her father, "it would have been inexcusable madness to fall for that one."

As proof of Charlotte's contradictions and Maximilian's hesitations, the couple left a few weeks later to make a round of the European courts to say good-bye before leaving for Mexico. Maximilian and Charlotte had still not received "the vote, or money, or any sort of guarantee," but nonetheless, in the confusion, they had prepared for their departure anyway.

Naturally, their trip began in Brussels. There was the sound of discord growing between them. "Everything is arranged," Charlotte declared. "Nothing is arranged," Maximilian cut her off in public. King Leopold perceived his son-in-law's foul mood, and tried to calm things by offering him wise advice.

At their next stop, in Paris, Charlotte and Maximilian were welcomed sumptuously, with all the honors accorded reigning sovereigns, and affectionately by their old friends, Napoleon III and Eugenie. "The empress was waiting for us at the door of a salon — graceful and beautiful, like a Greek statue sculpted by a Spanish chisel," Charlotte wrote. With curiosity, Charlotte entered the Tuileries, which she had not seen since childhood, and she noticed many changes. In her grandfather's time, the court, despite its undeniable dignity, had lacked a certain glamour, but now Charlotte was astounded by its splendor. Everything in the palace glittered. Wherever she looked, she saw gilded bronzes, rare marbles, and rich brocades, whose opulence turned her attention away from the Napoleonic portraits that had replaced those of the Orleans. Where had those quiet evenings gone, around Marie-Amelie's worktable, when her daughters had done needlepoint, King Louis-Philippe chatted in one of the corners with his friends, and Charlotte and her cousins had played with dolls? Now there were magnificent galas every night, balls that only ended at dawn, banquets of an abundance scarcely to be believed, perfumes, diamonds, flowers, silks, beautiful women, uniforms everywhere. Of course, so much show smelled a little ostentatious, but the whirlwind of parties given in her honor left Charlotte's head spinning.

She went from a presentation of *La Traviata* to a hunting party in the park of Versailles, to a thousand other attractions started afresh each day for more than a week. From Napoleon III, from Eugenie, and from their court, there was a train of gifts, of kindnesses, of curtsies, and even, from the head chef of the imperial kitchens, the creation of a succulent desert called, without irony, "Mexican bomb."

All these distractions did not, however, prevent serious discussion. French soldiers, Napoleon III announced, would not stay in Mexico forever, but let Maximilian rest assured that they would pull out gradually to give the new emperor enough time to consolidate his rule. As for money, they also needed to discuss the Jecker debt. Goaded by his half-brother Morny, who was expecting with growing impatience the thirty percent he had been promised in the affair, Napoleon asked that reimbursement be the first order of business. Jecker would be reimbursed, Maximilian assured. But then they must also take into account the costs of keeping French troops in Mexico, and Napoleon III gave him more and more astronomical figures. Fine, Maximilian responded, and proposed they work out a loan — for two hundred million gold francs. Always the businessman, Napoleon offered his conditions, which Maximilian agreed upon without exception. Of course, it would be necessary to put it all down on paper, so it was decided that they would sign the treaty at Miramar.

❖   ❖   ❖

Everything was going extremely well in this best possible of worlds, and yet . . . Napoleon's court was forever teeming with foreign kings and minor nobilities, attracted to the Tuileries as if by a magnet. As chance would have had it, at that precise moment, Charlotte's first cousin also happened to be staying there: Duke Ernest of Saxe-Coburg-Gotha, a bad character. At the last dinner given in honor of the future sovereigns of Mexico, the ambiance was even more glamorous and giddy. Charlotte was radiant. As they left the table, Napoleon III took the German duke aside, led him to a corner, turned around to stare thoughtfully at Maximilian, then commented, "It's a very bad deal . . . if I were he, I would never have accepted." Duke Ernest thought at first he had misheard, but no, the emperor repeated the same words several times.

Setting out from Paris, Charlotte and Maximilian moved on to London. After the Tuileries, without pedigree but glittering and fun, the British court felt like a tomb. Two years earlier, the prince consort Albert, beloved husband of Queen Victoria, had died, taking with him all his wife's joy and lust for life. Could the word "court" even be used to describe this somber existence without receptions or parties, within immense but silent palaces where a few courtiers wandered, forever in mourning? Victoria no longer felt enthusiasm for anything or anyone, and her minister, Lord Palmerston, was far too prudent to show the slightest sign of interest in the Mexican project. Thus the London visit was like a cold shower for the couple — a feeling that only continued to worsen upon their arrival in Claremont. Surrounded by her surviving children and grandchildren, Queen Marie-Amelie, now over eighty, received her favorite granddaughter and Maximilian with deep emotion. No matter how hard she tried to appear encouraging, she no longer had the strength for it, and instead of giving them her best wishes, she went so far as to urge them to change their minds and refuse the Mexican throne. She begged, she moaned, she cried. Maximilian was stunned; his eyes filled with tears, much to the surprise of little Blanche d'Orleans, the six-and-a-half-year-old daughter of the Duke of Nemours: "Usually it is the women who cry, this time it is the man." For her part, Charlotte remained unmoved. This coldness shocked her cousin Chiquita, who wondered what Charlotte could possibly have in place of a heart.

Given her age, Marie-Amelie knew that she would probably never see Charlotte and Maximilian again, so when they took their leave of her, she blessed them with all her love. She had regained her composure for the good-byes, but once their coach was out of sight, she collapsed and sobbed before her family: "They will be assassinated, they will be assassinated."

From there, Maximilian and Charlotte traveled to Vienna. They were welcomed with great pomp at the station by the emperor himself; that very evening, he also uncharacteristically offered them an enormous banquet at the palace. The Austrian court was the paragon of boredom. The empress was almost never there, and the emperor detested parties and frivolities with all the austerity of a boot-camp sergeant. But the gala that evening transfigured the palace. Out of the closets came the porcelain and the huge silver centerpieces from the eighteenth century. The Hungarian, Bohemian, and Polish uniforms of the court outdid each other in embroidery, stripes, and stitching. Fürstins and Gräfins, the most illustrious names in the Empire, had put on the historic jewels of their families. As for Empress Elisabeth, who made a rare appearance for the affair, she was as always the most beautiful, dressed in chiffon crinoline with diamond stars in her famously abundant hair. The emperor of Austria had gone to great expense to receive the emperor of Mexico. Maximilian and Charlotte were overwhelmed.

The next morning, the minister of foreign affairs, Count Rechberg, went to Maximilian's suite, where he was received with all due friendliness. Rechberg handed Maximilian a document, which he read with growing astonishment: it stated that Maximilian hereby renounced for himself and his descendants any and all rights to the crown of Austria, as well as his portion of the family fortune. In a word, Maximilian would no longer belong to the House of Austria. Rechberg handed him a pen, and said, "Sign here, your Royal and Imperial Highness."

"Never."

After the initial astonishment came indignation and deep suffering. Maximilian had the impression that his brother wanted to rip out his heart. Rechberg prudently withdrew and went straightaway to give a negative report to his master.

Refusing to discuss the matter directly with Maximilian, Francis-Joseph wrote him a letter from one room of the palace to another. If Maximilian did not sign, Francis-Joseph declared, he would not give his approval for Max to assume the crown of Mexico. Max choked with indignation. How could his brother have had the sneakiness to wait until the last minute to demand this renunciation? Of course, Maximilian was taking a few liberties with his wrath. A few months before, during an earlier visit to Vienna, Francis-Joseph had sent Count Rechberg to speak with Maximilian about the necessity of the renunciation. The archduke had not listened to a word of it. The very day before he had left for Brussels, Count Rechberg had again given him a memorandum outlining the arguments, and demonstrating the renunciation to be indispensable. Maximilian had read it inattentively: they would have the time to deal with the question later . . . in fact, in order not to face it, Maximilian had quite simply banished the question from his mind.

At the heart of this "injustice," as Charlotte called it, lay the jealousy and mistrust Francis-Joseph felt for his younger brother, who was so much more gifted and popular than himself, feelings that had not waned despite the countless times Maximilian had proved his loyalty and fidelity.

Maximilian now found himself in a horrible dilemma that taxed all his powers as a leader. He had committed himself so deeply to Mexico that he could no longer back out, but at the same time, he did not want to renounce Austria, the same Austria which, for him, represented his family. And was the imperial succession not otherwise represented only in a little boy, Archduke Rudolph? Who knew? If the boy should happen to die, Maximilian would be the next emperor. He was thus being asked to renounce his imperial privilege. The money did not matter as much as it did to see himself robbed of his part of an inheritance that had been passed down for almost one thousand years — that was unbearable. It was just as unbearable for him to think that, in the process, they would also rob him of his beloved Miramar.

A family dinner had been planned for that evening. Max declined, and Charlotte declared that nothing in the world could make her attend. Francis-Joseph sent his two youngest brothers to make them change their minds, but to no avail. Then, in their suite, appeared the person they were least expecting: Empress Elisabeth. According to Charlotte, "she was very sweet, she asked me to believe that her feelings for Max and for me were unchangeable, and I appreciated what she said." Still, this declaration of goodwill did nothing to improve Maximilian's situation, and since he did not know where else to turn, he brought his mother into the game.

Archduchess Sophie was also indignant at the humiliation inflicted upon her favorite son, and went about trying to sway Francis-Joseph, but in vain. The emperor would hear none of it. In an outrage, Sophie left the palace and retired to Laxenberg, a castle outside Vienna. Deciding that they would not spend another minute under the same roof as the emperor, Maximilian and Charlotte joined her. Laxenberg was small by Austrian imperial standards. Its tasteless décor, its utter coldness both in ambiance and in temperature—the heating did not work well and thus it was freezing inside—were only made gloomier by the winter. Lawns yellowed by frost stretched out between paths lined by leafless trees, whose sad silhouettes stood out against a cloudy sky. The weather was gray: a light rain fell, steady and bone-chilling, while inside the castle, it was moist and dank. All alone in the dim salon, Sophie, Max, and Charlotte fell into each other's arms and cried.

In the weakness of his position, Maximilian was well aware that resistance would be futile. He had no supporters. The court and the government would blindly obey Francis-Joseph, especially in a matter that exclusively concerned the imperial family. Even his mother, as he had just seen, was completely powerless in the face of his brother's stubbornness.

And yet he needed to act. Maximilian asked for an interview with Francis-Joseph, who could not refuse. It took place at Hofburg, in the presence of their wives. The four of them shut themselves away in Francis-Joseph's office, a huge, austere room with long tables covered with files. The interview lasted several hours. As Charlotte dutifully reported to her father, "Max had wanted me to be there. And we had one of those scenes you read about in history books but which seem to come straight out of a novel. Everything moving, lofty, and noble that a brother could say was said, but there were also justified and legitimate complaints, calls for justice, and appeals to family bonds and honor. Francis-Joseph was standing next to the table, his hand inside his uniform, his face twisted by some emotion I could not recognize. He was moved but unswayed, for within that gray tunic, there was no heart—no heart of a brother, no heart of honor. He is a sovereign born to make his people unhappy, one who believes that strength means imposing his will by force. I, on the other hand, think that a prince is called upon to feel more than others. This the emperor did not do."

Maximilian may as well have been talking to the wall. "Your Majesty will have the satisfaction of having ruined his most faithful servant," he said at the end. The more upset grew the younger brother, the stonier became the elder brother. Charlotte suffered to her very core; she tried to support her husband, but what could she do? "Oh God, give me the strength to accept my duty," Maximilian sighed. Charlotte's bitterness was so great that she sneered. Elisabeth, who still had a soft spot for Maximilian, saw a "base smile" on his wife's lips, and just at the moment when Maximilian was tempted to give in, she delivered a parting shot to her sister-in-law, calling her "the angel of Max's death." "Well, we're done here," Francis-Joseph spit out. And Charlotte concluded, "The emperor gave a stiff little salute that reminded me of the salutes that pretend kings give in comedies. The House of Austria had just called down upon itself the damnation of heaven by one of the blackest injustices that had taken place since Cain and Abel." When the two couples separated, a gaping abyss had forever been opened between them.

Maximilian and Charlotte could think of only one thing: taking refuge back home at Miramar. They were greeted by their Mexican guests, who were still waiting for the signal to leave for Mexico, and who were bluntly told to ask no questions, to expect nothing, and to return home until further notice. Charlotte ran to her writing desk to pour out some of her swirling emotions in a letter to her brother Philippe: "My dear friend, if you only knew what pain I have experienced of late, you would not ask me why we are leaving this country. Max suffered the deepest of infamies at the hands of his family, and I am not afraid to say it, even should this letter be brought directly to Emperor Francis-Joseph. They want to black-mail Max to force an unfair renunciation of his rights, to deprive him of his parents' inheritance, and to make him swear to every-thing with all the clauses and oaths you use to bind the conscience of a man you know you are deceiving—and all of it on the eve of a departure known and approved by Europe and the world. You will, of course, guess that this paper was not signed, but since, out of the blue, without preparation or forewarning, the emperor of Aus-tria made it the sine qua non condition to the acceptance of the Mexican throne, it means that the deputation has not yet been re-ceived. Between his honor as a man and as a prince—and the only future left for him after this nasty trick, for our only choice lies between a voluntary exile and a throne, however dangerous it is— Max did not waver, and he refused everything, both the condition and the throne that was its price. I wish with all my strength to leave this country—a country I will never again be able to love, no, that I began deep in my heart to hate a week ago—without upsetting the laws of justice and duty. All this is a blessing from above that kills in us whatever regrets we might have had in leaving. Imagine me there, witnessing everything as it happened, and trying to shower sarcasm on the agents of this injustice. All I wanted was to bite and spew venom: I could not tell whether we were in the fif-teenth or nineteenth century, if it was the Middle Ages or ancient times, a novel or history. Of course it was nothing of the sort, there was nothing noble or Christian about it, and the memory of it will haunt me on my deathbed. You can forgive, but never forget. I have just been savagely initiated to this fact. Nonetheless, whenever I had the chance, I defended Max as best I could. For my calm per-sonality to have risen to this fever pitch of indignation that comes out in what I am writing you, you can imagine the seriousness of the insult we suffered, and the sneaky duplicity with which we were maneuvered between a rock and a hard place."

The truth would have to be announced to the Mexicans. Maximilian and Charlotte summoned the most illustrious of them—their old acquaintances Hidalgo and Gutierrez d'Estrada—and then, in the presence of the indispensable Schertzenlechner, Maximilian told them what happened in Vienna. The Mexicans were heartbroken. Maximilian proposed that they ask the pope to intervene. The Mexicans shouted that the pope would be useless—the only person who could act was Napoleon III. Hidalgo telegraphed the Tuileries, where he had a certain access, to inform Napoleon III that Francis-Joseph's demands had rendered it impossible for Maximilian to accept the crown of Mexico. At the same time, Charlotte wrote a flood of emotions to Eugenie: an impenetrable decree from heaven had prevented Maximilian and her from contributing to the well-being of Mexico, for which they had been ready to sacrifice everything, including themselves. The conditions imposed by Francis-Joseph were incompatible with both Maximilian's honor and with the very future of what was to be the Mexican empire. The answer was no.

At the Tuileries, there was an uproar. At two o'clock in the morning, Eugenie wrote a note filled with bile to the Austrian ambassador, who was otherwise her good friend. As for Napoleon III, he had the impression that he was seeing his dearest dream collapse just at the moment that it had begun to come true. He was a strange character. Twenty days before, he had been whispering to the duke of Saxe-Coburg-Gotha that Maximilian had made the wrong choice. Now that Maximilian had renounced his decision, he bombarded him with telegrams: Maximilian had committed himself to Mexico, to France, and to him, Napoleon III. The treaties had not been signed, but they may just as well have been; he could not turn back now. Napoleon III did not want to meddle with the family affairs that only concerned the House of Austria, but he knew one thing: that Maximilian could not, and had no right to, pull himself out of Mexico.

❖   ❖   ❖

Right at this confluence of events, a man appeared at Miramar whom no one knew what to do with. A few months earlier, Charlotte had asked her father to recommend a trustworthy advisor to bring with her to Mexico. She wanted a Belgian. After long research, King Leopold had recommended the son of a notary, Felix Eloin. He had been summoned, and, of course, unaware of the latest developments, he arrived at Miramar with a lump in his throat. Put off by the four robust sailors standing guard at the door, he was led to a small salon filled with objets d'art and souvenirs that in unison formed quite a picturesque mess. Bombelles, who greeted him, found him gentle, intelligent, and likable.

Soon he was brought into Maximilian's office, where Maximilian told him everything at once. Eloin was impressed by the restraint with which Maximilian curbed his indignation and avoided using harsh words when he spoke of his betrayers. He was horrified by Francis-Joseph's demands, which stripped Maximilian of everything, "as if he wanted to declare him legally dead."

When he emerged from this long interview, he was brought to Charlotte's office, a corner room that looked out on three sides over the flat, gray winter sea. Charlotte kindly asked him to sit, then read him a long letter she was writing to King Leopold to inform him of what was going on. As she read, Eloin was overcome by the unnamable magnetism Charlotte radiated. He was struck by her proud indignation, by the loftiness of her sentiments, by the nobility of "this girl wounded in everything she holds most dear." In Brussels, he had been told that she was a remarkable princess, but that had been an understatement of the truth.

Thus, Eloin entered into the game and into the negotiations that kept the little society of Miramar busy from morning till night. The three voiced any possible remedy that crossed their minds, no matter how absurd—a secret departure for Mexico, proclamations

announced from neutral territory, formal protests, anything at all —
until Maximilian found the solution. They could add a secret clause
that would provide for him to recover everything he would have
renounced in Europe if ever he were to be chased out of Mexico.
Everyone applauded and they quickly sent the proposal to Vienna.
Vienna responded: the answer was no.

Next, General Frossard, the French emperor's aide-de-camp,
arrived at Miramar and handed Maximilian a rather harsh letter from
Napoleon III, to which he added his own remarks with a military
vigor and frankness. Maximilian had no right to break his promise
to Mexico. Habsburg infighting? This was something he neither
knew nor cared about. But Maximilian's promises? That he knew
something about. What about the French troops preparing the country for his arrival? What about the loan that was approved? And the
repayment of the debt? And the Mexicans waiting for their emperor?
How could Maximilian even consider changing his mind? What
would he have said if, despite his promises, Napoleon III suddenly
pulled his troops out of Mexico without warning? To soften the attack, Frossard announced a conciliatory gesture that he himself had
been able to obtain when, before coming to Miramar, he had passed
through Vienna.

This little gesture came to Maximilian in the form of three handwritten notes. If Maximilian signed the renunciation, Francis-Joseph
promised, he would continue to pay Maximilian's annual pension;
he would allow him to raise armies of Austrian volunteers; and finally, if, God forbid, Maximilian were to be chased from Mexico and
returned to Europe, he would never have reason to complain about
the fraternal love he would find waiting for him in his elder brother.
With Charlotte's support, Maximilian tried to argue for better conditions, and sent several telegrams to this end to Vienna.

Francis-Joseph, through Rechberg, finally got rough: he had
had enough of Maximilian's demands and had reached the extreme

limit of his concessions. Maximilian should get down on his knees in thanks rather than keep asking for more. He would not give another inch, and he would not be troubled on a daily basis by re-criminations from Miramar. Maximilian raised his arms to the heav-ens: "As far as I am concerned, if someone came to tell me that all bets were off, I would lock myself in my room and jump for joy, but Charlotte . . . ?" She would not give up, and offered to go to Vienna alone to try one last time with Francis-Joseph. Crushed by disgust for these sordid discussions, disappointed to his very core with his brother, and sick and tired of it all, Maximilian let her go.

Francis-Joseph made a show of the greatest kindness to his sister-in-law. He went in person to greet her at the train station, set her up in one of the most beautiful and least uncomfortable suites at Hofburg, and listened patiently as she developed her arguments. Then he answered that his duties to the dynasty alone had forced him to ask for the renunciation, and that those same duties now prevented him from giving ground. During a pause in the discus-sion, Charlotte wrote a telegram to her father, who, at the moment, was visiting at Windsor Castle: "Am at Vienna to negotiate. Result uncertain. Relations with emperor good, but if dilemma continues, do I go for future, renunciation, or compromise? Please advise, things are very muddled. Charlotte."

The discussion went on. Francis-Joseph was willing to make concessions. Max could enjoy certain dispositions in his relatives' wills, and if he were chased out of Mexico and if he came back to Europe, he would be given an honorable pension, but the renuncia-tion for him and his descendants of the Austrian throne and of his rights and honors as an archduke would be maintained. "Middle ground impossible," Charlotte sadly telegraphed her father. The only thing left for her to do was leave. Before she did, Francis-Joseph announced to her the unheard-of honor that he would be coming to Miramar in person to attend the signing of his brother's renunciation.

❊   ❊   ❊

Amid this intense agitation, no one noticed an important event. On this same fourth of April, 1864 — the same day the discouraging interview had taken place between Francis-Joseph and Charlotte — over in Washington, the House of Representatives had unanimously voted in favor of a bill opposing the recognition of a monarchy in Mexico. Charlotte was hardly worried about the United States, since she did not even know whether they would be going to Mexico at all. She had the idea of leaving Miramar in secret and of signing a renunciation in Rome or Algiers, far away from the Austrian empire — that way, the renunciation would be legally null, and contestable later on. Unable to bear any more discussions, proposals, or counterproposals, Maximilian rejected this suggestion out of hand. Charlotte finally gave up hope; as she wrote to her father, "Nothing gained from Vienna. Short of desertion, Max cannot leave Austria without renouncing. Emperor coming tomorrow to attend in person. Acceptance to follow, and Monday departure. If advice or observations, please be quick. Charlotte." Charlotte's handwriting, always so neat and firm, had become almost illegible in the draft of this telegram.

On April 9, 1864, early in the morning, Francis-Joseph's train came to a halt in Miramar's small private station. He descended surrounded by the entire Austrian imperial panoply: seven archdukes and a crowd of generals in uniforms and helmets with long bright-green feathers, and several ministers, including the indispensable Rechberg, in a uniform spangled with decorations. He was not there to be nice to Maximilian; he was there to fool public opinion. If word of his demands, his harshness, and his unfairness with his brother had gotten out, his popularity would have suffered. If Max had said something, Francis-Joseph would have been at great risk. But Max, in his loyalty, had kept his mouth shut.

The two brothers locked themselves away in the library for a final discussion. Max tried to sway him, knowing that the battle was lost before it had begun. Once this formality was through, they returned to the company awaiting them in the salon, where Max signed. Now that he had what he wanted, Francis-Joseph had no reason to stay around. Max walked him back to the little station. The snap of heels, the clanging of sabers, and the sharp movement of military salutes followed; Francis-Joseph was already standing on the step of the train car when he suddenly turned around and clasped his brother to his heart. "Max!" he shouted. Then he boarded the train. The two brothers would never see each other again.

Despite the suffering it caused him, Max had given in and Charlotte accepted his surrender despite her determination. Both of them were worn out, crushed between their Mexican destiny and Francis-Joseph's refusal to bend.

On the next day, April 10, the "coronation" took place. There was no throne room in Miramar, or rather it had not yet been finished, for the one Maximilian was having built on the second floor was still under construction. Thus, they decided to hold the ceremony in a rather small room on the first floor. Few people attended: only the members of Maximilian's house and those Mexican delegates still moping around in Trieste, most notably Gutierrez d'Estrada and Hidalgo. Following his custom, Maximilian was wearing his Austrian admiral's uniform. He was pale and tense. As agreed upon, the Mexicans had brought him the tally of the universal suffrage, which equated a list of "liberated" towns and villages, and next to their names a count of their population, for all the inhabitants of each of these towns had, it was said, voted in favor of Maximilian. Too bad if there had not actually been a vote; no one was going to quibble over details.

Gutierrez d'Estrada came forward and gave a speech in French, guaranteeing the devotion and love of all Mexicans for their new emperor, who in turn stepped up to deliver his speech in Spanish, promising to devote himself to his new task. The bishop of Trieste was called in to receive Maximilian's oath. The words "prosperity," "integrity," "independence," and "the people's well-being" appeared on the emperor's lips as they did in every oath, each of them as trite as the next.

It was now Charlotte's turn to come forward. In a pink dress, with a sparkling diamond diadem, she was radiant as she took the imperial oath. The Mexican flag was raised on Miramar's highest tower, and three or four warships anchored before the castle fired salvos in salute. Maximilian and Charlotte were now emperor and empress of Mexico.

Maximilian went into an adjoining room with the representative of France, General Frossard, and quickly signed the Miramar Treaty to formalize the conditions set down by Napoleon III. There was something pathetic about this ceremony, conducted in haste at a vacation castle, before the motley crew of a few dignitaries and a handful of expatriates who went hoarse shouting *"Dios salve a Maximiliano emperador de México!"* It left an impression of unreality, of being completely unconnected with the immense, massive, and mysterious empire so far away, now waiting for its new sovereigns.

The next day, April 11, was supposed to have been the day of departure, as Charlotte had telegraphed to King Leopold. The night before, however, after the "coronation," Maximilian had suddenly grown so pale and seemed so sick that his private doctor, Dr. Jilek, had examined him. He forbade him from appearing at the grand dinner, and thus it was Charlotte alone who presided at the officials' table. Jilek also prescribed three days of isolation and complete rest for Maximilian. Their departure was thus postponed, and Maximilian shut himself in at the Castelleto, the little house at the top of the park from which he had watched the progress of the work on his castle. He did not want to see anyone, and when Charlotte came to speak to him of preparations he needed to make, he dismissed her curtly: "I told you that I didn't want anyone talking to me about Mexico right now."

This situation could not last. On April 14, Maximilian emerged from his isolation. He walked around his beloved park one last time. Those of his servants who would not be coming with him to Mexico were all in tears. Trieste had come en masse to wish him good-bye, for he was still immensely popular. With Charlotte on his arm, he made his way through the crowd. The military orchestras played the Austrian imperial anthem, Haydn's slow and solemn music, and the brand-new Mexican imperial anthem. The spectators cheered.

Maximilian and Charlotte descended the marble steps that led to the pier of the tiny port. They boarded the launch, its mast adorned with the green, red, and white flag of Mexico, the center now emblazoned with the imperial crown.

A painting still to be seen at Miramar immortalizes the scene: the crowd, pressing in on the marble steps, waves hands and handkerchiefs. In the background, ships are lined up, their masts covered with flags. There is even Maximilian's yacht, the *Fantasy*, recognizable by its two tilted smokestacks. The sailors, with moustaches and sideburns, are preparing to row. The generals in uniform and the ladies-in-waiting in traveling clothes stand as stiffly as poles. At the stern of the launch, which is decorated in red carpets with golden trim, Maximilian and Charlotte stand staring at the spectators and the castle, their backs turned to the ship. He is wearing a dark, ordinary civilian's suit. Charlotte is wearing a little hat, the veil of which is floating in the breeze.

The launch passed before the granite Sphinx Maximilian had brought back from Egypt and reached the guardrail of the Austrian frigate, the *Novara*. Maximilian and Charlotte came aboard to the sound of the sailors' whistles. The Mexican flag was hoisted on the main mast, and the ship unfurled its sails and weighed anchor. It was followed by the French warship, *Themis*. Both ships set off slowly amid the salvos of salute and the joyful shouts of the crowd.

Maximilian had to make an effort to hide his distress. During those last weeks, the family fights, his brother's unexpected cruelty, and the harsh negotiations had all left him exhausted—exhausted to the point that he could no longer appreciate what he had wanted and had achieved, for he had indeed wanted the crown of Mexico with all his heart, so much so that he had given in to all of Napoleon III's conditions; he had even accepted an obvious deception for what was meant to be a legitimate result of universal suffrage in his favor. Since his childhood, his mother had endowed him, her favorite, with all her good qualities. Later, Charlotte had placed him on a pedestal. But was he as strong as those two strong women would have had him believe? Was he able to take on the lofty and crushing destiny that awaited him? These were exactly the things he was wondering, with an anguish that was pushing him toward depression.

Charlotte was as radiant on their journey as she had been when she had sat enthroned alone at the gala dinner on the night of her "coronation." She was happy to have a chance to put their abilities to the test: she was happy for this beautiful and grand mission she felt she and Maximilian were made for. Her happiness was so great that the trip became an escape for her, and she enjoyed writing about it to her father. The weather had been so rough that she had gotten seasick, and her bottle of smelling salts was useless. The *Novara* had sailed around the Italian peninsula, where they had landed at Civitavecchia, the Papal States' port that she haughtily judged to be "little more than a village." The French soldiers sent by Napoleon III to protect the pope had stood at attention, shouting "Long live the emperor!" as loudly as they could, and without being told to do so, as Charlotte noted. Accompanied by their entourage,

Maximilian and Charlotte had boarded a train so dilapidated that it tossed back and forth on ancient rails. Charlotte wrote, "It is the least civilized railway I know."

In Rome, there were still more soldiers to watch their procession pass by, along with many onlookers filled with affection and good wishes. They stayed at the Martinelli palace, which belonged to Gutierrez d'Estrada. The main purpose of this detour was to visit Pope Pius IX, and Charlotte described at length their arrival at the Vatican, the secret chamberlains in their cartwheel ruffs and Spanish outfits from the time of Henry IV, the Swiss guards in uniforms from the time of Julius II who led them, halberds in hand, up the Vatican's great marble staircase. Charlotte, wearing black as protocol dictated, with diamonds and pearls, and Maximilian, in formal uniform with full decorations, went through a series of richly carpeted salons. In the last one, Pius IX appeared and came toward them "with a sure step. Looking radiant and kind. He lifted us up with benevolence, and brought us into the adjoining room, where he seated us beneath a canopy on two armchairs." Everything went beautifully. Pius IX overflowed with kindness, and luckily they did not speak too much on the prickly question of clergy property seized by Benito Juárez. He kept them for lunch, invited them to a private mass the next day, and came to visit them at their home in the Martinelli palace. Charlotte went on and on about the overwhelming honors that were transforming her a little more each day into the empress of Mexico. As was her custom, she did not fail to tour the city, visiting the Colosseum by the light of the full moon, the Villa Borghese, the Fontana di Trevi, and other highlights of Rome.

At last, they reboarded the ship at Civitavecchia. The *Novara* crossed the Mediterranean, sailed along the Spanish coast, through the straits of Gibraltar, then undertook the long trip across the Atlantic with a single layover in Madeira, so laden with memories.

Although it was a warship, the *Novara* was equipped with many comforts. The imperial couple's cabins were spacious and looked out through wide windows over the sea. Charlotte spent most of her time there. Her entourage was surprised that, instead of taking the air and idling on deck, she remained locked in for hours at a time, hard at work. She was perfecting her Spanish, reading works on the history, economy, flora, and fauna of Mexico. Together with Maximilian, she worked out what her future court would look like, the public ceremonies, the decorations, the palace guard, the uniforms and livery, the number of officials, the ranks, protocols, and celebrations. Nothing was left to chance, and their reflections produced over six hundred handwritten pages of notes. Another priority, also instigated by Charlotte, was to protest the renunciation blackmailed against them by Emperor Francis-Joseph. In a document that she herself wrote, both of them swore that they had never had the chance to read the renunciation Maximilian signed, and that they had been put under unbearable pressure. Since they needed two witnesses, they called on Schertzenlechner, who of course had come along with his master, and the newcomer, Felix Eloin, the Belgian advisor sent by King Leopold.

Not only had they kept Eloin, but they were now bringing him along to Mexico with the other members of the household: Bombelles, Maximilian's childhood friend, and Kuhacsevich, the treasurer, and his wife. The members of this tight little society were jealous of each other, sometimes hated each other, and tried to avoid each other, which was no simple task on a ship. The days drifted by, each one the same as the last. Only when they reached the Caribbean, which is to say, the American continent, did Charlotte emerge from her cabin to appear on deck in all her radiance. During the layovers in Martinique and Jamaica, she had stared in wonder at the white beaches, the coconut trees, the parrots and lush vegetation, the transparent sea. This exotic vista seemed to her a delicious foretaste of what was awaiting her in Mexico. She was more and more impatient to arrive. On May 28, 1864, the appointed day, she was on deck at dawn, scanning the horizon where the sea and sky blended together in a gray-blue haze, until the precise moment when a slightly darker line appeared, growing clearer with each passing second. Finally, she could make out a coastline: Mexico.

Charlotte returned to her writing desk and her thoughts went back to her grandmother, Queen Marie-Amelie. "Within view of Veracruz. My beloved grandmother, our trip reaped the rewards of your blessing and best wishes. It could not have been happier, not at all fatiguing, and it was even interesting and pleasant. I am thrilled by the Tropics and all my dreams are filled with butterflies and hummingbirds. In hummingbirds, nature has formed creatures with all the graceful poetry it could muster. The beauty of the nature here, so varied and rich, escapes words. I could not express it with any description and my heart has already begun to become attached to it, but without any suffering to my body. I would never have thought that, with respect to the region where we will be living, my wishes could ever come so completely true. . . ."

She put down the pen and looked out the window. The rising sun flooded the land of her empire with an orange light. Might Mexico be for her those butterflies and hummingbirds of her dreams!

6

The sun had at last fully risen that spring morning when Charlotte discovered that what she saw by the light of day lacked the golden beauty it had had at the first light of dawn. Before her, the fort of San Juan de Ulua blocked her view, a foreboding, thick, and sinister fortress where thousands of prisoners had died over the centuries. The dark reefs barring access to the shore were strewn with the breached carcasses of ships they had disemboweled, their forlorn masts still sticking out of the water in places. The coastline looked completely yellow to Charlotte, the yellow sand dunes whipped by equally yellow dust devils. There was almost no plant life to be seen.

From afar, Veracruz was little more than a dark stain pricked by the needles of its many steeples. The townspeople had done what was necessary to receive their new sovereigns. A tent of honor had been raised to welcome them. A large sum of money had been set aside to organize a banquet, a ball, and decent lighting. The only thing missing was the delegation from Mexico City, so the official landing was postponed.

The day was spent waiting. The *Novara* swayed gently, and it was very hot. Maximilian and Charlotte watched the land tirelessly, the land of their empire that they could not wait to touch.

At around six o'clock in the evening, the delegation finally arrived and came aboard, led by Almonte, who had been the first in his letters to salute Maximilian by his imperial title. Yet still, he broke protocol: instead of respectfully bowing before his sovereign, he vigorously shook his hand. Señora Almonte went so far as to permit herself a hug, the Mexican *abrazo*. Maximilian and Charlotte cringed. Taking no notice, Señora Almonte pulled a pack of cigarettes out of the pocket of her petticoat and kindly offered it to Charlotte: "*Gusta usted?* Do you want one?"

During the night, the strong wind had grown into a storm, wailing through the *Novara*'s rigging as it had pitched. The coastline and the town had disappeared under clouds of sand.

The next morning, the twenty-ninth of May, 1864, Charlotte and Maximilian rose before dawn and attended mass aboard ship. By the time the hour for the official landing tolled, the storm had finally died down, but the wind was still blowing violently, whipping up white crests across the sea. The Veracruz fort's cannons shot off honor salvos that were picked up by the French fleet anchored off the town. It was five o'clock in the morning when the imperial launch reached the dock. There were no courtiers, no dignitaries, not even any onlookers. That early in the morning, everyone was still asleep. Not even a new emperor was enough to make the Mexicans get up so early! In the straight, deserted streets of the low city, there lingered a vague stench of death, for Veracruz agonized under the *vomito negro,* the chronic epidemic of the Tropics. The dead numbered in the hundreds and the townspeople cringed in hiding at home.

The dawn's coolness soon disappeared. The sky was veiled with a haze of heat, the air became stifling, and swarms of mosquitoes descended upon the newcomers. On top of it all, the two cloth and wooden arches of triumph erected in honor of the new sovereigns had been knocked over during the night by gusts of wind, so that Maximilian and Charlotte had to make their way alongside the debris. Overcome by discouragement, he was stunned silent while she, despite her great self-control, had tears in her eyes.

They rushed to the train station, where the sovereigns, their entourage, the French officers, the domestic help, and dozens of trunks were loaded onto a special train that set off with a huff. The wooden compartments with their hard seats were particularly uncomfortable, and the travelers were violently tossed about. The convoy crossed sandy expanses stuck through with shriveled trees and cacti. The train stopped long enough for a luncheon at La Soledad, where Indian onlookers showed clear signs of their goodwill—a good beginning.

Less of a good sign was the note that mysteriously landed in Maximilian and Charlotte's hands: "A man, dear sir, may well trample others' rights, seize their belongings, attack those who defend their nation, and make their virtues into crimes, but there is one thing that such depravity cannot prevent, and that is the terrible verdict of History. . . ."—signed, Benito Juárez. With their heads held high to hide their sadness, Maximilian and Charlotte boarded the train again, which continued on for another six miles to Laloma Alta, where the tracks abruptly ended at the foot of the mountains blocking the plain.

They were forced to take what the native people called "stagecoaches of the republic," which were fast but extremely uncomfortable: there were only six of them to transport the emperor, the empress, and their entourage, as well as the cavalry in gleaming uniforms that made up their Mexican escort. The convoy scaled the mountains' steep cliffs, where the villages' names—such as Sal Si Puedes, "Get out if you can"—nicely encapsulated the traveling conditions. To make things worse, the sky had darkened, and it had begun to rain with violent winds. One coach broke an axle; another toppled over and just missed falling into a ravine, miraculously sparing the life of one of the new emperor's ministers.

As usual, Charlotte hid her true feelings. In the description she sent back to King Leopold, there was not a single word of the miserable landing at Veracruz. "Here are my impressions of this country: it is a lot less bad than I thought it would be. Its people are enthusiastic and truly affectionate." She then described the deserts she was crossing, which "weren't at all cheerful. I admit that my heart ached a little at the sight. Our mission was starting to feel a little burdensome to me. You can't imagine the roads—they defy expression. At first, there seems to be no trace of them, as if no engineer had ever worked on them before. Rocks that are yards long are strewn everywhere, and then there are the floodplains. Every few minutes, you think that the axles will break, that they will break right then and there, but then nothing happens."

The numerous stops slowed them down even further. Night had fallen, and now the time scheduled for their arrival in Cordoba had long passed. Despite the darkness, Charlotte could feel that the landscape around her had changed. Tropical sultriness had given way to a delicious coolness exhaled by thick vegetation. She heard the tinkling flow of springwater. She could just make out the coffee, tobacco, and banana plantations ringed round by dried earth hedges and lush gardens.

They arrived at Cordoba at two o'clock in the morning, half
dead from fatigue and hunger. Whatever natives were not asleep
expressed their enthusiasm noisily. In a flash, Maximilian and
Charlotte roused from their torpor and took heart again.

After a night's sleep, they were greeted with the news that bandits had held up a government coach loaded with cash for them.
Millions of coins had vanished into the forest. They left immediately afterward and set out for the town of Orizaba. As the road
rose, the plant life thickened. Riding alongside boulders with mudslides sweeping down their sides, they finally reached a green valley surrounded by the peaks of ancient volcanoes. In the middle,
the little town of Orizaba huddled around its cathedral. Charlotte
wondered what welcome was in store for them in this hotbed of
republicanism, where a large crowd, visible from afar, was waiting. She was wrong to worry, for she and Maximilian were greeted
with unheard-of enthusiasm that she happily described to her
family. The Indians wanted to unhitch their stagecoach, and more
than ten thousand people had come to shout *"Viva el emperador!"*
with deafening screams. The feelings expressed by the Mexicans
reminded her of those she had experienced in Belgium: that con-
nection between a sovereign and a people. She thought the landscape looked like the Tyrolean Alps, "a cheerful greenness, and
air of incomparable purity and lightness."

It did not matter that the town was not very pretty, or that its
streets were poorly laid out and lined with low, sad houses jutting
out with flimsy awnings to protect against sun and rain. Charlotte
only had eyes for the motley population cheering her. Like the
amateur painter she was, as she received her homage, she carefully
observed the varieties of dress bespeaking the diversity of races.
Those who were proud to have Spanish blood saluted her in the
European way. With their wide sombreros, short jackets held in
by silver-inlaid belts, and wide pants tucked into leather boots, the

men sharply bowed their heads. Their hair brightened with flowers, women curtsied in their embroidered boleros, short skirts, and
mantillas. The Indians, simply dressed in wide shirts floating loose
over their pants, wearing blankets with holes in the middle for their
heads to pass through — the national serape — were smiling widely
with happiness. The Indian women, in white skirts and draped in
flowered rebozos, showered the empress with flowers they had
picked in the fields.

Two days later, they set off again toward Mexico City. Along the
roads and in every village they passed, enthusiastic Indians appeared to watch their sovereigns pass by. "We were everywhere
overwhelmed with flowers, poetry, golden confetti. What strikes
me is that these people were truly hungry for a monarchy, that they
say they had felt a great void in their hearts for a long time — that is
the feeling they express most. Especially the Indians who turn up
on the roadside with their chieftains' staffs and long carnation scep-
ters who look at us with an indefinable curiosity: they have been
apathetic and oppressed for so long that they do not show their
emotions right away, but when they finally do, they do it with their
entire soul," Charlotte wrote.

Soon the road became so steep that they were forced to abandon the "stagecoaches of the republic" and continue on horseback.
They stopped at the Acultzingo pass, two thousand meters above
sea level. The Indians had prepared a breakfast, and for the first
time in their lives, Maximilian and Charlotte tried guacamole;
frijoles, various beans; and *tortillas enchiladas,* thin corn pancakes
stuffed with shredded meat spiced beyond belief. Their entourage
was stunned to watch them swallow these exotic, red-hot dishes as
if they were the latest delicacies cooked by Europe's royal chefs.
For Charlotte, any meal was succulent, any bed was comfortable:

"We have been beautifully housed and wonderfully fed wherever we have stopped." This was far from her entourage's opinion, after they had been attacked by fleas, bruised by hard mattresses, disheartened by the lack of service, and numbed by humidity.

One evening, they arrived at the gates of Puebla, where they spent the night at a hacienda perched on the heights surrounding the city. The next morning, Charlotte witnessed an extraordinary spectacle: situated in the middle of a plain, Puebla looked like an immense checkerboard of gardens and palatial terraces topped with innumerable domes and steeples. A belt of opulent sheep meadows and prosperous farms surrounded the city, and on the horizon rose the two tallest volcanoes in Mexico, Ixtaccihuatl and the legendary Popocatepetl, whose peaks were forever blanketed in snow. Everyone who was anyone in Puebla had come out of the city on horseback or by coach to meet Charlotte and Maximilian. The cheers were deafening. Faced with this welcome, Charlotte began to see that there were traditions here, the beginnings of a culture superior in some ways to that of old Europe, a civilization in stark contrast with the rough-hewn roads she had taken and the savagery of the deserts she had crossed.

Their triumphant entrance into Puebla had left Charlotte with a wonderful impression. The natives' enthusiasm was unimaginable. From all the roofs and terraces, there had been a shower of golden paper crowns and flowers that smelled so strongly she later said they almost "suffocated" her. Amid the cries of *"Viva el emperador! Viva la emperatriz!"* they could hear a few *"Vive l'empereur! Vive l'impératrice!"* shouted by the French soldiers. These might have served to remind her that Mexico was an occupied country, and that her empire was held together only by their presence, but those thoughts remained far from her mind. For Charlotte, the soldiers' shouts were simply "nice."

The cortège came to a halt in front of the cathedral, one of the most imposing monuments in Mexico, where they were to hear a *Te Deum* in their honor. Charlotte admired the forest of white statues decorating its façade, the green and yellow varnished domes, the huge cedar doors. Inside, it looked like Ali Baba's cave, replete with monstrances, candlesticks, reliquaries and altars, and solid silver chandeliers encrusted with gold, all of them of immense proportions. Upon nightfall, French gunners shot off a spectacular fireworks show from the surrounding hills.

At last fully triumphant, their advance carried on. The sovereigns stopped at Cholula, once the Aztecs' most important city. Charlotte prayed at the sanctuary of Remedios, built on the very *tocali* where, in earlier times, human sacrifices were made. They rode through the Puerto Aire pass — appropriately named "Port of the Air," since it stood at an elevation of three thousand two hundred meters — then they set out across the Sierra Nevada, past the foot of Popocatepetl, and finally began to descend toward the Mexico City plateau. Suddenly, far beneath them, they spotted a few pale expanses. These were the lakes surrounding the capital: "It was a solemn moment; we felt just like the Crusaders must have when they finally saw Jerusalem. We got down from the coach with an almost religious enthusiasm. And indeed, the spectacle was grand. It had struck Cortés three hundred years ago, it had been the center of migration for great peoples, it had stopped the Aztecs as well as the Spanish, and now it could see us coming."

Maximilian, but especially Charlotte, had decided that before they entered Mexico City, they would stop by at the Santa Maria de Guadalupe sanctuary where the Virgin had appeared. This sanctuary remained the most important place of pilgrimage in all of Mexico, but it was also a rallying point, a national symbol that all Mexicans, even atheists, carried with them in their hearts. Charlotte also had another motive in going there: "An old prophecy holds that a young blond man coming from the east will enter Mexico City through Guadalupe, and that he will found an empire there that will make the Indian race flourish again."

Just as in Puebla, the notables and the rich had come out to greet their sovereigns. But this time it had been not hundreds, but thousands of gentlemen and ladies shouting from their coaches: "*Viva México independiente!*" "*Viva el imperio mexicano!*" "*Viva Maximiliano primero!*" "*Viva Napoleone tercero!*" "*Viva el rey de los Belgas!*" and "*Viva Leopold primero!*" These last cheers brought tears to Charlotte's eyes.

As they entered Guadalupe, they climbed up into an elegant coach driven by coachmen in red livery—the very livery that had belonged to Benito Juárez—and Charlotte saw in that the intention to set up the new power with the old one's furniture. When they stopped before the sanctuary, the crowd broke through the guards' barricades and rushed at them, dying to touch them. If they had not been fairly tall, Charlotte had noted, they would have been crushed. "I have never seen such enthusiasm; it was more than delirium, it was a frenzy."

Charlotte and Maximilian prostrated themselves before the miraculous statue of the dark-faced Virgin. During the *Te Deum*, the *Domine salvum fac imperatorem*—the hymn sung in all the European courts for the sovereigns' health—sounded out for the first time in Mexico. It was also the first time that the honor so familiar to their ears was sung to Maximilian and Charlotte. Their throats constricted with emotion.

Later on, in the Chapter House, they received the capital's notables. Among them, a thickly moustachioed soldier strode up imposingly, his chubby face contradicted by little dark eyes half-hidden behind heavy lids. It was General Bazaine, commander in chief of the French forces. Maximilian and Charlotte greeted him with extreme kindness, as they were well aware that their fate depended on him. Only when the French troops had cleaned up the last pockets still held by Juárez's partisans, and thus pacified the country, would Maximilian and Charlotte finally be able to begin their reign.

Despite his experienced courtier's subtle subservience and his gift for crafty words, Bazaine immediately judged the couple harshly. He felt himself to be superior to the emperor and empress. For their part, they instinctively understood that they had to watch out for him.

On the next day, the twelfth of June, 1864, Maximilian and Charlotte once again boarded the train. "A little fifteen-minute trip" would bring them to the gates of the capital. Charlotte could not peel herself away from the window, her eyes wide before the spectacle of her capital's suburbs. "The outskirts are those of a big city; it felt as if I were arriving at Paris." This comparison was perhaps a bit exaggerated, stemming from overflowing enthusiasm. At the station, an elegant convertible coach picked them up and paraded them through festooned streets, as they passed beneath the arches of triumph erected for the event. A shower of calligraphy poems, flowers, and paper crowns rained down from the balconies. The entire city was in the streets to cheer them. Gone were the class distinctions and differences of political opinion — even if the poor stood in the streets while the rich had paid up to four hundred francs for a place at a window and up to two thousand five hundred for a seat on a balcony. The republicans shouted their cheers along with the conservatives. Losing all fear of the escort's horses in her excitement, a woman well known for her liberal opinions even rushed to the imperial coach to offer a bouquet of flowers that Maximilian caught on the fly while shouting, "Watch out, watch out for the horses!" Next to the coach, General Bazaine was on horseback in dress uniform, flanked by his entire staff. Charlotte was waving back to the cheers. She observed the crowd so warmly welcoming her, and then her eyes drifted back to the French uniforms she had had a soft spot for ever since her childhood. "The shouts of *'Viva el emperador!'* were only interrupted by other shouts of *'Vive l'empereur!'*; it was like a symbol of the important alliance that we ourselves hold together. For the very reason we are here is that the Mexicans elected us and France wanted us. We are the bond between them, and I hope we will remain so.".

Maximilian was thinking about entirely different things. His eyes landed on Colonel Miguel Lopez, who was riding in front of the coach at the head of the Mexican escort. His blond hair, pale skin, and blue eyes made him appear more French than Mexican. Handsome, elegant, and glamorous with his *hidalgo*'s manners, he had been sent by Almonte to greet the emperor at Veracruz; he had impressed Maximilian right away, so much so that Maximilian had immediately named him chief of the imperial escort. Miguel Lopez had followed his sovereigns from the coast to the capital, laying his deference on thickly, prancing about on his horse like a virtuoso, never once missing a chance to be noticed by his emperor.

Bathed in the screams of the near-hysterical crowd, the procession reached the capital's most venerable site: the Zocalo, an ancient sacred center of the Aztecs and the most mystical place in their religion, where one of their leaders had once sacrificed twenty thousand prisoners in thanks for a single victory. Later, the pyramids had been razed by the Spanish to make way for the opulent baroque cathedral, and for the gigantic palace of the old viceroys.

Maximilian and Charlotte crossed the Zocalo on foot and entered the building that would be their residence. Notables and dignitaries were waiting for them there, to whom Maximilian delivered a short speech filled with good sentiments.

That night, the entire city was floodlit. The Mexicans did not want to leave the Zocalo, and called their emperor and empress out onto the balcony ten, twenty times. A dazzling fireworks show began, and as the taste of the time dictated, the rockets traced various figures, most notably that of Miramar Castle. Miramar drawn in Aztec lights! With her enthusiasm still going strong, Charlotte noticed that the Mexicans had the most beautiful fireworks in the world: "Among many others, there is one that goes back and forth like a will-o'-the-wisp that is called the Correo."

Finally the couple was able to retire to find a little peace. But where? The building that people were already calling the Imperial Palace was not yet ready to receive them. They had to resign themselves to the inevitable; Maximilian lay down on the billiards table and Charlotte set herself up in an ugly little armchair. Discomfort mixed with the day's exaltation prevented her from sleeping. She turned over and over, paced back and forth, sat back down again. She heard the city's noises, echoes so different from the ones she had been used to in Europe. She was happy at last to find herself in "this old palace of the viceroys, which, from Montezuma all the way down to Juárez, has always housed whatever power there has been in this country." Henceforth, she and Maximilian were that power, and they lived in its seat. No matter that the old palace was poorly furnished, uncomfortable, and even unhealthy; no matter that it was infested with fleas and bedbugs. When your name was Charlotte and a nation unanimously offered you power on a silver platter, you could deal with all the insects in the world.

The next morning and all through the day, this same nation returned to the Zocalo to continue showing its affection to its sovereigns. Even though the square was one of the biggest in the world, there was not enough room "for a pin to drop," so tightly were the crowds packed in. "We couldn't hear any *viva*'s anymore; now it was just the confused mumble of people talking at the same time, and who have so much to say that their words come out as inarticulate noises." Over and over, they heard the same piercing scream, "*Que salga el emperador!,*" "Let the emperor come out!" All that Maximilian and Charlotte had to do was step outside for a moment, and the confused mumble instantly transformed into frenzied *viva*'s.

That night, there was a gala presentation at the National Theater. Señora de Miramon, the wife of a former president of the republic recently come over to Maximilian's side, was invited. Despite her taste for worldly pleasures, she kept a critical eye and tongue trained at the members of the diplomatic corps, the court, the politicians, high Mexican society, the men in tuxedos and medals, and the women vying with each other in elegance. The hall had been brilliantly illuminated and decorated with thick garlands of flowers tied to the crimson velvet wall tapestries. Every box had been reserved for an exorbitant price. Señora de Miramon watched the emperor and empress come in, lofty and graceful, the very image of what monarchs should be: he in tails, his chest wrapped in the sash of the brand new Order of Guadalupe, she in white crinoline covered with priceless Valenciennes lace, a jeweled diadem in her hair, and a string of enormous pearls around her neck. Once she had reached her box, Charlotte scanned the assembly. She had her new lady-in-waiting, Madam Almonte, point out the most notable personalities. When Charlotte noticed Señora de Miramon, she asked that she be summoned. "Oh no, Your Majesty, since she was the president's wife and she is very proud, she will never accept." This "venomous" remark of Madam Almonte's would be reported back to Señora de Miramon by her friend, the countess del Valle, recently named high mistress of the court.

Some time later, Señora de Miramon and her husband were invited to a luncheon, for Charlotte had certainly not forgotten her. With his inborn talent for decoration, Maximilian had quickly transformed the palace, so much so that Señora de Miramon scarcely recognized the place where she had once lived. The emperor had demolished several walls of the halls lining the main façade and turned them into a huge Ambassadors' Salon. He had had the floor covered with a Bordeaux carpet brought from Europe, and the walls with tapestries bearing the coat of arms of the new empire: an eagle clutching a serpent in its talons, an image inspired by Aztec mythology, and the fairly prosaic motto he himself invented, "Equity in Justice." While he had been pacing about in one of the least well-maintained halls of his new palace, he had noticed bits of stucco that had fallen from the ceiling to the floor below. Lifting his eyes, he had spotted painted beams between the cracks. He had had the stucco cleared off only to discover beautiful ceilings decorated in the time of Cortés, and he immediately had had their former luster restored.

Señora de Miramon was astounded by the immense Venetian mirrors, the marble vases, and the statues now populating the hallways she had last seen deserted, but especially by the gigantic Japanese porcelain candlesticks whose bronze branches rose to hold the candles aloft. She wondered how the royal couple could possibly have brought all those treasures to Mexico so quickly.

Once the grand chamberlain announced them, the imperial couple appeared in the salon's doorway. That day, Charlotte was wearing a gray silk dress decorated with embroidery and needlepoint, diamond earrings, and in her hair, a jeweled aigrette. The sovereigns greeted their guests with a kind word to everyone, and finally they went into the dining room, which had also been entirely redecorated. Once again, Señora de Miramon swooned over the service of Sèvres porcelain, the Bohême crystal, the finely worked silverware. She did not know that it was not real silver, but rather an imitation invented by the House of Christofle. Maximilian and Charlotte had wanted to put on a good show to impress their subjects, but since their credit was by no means unlimited, sometimes they had to make do with fakes.

The festivities continued day after day: military reviews, galas, banquets, and even a Venetian masquerade ball sponsored by the municipality. The people rushed to watch and cheer. High society was stricken with a widespread frenzy: there had been good things about the republic, but it had been mostly bad; it had abolished the nobility's titles and other "baubles of vanity" that the Spanish had invented and doled out at the time of the viceroys. The dismayed modern beneficiaries had had to relegate to the depths of drawers and closets those beautifully illuminated parchments listing their noble distinctions. But now, the empire was rising from the dust.

The Mexicans descended from old families, as Señora de Miramon told it, had one day realized that they were counts, marquises, grand names of Spain . . . one woman of her acquaintance had demanded special treatment since, she claimed, she descended directly from Montezuma, the last Aztec sovereign. This elegant and refined society, which had known how to live better than the aristocrats of Europe, and whom years of the republic had trained to act casually, now joyfully threw itself headlong into the rigors of a protocol that their sovereigns had brought with them in their suitcases.

Charlotte was having a great time discovering the city, crisscrossing it every day in her convertible coach, surrounded by a platoon of cavalry. Perhaps it was not the Paris she had previously described, but Mexico City, in its proportions and the wideness of its avenues, did have a certain grandeur. The monuments were beautiful, erected by the Spanish to prove the incontestable greatness of their empire. Private palaces bore witness to the old families' wealth. Houses with more than one floor were still rare, and the homes were built in the Arab tradition, around a central patio onto which halls and bedrooms opened out. But unlike the Arabs, the Mexicans had opened their homes to the street, with full-length windows protected by *rejas*, elegantly twisted grates. The capital extended out into unending suburbs whose straight streets were bordered by low mud houses crammed full of Indians and mestizos.

Charlotte also spent long hours on her balcony, shaded by a striped awning. She came to know her subjects by watching their comings and goings. A horse galloped by, ridden by a *jinete*, or knight; his legs were stiff, and his body leaned forward; the saddle was encrusted with silver, and there was a skin tossed over the horse's flanks. She heard a donkey bray: Indians from the country were coming to town. Swaying in their straw hats, they walked at a lazy gait. When the rain began to fall, they wrapped themselves in their serapes. The Indians went by foot, while the descendants of the white conquerors, in their riding coats and European hats, circulated only on horseback. Sometimes they wore the ranchero costume, half Andalusian, half Arabic, something between a *majo* and a lasso-thrower.

The only women to be seen in the streets were Indian. Ladies of social standing never left the house except to go to mass, and even then, their faces remained hidden behind a mantilla.

The Zouaves walked in pairs beneath Charlotte's balcony, looking "mischievous and relaxed, even gallant, as they would say in Paris," with their red fezzes tilted back and bayonets or sabers at their sides. These officers wore a sort of cross between trousers and petticoats, tight at the waist, which from Charlotte's balcony made them look like pyramids or bells.

The hours passed by but still she never grew tired of the endlessly exotic spectacle. She felt at peace and confident. Gone were
the doubts that had plagued Maximilian and Charlotte before they
had accepted the throne—all they had had to do was appear for
the entire country to rally to them: the aristocrats, of course, the
clergy and conservatives, but also the middle class and especially
the Indians, even the republicans, all the more so since their leader,
in everyone's opinion, was done for.

Barely had Maximilian set foot in Mexico than Juárez had
begun his retreat north. Though Maximilian had stopped at Mexico
City, "the pathetic caravan of the republic," pursued by French troops
and undermined by defections, kept pushing on. Out of sheer exhaustion, they had come to a halt in Monterrey. A single attack by
Bazaine, and Juárez would be erased from the Earth forever. The
Mexican empire, founded more or less on acceptable pretexts, had
become a reality, thanks to Maximilian and Charlotte's conviction.
Theirs was a conviction that had been built not only on their abilities
and skills, but also on their desire to devote themselves body and soul
to Mexico. The new empire would wipe clean all memory of the republic, for it was made to take root, to last, and to prosper. Charlotte
believed it, Maximilian believed it, and Mexico believed it.

As she was expected to, Charlotte began to hold receptions at the palace. Each Monday, she hosted intimate balls, more exclusive and
envied than official ceremonies, with fewer, carefully chosen guests.
Before each party began, Maximilian inspected everything, even
the ladies' powder room. At eight-thirty, the sovereigns entered the
small salon reserved for the diplomatic corps and the court's higher
officials. Maximilian wore his uniform, decorated with the Order
of the Golden Fleece and the sash of the Order of Guadalupe.
Charlotte favored pale tones: white, pink, yellow. She sparkled with

diamonds and enormous pearls, and her chest was wrapped in the wide sash of the Order of San Carlos that she had founded for women. The master of ceremonies, Count del Valle, opened the double doors and with a stentorian voice announced, "Sirs, Their Majesties." The sovereigns rushed through the salons where their guests, Mexico City's highest society, were waiting for them. Caballeros and señoritas all thrilled at the sight of the magnificent couple. Both of them tall and glamorous, he blond, she with hair as black as night, both gifted with natural ease, they presented the image of a perfect union: a deep love that illuminated them from within with grace and allure.

One such night, Countess del Valle imitated Charlotte, wearing a white gown covered with lace and even diamonds, though ones smaller than the empress's. In her red gown stitched with real flowers, Señora de Sanchez Navarro looked like a Virgin Mary painted by Murillo. Señora de Arrigunaya, a famous beauty, had the smallest feet in the world. One of the prettiest girls in Mexico, a living springtime for the eyes, Enriqueta Servantes raised her silvery voice as she spoke with Antonia Barandiaran, herself a seeming Greek goddess. Behind their flittering fans, all of them were mocking the canoness—that was the title borne by one of the ladies-in-waiting whom Charlotte had brought from Austria. She was very tall, even gigantic, always dressed in black, and on her chest, she wore the red ribbon indicating her rank. Between bursts of laughter, the Mexican women compared her to an elephant.

Of course, the Almontes were there, the Miramons, General Bazaine, and all the high-ranking French officers. Their Majesties began by making a "court circle," which meant that they proceeded slowly between two lines of guests, stopping before each one to say a few words. Then the actual ball began, and it was a wonder to behold those pretty girls waltzing with Austrian, Mexican, and French officers. The sheer number of uniforms drowned out the few gloomy black tuxedos.

Pepita de la Pena was seventeen years old, with beautiful black hair and a very Spanish, very expressive personality. A ravishing beauty, she came from an excellent family, though unfortunately she had lost her father. Perfectly educated, she spoke French. That night, she was having wild fun, dancing with Captain Detroya, a seductive officer from the French navy, when suddenly General Almonte, whom she had known since childhood, tapped her on the shoulder.

"Pepita, let me introduce you to General Bazaine, who would like to make your acquaintance."

He stole her away from Detroya and walked her over to the commander in chief. Bazaine stared at her at length, and then, as a first compliment, he told her that she strangely resembled his beloved wife, now dead for just over a year. To make up for that gaffe, he asked her to dance, not in the young people's room, but rather in the hall where the empress was dancing the quadrille with the city's leading ladies—a quadrille from which young women like Pepita were excluded, but then, nothing was denied General Bazaine. Thanks to him, Pepita advanced gracefully before Charlotte's astonished stare.

Finally it was suppertime. The guests stormed the buffet where the latest rage, pink champagne, flowed like water. The Austrian majordomos had had time to train the waiters, all of them Mexican, and their service was impeccable. The emperor dined with the diplomatic corps, the empress with the most important ladies. The young men and women had been gathered at the most distant table, and were having the most fun.

All of a sudden, Bazaine asked Maximilian for permission to dine not with him, but rather to sit with the beautiful Pepita at the young people's table. Maximilian agreed with a smile, then whispered to a friend, "Tonight, Bazaine has fallen head over heels for Señorita de la Pena."

As the hours passed by, fatigue began to douse the party's fervor. After midnight, the masks came off. Señora de Miramon continued her observation, particularly of the new sovereigns: Maximilian was the same age as her husband, the ex-president, barely thirty years old. He had regular features, a majestic bearing, skin as white as ivory, blond hair. The expressiveness of his blue eyes gave his face a particularly friendly look. His character seemed jovial—and indeed he loved jokes, which he told elegantly, though sometimes with a biting, even bitter ending. He had a passion for the fine arts, literature, and poetry, and he knew a great deal about botany. His wife's ladies-in-waiting, all of them in love with him, told Señora de Miramon that when Maximilian left the palace, everything, "even the plants in the garden," drooped with sadness.

On to Charlotte. Señora de Miramon found Charlotte's head to be a little small for her stature. She had a round face with blushes on her cheekbones, just above her pale cheeks, and hair as black as her eyes. Her eyes drifted off into space for long periods of time. Very intelligent, very cultivated, she spoke six or seven languages fluently, including Latin. She knew a great deal about many subjects, even about the art of sailing. But she lacked a certain softness. Her pride sometimes stung the ladies of her entourage. During the audience that Charlotte permitted Countess del Valle, she made her stand even though she was pregnant. When she went out for coach rides, she enjoyed asking her ladies-in-waiting questions none of them knew the answer to: "Under what viceroy was the School of Mining built?" Silence. "Who sculpted the Tlaxaba fountain and the façade of the Sacred Heart Church?" Silence. Charlotte's expression let her ladies know that she considered them all hopelessly ignorant.

Nor was Charlotte any less demanding with the French army. In her opinion, the generals were resting on their laurels. Bazaine and his top officers did not walk down the street unless they had a horde of aides with them. It was not a crime, but Charlotte saw in it a "symptom of idleness." All things considered, Bazaine was not the hawk Charlotte had made him out to be. He had received all honors imaginable, even the Legion of Honor, but, in her opinion, all they had done was make him lazy. For indeed, the republican party was not dead yet.

At last, Bazaine, perhaps goaded on by Charlotte, took action. In the south, his troops beat those of General Uraga, the last one to hold out against Maximilian. The only pocket of resistance then left in the area was at Oaxaca, which was held by a certain Porfirio Diaz, a half-breed native to the region, like Juárez. Also from a poor family, Diaz had chosen adventure over titles. As a guerrilla, he had known prison, and his short existence had been punctuated with the most bizarre events. Despite his modest origin, he instinctively possessed a panache that the colder, more reserved, and calculating Juárez lacked. They were both equally cunning. Juárez was a politician, but Diaz was a leader.

Even though there was already quite a bit of talk about Diaz, Bazaine considered him a negligible nuisance that he would take care of in good time. His principal targets were Monterrey and, in it, Juárez. His troops marched north, destroying everything in their path. Juárez was forced to retreat hastily. He did not stop until hundreds of miles later, in Chihuahua; prudently, he sent his wife and children off to the United States. Around him, all that was left was a handful of the faithful, living in squalor and losing a little more hope every day.

This impressive series of successes changed Charlotte's opinion of the commander in chief of the French forces. "Bazaine is a man of a somewhat cold mind, entirely under the charm of Max, who is able to move him however he likes, and even make him cry from tenderness. Bazaine had not done a thing for six months, and when he is not doing anything, he does not like to see others doing anything either. Luckily our arrival shook him out of his torpor."

To complete the "pacification," Bazaine had not shied away from brutality. When Maximilian learned of this, he became angry and had his principal private secretary, the faithful Eloin, write the commander in chief. Eloin carefully listed the French "atrocities": the town of Zacualtipán had been burned to the ground; Huauchinango had been sacked "with a barbarity worthy of an earlier century"; and in Tulancingo, several rebels had been shot in a firing line, and so on. "His Majesty would like to believe that this news is false."

For her part, Charlotte was still gathering her observations of her subjects and sending them to her father. This Mexican nation that Juárez used to call *El Soberano*—the Sovereign—was not a nation at all, but a patchwork of races, languages, and characters, all of completely distinct origins. Only the love of independence united Mexicans, an independence now manifest in Maximilian. Charlotte was truly astounded by their docility, which made her and Maximilian's task so much easier than that of their European counterparts. Yet that task was still enormous. Everywhere they needed to push people into action, to combat laziness and apathy, and that was the hardest job of all. There was no one else to depend on. The government did nothing but produce paper. They passed their bills and laws, all of which remained without effect. The chaos she and Maximilian faced sometimes left her feeling powerless.

But they had no time for discouragement, no matter how fleeting. Maximilian remained chained to his desk the entire day, granting audiences, studying files, and writing instructions. Charlotte, on the other hand, dealt with official obligations on a day-to-day basis. As she wrote her father, "Yesterday I had to bear myself with unheard-of majesty the whole day through. I went to mass and to the *Te Deum* with a court coat made of red velvet, and for twenty-four hours, I gathered within myself all the dignity of the monarchy."

She was twenty-four years old. Her new position left her feeling exalted, but, because she had been raised in democratic Belgium, she also knew how to put a stop to overblown honors. She did not allow Bazaine to erect a bust of her in a public square, and she did away with the canopy under which she and Maximilian had used to enter shrines. If they went on like that, she joked, the Indians would start taking them for gods on Earth.

Maximilian and Charlotte had been so overworked and their imperial palace so cold and official that they had decided to look for a country retreat. They found it one day when their daily ride brought them to the locality known as Chapultepec. A mile or two outside the city, it was a characterless house dating from the end of the eighteenth century, built by the Spanish viceroys as a vacation home. The mansion had since become a barracks, and then a hospital, before it had finally been abandoned. It occupied an exceptional site on an enormous rock face that looked out over the entire plain. From its terraces, all of Mexico City stretched out wide beneath it, including its lakes and the distant fields, and all the way at the horizon, its inaccessible volcanoes. Around the residence, there was an expansive forest of giant tamarisks, cedars, and cypresses, which kept the place deliciously cool.

Maximilian and Charlotte were seduced by Chapultepec. The emperor immediately got down to work. He was his own architect and interior designer. In place of the viceroys' modest mansion, he built a huge French-style castle with colonnades, a covered terrace, arcades, and verandas. He transformed the rooms that were already there, invented new ones, and then carpeted and furnished all with shiploads of cargo brought over entirely from Europe. He decided to connect his pleasure home to the capital with a long avenue that he would border with eucalyptus trees and wide lawns. The Paseo de Carlotta, as he baptized it, would not be completed until long after his reign; even now, renamed the Paseo de la Reforma, it remains one of the Mexican capital's major arteries.

Charlotte and Maximilian moved into Chapultepec without delay. For his suite, Maximilian had chosen the calmest section, for he was a light sleeper and the slightest noise woke him. He jumped out of bed at four o'clock in the morning to go horseback riding in the freshness of the coming dawn. By nine o'clock, he was at his desk, and took a break only to go swimming in a pond he had discovered in the woods, where, according to legend, Malinche, the famous mistress of Cortés, used to come to bathe.

Charlotte woke up later than Maximilian and had her breakfast in her suite. She also went out horseback riding, her favorite sport. She galloped down the sandy paths that wound through the immense prehistoric-looking trees. Then, either with Maximilian or separately, she went by coach to the office, the Imperial Palace in Mexico City—he to receive his ministers, she to preside over charity councils. They met back at Chapultepec at four o'clock for dinner, which took place in the presence of both their entourages. The conversation there was freewheeling and relaxed—they could speak about anything except politics. Then Charlotte retired with the ladies to her boudoir, while Maximilian led the men into his smoking room. By Mexican standards, it was still early when the fires were extinguished and Maximilian and Charlotte finally found themselves alone.

Once upon a time, Charlotte had seen Miramar as a cocoon Maximilian had thought up as a shelter for their love. Since she had never had a chance to find out whether that was the case, she hoped with all her heart that Chapultepec would play that role from now on, that their castle deep in the forest would protect them and enclose them so that they could love each other freely and with all their strength.

But as soon as they had moved in, Maximilian announced he would be leaving.

7

During that summer of 1864, Maximilian had decided to undertake a tour of the provinces. He knew that his presence strengthened old loyalties and won over new ones. Of course, Charlotte was included, or rather, *had been* included, for she was abruptly uninvited. She was unable to hide her deep disappointment from her father: "In my last letter, I spoke to you of a trip to the north, but fate has ruled against me, and instead, Max will be going alone." Thereupon followed explanations and excuses: Maximilian wanted to travel quickly and far, so it was wiser for Charlotte not to accompany him on roads so unhealthy in that season. Then, of course, someone had to stay at home. People did so enjoy seeing the palace lived in. Finally, Maximilian had given Charlotte the task of presiding over the cabinet, and so she needed to stay where she was. All lines of reasoning at once plausible and implausible. Obviously, Charlotte had been greatly looking forward to the trip with her beloved Max, and the reasons she offered to justify his leaving her alone in Mexico City were not very convincing.

Once again, Charlotte held her tongue, and yet, when she saw her husband depart, her heartache was so deep that she fell ill. As she told him: "Yesterday and today, I spent several hours in bed, I have stomach pains and probably also diarrhea—it is just as I told you before you left, but even worse now, so that I can only manage soup. I hope it will pass in a few days. . . . I can't tell whether my pain is physical or mental . . . you see that I'm not having a very good time of it. After living such an uninteresting life, I feel paralyzed by your departure. . . . I want to stop this whining, which only serves to show you that I'm not in my normal state, because I feel sad, idle, useless."

Barely had he left than she began to pine for his return. For consolation, she bought green hummingbirds with lilac breasts, and fed them herself with orange blossoms and sugar-water. She observed them at length, sucking the flowers' juices while hovering still in the air. Their wings buzzed so much that they reminded Charlotte of swarms of flies, and when she came close to their cage, she felt drafts of air, as if from a fan.

Meanwhile, Max was heading north. Six coaches made up the convoy, surrounded by platoons of French and Mexican cavalry. He had brought Schertzenlechner along, or rather, Schertzenlechner had gotten himself invited. Schertzenlechner hated and envied Eloin, the Belgian who had gained such influence over the imperial couple. But Eloin had stayed in Mexico City to assist Charlotte, and Schertzenlechner was determined to use this trip to win back his hold over Max. A newcomer was also present: Joseph Loysel, thirty-nine years old, a Breton, and a graduate of the Saint-Cyr military academy. Bazaine had assigned him to Maximilian, who had soon grown fond of the discreet and loyal officer.

Leaving on the tenth of August, Maximilian found himself five days later at San Juan del Rio, eighty-five miles out on the north road, to celebrate with due decorum the official feast of the French emperor. He soon reached the next leg of his journey, Queretaro. He wrote letter after letter to Charlotte: "*Angel de mi corazon,*" "*Señora de mis deseos*" — "Angel of my heart," "Lady of my desires," and then, "I can never be fully happy when I'm not with the star of my life." These declarations, repeated tirelessly, should have been the expressions of an all-consuming passion. And yet it was Maximilian who had not wanted to bring Charlotte along. Might he have loved her only with distance between them?

From Mexico City, Charlotte poured out her heart in long letters to her father, in which she told him everything that crossed her mind, especially her thoughts on the Mexicans, an inexhaustible subject: it was impossible to use them in government, she said. In fact, you could really trust only foreigners. If the foreigners were suddenly to leave the country for one reason or another, the whole of Mexico's future would be in jeopardy. And yet the Hispano-American race, as Charlotte called it, was extremely intelligent — they learned everything quickly and well, they showed themselves gifted for the arts, but what ghastly laziness, what a lack of obedience, discipline, and logical thought. Charlotte was probably the first among the European powers to take an interest in the Indians, who comprised the majority of the Mexican people. The land they worked did not belong to them. They remained, she noticed, in a state of subjugation similar to slavery. The landowners, whose property sometimes covered entire provinces, treated the Indians little better than cattle. How, under these circumstances, was one to demand courage, initiative, and devotion of them? And yet, despite their inertia, they did experience love and trust.

In each city, Maximilian was met with "frenzied" enthusiasm, for he truly knew his business, as Charlotte proudly told her father. He convinced the Mexicans that he expected everything of them; he told them over and over how he admired them; he did everything to encourage them. To the intimidated masses, he displayed a gentleness and benevolence that sent them into rapture. In short, Maximilian treated the Mexicans like children who had to be entertained, and who could not be told the same things too often lest they grow bored. He could have certain hopes for Mexico and for the Mexicans, but in the meantime, there could be "no law, no equality, no clergy worth their salt. All the branches of government and the administration together can do nothing." For her part, Charlotte had not failed to notice that deep down, her subjects were horrified by foreigners, even when they came bearing useful innovations.

Max passed through Celaya, and in the beginning of September, he arrived at Irapuato, where he hosted a dinner for General Uraga, yesterday chief of the rebels, now entirely devoted to Maximilian. The next day, the emperor fell ill. He had caught a sore throat, and with his fever, he could neither get out of bed nor speak. In his distress, he turned to Charlotte, writing to her how lonely and lost he felt, how much he missed her. For several days, Charlotte was racked with worry, and her distance from Maximilian only worsened her suffering. Finally, after a few days, he recovered. It was only a false alarm. "Thank God you're feeling better," Charlotte wrote. "The fright I took from your illness gave me a few bad days. Just yesterday, I was terrified that news would come that you were still in pain. You are not like other people, so I always fear you will fall ill, and more seriously than people will tell me. I no longer even know if you have a body, for the tales of your trip fill me with such admiration that I am starting to consider you more of an angel than a man. I am jealous of all the good you're doing without me, and especially of your quick and practical ideas. . . ."

Nonetheless, from Brussels, King Leopold was growing anxious. He recommended that Charlotte prevent Maximilian from doing anything rash, which is what Leopold feared he always tended to do. "Don't be overzealous, and make sure you get enough sleep, otherwise you will weaken yourselves and get sick," he told her. To raise her spirits, her father announced that all the European nations had officially recognized them as the sovereigns of Mexico — one worry less for an empress burdened every day with more and more responsibilities.

When he left, Maximilian had asked Charlotte to preside over the council of ministers whenever it was necessary, but the growing number of emergencies had pushed her to assume a veritable regency. Bazaine came to report to her every week, just as he would have to Maximilian. She took the initiative of offering public audiences on Sundays, when she received whomever wanted to speak with her. As a consequence, the petitions flooded in, and she admitted that she was sometimes horrified by what people asked of her and by the casualness with which they asked it. But Charlotte was no one's fool — neither the French commander in chief's nor the petitioners'. Forever unruffled, she delivered speeches, presided over charitable ceremonies, and inspected institutions. She had long interviews with Corta, a French deputy lent to Maximilian to clear up Mexico's finances, a colossal task.

Charlotte enjoyed reading the files attentively, examining financial questions, and finding solutions. The necessity of standing
in for Max at a moment's notice gave her the chance to discover
what she was truly capable of. She was pleased to tell her father
that, at the end of a long discussion with Corta, they had both decided not to grant the cities the subsidies they asked for, which
meant a great savings for the state.

If only there had been nothing but financial problems! In
September, Charlotte had her first alarm: she found out by telegram that ten thousand men of the French contingent had suddenly
been recalled. She almost fell out of her chair, until she realized that
the decision had been dictated solely by politics, to Napoleon III's
profit. That's fine, she told herself, Bazaine will stand up for us, he
will know how to send the men back in dribs and drabs, starting
with the sick and those on leave. Even still, to maintain order in an
empire as vast as Mexico's, they would need a great deal of French
troops. Hanging a Zouave's red trousers in a tree, she confided to
her father, would be more effective in defending a village than all
the Mexican soldiers put together.

The announced pullout of a part of the occupying troops worried her,
all the more so in that, for some time, she had begun noticing a
certain laxness in the French. Take customs, for example. Ever since
the French administration had stopped looking so closely, people
had been taking their sweet time paying customs duties. Or thieves:
ever since the French had been easing up on their crackdown, the
number of thieves had been increasing, and they had even begun
robbing around the capital. There were almost one hundred thousand of them in the country, "without mentioning the other bandits, or the ones who steal from homes and businesses—the greater

part of the nation's employees." Of course, Maximilian and Charlotte had won the Mexicans' hearts more solidly than any president had in the past, but the French served their purpose too.

Then there were the priests. Charlotte had been raised by her mother to be very religious, and then by her governess, but her grandfather Louis-Philippe had never believed in anything at all, and her uncles were all freethinkers. She tended to agree with them when it came to judging the Mexican clergy. The church in Mexico was preoccupied with political passion and especially money. Despite the end of privileges held over from colonial times, despite Juárez's seizing of the clergy's property, there remained certain prelates who took themselves for feudal lords, grasping and ferocious. It was of no consequence that the people were dying without education, without sacraments or consolation—the priests did not care as long as they won back their privileges and property.

Charlotte realized that the question of the clergy's property was Mexico's first order of business. As fate would have it, she had just been sent word of the arrival of a special envoy whom the pope had sent to settle the matter. Charlotte had no doubt that they would reach an agreement with the nuncio, and if they did not, they could continue on without him.

In the midst of all these worries, Charlotte became acquainted with a special characteristic of Mexico that she had not known about before. During the night of October 3, 1864, the clock had just tolled two o'clock in the morning when she was woken by a loud noise and cracking sounds that shook the entire building. The entire palace felt to her like a ship trying to move forward while grapnels were pulling it back. After a few minutes, the motion subsided. Her first thought was that a mine must have exploded beneath the palace, but actually, it had been an earthquake. She had not been afraid for a second.

❀   ❀   ❀

Maximilian's grand tour carried on triumphantly: his people discovered him and came to love him. He had traveled through Dolores Hidalgo, through León, and finally reached the ancient and magnificent town of Morelia. Every day, he listened as his faithful Schertzenlechner repeated that the French only wanted to cast a shadow over his crown, and that Maximilian could get by without them. As for the clergy, Maximilian would have to whip them back into line with vigor, a refrain that the emperor was only too ready to hear.

Finally, the moment of his return, so desired by Charlotte, was at hand. She constantly thought of the happiness she would feel upon seeing him again, imagining the scene when he first came home. She was so impatient that she decided to go meet him. On October 24, 1864, she left Mexico City at six o'clock on a beautiful morning. The sun had begun to burn away the fog gathered at the top of the mountains. Around eight o'clock, at Santa Fe, a hamlet that looked out over Mexico City, she got down from the carriage to go by horseback. Bazaine was waiting for her and proposed accompanying her with all his senior staff. He was riding a magnificent white horse, as Charlotte wrote her father. Almonte rode on her other side. Toward one o'clock, the cortège arrived at Llano de San Lazaro, a beautiful valley crossed by a brook and bordered by fields of flowers and immense, dark-green pine trees. An African tracker was standing on the lookout, stiff as a statue on his horse, way up on high. Charlotte spotted the white tents of an improvised French camp.

Bazaine invited her to have lunch in the middle of his headquarters. She had a good time among his officers, all of whom she found likable, especially "the good marshal, who had been beaming with satisfaction." And "beaming" he had been indeed, for he had just been named marshal of France. After lunch, Charlotte took a siesta in a tent a little bit larger than the others. All was peace and quiet. Around her, the silence was broken only by the sound of sentries being relieved, horses drinking at the brook, and the low murmur of commands given and received.

A little later, they headed off again. The landscapes they crossed reminded Charlotte of Austria: verdant forests and copses interspersed with fields of corn. And the plant life changed every fifteen minutes. The flowers were yellow, pink, and blue, and here and there sprouted red sage. Two leagues away from the town of Lerma, where they planned to spend the night, a crowd of soldiers appeared before her and shouted "*Viva la emperatriz! Viva el mariscal Bazaine!*" Though she tried to act casually, she was deeply touched. Then a storm broke out and rain fell, forcing them to ride to Lerma at a full gallop.

The next morning, after the mass, they left for Toluca. Charlotte was in the coach with Almonte. They had barely arrived at the city when Charlotte was told that Max would reach her in two hours. She rushed back into the coach to go meet him. Bazaine rode ahead of her with his officers, all of them draped in burnooses "like in the times of the desert Bedouins." Along the way, they came across a French officer who warned them that Maximilian was only a league away. At last, Charlotte spotted the troop of soldiers that made up Maximilian's Mexican escort. Bazaine discreetly slowed down to let the empress's coach go on ahead. A few moments later, Max and Charlotte fell into each other's arms, crying with joy as if the crowd were not there. Never had Charlotte felt so entirely happy, and she was thrilled to see that Max shared the same emotion. The long separation had rekindled their love, which exploded into passion the moment they saw each other.

Max tore himself away from Charlotte just long enough to shake Bazaine's hand. Charlotte eyed the Mexican outfit her husband had recently adopted and thought it looked dashing on him:

the wide sombrero, the black jacket, the trousers with silver buttons. Max and Bazaine's chiefs of staff saluted each other, and as Charlotte wrote, "With Max, there is chief of staff Loysel, a good officer, very proper and tactful . . ."

The next day, Maximilian and Charlotte were out horseback riding when suddenly they noticed a few suspicious-looking men. These were guerrillas belonging to one of the gangs that infested the region. The couple did not have the time to be afraid, because a patrol of French soldiers immediately showed up to pursue them, and both groups soon disappeared into the hills.

Were these outlaws just bandits or were they political opponents? Perhaps both at the same time. Since its independence, Mexico had lived in a constant state of endemic insecurity. Kidnappings, pillaging, and armed attacks were all part of everyday life. Once in a while, a political cause sprang up to channel the violence and give it a name. In the process, the bandits became the defenders of an ideal, though without bothering to change their methods. It was difficult, therefore, to tell a highway robber from a freedom fighter, for sometimes the same man was both.

In any case, be they pillagers or republicans, in Maximilian's eyes, the men he saw that day were rebels. It was the first time he had seen any: during his entire trip, they had remained hidden. So they still existed, those "dissidents" whom he had been assured had been wiped out. The "pacification" was not yet complete, whatever Bazaine said. Furious at the discovery, Maximilian decided on the spot that from then on, no guilty verdict passed by a French military tribunal was to be questioned, no appeal would be heard, no pardon given, and the sentence would be carried out immediately. This severity was music to Bazaine's ears, for Maximilian's stubborn indulgence had been irking him for a long time. It also gladdened Charlotte, for she had heard how the guerrillas harassed peasants, pillaging their fields and attacking their flocks and homes, holding them for ransom when they were very poor. Once they were delivered from the criminals, the unfortunate peasants grew even more enthusiastic for their liberator: *"Viva nuestro emperador, viva quien nos dará libertad, viva nuestro padre!"*

Setting out from Toluca, Maximilian and Charlotte headed back to the capital. They reached Carajamalpa by nightfall, where Bazaine had set up camp and was awaiting them with his staff. The tents had been raised on a great lawn from which Charlotte looked around at the beautiful landscape: on the left, a big forest; in front, lakes and mountains; and far off in the distance, Mexico City, bathing in the rays of the setting sun. A large tent topped with the Mexican imperial standard had been prepared for them. The Zouaves climbed up the trees "like cats" to cut down branches for firewood and torches. The military commotion in the lovely natural setting spoke to Charlotte's heart.

Once darkness fell, the soldiers set off fireworks that sounded like bombs to Charlotte. After a calm night of deep sleep, she greeted the rising sun to the sound of the Foreign Legion playing the soothing and plaintive notes of the Austrian national anthem. In front of the imperial tent, the engineers were erecting an altar for morning mass, surrounding it with boughs and branches, and topping it with a leafy cross. At seven o'clock, the chaplain began the service by chanting *"Per Maximilianum imperatorem nostrum,"* and Charlotte's eyes drifted to the soldiers around her, to those tanned faces weathered by the sun of one hundred campaigns fought at the ends of the Earth.

As they rode toward Mexico City, the sun was burning down on them, the sky hazy and white with heat. From Santa Fe on, they met Mexican dignitaries and French officers who had come to meet the sovereigns, but also ladies of Mexican high society who took

shelter from the sun beneath pavilions. The closer they came to
Mexico City, the thicker the crowd became. The welcome was even
more frenzied than it had been at Maximilian and Charlotte's official entrance into Mexico, and when they reached the palace, the
cathedral's huge bell tolled madly.

First, Charlotte handed the house's accounts back over to her husband,
which meant that she gave a report on the events of her "regency."
Despite their numbers, the thieves had been chased from the region around the capital, and many streets had been repaired and
paved. Charlotte had also been able to make peace between the
commander of the square of Mexico and the prelate, who had constantly been at each other's throats. She had put a halt to an irri-
tating story in the newspapers, and she had celebrated Mexican
Independence Day with particular solemnity, in order to "rub the
foreign ministers' noses in it." She had gotten to the bottom of a
hundred minor schemes, she had overcome pervasive inertia in a
hundred minor affairs. She had smoothed ruffled feathers, worked
out arguments, and calmed resentments. Maximilian listened to her,
stroking his blond beard distractedly. His eyes were as gentle as
they were impenetrable. He thanked Charlotte but the congratulations she was expecting never came.

The arrival of Belgian volunteers gave her great joy. Supporting the throne, there were already the Austrian legionnaires Francis-
Joseph had sent to his brother. But this time, King Leopold had
decided to give his daughter a gift, allowing his subjects to freely enlist
to go to Mexico and form a sort of personal guard around the empress. They landed in Veracruz toward the end of November.

Charlotte learned that the French had welcomed the Belgian
volunteers with open arms. At Orizaba, Commander d'Ornano
and the soldiers of the African battalion, nicknamed the Zephyrs,

had come out of the town on horseback to meet them. Naturally, Maximilian and Charlotte went to the gates of Mexico City in greeting.

The former princess of Belgium's emotions upon seeing the Belgians was so great that she feared she would fall out of her carriage. She was so worked up that she could not even cry, and her heart was beating wildly. She felt as if she was receiving family, for as she wrote her father, "Belgium is you." She stared at the men at length, all of them young and handsome, beaming back at her; she noticed the elegance of their uniforms and their white hats. Their commander attracted everyone's attention with his sunburned face and harshly chiseled features. He radiated energy, indomitable courage, and a fiery personality. He would also prove to be a desperado: violent, even cruel, obeying no one, least of all his superiors. His name was Alfred Van der Smissen. In the long description Charlotte gave of this exciting day, there was strangely no mention of him. And yet . . .

In the beginning of December 1864, the pope's special envoy, Nuncio Meglia, arrived in Mexico City to discuss the matter of the clergy's property which had been seized by Juárez.

Charlotte and Maximilian invited him to a gala at the palace. He made a good impression on Charlotte, who judged him to be a decent man. He had just been given a little memorandum that Maximilian happened to have concocted with his ministers. In it, there was not too much mention of material property, but to please the liberals, there was a lot of talk of religious freedom. The nuncio did not much like the memorandum, and he had even raised his eyebrows at a few paragraphs, but he did appreciate their frankness. Charlotte had no doubt that, after a few meetings, he would end up giving in. Although during her visit to the Vatican, Pope

Pius IX had seemed a fairly indulgent man to Charlotte, she was nonetheless alarmed at some of his views as they were expressed by his representative.

It seemed to Charlotte that the head of the Church had no understanding whatsoever of the issue. But did the Holy Father's personal opinion really count in the face of Mexico's reality?

Much to Maximilian's surprise, the nuncio imposed a veritable diktat: there would be an immediate restitution of the clergy's property, and furthermore, there would be no tolerance of other religions. Only Catholicism would be recognized. Such intransigence struck like a bolt from the blue. Charlotte thought the nuncio had gone mad. "There is only one solution," she whispered to Bazaine, who burst out laughing: "We must throw him out the window." Maximilian sent one of his counselors to make him see reason. Monsignor Meglia replied that he had been given no order to negotiate, and that his sole reason for coming to Mexico was to enforce the Holy Father's will.

They had to find a way out of such an impasse. Charlotte was convinced that if there was a chance, she was the one who had to take it. The nuncio seemed open to serious arguments based in fact. He would see reason.

Charlotte received him in her salon in the Mexico City palace. All along the walls hung portraits of her parents, her brothers, and her grandparents. A copper brazier radiated feeble heat, and the windows remained shut against the biting cold of the Mexican winter. The tables were covered with piles of the books Charlotte was voraciously reading, the vases brimming with the Mexican flowers she loved so much. She gave the word and the nuncio was led in, a stocky man with a round face, a stubborn expression, and features frozen in a bitter grimace. She slowly walked him through the logic of her arguments, which she knew few could resist. But Meglia did resist. She felt as if she were speaking to the wall—he did not seem to understand a thing she was saying, and her arguments slid off him like water on marble. She was face-to-face with nothing short of hell: "for what is hell if not an eternal impasse?"

Meglia did not back down from even one of his demands: the clergy's property was to be returned, and there was to be no religious tolerance. This was only fair, for who put Maximilian on the Mexican throne but the clergy? It was the clergy who built the empire. Charlotte blushed upon hearing this argument, which smacked her like an insult. Her black eyes aflame, she rose up from her armchair so quickly that she almost fell over. "Just a minute: it is not the clergy that made the empire, it was the emperor, the day he arrived here." The nuncio walked out and slammed the door behind him. Charlotte was left in utter confusion.

Max, on the other hand, was insane with rage. In him, there was a conflict between the reverence for the Church he felt as a Catholic and as an Austrian, and the eternal mistrust kings had for the ever-meddlesome and conniving Vatican. In short order, Maximilian published a decree confirming Juárez's previous one on the nationalization of the clergy's property. The empire was following in the republic's footsteps. The nuncio and the priests would just have to accept it.

But the clergy was far from beaten. In an explosion of outrage, they attacked. Mortally wounded in what they held most dear— their wealth—they reacted with unheard-of violence, fanaticism, and cunning, dragging all the conservative parties along with them in their screams for Maximilian's blood.

Charlotte wondered where their intrigues would lead. She almost suspected them of reviving the flagging energies of their most dogged adversaries, the very Juárez rebels who had stripped them of their money in the first place. As if to prove that suspicion true, when Bazaine left to take the town of Oaxaca, which was still holding out, but which everyone expected to fall without any trouble, the town defended itself vigorously, thanks to Juárez's lieutenant, the picaresque Porfirio Diaz, who, with his obvious panache, again revealed the makings of a military genius. Taking up position in the immense, baroque convent of Santo Domingo, he transformed it into a fortress and withstood all assaults and bombardments. Priests and conservatives agreed on regarding the bizarre alliance forming between them and the dissidents as a sign from heaven condemning Maximilian.

At last, Charlotte fell victim to discouragement. She held the pope responsible for the recent string of calamities. The pope was well known for possessing the *iettatura* — the evil eye — and she was forced to admit that nothing had gone well for them since the moment his representative had set foot in Mexico.

Iettatura or no *iettatura*, the Mexican empire was in crisis. If it recovered, all would be well, but if it did not, the imperial couple's fate was in the hands of God. Anything could happen. "For the first six months, everyone finds the government charming, but touch anything, try to get down to work, and the world curses you. Chaos will not be dethroned. It was easier to raise the pyramids in Egypt than it will be to defeat the Mexican abyss."

Everything now depended on Bazaine. Between him and the imperial couple, the honeymoon, it would seem, went on. Maximilian truly liked him and Charlotte esteemed him, though not without having examined him closely. In him, she saw noble sentiments, uncommon intelligence, and the mental acumen of a superior man. She admired the way he never said or showed anything more than he wanted to. He had an answer for everything, and he was never caught off guard. Deep down, he was an upstanding man, with a loyal and decent heart strengthened by courage, quickness of insight, and the ability to surprise.

The only problem was that the fifty-year-old marshal was in love like a teenager. The ravishing Pepita de la Pena, in whose ear he had been whispering sweet nothings at the empress's ball, had so captivated his heart that he could not stop thinking about her, so much so that he confided in Charlotte that he loved her and wanted to marry her, though he begged the empress to keep it secret. She promised, only to rush immediately to announce the mismatched engagement to her great friend, Empress Eugenie. Such a pairing would have simply seemed silly if it had not been distracting the commander in chief of the French forces from his duties. You could not be in love with a girl and crush a rebellion at the same time. Naturally, Juárez's men took advantage of the situation to attack Toluca, the very town where, a few weeks before, Charlotte had joined Maximilian. The blow was so hard that Charlotte feared the rebels would soon be marching right up to the gates of the capital.

She quickly summoned Bazaine and nervously asked him what measures he was going to take. "It is blown all out of proportion," the marshal answered her with a big smile. From then on, Charlotte's tone slowly began to change. She continued to praise the marshal, but complained of his "indulgence" to Empress Eugenie. She did not dare write "negligence," but thought it all the same. As her insecurity grew, she blamed Bazaine. Were they rebels or bandits, these men who kidnapped people and held them for ransom, who robbed and killed with such frequency that you could not even leave the capital without a gun?

In this deep and widespread tension, what they needed was a scapegoat.

Just as it should be, Maximilian and Charlotte's entourages hated each other. Max's childhood friend, Bombelles, had an alliance with Kuhacsevich, the treasurer, also an Austrian, against the Belgian, Eloin. The Frenchman Loysel, lent by Bazaine, also had Maximilian's ear. He had been carefully keeping to the shadows, observing the others, pulling their strings. But everyone could come together in their common hatred of the most powerful and odious among them, the ex-butler Schertzenlechner, whom they nicknamed "the big Muh," "the big cow." He was unpleasant and vulgar even with the emperor, but still Maximilian ran after him for advice. Unbearable even in his better moments, Schertzenlechner was even worse when he was feeling ill. Since he kept all the responsibilities for himself, when he took sick days, there was such confusion that in the end, the others were glad to see him come back to work. Madame Kuhacsevich had even been caught sighing, "The big Muh is sick again, he's in a bad mood, and he's being vulgar. The chaos is as widespread as always. What a circus!"

The relationship between the proud Habsburg and the ex-servant was very curious. Perhaps Maximilian felt at ease only with his social inferiors. But how can it be explained that he let an ignorant brute gain such control over him? It was Schertzenlechner who had pushed Max to stand up to the nuncio with such disastrous stubbornness, and Eloin could not forgive him for that—so he decided that it was time to do away with the big Muh.

Rummaging through the records, Eloin discovered that Schertzenlechner was still secretly getting his butler's salary from the Austrian court, a job incompatible with his lofty position as the powerful adviser to His Imperial Majesty of Mexico. Eloin sneakily slipped the information to Maximilian, who naturally took offense. Full of himself after what he considered to be his great victory over the nuncio, Schertzenlechner counterattacked. He won the Mexican members of the court over to his side, and together they besieged Maximilian, whispering horrors about Eloin in his ear from morning till night. But Maximilian was not so easily taken in. "Don't lie!" he yelled at his favorite.

Hearing of what was going on, Eloin ran to Maximilian's office, where he found Schertzenlechner. The two enemies had their showdown. The arrogant and stupid Austrian looked down on Eloin and treated him the only way he knew how—with the utmost vulgarity. But the tall, fat, bald Belgian, with his beautiful moustache, had come to the end of his patience and now exploded. Even though Maximilian was there with them, the two men traded increasingly violent accusations, then insults, and finally almost came to blows. Schertzenlechner had never had any self-control, and for once, Eloin was furious. It began to look as if the two men would kill each other in the emperor's very office. Loysel was there, but receded into the background; he kept score with glee, for he knew that whoever the winner would be, he would emerge weakened, while Loysel, and through him France, would have a better position than ever.

The ruckus continued, and not even Maximilian was able to stop it.

It was then that the big Muh committed the stupidity common to the mediocre the world over: he blurted out his resignation to the emperor, sure that he would beg him to reconsider. In his fury, he ripped off his Mexican medal, threw it on the floor, and left so violently that the door and windows rattled.

Maximilian accepted Schertzenlechner's resignation without a moment's hesitation. Joy spread through the court, and Madame Kuhacsevich in her happiness noted, "Bombelles is resurrected from the dead."

To calm the big Muh, Maximilian offered him a title and a pension, and the opportunity to live in one of his castles once he returned to Europe. He even invited him to Chapultepec. Schertzenlechner refused these honors with disdain and announced that thousands of Mexicans angered by his disgrace were on their way to Mexico City to demand that the emperor reinstate him. This ridiculous statement obviously had no basis in fact, as was soon discovered, but Maximilian nonetheless took the precaution of having the big Muh's papers gone through. At the same time, he persisted in wanting to make peace with him. Schertzenlechner knew too much for Maximilian to let him become an enemy. Meanwhile, Schertzenlechner was shouting to anyone who would listen that he had enough power and information to force the emperor to bow down before him. So Maximilian continued to offer him titles, pensions, castles, trips, and even the permission to show Miramar to the certain redhead of dubious background whom he paraded about at his side. Schertzenlechner refused it all: *"Naδa! Naδa!"* he shouted. Maximilian even stooped low enough to write a letter brimming with friendship and reconciliation. The big Muh did not even deign to respond, and amid the relief of the entire court, he left for Europe.

This striking episode only thickened the mystery surrounding Maximilian's true nature and certain aspects of his existence. Strangely, finally rid of his favorite, he did not show the slightest regret. For her part, Charlotte preferred to pretend that the unreal fight and the resounding disgrace had never taken place. She had just received a letter from her father that was like a balm for her soul, for in it, he expressed his feelings as he had never before: "My dear treasure, my beloved child, the image of you is always in my mind, and I am confident that my dear, beautiful children will be rewarded for their courage with the most glorious success." Once again, he praised Maximilian, but especially Charlotte, for leaving everything—their families, their homes, Europe—behind, to undertake such a formidable task. They would succeed because they had courage and determination. Over in Brussels, the king missed Charlotte more every day, and would even be willing to make the long trip to Mexico if only he had not felt so old and weak—he went on about the various ailments overwhelming him. If only he had his Charlotte by his side! The rest of the family disappointed him. His heir, the duke of Brabant, was, as always, on the other side of the world, on pleasure cruises. God only knew where he got his strange character from. At least his second son, Philippe, showed some goodness, the goodness so lacking in his elder brother, but in his father's opinion, he was not the most brilliant person in the world. As for his daughter-in-law, young Leopold's wife Marie, he had no choice but to admit that she was useless. The old king felt more and more lonely, and bewailed his dear Charlotte.

Forgetting the nuncio, the rebellion, and the unrest, Charlotte calmly returned to her activities and obligations, down to the smallest details. She named a new chamberlain, she awarded medals of her Order of San Carlos right and left, she had her diamond-studded monogram sent from Paris and distributed it among her ladies-in-waiting. On Sundays, like any couple, she and Maximilian went strolling among the people along a canal. The Indians, wearing poppy wreaths and dancing the *jarabé* with joy, recognized them and called out to them in a frenzy.

But worries finally caught up with Charlotte. The Belgian volunteers had been promised that they would be allowed to guard the door of their former princess, now empress of Mexico. But their commander, Van der Smissen, had other ideas in mind. No one, least of all the emperor, had any love for that violent and undisciplined man who criticized everything. In Van der Smissen's opinion, the Mexican army was nothing more than a group of a few thousand bandits, mule-drivers, and butcher-boys made colonels. The soldiers had all been recruited by force, and marched to the base between two rows of bayonets. As soon as they came across a sugarcane field where they could hide, they deserted. It was not with soldiers of their kind that Maximilian would stay on the throne. He would reign only as long as the country remained occupied by the French . . . and Belgians. Van der Smissen and his men had not come all the way from Belgium just to be ceremonial guards, but to fight.

Bazaine decided to take him at his word. The Belgians wanted to fight? Fine, let them fight! He sent them to the province of

Michoacán, east of Mexico City, under the command of a French-
man. Choking with rage, Van der Smissen had no choice but to
accept. The French colonel sent Van der Smissen to Morelia.
Meanwhile, he dispatched two hundred Belgians in another direction, to organize the defense of the small town of Tacambaro,
under the command of a brave man from Gent. Once they arrived,
the first thing they did was tear out the wooden crosses from the
graves of the town cemetery and make a big fire. Then they set
up a little café in the middle of all of it. Coming down from the
heights surrounding the city, the rebels attacked, weapons in
hand. Taken by surprise, the Belgians were shot at from close
range, and what few survivors there were took refuge in a church
whose roof soon went up in flames. Trapped, they surrendered.
The results: two officers and twenty-seven soldiers dead; the rest,
more than two hundred men, taken prisoner by the rebels! Van
der Smissen had come as soon as he was informed, but it had been
too late. He poured out his rage so violently on the poor, mortally
wounded commander from Gent that it finished him off.

"This horrendous catastrophe" left Charlotte distraught. Me-
thodic and conscientious, she had had high-ranking officers give
her lessons in the art of war, and she was perfectly capable of analyzing the defeat at Tacambaro. Her countrymen, the volunteers,
possessed all the right qualities; the only problem was that they were
too young and inexperienced. One doesn't learn war from books,
but in action, and the men had never before fought for real. Charlotte had told the French over and over: do not send the Belgians
to fight alone, surround them, give them orders, teach them. The
French had not listened to her, and this was the result. Van der
Smissen was furious—and anyone he came across who smelled even
the slightest bit like a rebel paid the price dearly. There was even
talk of the atrocities he had committed. A few months later, he won

a resounding victory over one of Juárez's most brilliant generals at La Loma. Charlotte was thrilled and at last seemed to realize that Van der Smissen existed.

A victory could counterbalance a defeat. But the Mexican empire's finances, even after all of Charlotte's efforts during her "regency," were still sinking into a bottomless pit. The first loan had evaporated into thin air before it could be used. Maximilian had thought to organize Mexican finances with the little money that remained, but Mexican inertia had paralyzed him.

He had turned to Corta, the French civil servant sent by Napoleon III who had worked so well with Charlotte. After a few weeks spent poring over the files, Corta had thrown up his arms in surrender and hurried back to France. There had been no choice but to take on another loan.

Corta had kindly agreed to take up Maximilian's cause, and he urged the parliament to convince a French investor to underwrite the loan. He succeeded. The French investor believed in Mexico and pulled another two hundred fifty million francs out of his mattress. Much of it dissolved immediately as unpaid interest deducted automatically, or as commissions. Maximilian protested against Bazaine's ballooning budget. "He is the biggest spender in the army," Corta sighed, and again lifted his arms to the sky. Maximilian now had only seventy million at his disposal of the two hundred fifty million he had signed for . . . plus he owed five hundred million to France. He complained to Napoleon, who in turn complained to him. How was it possible that the emperor of Mexico had not yet straightened out his finances? Why were customs fees, Mexico's greatest resource, not bringing in any revenue? Poor Maximilian had no answer.

Now Maximilian called upon his new favorite, the Frenchman Loysel, and began to work with him. To breathe new life into the finances, they needed to get them in order, and to get them in order, they created an impressive number of civil servants, the cost of whom only weighed the budget down further. They issued order after order, whole volumes of instructions that no one would ever follow. Convinced that he had gotten the problem under control, Maximilian set out again to tour his country, fully confident in his method of making appearances in order to rally the people to him.

First he returned to Orizaba, where he had stopped when he had first come to Mexico, whose beauty he had not forgotten. He chose to stay just outside the town, in the Jalapilla hacienda. There he banished protocol and uniforms, courtiers and duties. He dressed only in civilian clothes. He went to bed late, woke up early. He took long walks through the tropical forest, scaled the wooded cliffs of extinct volcanoes, and descended into deep valleys where crystal water flowed beneath greenery in bloom. Indeed, this triumphant tour looked suspiciously like nothing less than a vacation.

Happy to unload his troubles on Charlotte, Maximilian had left her to her regency again. Though it had not been long since she had been cut out completely, she suddenly had all duties thrust upon her. She went about the business conscientiously, especially the duties of her station. At the Mexico City palace, she gave dinners which some found lacking, despite the systematic lavishness of the courses. For lack of new arrivals, the guests were almost always the same. Charlotte nonetheless insisted on the banquets as a way to show off life at the court. As much as Maximilian preferred simplicity, Charlotte surrounded herself in pomp, not so much by taste as by the conviction that that is what monarchs should do, especially in Mexico, where they had to impress the natives. Charlotte would only appear in the center of a swarm of ladies-in-waiting, aides, and chamberlains.

At the same time, she was leading a very regular and studious life. She spent more and more time at Chapultepec, whose park allowed her to indulge in her favorite sport, horseback riding. From there, she traveled every day to the Mexico City palace in a coach pulled by six mules with silver bells, surrounded by a squadron of cavalry. Then she presided over the ministers' council and granted audiences to civil servants. She stayed up late at night to analyze files thoroughly in order to arrive at each meeting completely informed, stunning those presenting reports with her seriousness and the breadth of her knowledge. Maximilian, however, had been allowing his ministers to express their opinions, and especially, in accordance with local custom, to put off till tomorrow whatever work might have been done today. Charlotte took advantage of the fact that her ministers, as good Mexicans, had not read a word of the files to be discussed, and used it to force their hand and push them into making whatever decision she wanted. We are in agreement then, dear ministers? They nodded their heads and sent the decree off to the *Official Journal.* Neither time nor fatigue had any effect on Charlotte; she could stay at the council's table for hours, going over every item of business, every issue at hand. She loved work, and especially work well done. For her, work meant governing, a task she had been born for. She had the mind and the character of a man—and more precisely, of a man of state.

But still she was a woman, and she never forgot compassion for a minute. Her acts of charity were nothing like those of the usual ladies from benevolent societies. She thought things through, spreading good deeds to large swathes of the population. Charlotte had taken to heart the plight of Mexico's poorest; she had studied their problems, and proposed solutions that stunned the Mexicans so inured to the spectacle of abject poverty. She described her work modestly: "As the last time, my mission is to quietly insure nothing goes wrong or awry while the master of the house is away." Yet the task was so great that at times she felt extremely lonely. Maximilian had taken the faithful Eloin with him, along with other court favorites and counselors. He had left Charlotte with but a single assistant: "All I have here is the chief of the military cabinet, a Frenchman, Monsieur Loysel, the chief of the headquarters' squadron, in whom we have placed our confidence . . ."

8

Charlotte dearly needed Loysel's help to face the crisis that then occurred. On April 9, 1865, General Robert E. Lee, commander in chief of the Confederate forces, surrendered to General Ulysses S. Grant, commander in chief of the Union forces. It was the end of the Civil War. The North had won—the same North so fiercely opposed to the Mexican empire, which had itself made pacts with the South. Charlotte immediately wondered whether Washington would try to exact revenge. *We can't very well raise a wall between Mexico and the United States by severing bridges, roads, railway tracks, and telegraph lines,* she sadly admitted to herself.

She summoned the ministers' council together to present her views: "We are on this ever-changing continent where the colossus is stirring, the colossus that strips virgin forests, takes in the world's outcasts, and shelters all forms of human thought under the vast cloak of its liberties. The colossus is at our gates. It is just now emerging victorious from a war of giants. It is not considering physical annexation, but rather moral conquest. . . ." A moral conquest perhaps, but, if worst came to worst, one which some day might still have meant war. Luckily, the victorious Abraham Lincoln publicly declared, "I do not know what the nation wants: all I know is that there will be no more war while I am president." Charlotte was a little reassured, all the more so once she discovered that the Confederacy's defeat was not all bad for Mexico. Entire families — even whole villages — were crossing the border into Mexico with their covered wagons and cattle, harassed by Indians and defended by cowboys, in a cloud of dust and a cacophony of men's shouts and bulls' lowing.

Charlotte perceived this as a gain for her empire. Instead of chasing them back, let's let those hardworking American farmers come. Let us give them the land that Juárez confiscated from the Church. They will settle in, clear the inhospitable terrain, and develop whole provinces, sweeping the natives along with them to form a barrage of stability.

Suddenly the bombshell hit: President Lincoln had been assassinated. Secretary of State Seward, the inexorable foe of the Mexican empire, had also been the victim of an assassination attempt. "Like all of us, you must have been shocked by Lincoln and Seward's deaths," Maximilian wrote Charlotte. "This event might be better for us, but it is a tragedy all the same." As dictated by the American constitution, Vice President Andrew Johnson automatically succeeded Lincoln.

Charlotte had no idea what this newcomer's ideas might be, or what his intentions were for Mexico. She immediately wrote a draft of a letter of condolence, brimming with the warmest sentiments for the victim as well as for his replacement. She sent the letter to Maximilian so he could sign it, then dispatched a special envoy, Mariano Degollado, to bring it to Washington.

Charlotte did not need to wait long for the results of her action. Degollado brought the letter back from Washington unopened. President Johnson had refused to see him, or even to accept the letter. The United States would only recognize a Republic of Mexico.

But that was a republic in dire straits. Bazaine finally took Oaxaca, and at the moment, Porfirio Diaz seemed to have disappeared. The last provinces still loyal to the republic had at last rallied to the empire, and the republicans had all the reason in the world to call 1865 *"el año terrible."* Then Juárez, in his despair, decided to send his trusty Romero to Washington.

Despite his serious injuries, Seward was not dead, as Maximilian and Charlotte had hoped. Once he had recovered, he rushed to receive Juárez's envoy.

Romero asked him to send the American army to chase out Maximilian and reestablish the republic. The secretary of state was indignant: we will give you moral support, but military assistance, never! The United States is not imperialistic, he said. But inwardly, Seward dreamed of transforming Mexico into a protectorate "in all but name." An out-and-out invasion would have brought the fury of Europe down upon him, so instead Seward tried to place nicely docile Mexicans in power. Only he was not at all sure that Juárez was the ideal candidate.

Meanwhile, Charlotte had taken the American president's refusal of her letter very badly. "The United States will not go to war with us," she told her ministers over and over. "There is no need to panic." But, despite everything, what if they did attack? Then France and England, the empire's two guarantors, would rush to Mexico's aid, or at least, there was a hope that they would. To be sure one way or the other, there was no better solution than to send a man of confidence off to Paris and London. Consulted from afar by Charlotte, Maximilian chose Eloin to be the envoy, perhaps as a pretext to be rid of him. Since Schertzenlechner's elimination, Loysel's goal had been to drive a wedge between the imperial couple and the Belgian, so that he might occupy the place alone.

Charlotte felt no remorse at having somewhat sacrificed Eloin to Loysel. It was good politics, she told herself, for to put a French-man in such a position of trust could only flatter Napoleon III, who could then only become more generous to Mexico. Loysel, the forty-year-old from Brittany, was not handsome. Tall, thin, with an an-gular face and a poorly shaped goatee, he had melancholy eyes that were sometimes lit from within. Under the slightly boring exterior of an overly conscientious officer, there must have been a certain romanticism and even some sort of hidden charm there for Char-lotte to have talked about him at such lengths with her father: "The Bretons are a truly special race. Loysel is not like any other French-man. He is very calm, very serious and hard-working, and very capable in every field, with infinite insight; I think he is entirely devoted to us. He proves it because he had himself discharged in order to serve us. Yet he certainly would have had a quick rise through the ranks in the French army, for he is one of the best of-ficers at the headquarters. He also understands a great number of civilian affairs, and I am happy to hear his opinion on anything." For anyone accustomed to Charlotte's usual reserve, such high praise from her was quite exceptional. During the long weeks of Maximilian's absence, Charlotte and Loysel had seen each other almost every day, and she had come to depend on him, perhaps more than she would have liked to admit. Indeed, he was the only per-son she confided in.

Finally, it was time for Maximilian's return. But he was mov-ing at a leisurely pace, leaving Charlotte the chance to continue taking advantage of Loysel's company. The emperor took thirty-six days, from May 19 to June 24, to cover the distance from Orizaba to Mexico City. This slow voyage, like the others, was punctuated by applause from the crowds running to see their emperor; by expeditions into the jungle and to the mountaintops dear to this natural-born tourist; and by the illnesses caused by his weak constitution. He shivered, he had to cover himself with several blankets, he had contracted dysentery. He wrote to Charlotte to summon her to him at Puebla: if she would come to meet him, he explained, it would make a good impression.

The day before she left, Charlotte held a last meeting with Loysel and Bonnefond, yet another French civil servant sent to deal with Mexico's finances. Four years later, Charlotte herself would remind Loysel of the scene: "When we parted on June 5, 1865, when I was setting out for Puebla, and we had been seeing each other most respectably for a month to deal with politics, you, who were about to turn forty years old, who had seen the enemy, gunpowder, and battles, you were crying and I was too. And we felt something indescribable in our souls, something bigger than the tears. Luckily Mr. Bonnefond had had his columns of numbers and figures drawn up almost illegibly, and that was a distraction. Commander Loysel smoothed out financial difficulties with his hard work, and the empress of Mexico let him do it. You went off with your obscure plans, and I left for Puebla." Everything was said in this simple paragraph.

In this woman so proud of her rank, so indefatigable in work, and so masculine in character, there was little space left for romanticism, and even less for an affair. Nor could the idea ever have come to the mind of the shy and efficient officer, so bereft of imagination, to lunge into the empress's arms. But if not love, at least strong feelings did undeniably exist between them, feelings that developed during their long daily meetings. A few glances, gestures abruptly halted in midair, were enough to make those feelings known.

❊   ❊   ❊

The next day, escorted by Bombelles, Charlotte set out for Puebla. The trip progressed normally: in each town, she found arches of triumph, long speeches, and frenzied masses that unhitched her horses in order to drag her carriage through the crowded streets. She smiled, she answered their cheers, and she thought of Loysel, so much so that she gathered the courage to ask Bombelles the question that had been on the tip of her tongue. She chose her moment strangely, just as the procession was crossing a raging river. The sun was shining, nature was at its most lush, Charlotte's horse was wading among the armed guards. Amid the thunder of the rushing water, there was the clatter of sabers. As was his duty, Bombelles was riding beside her.

"Tell me, Bombelles, do you think the emperor will have Loysel come to Puebla, just as he has summoned me?"

"Under no circumstances, Madam."

She had expected that answer, she admitted later, and yet the thought of not seeing her friend at Puebla saddened her for the rest of the day.

On the sixth of June, Maximilian arrived at Puebla at dawn. He immediately went to inspect the accommodations reserved for him and the empress. Blasio, his new Mexican butler, went with him. The emperor entered their room to find the huge double bed draped with lace curtains, as beautiful as they were seductive. Maximilian said he was satisfied and Blasio was very happy to have been able to guess his new master's wishes. But the emperor had barely stepped out of the room when his foot servants came back to break Blasio's heart: by imperial command, there were to be several modifications made to the living arrangements. The emperor was to be set up in another bedroom, the room farthest away from this one, and it was to be furnished with the single iron bed he traveled with, and that would be where he spent his nights. Surprised and saddened, Blasio could not understand. But the fact was right in front of him and he was forced to accept it: the emperor and empress slept separately, and perhaps they had been doing so for a while, for Blasio could not imagine that Maximilian would have chosen this particular moment to make such a fundamental change. "What marital drama was hidden behind this decision?" he wondered. How was it possible that the married couple—so young and beautiful, united by love as everyone knew, in the full heat of youth—could have no life as man and wife? How could the husband be almost irritated by the thought of having to spend the night in the same bed as his lovely wife?

A little before noon, Maximilian left Puebla in a luxurious four-horse coach. His officials and aides followed him. At the scheduled time, a traveling coach appeared bearing Charlotte, her matron of honor, and Bombelles. The palace guard that Bombelles commanded escorted them. The domestic help followed in other coaches.

The emperor stepped down from his coach, joined his wife, and, standing in Charlotte's open carriage, husband and wife embraced surrounded by Mexicans who cheered for the love that bound their two sovereigns. Carried forth amid universal enthusiasm under the arches of triumph, they made their entrance into Puebla through a rain of flowers. Some of the bouquets were so large that Charlotte almost yelped when they landed on her lap.

When she entered the double bedroom alone, she was not surprised. She had become used to it by then.

On the next day, June 7, 1865, Charlotte was woken up at dawn by cannon salvos. It was her birthday, and the celebrations went on all day. After the cannon shots came the bells of the old city's countless churches, as well as that Mexican specialty, the *cohetes*—firecrackers that flew off in all directions. The entire town was joyful. But the *festejada*, Charlotte, the birthday girl, felt sad, and she could not admit to herself that she missed Loysel. She smiled again only when Maximilian, without a clue as to the reasons for his wife's mood, began to speak to her affectionately of Loysel, praising his merits.

Soon they set off again for Mexico City. Maximilian and Charlotte traveled in two separate coaches. His curiosity now aroused, Blasio noticed that again the couple slept apart when they stopped at Zoquiapan. Blasio watched Charlotte go into the bedroom alone, and his greatest surprise came from the fact that Charlotte was not surprised at all.

Returning to his office in the unbearable heat of that summer of 1865 brought a frown to Maximilian's lips and darkened even more the pessimistic analysis of the situation that he gave his ministers. Guanajuato and Guadalajara were at risk; Morelia was under siege by the rebels; Acapulco had already been lost; San Luis Potosí was in danger. In short, the situation was ten times worse than it had been the previous year. Precious time had been lost, the country's treasury was gone, public confidence had been shaken, and why? Because reports sent back to Paris said that the "pacification" had been carried out gloriously.

By "reports sent back to Paris," Maximilian obviously meant Bazaine's. Acting on Bazaine's false information, the French government had recalled part of its troops, though still requiring the empire to pay the upkeep of the full force. Two major problems remained: the lack of manpower, and the insane amounts of money that were being swallowed up by this slow and shameful war. "If there is even the hint of a scandal, I, Maximilian, hold Bazaine responsible."

At the same time, Charlotte wrote Philippe: "Here everything is going ahead with giant steps." When they returned to Mexico City, she and Maximilian had been greeted with so much fervor that she was moved to tears. Maximilian governed with the greatest talent, and she herself did not do a bad job when affairs were given over to her. The empire was coming together a little more each day, thanks also to the good troops that soon cleared up the military problem. "Nothing stands in the way of Mexico anymore, or of the successful completion of the work we are undertaking."

The difference between these two assessments of the same situation was surprising. On one hand, the defeats Maximilian enumerated were all too real, but on the other, Charlotte's optimism was based on solid facts, since the empire's consolidation grew surer every day. The Mexicans were torn between two polarities, especially when the alarmism of the republicans' and Juárez's followers was thrown into the mix. It was a further characteristic of the forever ungraspable Mexican reality, rooted in an immense and unfathomable people who were at once exuberant and silent, violent and meek. Their leaders, even the ones who were born among them, found them incomprehensible. Mexican reality was a hodgepodge of diversity, made up of contradictory elements bound together in a way no one could understand. It escaped any unity, any unanimity, and it was propelled forward by the most starkly opposed opinions, which never faded away, but only swelled in number as new contradictions were accumulated.

One girl shared Charlotte's optimism: Pepita de la Pena, Bazaine's fiancée, who witnessed Maximilian and Charlotte's return to Mexico City with her own eyes. How could anyone say the empire was unpopular, when she herself saw the spectacle? All classes were joined together, from the nobility all the way to the Indians—all rushed toward the imperial couple just to catch a glimpse. Pretty Pepita idolized Charlotte, especially since Charlotte had scheduled her marriage for June, just a few weeks away. And on a Monday, the empress had added, for that was the day she herself had gotten married. She hoped those joyful auspices would guarantee the fiancés' happiness.

Bazaine and Pepita were married in the Mexico City Imperial Palace. The court's protocol office published a program several pages long. The best man and matron of honor were, of course, the emperor and empress. The civil ceremony took place in the council hall, and then the archbishop conducted the religious ceremony in the imperial chapel. The entire court was in attendance, together with the municipal authorities and officers from the French military headquarters. For the luncheon, a special hall had been built. The table was set with new, ornate dishware ordered just for the occasion from Europe. Then the marshal, in his mid-fifties, and the seventeen-year-old Mexican girl, set off on their honeymoon . . . to the Mexico City army base, where they would reside, and which the commander in chief of French forces could not leave. The sovereigns' shows of kindness filled them with gratitude. Despite recent politics, a deep and heartfelt closeness and affection reigned between the two couples.

Barely ten days later, on the sixth of July, it was Maximilian's birthday. Even though the procession did not have far to go between the Imperial Palace and the cathedral, the Mexicans, always eager for spectacles, were overwhelmed by what they witnessed. The palace's heavy doors opened, and the parade of French and Mexican troops set out; next came the mounted officers in their striped and embroidered dress uniforms; then the chamberlains in waistcoats sparkling with gold; then the court coaches with ladies-in-waiting dripping with jewels; and finally, surrounded by guards and pages, the imperial coach, an enormous carriage laden with sculptures and gold, all of it overhung by a large imperial crown brought just for the occasion from Vienna. Majestic on the cushions, Charlotte smiled with solemn restraint.

But Charlotte was alone. Maximilian had remained at Chapultepec—such huge productions always bored him. The carriage rode around the plaza, then came to a halt before the cathedral. The butlers lowered the step, and as Charlotte stepped down, Bazaine offered his hand, and together they slowly crossed the esplanade. She was wearing a white gown embroidered with gold, a long scarlet cloak that also glinted with gold, about her neck were diamonds and pearls, and upon her head, her diamond-encrusted diadem. The *Te Deum* went on interminably, but Charlotte continued to stand completely straight, impassable, impenetrable, the very image of sovereignty. Once the ceremony was complete, she appeared at the doors of the cathedral, and was greeted with long joyful cheers from the crowd. Then, after unending ovations, she returned to the palace where speeches, receptions, and a banquet awaited her.

The reporters were in rapture—at last they had something to write about. That day they filled several columns in their newspapers, the same newspapers that several weeks would later end up on Queen Marie-Amelie's table at Claremont, in the bedroom Charlotte knew so well. The grandmother and granddaughter had been keeping up a regular correspondence, but ever since Charlotte had assumed such various and time-consuming responsibilities, her letters had been growing less frequent. Marie-Amelie thus followed recent events in newspapers, where she hunted out any information concerning her granddaughter.

This time, as she carefully read the description of the July 6 ceremony, she was not at all pleased, and she sent Charlotte a letter filled with affectionate reproaches. First of all, what had she been thinking to appear at a *Te Deum* without her husband? Remember, Charlotte, she said, you are not the sovereign, you are only the wife of the sovereign. It is unheard of for the wife of a sovereign to appear with such a display of opulence. And what of the big red and gold cloak and the jewels—was that not just a bit ostentatious? Would not a little understatement have been preferable? And if Maximilian was indisposed, would it not have been better not to have made an appearance at all? Vanity is a terrible vice, and all the more dangerous in a sovereign, Charlotte should remember.

When, several weeks later, Charlotte received this gentle reprimand, she hurried to her desk in vexation, and with her slanted, regular penmanship, wrote a response several pages long to her grandmother. She had gone beforehand to show Marie-Amelie's letter to Max, and it was thus armed with her husband's authority that she explained that the only reason she appeared alone at the July 6 ceremony was because her husband had expressly ordered her to, and because there was no one else able to represent him. As for the offending cloak, it was the same one she had received in her bridal trousseau. The reporters stupidly described it each time as if it were a stunning novelty, when actually she had never stopped wearing it to every function. Grandmother spoke of vanity—what vanity? When Charlotte was young, it is true that she loved the cheers of the crowd, but really, she had grown a little since then. She had gotten old . . . twenty-five years old, in fact! Of all the pomp that surrounded her, Max had been the one who had wanted it—Max who had arranged everything down to the smallest detail. She had only acquiesced to it after fighting tooth and nail against it.

Slowly but surely, Charlotte began to confide in her grandmother, a rare thing for her. She was fully aware, having read the newspapers herself, of the unfair reproaches leveled at her. They claimed that she was the one who decided everything, and that she influenced Max. But how could that be possible when Max was so superior to her? How could she inspire him with any idea when he knew so much more than she did, when he was so much wiser than she? Let her grandmother make no mistake! Max did not tell everything to Charlotte, and when he refused to speak about a state secret, she was much too discreet to ask him. If she did carry on a regency, it was only because Max had told her to. She was happy to make his work easier and to spare him wasted time whenever he came back from his tours. She helped Max only within the limits that both her abilities and Max had set for her. And was that not the role of a wife, especially when she was not yet a mother and thus had all her time to devote to her husband? A virago, that was the word going about: some sort of woman of great strength and stature—perhaps overbearingly so—that the Italian newspapers, for one, described when they spoke of Charlotte. But let Grandmother rest assured, her little Charlotte had not changed one bit. She was more detached than ever from vanity, egotism, and ambition. As for ambitions, she had only one: to do some good. For the rest, *vanitas vanitatis et omnia vanitas*, she repeated to herself every day.

Did she realize that if she depicted herself as a woman entirely subservient to her husband, it was only because she was superior to him in intelligence and character? The more aware Charlotte became of it, the more she groveled at his feet, ready to indulge his slightest whims.

For the moment, Maximilian was consumed by the bitterness he felt toward Bazaine, about whom his feelings had shifted in the space of a few weeks from the most demonstrative affection to the deepest mistrust. Like a bottomless abyss, Bazaine continued to swallow huge amounts of cash, but still the bandits kept multiplying like rabbits. In her writings, Charlotte analyzed the problem as she saw it: take

an average Mexican. He was ready for anything but work. Since he
was also brave and bold, one day he picked up his gun and headed
off into the countryside, not caring whether he would be caught and
executed, for he was a fatalist who was so bored with his former life
that he could only dream of adventure, excitement, and gold. In the
country, he found five or six other men with the same ideas. They
started out by attacking a hacienda and stealing the cattle. "That is
the baptism into the career." Immediately, the local population began speaking of guerrillas. The newspapers picked up the news and
reported that a dangerous gang was lurking in the vicinity. Puffed
up with their newfound importance, the bandits attacked stagecoaches and kidnapped a few of the rich. With the police on their
tail, they hid out in the sierras, and took back roads to a region as yet
untouched by their crimes. There, they met another gang and joined
up with them, and maybe then with a third gang. They had set out
as six men, and soon could easily find themselves numbering two to
three thousand. Now they were ready to set up a headquarters.

The danger was that they were clever and knew how to count,
particularly when it came to the number of French troops sent to
hunt them down. What could one miserable garrison do against
thousands of little sneaks? When the French soldiers left a town
through one gate, the bandits came in through the other, unless they
decided to ambush them. On the other hand, if the French were
there in number, the gang ran away on the spot, refusing a fight.
You should not treat them with indifference: and by this "you,"
Charlotte and Maximilian meant Bazaine.

Every day, the emperor whispered his complaints about the
marshal in Loysel's ear, even though Bazaine himself had assigned
Loysel to the emperor. In the crowd of aides, Maximilian tried
everyone, but there was no one to help him.

They were all the same, lazy and incompetent—Bonnefond,
Eloin, and all the others. Only dear Loysel stood out. But even

Loysel, despite his good wishes, could take no action against his superior, the commander in chief of the French forces. So Maximilian exploded in a rage against the French — not the good French, who had served Mexico so well and generously, but the bad French who shamed Napoleon III and France itself: the bureaucrats who were sucking the lifeblood out of Mexico, the generals who spoke of victories while suffering defeat after defeat, who threw their brave soldiers' lives away, who allowed Juárez to escape and laugh at them, and who, by their abject uselessness, worsened the situation instead of improving it. These generals took no account of their promises and hoodwinked both emperors, Mexican and French. And their leader, more to blame than anyone else, was the worst of all: Marshal Bazaine.

This mistrust had been building for some time, though constantly checked and hidden, either out of the necessity to make a good impression on Bazaine, or by Bazaine's charm and skill of persuasion. But the situation had become so troubling that cracks were appearing in the fragile façade. Action was needed urgently and still the commander in chief of French forces did nothing. So what did Maximilian decide to do? He left on another tour.

August was hot in Mexico City. The emperor decided to go canoeing on the lake of Texcoco, just outside the city gates. He traveled from there to Teotihuacán, and despite the heat, climbed up the famous Sun and Moon Pyramids, the most impressive monuments in Mexico. Then he proceeded north to visit the silver mines. Finally, giving up all pretext of making a propaganda tour, he took ten days of pure vacation and did what he loved best: sightseeing.

As he had done in the past, Maximilian left the regency to Charlotte, with one crucial difference: he wrote down long instructions which limited his wife's powers. The civilian and military cabinets' reports would still go to Charlotte, but only Maximilian would have the right to sign anything. The documents would be sent to him on a daily basis for his written approval. Moreover, he reserved for himself all matters dealing with legislation, nominations, promotions, important diplomatic correspondence, extra-budgetary expenditures, troop changes, and judicial affairs. The empress could preside in his name over the council of ministers, she could give public audiences and open correspondence coming from Europe, but letters addressed to Maximilian marked "private" or "personal" were to be forwarded, unopened, directly to him wherever he might be. In other words, she would only inhabit the shadow of power, limited to the role of representative.

Despite such a humiliation, Charlotte gave no reaction. Her self-control enabled her to hide her feelings, as always. She even seemed to redouble her initiatives.

For example, she used her time in the spotlight to pose the Indian question to the table of the council of ministers. Ever since their arrival, she and Maximilian had been horrified by the treatment afforded the Indians. They had received reports exposing the abominable state that the majority of the population was reduced to, the frightening cruelty and torture they lived through every day. Much to the surprise of the Mexicans, who had long been accustomed to the abomination, Maximilian and Charlotte were scandalized, and, overcome by indignation, they were determined to put an end to it. Charlotte brought the burning debate before the ministers, though not without first having obtained Maximilian's express order to do so. A committee prepared the necessary documentation, which the emperor examined and then sent on to Charlotte, who absorbed and digested it down to its smallest detail. When she spoke, well versed in her subject, she began by describing the unbearable situation in which millions of Indians were rotting away, and then presented the urgency of granting them the status of human beings. "Here, honorable ministers, is the law that I have had drafted, of which you will certainly approve."

To her astonishment, a voice rose in protest, that of Minister Silicio: "The Indians remain at peace only because of their social degradation; by their innate character and the nature of their race, as soon as they are worked up and allowed to look upon the white man as their equal, we will see the moment of insurrection and vengeance at hand, and that will spell disaster for Mexicans."

Despite this protest, Charlotte managed to win over the other ministers. The reform was passed, and, with such measures as the abolishment of corporal punishment, it radically transformed the Indians' status.

As soon as she left the council, Charlotte triumphantly wrote Maximilian that she had had success all the way down the line. With the exception of a single dissenter, everyone approved of their decision to put an end to a national wound that independence had not remedied in the least: "though de facto citizens, the Indians had nonetheless remained in catastrophic squalor and abasement."

In the beginning of September, Maximilian returned to Mexico City, and instead of congratulating Charlotte, he relieved her of whatever power she had left. She found herself limited exclusively to social issues and the national education system, fields to which she devoted an enormous amount of energy. She was no longer allowed to attend the council of ministers unless Maximilian expressly invited her, and, even then, if during the course of discussions he winked at her, she was to rise immediately and leave the room without a word. She was no longer permitted to enter his office unannounced, and, if things continued along this path, soon she would have to ask him for an audience like any other of his subordinates. In a word, Maximilian publicly considered her as negligible, and

kept her in an inferior station. Such a transformation did not come
about in one day: the progression had been obvious for months, but
it was only upon Maximilian's homecoming, in September 1865,
that the full extent of it could be felt. It was no longer possible to
hide the truth, even for Charlotte.

Maximilian pushed her out of politics not because she failed,
but because she succeeded too well. Despite her repeated attempts
at submission and obedience, Charlotte's abundance of talent had
awakened her husband's jealousy. Like all weak people, he had a
contradictory attitude toward Charlotte. He was impressed with
her gift for governing, but at the same time, he was painfully aware
of her superiority. He could not get by without her strength, so he
rejected her. Ever since they had been sleeping in different bedrooms, Charlotte had hoped a good working relationship would
build up between them, and she had struggled to encourage it.
Maximilian destroyed that hope.

Charlotte's loneliness ran deep. The Austrian ladies who had come
with her to Mexico had all returned to Europe, and the Mexican
ladies could hardly fill their shoes. Nonetheless, she bravely continued her routine, visiting charitable foundations and schools. She
went horseback riding every day, and every day she locked herself
in her room for hours on end to read texts on politics, economics,
history, and law . . . but to what end, since all her knowledge was
going to waste? Then she paced back and forth in the palace's halls,
tearing her lace handkerchief between her teeth, especially the corner bearing her crowned monogram. She ran no risk whatsoever
of running into Maximilian, who lived completely apart from her —
in Chapultepec when she was in Mexico City, and in Mexico City
when she was in Chapultepec.

And what of Loysel? Loysel had resumed his role as Maximilian's faithful counselor and confidant, and he no longer seemed to count in Charlotte's eyes. Though she was completely alone, to think she might complain about it would betray a misunderstanding of her character. On the contrary, she retreated into her wounded pride. She became haughty, even harsh, and particularly demanding in matters of protocol. One day, she descended from her carriage to rebuke a group of caballeros who had failed to recognize her and had not removed their hats. She forbade the butlers from serving ladies-in-waiting who had arrived late for lunch. Pain had transformed her personality, turning it to ice. This is visible in photographs from the period: not a single smile, her small eyes squinting from nearsightedness, a somber and unmoving expression, a frown, and a closed, almost sarcastic look. She had no grace, no desire to seduce. The feathers and diamonds, the lace and silk that covered her, all the trappings of a pampered sovereign couldn't hide the look of a wounded woman.

And yet Charlotte had not come to the end of her sorrows. Maximilian was getting ready to hurt her again, this time even worse. The Mexican dynasty needed an heir to insure the continuity of the throne, especially since the throne was so new and shaky. Charlotte had gone on a pilgrimage to Santa Maria de Guadalupe, renowned for granting the prayers of women wanting to have children. Not longer after, a pamphlet written by republicans had been spread throughout Mexico, accusing Maximilian of having a venereal disease, of infecting his wife with it, and thus of rendering her sterile. It became urgent for her to give birth. A thirty-three-year-old man and a twenty-five-year-old woman, both in the pink of health, could still maintain their hopes. The only problem was that this same man and woman, in the secrecy of their palace, were leading completely separate lives.

Suddenly, out of nowhere, Maximilian announced his decision to adopt an heir. Without going into details or accusing anyone — for it would have been unthinkable to disclose the imperial couple's private life to public opinion — he revealed in the most garish fashion that he and Charlotte had given up all hope of having children.

Their intimates — that is to say, the domestic help — knew the situation quite well. The maids slept not far from Charlotte, and the butlers spent their nights in the room next to Maximilian's. They were wild with curiosity, asking each other thousands of questions: had the emperor been unfaithful to his wife? Did he suffer from a physiological defect? Was he impotent, as some people said? And yet, Maximilian and Charlotte had married for love; they had had the most beautiful honeymoon. Everyone knew that, all of Mexico repeated it. Maximilian was handsome, attractive, charming. Before his marriage, when he was traveling throughout Greece, Asia Minor, and across the globe, he had had affairs of the heart, as Maximilian's Austrian servants had amply informed Blasio, the new butler, and his fellow Mexicans. Since his marriage, however, he had been above reproach. The empire's best-kept secret remained a mystery.

As for the rest of the world, the situation was not hard to understand. At the time, if a couple could not have a child, it was always seen as the woman's fault. Maximilian thus left Charlotte exposed to the waves of public curiosity and speculation unleashed by the announcement of the adoption. The hypotheses and suspicions all boiled down to one thing: Charlotte was sterile. Upon hearing this accusation, most devastating and cruel for a woman, Charlotte responded in her usual way, lifting her head high and pursing her lips even more tightly.

Where should they look for an heir? Maximilian chose him from the family of Iturbide, Mexico's erstwhile emperor from the turn of the century. The boy was named Augustin Iturbide, a beautiful child then two-and-a-half years old. He had relatives, a family to negotiate with; when they caused difficulties, Charlotte supported Maximilian and got involved in the matter that was cutting her to the quick. "There are problems with the Iturbide family," she wrote him. "No victory is won without glory, but you must gain ground foot by foot, inch by inch. I always press them to understand that if they do not accept all our terms, nothing will come of it for any of them. . . ."

Finally, young Augustin's father and uncles were extradited to the United States, though not without monetary compensation. They were bad subjects, Charlotte liked to say. The mother, Doña Alicia, proved even more stubborn. Charlotte sent her bouquet after bouquet, she invited her to dinner, but the young and pretty American loved her son. She protested, she cried for ten days, but one hundred forty thousand piastres helped make up her mind, and she too left for the United States.

So that the child would not be lonely, one of his cousins, Salvatore, was brought along, and they were put in the care of their aunt, Doña Josephina, who was the sort of governess one might find in a comedy.

Charlotte had the wherewithal to go in person to pick up the child, whose elevation to the rank of heir was the deepest insult to her. She concluded her report to Maximilian with this cryptic sentence: "I kiss you with all my heart and am abundantly happy with the beauty of a paradise that is now closed to me." The child, his cousin, and his aunt received the titles of prince and princess, which caused countless protocol problems that Charlotte attempted to solve. She wrote a long letter to Hidalgo, who had become the empire's ambassador to France, requesting that he make inquiries at Napoleon III's court. The young Iturbide princes were in a position analogous to that of the Murat princes, boys who were somehow related to the French emperor without being full members of the imperial family.

Hidalgo's mission was thus to find out how the Murats were treated, so that similar treatment could be given to the Iturbides. In her instructions, Charlotte did not omit a single aspect of the question, using her perfect knowledge of etiquette in favor of a little boy whose new rank and presence would be a constant reminder to her that she would never have a child of her own. . . . The scandal of the adoption and its far-reaching implications could thus be diluted in the nuances of protocol.

Meanwhile, in the United States, public opinion against the Mexican empire had been growing even more virulent. The American media, already in liberal hands, categorically refused to support a monarchy. Maximilian tried a diversion. He sent an emissary to convince industrialists and bankers to invest in various aspects of the Mexican economy. American capital did not so much as nibble at the bait. The United States knew full well that a monarchy in Mexico, as anywhere else, guaranteed the country's independence, and that the United States would be able to milk the Mexican cow for a lot more if it were to become a republic. The Americans thus preferred to calmly wait for Mexico to become a republic in order to reap the maximum profits.

To this end, Secretary of State Seward was still looking for the best candidate to bring such a transformation about.

He thought of Gonzalez Ortega. The Mexican republicans, though reduced in number and everywhere persecuted by the French, still kept up appearances of the republic's legal continuity. There were even meetings of representatives and a presidential election. Juárez had lost, and Gonzalez Ortega had been elected to replace him. While he was awaiting his inauguration, the new "president of the Republic of Mexico" had hastened to visit the United States. Seward and his administration were already recognizing him as Juárez's successor when an absurd case involving debts and a minor American judge's excess of zeal stopped Ortega in his tracks and prevented him from returning to Mexico. Juárez jumped on the opportunity. He published one decree extending his presidential powers until the Ortega affair was cleared up, and another ordering that Ortega be arrested the moment he stepped foot in Mexico. The game was forfeited for lack of players, and Seward had no choice but to choose Juárez to overthrow the empire and to plant the American flag in Mexico. In a show of goodwill, he immediately sent twenty million pesos to his brand-new champion.

The new champion, however, had never had it so bad. Continuing their offensive, the French had chased him out of Chihuahua. Juárez had had to take refuge at Paso del Norte on the American border. The Republic of Mexico's entire territory was thus comprised of a modest mud house, which the officials shared with a few shepherds and their flocks. If he were pushed one step further, Juárez would be out of Mexico and in the United States. This was so close to becoming reality that already the news of his defeat had spread throughout Mexico and was considered certain: Juárez had abandoned Mexico.

And he had taken the republic with him, Charlotte concluded. There might be no republic any longer, but the same could not be said for the republicans, who, strangely enough, seemed to be multiplying. It was an absurd and unbearable situation, one that needed to end now, by whatever means necessary.

At that moment, a newcomer arrived on the scene: Fischer. Born a poor German, Fischer had emigrated to the United States and moved to Texas, where he lived in squalid poverty as a farmhand. When the gold rush began, he hurried to California and scratched the earth with thousands of others in search of the precious metal. He rubbed shoulders with the dregs of society, with gangsters and loose women; the former suited his taste for adventure, the latter his sexual appetite. One day, the Jesuits spotted him. If God couldn't explain why, perhaps the devil might be able to: not only did they convert the Protestant to Catholicism, but they even ordained him a priest. Fischer found himself employed as a bishop's secretary, but the scandals of his former life with women and bastard children soon ended that. He disappeared, only to reappear in Maximilian's intimate entourage. He had begun by writing brilliant reports. Then he had been sent on missions of increasing importance and secrecy. He was liked from the outset. He was a fighter, but there was nothing low-class about him. On the contrary, he was a cultivated and civilized man who knew how to charm, engage, and convince. Maximilian was always looking for strong men to surround him, but he used them up so quickly that there was always room for a newcomer. Though he had once seemed all-powerful, Loysel was now on the decline, and Fischer could not have chosen his moment better.

Fischer's rapid ascension could not be explained solely by his virtues, however, if indeed he possessed any virtues worthy of mention. It looked as if powerful interests had managed to place him in Maximilian's path. The Jesuits, and with them the conservatives, were the best suspects. Gossip had it that the good father had begun his career by suggesting the disastrous adoption of young Iturbide. Once that decision had consolidated his position, he worked on his new project, in German, since of course he spoke his native language with the emperor. With Juárez out of Mexico and the republic crushed, the republicans were no longer political opponents—they were simply rebels, little better than criminals. With that change in status, they deserved one thing and one thing only: the firing squad. Bazaine whispered it in Maximilian's ear over and over. In his exasperation over the quagmire Mexico was becoming, Napoleon III repeatedly urged Maximilian to take firmer action. Finally convinced, Maximilian stopped hesitating, and on

October 3, 1865, with the blessing of Father Fischer, he published a decree ordering any rebel caught with a weapon in his hands to be shot on the spot without a trial.

Finally receiving the signal they had been waiting for, the loyalists immediately let loose their rage. Arbitrary arrests and summary executions filled the country with gunfire and misery. But far from giving in, the rebels repaid the horror in kind. Captured soldiers and officers were massacred. Ghastly reports, calls for clemency, and petitions flooded Maximilian's desk; unswayed, he announced to Loysel that from then on, he was through pardoning prisoners.

Maximilian was not a bloodthirsty man, but he was a weak one. Awareness of his weakness threw him into fits of action in which he confused brutality for firmness. And Charlotte, who was not cruel either, nonetheless supported Maximilian in whatever decisions he made. She had not taken part in drawing up the murderous decree, but once it was published, she backed it, out of faithfulness to her husband, and out of love for him.

Her French family was shocked. Her favorite uncle, Joinville, wrote her in horror for the blood spilled. He had heard of countless executions and terrifying statistics: four hundred fifty lined up and shot in the town of Sacatecas; innocents hanged by mistake in Tampico; all the victims branded with the generic label of "bandits." Joinville wept to see his niece responsible, however indirectly, for these atrocities. Charlotte did not answer his letter. She did not hear the firing squads, she did not see the corpses. Two weeks after the decree was published, as the executions were taking place all around her, Charlotte wrote her brother that all was well. There was no more tension with the United States or with the pope, there was a new confidence surging through the country, and the small opposition parties had all either disappeared or calmed down. Of course, some problems remained, some of them quite serious, but there was no longer any risk that the country could fall apart, no worry for the future. "The machine is working. . . . This nation once so burdened by apathy, demagogy, and chaos is finally rediscovering something akin to hope and enthusiasm; it is confident again in its strengths, in its uncontested intelligence, and at the same time, in its destiny."

Also out of love for Maximilian, Charlotte once again accepted being separated from him. This time, however, she was the one who left.

Months before, the emperor had decided to visit the distant province of Yucatán. But now, because of the situation's growing danger, his advisers urged him to stay in the capital. Maximilian said nothing until the autumn of 1865, when he suddenly announced that he and Charlotte would be leaving. The problem was that roads barely existed, so in order to go to that province, they would first have to travel to Veracruz and then take a ship to Mérida. The European newspapers screamed that the only reason Maximilian and Charlotte were going to Veracruz was to sneak out of Mexico under their subjects' and the French troops' noses. The baseless accusation so startled Maximilian that he decided on the spot not to leave for the trip. Charlotte took his place and left alone, armed with the most detailed instructions.

She left Mexico City in November, accompanied by two ministers, an ambassador, a chaplain, a doctor, two ladies-in-waiting, and Eloin, who meanwhile had returned from his mission to Europe. Barely had she left than Maximilian immediately felt lonely, as he did each time they parted. "My dearest angel, after the sorrow of our good-byes, I had a gloomy and mournful day. Everything seemed so deserted and sad. I wandered through the palace like a man abandoned."

The Yucatán, in the second half of the nineteenth century, was a world onto itself. This immense province occupied the empire's entire southwest peninsula. It was covered by thick forests abounding in the most ferocious animals, the most venomous snakes, and the most voracious insects. In the stifling climate, fevers and sickness were everywhere. Spanish colonists had barely been able to make headway into it, just enough to found a few cities. The rare travelers who had explored it had come back with tales of dead cities buried under lush vegetation. Charlotte, who had read everything on Mexico, knew that ancient civilizations had sparkled in the Yucatán before mysteriously disappearing. The risks of this voyage did not stop the empress of Mexico for a moment; in fact, they thrilled her.

The adventure began at the gates of Mexico City. On the road connecting the capital with Veracruz, a road she knew so well, Charlotte had to deal with torrential rain and oceans of mud that hindered the soldiers of her French escort from pitching their tents. The poor condition of the roads only added to the insecurity caused by bandits, rebels, and even French deserters, which prevented them from traveling at night. The towns they crossed, Puebla and Orizaba, offered discouraging welcomes. A few months earlier, these same towns had greeted their sovereigns with enthusiasm. But now, Charlotte could feel the people's coldness. Her heart was pained but she said nothing. Maximilian's letters saddened her: "The farther you go, the more I miss you and the more melancholy I feel. I wander like a lost soul through these empty halls, and to add to my depression, the weather is frightfully cold."

In these words, we hear the Maximilian who needed Charlotte so much that he was unable to get by without her. When they were together, he cloistered her in her apartments. But when they were apart, he discovered just how important and how great a support she was to him. His foul mood, in conjunction with the weather, began to affect his health. No matter how much iron and quinine he took, he felt ill and alone, and his sorrow, which was palpable in his letter, weighed heavily on Charlotte's spirit.

She was approaching Veracruz, that republican stronghold that had so unfavorably impressed her when she landed in Mexico, and she anxiously inquired after the welcome she had in store. Contrary to all expectations, she received the most enthusiastic greetings, but then again, Mexico never failed to surprise. They traveled the last miles in a train, and from the station all the way to her residence, the entire population had come together to cheer her. Despite the stifling heat, the townswomen were dressed in the latest European fashions in her honor. The city government had even had a sort of triumphant chariot built, and Charlotte had little choice but to climb aboard for a ride. She herself was shocked by her popularity. The heat increased and was compounded with tropical downpours that delayed her trip to the Yucatán for two mosquito-infested days. But Charlotte did not care—she was popular, as her subjects were showing her, and that was enough for her. She could not help telling Maximilian that the Belgian minister never failed to say that the empress's presence was worth more than that of an entire army. After such an outburst of vanity, she checked herself: "The cheers are not for me, but because I am your wife."

Finally the weather cleared and she was able to board her ship. She found a luxurious Austrian corvette awaiting her. Charlotte protested that the empress of Mexico could sail only aboard a Mexican vessel, and she chose a squalid steamship that at least flew the national flag.

She recorded the tale of her trip with the clarity and precision so characteristic of her. She remained at Mérida, capital of the Yucatán, for more than a week. She loved this beautiful, white city

and its straight streets, whose lack of notable monuments was com-
pensated for by a powerful charm. She did not remain idle. She presided over balls, banquets, fireworks displays, and performances
of folk dance, but she also visited the prison, schools, hospitals, and
industry and agriculture expositions. She held public audiences, and
attended a grand reception where gleeful women covered her feet
with flowers while their husbands shouted, "Long live the salvation of the Yucatán, long live the protectress of the Yucatecs, long
live our empress!"

At this pace, fatigue soon overwhelmed her, and during the
night, Charlotte came down with a painful sore throat. This did not
stop her from attending the inauguration of a textile factory and a
ball the next day. The strain worsened her condition, and she was
forced to take to bed. Her sore throat kept her awake all night, but
fortunately, she had no fever. On the second day, she felt well
enough to resume her activities. In every village, Indians led by their
chieftains came to meet her, and at nightfall, they lit torches that
transformed the scene into a magical spectacle.

After Mérida, she made a detour to visit Uxmal. Only a few
archeologists and the local Indians knew of this immense field of
ruins that had withstood centuries of the forest's encroachments.
Charlotte was without a doubt the first European woman to have
reached it. Even today, the trip is not without its perils for novices,
because of its high and slippery steps, the ubiquitous and treach-
erous vegetation, the reptiles and insects whose only aim seems to
be to sting and poison the unsuspecting tourist. At the time, the site
had not yet been cleared, which made exploration extremely dangerous. Fearless, Charlotte seemed to have forgotten her fatigue. In
her long skirt with a light bolero over her blouse and a wide-
brimmed straw hat on her head, she jumped from stone to stone
and climbed up the lofty pyramids like a gazelle. She enthusiastically discovered the grandiose monuments with their sophisticated

architecture and elegant ornamentation. She visited everything: the Pyramid of the Soothsayer, the Nuns' Rectangle, the Palace of the Doves, the Governor's House, the Stone of Punishment, and her descriptions surpass even those of the best tourist guides in their precision. She went so far as to draw a map of the ruins that is still valid today. She inquired after the customs of the site's former inhabitants, the Maya, whose name was still barely known at the time. She learned of the bloody rituals of their religion, and listened to descriptions of their human sacrifices. Then, despite her enthusiasm, whether from the heat or from the sinister tales, she was overwhelmed by depression: "I suddenly felt tormented by sad thoughts."

Though this feeling was rare in Charlotte, Maximilian had been prey to it ever since his wife's departure: "My dear angel, a thousand thanks for your many and happy telegrams which did much to reassure me. I had spent several days in horrible anguish and dark melancholy. . . . In my melancholy, I have completely retired to Chapultepec, to the high, solitary rock I like so much, and there, in the calm, I have recovered my senses a bit. . . ."

The day after her visit to Uxmal, Charlotte woke before dawn, for their departure had been scheduled for four o'clock in the morning. Giddiness had replaced her sad thoughts of the day before. At the village of Becal, the old parish priest had adorned his house with a wide banner that read: "Long live King Leopold and glory to the great monarch!" At the next village, the same thing happened: as Charlotte passed by, the Indians shouted "Long live great Leopold!" Charlotte was deeply touched by these cheers for her father, but wondered what made the Indians mention him. That night, during their layover in Calkini, she found and spent time with her good friend, the beautiful Madam Arrigunaga, daughter of Gutierrez d'Estrada, one of the first and most enthusiastic of Maximilian's supporters. Throughout the evening, Charlotte was overcome by

a serenity that she tried to describe: "My soul felt a gentle and profound joy more akin to the one when God makes his presence felt
than to any of this world. From that moment on, I have not stopped
feeling more pious and making the best resolutions. . . ." She herself was taken aback by her unexpected state of mind, but she had
no time to dwell on it, since it was already time to get back on the
road again. They approached Campeche, the great commercial port
that once upon a time was a magnet for pirates, and suffered because of it. Groups of inhabitants had come out from the city to meet
Charlotte. Their numbers increased but their greetings remained
muted. It was as if they were trying to preserve for Charlotte the
surprise of the indescribable enthusiasm awaiting her as soon as
she reached the city's outlying districts. The entire population
rushed her coach. In a second, the escort was submerged in the
crowd and the horses disappeared, only to be replaced as if by magic
by cheering people. Charlotte tried to make her voice heard—she
would have liked to come down from the coach—but the people
prevented her, and she made her entrance into Campeche in a coach
pulled by men. She spent the night in a huge home with a foreboding façade decorated with geometric motifs. Despite the height of
the ceilings, the heat was so atrocious that she spent the night bathed
in sweat, but nonetheless, she had to follow the same, inexorable
schedule in every town: visits to the schools, charitable institutions,
hospitals, the prison, grand balls, solemn high mass in the half-light
of the local cathedral in the presence of all the city's magistrates.

Finally, on December 16, after four weeks of traveling and
attending ceremonies conducted at a fever pitch, Charlotte reached
"the Gateway of the Sea," and boarded her ship at the little port of
Lerma, outside of Campeche.

The empress could finally say that she had now fulfilled her
mission—and that mission had not simply been to go to the empire's
edges to win popularity in far-off provinces. For one, Maximilian

had asked Charlotte to have the formal ban against exporting the Yucatán's antiquities abroad passed into law. At a time when no one gave a thought to this sort of trafficking, he was anxious to put a stop to this hemorrhage of masterpieces that even today is slowly bleeding Mexico dry.

Even more importantly, Maximilian knew that the Maya hated the Mexicans, and vice versa, as he himself wrote in his instructions. He ordered her to establish the groundwork for autonomy in the Yucatán, and she attempted to do so all the more willingly in that she was now brimming over with enthusiasm for the land. Nothing she had seen in Mexico had inspired such feeling in her. The province had remained very different from the rest of the country, for it was barely touched by "the evils of colonization." Amid the widespread destruction that reigned everywhere else, the people had found the strength to survive the most aberrant and dangerous doctrines with their energy, patriotism and society intact. The Yucatán, Charlotte noted, knew neither theft nor civil war; everything had a patriarchal and almost celestial atmosphere, where, under a cloudless sky, amid sumptuous flowers blooming in the exuberance of an eternal springtime, the population went about its peaceful occupations. The empress also noticed that in that particularly romantic region, poets abounded. The paradise that she discovered on the outskirts of her empire corresponded to Maximilian's secret desire to transform Mexico into the giant of Central America. An autonomous Yucatán would draw in investors, and bind together all the territories and countries in the region. Following his vision, Maximilian was already planning a division of the American continent into three great empires: the United States, Mexico, and, farther to the south, Brazil.

Charlotte had fallen in love with the Yucatán, but she returned from it exhausted. The tropical climate sapping energy and will, the inedible food, the never-ending activities on her schedule, the long hours spent on horseback in the middle of the jungle, the uncertainty, never admitted to, of what sort of welcome she would receive in the cities, perhaps even the mysteriously threatening shadows that still lingered over Uxmal—all had quite literally wiped her out. Several remarks she let slip indicate that she was on the verge of a nervous breakdown.

9

Maximilian met up with Charlotte at San Martín de Texmelucan, sixty miles from Mexico City, and her joy at seeing him again knew no bounds. As she wrote to her dear grandmother Marie-Amelie: "Max and I are so united in policy as in all other things that there is no danger that anyone might try to separate us in anything, and if I have my isolated successes, I bring them all back to him, and he is always royally proud and satisfied, as he is with what just happened in the Yucatán."

The emperor and empress did not return immediately to the capital. Instead, they played hooky like a couple of lovebirds. Maximilian had telegraphed her, "If you are not too tired from the trip, I thought I would go with you to Cuernavaca, a town filled with tenderness for us, and which I promised I would visit soon. We could spend a few days there. . . ." Thus they made a detour that led them through tiny passes between wooded hills.

On January 3, at one-thirty in the afternoon, cannon salvos announced to the population of the little town that their sovereigns had arrived. Charlotte and Maximilian discovered an enchanting village, set in a valley "blessed by heaven" that looked to them like a golden cup resting in the center of a chain of mountains stretching out in hues of pink, purple, violet, and blue—some of them jagged and uneven like towers piled on top of one another, others high and forest-covered, like the mountains of Switzerland, and far in the distance, the snow-capped summits of gigantic volcanoes against a crystalline sky. There were no seasons in this golden cup, so all year long the most abundant tropical vegetation flourished, inebriating scents wafted through the air, and exotic fruit bobbed in the trees. The climate was eternally gentle and the people handsome, likeable, and honest.

Before them, Cortés had loved Cuernavaca, so much so that he had had a palace built there. Although it was falling a bit to ruins, Maximilian and Charlotte set themselves up in it, for, in the hope that they would linger a while, the town had offered it to them. Suddenly Charlotte fell ill. She was overcome by migraines, discomfort, and dizziness, and she was unable to sleep. What was the cause of these strange pains, normally so foreign to her robust health? "I have been poisoned," she concluded. Poisoned? But by whom, when, why? "I do not know, I only know that I have been poisoned," she insisted to Maximilian, who could not believe his ears.

A few days later, she felt a little better, and Maximilian took advantage of this improvement to bring her for a ride in the surrounding country. They crossed through Indian villages, walked on sandy paths among the orange blossoms and laurels, beneath immense trees "that have no name in French." In the evening's peace and nature's beauty, they forgot their worries, and joyful, hand in hand, they came back home to Cortés' palace.

The next day was the Feast of the Three Kings, or Epiphany, which is celebrated with particular gusto by the Mexican church. Maximilian came into Charlotte's bedroom in tears, unable to speak. In his trembling hand, he held out a telegram to her. Far away in Brussels, King Leopold had been dead for almost a month. Charlotte threw herself into her husband's arms, and they cried together, holding each other tightly.

The news spread like wildfire throughout the town, and by their own initiative, without any order to do so, the Indians dismantled the arches of triumph and decorations set up for their sovereigns' visit. They somehow managed to unearth black crêpe paper, and they covered everything they could in it. The next day, Maximilian and Charlotte crossed the town in mourning, accompanied by a huge and silent crowd who had come to see them off. They left their paradise, which had become for them a place of sadness. As she sunk into her black thoughts, Charlotte remembered three strange things that had happened during her trip to the Yucatán: the unexpected depression that came over her among the ruins of Uxmal; the strangely misplaced banner, "Long live the great Leopold," that had greeted her in an Indian village; and those Indians who had called out her father's name on the same day that, thousands of miles away, he was on his deathbed.

The couple returned directly to Chapultepec, where they locked themselves away. The capital had covered its balconies in black. Charlotte's heartache was all the more painful in that she had not seen her father since she left for Mexico, and she would never have the chance to see him again. From the depths of her sadness, she sought consolation in the expressions of condolence flooding in from everywhere. She read thousands of letters and telegrams.

One of these messages particularly attracted her attention, coming from the Grand Orient of Mexico: "Your Majesty's august father was once willing to remove his royal crown in order to don the humble Masonic cloak. Six million Free Masons spread across the entire surface of the globe join together in a final homage to the ILLUSTRIOUS BROTHER they have lost. The Free Masons of Mexico pray that the GREAT ARCHITECT OF THE UNI-VERSE will throw his balm upon Your Majesty's aching heart."

In letters arriving from Europe, Charlotte learned the details of her father's last days, which she probably should not have done. Before his death, Leopold's depression and desire for isolation had so worsened that he refused to see his family. He did not, however, refuse to see the beautiful Arcadie, who was still living in the square. She would come to Laeken every day from the little castle outside of Stuyvenberg that Leopold had bought her. Her presence singularly annoyed the court and the palace staff, even if, over time, she had become more discreet. Every night, two policemen would escort her back home.

As the king's health declined, he had had no choice but to open the doors to his family. He would not hear a word about his sons, but he agreed to receive his daughter-in-law, Marie-Henriette, the elder son's wife. He had recently changed his mind about her; he no longer found her useless, and instead, he had come to like the prudent and stable woman, who grew on people the longer they knew her. Since she had gained Leopold's confidence, the family had taken advantage of the fact to suggest a plan of final action. Though he was the king of a Catholic country, the father of Catholic princes, and the widower of the very Catholic Louise d'Orleans, Leopold was dying a Protestant, and that was intolerable. Which is why, evoking Louise d'Orleans' name, Marie-Henriette gently suggested to her father-in-law that he convert on his deathbed. A resounding "Nein" cut her attempt short.

Then the old king had fallen into a semi-coma. He repeated over and over again, "Mexico, Charlotte. Charlotte, Mexico." When death had finally begun, the doors of his bedroom were opened wide. His children, his servants, and even the ministers and representatives of the state who had come running to Laeken all entered the vast room.

King Leopold died in the space of a breath with the name "Charlotte" on his lips.

Arcadie hastened to disappear, and the new king, Leopold II, bought back from her the castle at Stuyvenberg, which from then on would serve as a residence for the widowed queens of Belgium. But Arcadie had more than one trick up her sleeve. She had had the prudence to send her nest egg abroad. Soon she reappeared near Düsseldorf, in a very cute villa, under the title of Baroness von Eppinghoven. As for the two sons she had had by Leopold, they were insured a career at the Coburg court, from which, so long ago, the first king of Belgium had sprung.

While Charlotte cried for her father, Maximilian received only the best of news: First, Bazaine solemnly swore to him that he was formally resolved to take widespread action to crush the rebellion once and for all. Next, Father Fischer, whom Maximilian had sent to Rome to settle the question of the clergy's property, assured him that the pope was full of goodwill for him and would be understanding. Finally, an unofficial envoy from Washington informed him that the dark clouds existing between the United States and Mexico would quickly disappear, and would soon be nothing more than "phantoms."

For all of these reasons, Maximilian judged the time perfect for a vacation, and he also felt it would be the best thing for Charlotte at that time. And where should they go but to the blessed

Cuernavaca they had just discovered? This time, they would not put up in Cortés' palace, which was really too uncomfortable and dilapidated. Instead, they found a heavenly place, the Borda garden, named after its creator, a Frenchman who had made his fortune in the mines. No sooner had they found it than Maximilian acquired it. Charlotte and he could take all the time they wanted to explore the site, which today still maintains its power to enchant. A botanist's masterpiece, the garden was planted with essences from all over the world. It had a profusion of rare and immense trees, of prickly bushes and wreaths of flowers otherwise unknown to Mexico, and it was also a water garden. Staircases and bowers covered with creeping vines led from one fountain to another. From thin canals, the water emptied out into lakes, at the edges of which rose pavilions that lent a calming shade. The Borda garden was not very big, and yet Maximilian and Charlotte strolled from surprise to surprise in the cool and multicolored labyrinth that gave them the impression of an immense domain. Behind a wall of old stones, they spotted the bell towers of a church that they would use as their chapel.

The house was modest, big enough to live in but nothing else. Their suite would be in a nearby building that had an attractive patio. Under the verandas, in front of the bedrooms, white hammocks were stretched out, and above them fluttered birds of all shapes and colors, chirping every note imaginable.

Maximilian had brought along on this vacation the heir he had chosen for himself, young Iturbide, as well as his aunt and governess, Doña Josephina. As the child ran and shouted for joy and the aunt fanned herself on a huge straw armchair, Maximilian let his imagination roam free along the paths traced out by the enchanting natural surroundings. Old memories bubbled up to the surface, and as he thought about the past, he realized that nothing could make him give up his present situation. Of course, there were difficulties and obstacles, but he loved the fight. He was enjoying this free and unhindered life, "without all that clutter of old, enfeebled Europe." Charlotte and he had become true Mexicans. Over in Europe, they did not understand, especially the press, but "we children of the new continent" did not care about European gossip. "*Adelante!* Forward!" they cried, and over their shoulders they looked behind them with pity at poor withered Europe.

Maximilian wrote his friends on the Continent that they should not think he had become lazy. On the contrary, he worked between ten and twelve hours per day. He felt stronger and more robust than ever. His beard came down to his chest, and his moustache was so long that it would make a Hungarian turn green with envy. On the other hand, he was going slightly bald. He lived his happiness with "my dear better half, so light and cheerful," who shared his dangers and his exertions, and who, with him, was forever crossing their vast empire.

Their entourage had also taken to Mexico better than Maximilian and Charlotte could have hoped. Maximilian smiled as he watched his treasurer, old Kuhacsevich, "as round as a barrel," galloping on a spirited steed and winning the natives' admiration for his equestrian dexterity. As for Madame Kuhacsevich, she had become a true Creole, perhaps a bit thick about the hips, but "flourishing with health," swaying in her hammock in the shade of the orange blossoms and giving mute orders to her many servants with a flick of her fan.

They had also brought along a dear friend to Cuernavaca, Professor Billimek, an Austrian entomologist. All day long, he wandered the countryside looking for rare insects and reptiles that he brought back home at night to classify and discuss before the excited sovereigns. Together with him, Charlotte, but also Maximilian, hunted the marvelous butterflies that populated Mexico in an extraordinary variety of sizes, shapes, and colors. Charlotte also spent a great deal of time in her rose garden, which she had copied from those she saw in Europe. Since they were first planted, the rosebushes had grown bigger and older. Within the old walls, there were also some of the flowers that made the trip over from the old Continent that Charlotte cherished so lovingly.

Charlotte and Maximilian took long rides on horseback in the lands surrounding Cuernavaca. They could never get enough of discovering new villages, valleys invisible from afar, opulent or abandoned haciendas that sprouted in the middle of little jungles. Sometimes they rode separately, for Charlotte preferred to ride in the morning, Maximilian in the evening. Setting out one day at nightfall, Maximilian let his horse lazily descend the slope on which Cuernavaca was built. He crossed fields bristling with cacti that alternated with lush meadows held within walls of dried earth. He reached the locality of Acapazingo, where he happened upon a little house enclosing a miniature patio, where bushes with dark leaves and bright flowers grew tightly. Fruit trees grew all around the patio, lined up in order. From the top of the few steps that led to the patio, he discovered an immense view looking out over the plain below.

He immediately fell so in love with the modest farm that he acquired it on the spot. He had some work done quickly and in secret, for he wanted to surprise Charlotte with the refuge he had bought just for her. And he had already come up with a meaningful name for it: La Quinta del Olvido—the Farm of Forgetfulness.

Cuernavaca was not just a vacation home, for work followed the couple everywhere. Charlotte read a great deal and took care of the charitable institutions she had founded. For his part, Maximilian governed from the Borda garden, with home secretaries and ministers who commuted back and forth from Mexico City. He liked to work in the coolest place in the house, a breezy veranda where he had set up a small table. Reports and files were piled up high on the floor tiles. Whenever Maximilian lifted his nose out of his papers, he looked down the long lane bordered by tall trees that looked like umbrellas of many colors. When he found time to relax and let his attention wander, the gurgle of flowing water or the songs of exotic birds gave him great pleasure. He also granted audiences to his visitors there.

It was also in the garden that, one winter morning, he received a special envoy from Napoleon III. Baron Saillard was a short, distinctly dislikable man. He seemed astonished by the mixture of simplicity and exoticism in Maximilian's entourage. As he approached the little table behind which the emperor was working, Maximilian stood to greet him. Saillard noticed that Maximilian looked bigger than he actually was, so noble and majestic was his bearing. Saillard bowed his head as a sign of respect, then stiffly handed over a letter from the emperor of the French: "My dear brother, it is not without a feeling of sorrow that I write to Your Majesty, for I am forced to inform him of the determination I have had to make in relation to all the difficulties the Mexican issue has been causing me. . . . The impossibility of asking for new subsidies from the legislative branch for the upkeep of the Mexican army, as well as Your Majesty's own inability to contribute to the same expense, force me to fix a definitive date for the end of French occupation. In my opinion, this end should come as soon as possible. . . ."

Thunder cracked, lightning struck, the Earth quaked. With only a tenth of the country truly pacified, the treasury empty, and no national army at all, pulling the French troops out meant condemning the Mexican empire to death.

Napoleon III knew the consequences of his decision full well, but he also had to take into consideration French public opinion that was growing more and more opposed to the Mexican expedition, and most of all its cost. Although Napoleon III's reign was still quite strong, he could not risk turning the parliament against him. Moreover, the European skies were already darkening. The rising star of European politics, Bismarck, was rattling his saber more forcefully every day. To test out his power, he had already brought poor little Denmark to its knees, snatching up a third of its territory, and now he was eyeing the Austrian empire. He growled and threatened, throwing governments into an uproar, and Napoleon III into panic.

From the flowery shelter of his Cuernavaca retreat, Maximilian had no clue that his country was in danger. But most of all, he was unaware of the United States' role in Napoleon III's decision. He was still under the illusion that he would be able to reach an agreement with Washington, and he did not suspect that at that very minute, Seward, the seeming unremovable secretary of state, was urging Napoleon III to immediately withdraw all his troops from Mexico or face dire consequences. His threats had been enough to make the French emperor give in.

Napoleon III followed up his lethal blow with a few concessions. The French troops, he specified, would leave gradually, according to a timetable to be approved by the emperor of Mexico, and the foreign legions, both Austrian and Belgian, would stay. Pushing aside these crumbs, Maximilian responded right away, refusing to negotiate or beg. There would be no procrastination with Napoleon III. "I thus propose with a cordiality equal to your own to withdraw your troops immediately from the American continent." Only on one point did Maximilian prove intransigent: there would be no question of his abandoning Mexico.

To clarify things and make sure nothing more was to be expected from France, or even from Europe, Maximilian decided to send Eloin once again, and for added weight, he sent Loysel right after him.

❀   ❀   ❀

Charlotte had barely had the time to digest the stunning news of the
French troops' withdrawal from Mexico when she was forced to
deal with an official delegation from Belgium that showed up in
Mexico City. In her anxiety, she was truly relieved to see old acquaintances. Maximilian feigned illness to get out of the chore, and
left his wife alone to receive her fellow countrymen, who were led
by Baron of Huart, a good friend of her favorite brother, Philippe.

The reunion was not, however, a complete joy for the empress.
The new king of Belgium, Leopold II, had never been close with
his sister. He showed himself to be much less enthusiastic for the
Mexican project than his father had been. First of all, he did not
feel that the Belgian volunteers had been well treated. Second, they
needed to discuss inheritance questions raised by Leopold I's
death—and inheritance questions meant friction, even if cloaked
in the genteel terms befitting a royal family.

The Belgians stayed only a week. Upon their departure, despite
the danger on the roads, the French provided them with only a mini-
mal escort. Their procession headed off into the dust, crossed the plain
surrounding Mexico City, and soon reached the sierra foothills at the
locality known as Rio Frio, or "Cold River," a rocky pass that led
toward the mountains. The detachment of French soldiers had expected to be relieved, but no one was there to meet them at the rendezvous point. Without waiting a minute more, the French turned
around and went back to Mexico City. The Belgian coach thus proceeded without protection onto the pass. The road was so bad, but
the landscape so beautiful, that Baron of Huart decided that if he had
to be shaken anyway, he might as well climb up top and sit with the
coachman. He was admiring the wild savagery of rocky nature when
gunshots suddenly erupted from the heights. A group of about twenty
men, whether bandits, rebels, or deserters, shot point-blank at the
Belgians. Huart, hit in the forehead, collapsed.

A telegram brought Maximilian the news at Cuernavaca. He jumped onto his horse with as many men as he could find, his personal doctor and Bombelles among them, and rushed to the scene of the tragedy. But the roads were so bad that he reached it only at five o'clock the next morning, after riding all afternoon and all night. When he arrived, there was nothing left for him to do but confirm that Baron of Huart was dead. There was no chance of pursuing the murderers — they were already long gone, and it would be impossible to track them through the mountains. Shaken by such a tragic death of a friend, Charlotte needed a few days before she could find the strength to write to her brother Philippe: "I have very sad news for you, and my heart weeps as I pick up my pen. Your poor Huart is no more, God has called him back." Charlotte was well aware what effects this murder would have in Europe, just as Napoleon III was smugly telling everyone that it was impossible to establish a lasting empire in Mexico, and especially in Belgium, as Leopold II was complaining about having to keep Belgian volunteers there. Whether his reaction was sincere or just a bit of political theatricality, Leopold II seemed deeply upset by his envoy's death. "The tragedy of Rio Frio has filled me with horror; you would have to go all the way to the cannibalistic blacks in the heart of Africa to find similar scenes of savagery," he wrote. Charlotte was ashamed for Mexico, for the Empire, for Maximilian, and for herself.

But as always, she dealt with her problems. She sent letter after letter to her favorite brother Philippe, to her former governess the countess of Hulste, to old friends. She said the same thing to everyone. It was only to excuse the inexcusable and attempt to justify the withdrawal of French troops that the French government and press were screaming that there was no chance for the empire to take root in Mexico. "Don't listen to those tales, those lies, that libel," Charlotte insisted. "Don't listen to the French press, don't listen to the rumors spreading around Europe. Mexico is doing just fine."

In a letter to Philippe, Charlotte permitted herself a diatribe against those truly responsible for the French troops' pullout and for the empire's hardships: "The Americans have been the enemies of peace in all Spanish-speaking countries ever since their independence. They lurk around like wolves eyeing their prey. They stir up dissension under the pretext of freedom. Half the civil wars have no other cause but the U.S., and now that they see Mexico finally coming together and back to life, when they have so long profited from its corpse, they bombard us with lies, complaints, and recriminations. . . ."

Ironically, Charlotte did not even know that at that very moment in Washington, President Johnson was glamorously entertaining the wife of Benito Juárez, propelling her from banquet to banquet, from ceremony to ceremony, all the while filling her head with republican speeches. The same President Johnson had also just named a rabid antimonarchist as his official representative to President Juárez.

Despite everything, Maximilian was falling more and more in love with Cuernavaca. The few days that he was supposed to be staying there stretched out to a week, then ten days. He sometimes stayed there for two weeks at a time, spending the other half of his months at Chapultepec, for he now refused to reside in the overly large and formal Mexico City palace.

At the Borda garden, visitors checked protocol at the door. The heat was so great that, despite the official mourning still imposed on the court for King Leopold's death, everyone, starting with the emperor himself, dressed in white. Only Charlotte insisted on wearing black from head to toe. It wasn't long, however, before the temperature forced her to wear white, though she kept her black belts and trimmings as a reminder of her loss, and as a constant reproach to the others. For around her, everyone was having a grand old time: luncheons and dinners went on for hours. Maximilian had summoned the members of his court to Cuernavaca, but also some Austrians he once knew or who belonged to the legion sent by Francis-Joseph. They spoke of women, even in Charlotte's presence, each man waxing lyrical on the wonders of this beauty or that. Maximilian spoke like an old sage on the matter, teasing the men on their true or imaginary affairs. His particular target was the minister Don Martin Castillo, who was rumored to have fallen in love with a local girl.

Charlotte said nothing during these somewhat bawdy and innuendo-ridden exchanges. She simply put on a sad smile, and only lifted her eyes to cast melancholy looks upon her husband — a detail that escaped no one, least of all the butler Blasio.

Sometimes, at night, the mayor hosted a modest ball, and everyone at the Borda garden hastened to attend. The young women and girls from local society put on bright dresses and embroidered silk shawls, and in their hair, they pinned the most beautiful flowers that grew in their gardens. All the women knew how to dance the languid Pacific coast dances beautifully, and the men joined them joyfully. Even if Maximilian did not dance, his eye jumped from one woman to the next — so much so that Maximilian often took advantage of the ball to invite the most beautiful women to a party at the Borda garden. Charlotte saw it all, and her mood declined visibly.

Bit by bit, rumors started to circulate. Blasio overheard little asides and whispered comments: the emperor was cheating on the empress, the emperor had mistresses. Or maybe just one mistress, an Indian, the daughter of a government official from Cuernavaca. She was seventeen years old and stunning. She was the same woman rumored to have driven the minister, Don Martin Castillo, the butt of Maximilian's jokes, to distraction.

Blasio wanted to check into this rumor. How could the emperor have cheated on the empress when Blasio stayed with him day and night? He knocked at Maximilian's door at dawn, and between the horseback rides, the work sessions, and meals with the court, did not leave his master's side until nighttime. It was true that his duties ended at eight o'clock, and that the emperor spent his evenings as he saw fit. But then there was the empress, a constant fixture at Cuernavaca. There again, rumor had it that the only reason she was always there was not because she loved her husband, but because she was filled with jealousy and determined to spy on him. Now, Charlotte was no night owl. She spent the hours after dinner with her ladies-in-waiting, reading aloud or knitting, then at ten o'clock, she retired to her room and her surveillance ended. What did Maximilian do then? That is what Blasio wanted to find out.

The emperor had changed. The climate, food, and atmosphere of this lavish and attractive, though disorienting and even confusing, country had had an effect on him. The overly spicy foods that he washed down with too much wine and champagne had ruined his liver. He suffered almost constantly from a form of malaria that made him shake with chronic dysentery. Once so careful about his person, he no longer even got dressed. He passed from the deepest melancholy that left him listless for hours to an almost frenzied optimism for unrealistic plans. His normally sarcastic personality was drifting into bitterness. The haughty son of Austrian kaisers had become an epitome of the many Europeans that this seductive and poisonous country ground down into tragic figures. In this setting, it is easy to imagine the former archduke, unshaven and listless, his foot dangling from his hammock, spending his time listening to the strange cries of exotic birds and calling for tequila from the Indian *niña* whose long braids were tied with pink ribbons.

Perhaps Maximilian had not sunk so low, and yet . . . centuries of Spanish Catholic oppression had never succeeded in transforming Mexicans, and especially Mexican women, into prudes. And in Cuernavaca especially, there floated over the sovereigns a feeling of freedom, even permissiveness, that could never have existed in the capital. Whereas, at the Imperial Palace or at Chapultepec, the white representatives of European extraction formed a barrier around the couple, at Cuernavaca, Indian society had complete access to them. Moreover, for millennia, the Indians of Mexico had been among the most expert in matters of drugs, concocted from strange plants unknown to Europe. These infamous drugs, dating from the most ancient pre-Columbian history and celebrated in the literature of the 1930s, transport their users into a paradise some claim is artificial, and amplify sexual potency. The Spanish colonists had enthusiastically adopted the previously unknown recipes and consumed them in huge quantities. Like the masses, Mexican high society continued to use them in the most natural way in the world.

Why would Maximilian have been an exception? There is no doubt that his entourage had experimented. Why would he, so curious and weak before temptation, not have done the same? Picture Maximilian's parties in the Borda garden: Charlotte had retired to go knit or read with her ladies. Only men were left, and conversation had become looser and more licentious. Everyone told of his experiences and adventures, duly spiced with the normal bragging. Under the hot and starry night, Maximilian listened without trying to hide his interest.

"What, sire, you have never tried it? You feel so good afterward."

The cup or glass materialized. Maximilian hesitated but a moment, then swallowed it down. Within moments, the world appeared transformed, his worries melted away, no matter how serious they were, his problems seemed to solve themselves. The Indian women at Cuernavaca did not intimidate him in the least. On the short side, with skin of a copper hue, immense, dark eyes, brilliant smiles, and the familiarity inherent in the Tropics, they came and went, they enticed, they made love naturally with whomever they pleased. One or another of them slipped into Maximilian's bedroom or waited for him in a garden pavilion near the moonlit fountain. Thanks to their caresses, his inhibitions, already undermined by the drugs, then completely faded away. If they did not give him back all his potency, at least they seemed to, and that was what was important. He felt his manhood; he reveled in his power and strength . . . at least until the next morning, when he had to emerge from the drugs' mists. Meanwhile, Charlotte, whom in his drug-filled haze, he had seen ramrod erect and straight-laced in her black dresses, no longer impressed him. She reminded him so much of his mother, Archduchess Sophie. These two women of character, whom he adored, tried to govern and control him. How many times had he given in, especially to his wife? But his wife had paid the price, and that price was his desire—and for some time, he had felt no attraction for the beautiful and seductive woman, whose superiority had left him frigid.

Archduchess Sophie had coddled her favorite son who, as he had admitted to his brother-in-law Leopold, had married when he was still a virgin. He loved Charlotte, he still loved her, he could not live without her, but she killed all desire in him. Blasio noticed that they slept apart, and in a gossip-hungry court that would have reported the slightest occurrence, there was no mention of Maximilian ever having a mistress—until he began staying at Cuernavaca. The talk on everyone's lips was the affair he may have had with this or that local beauty, always an Indian or half-Indian.

Charlotte knew, or, even worse, sensed everything. Maximilian began by abandoning her physically; then he went on to deprive her of power and to reduce her to a secondary role. Now he was cheating on her with natives. All this when King Leopold, her father, support, and counselor, the source of her strength, had just died. Never before had Charlotte felt so completely alone. Not a word, not a single complaint slipped past her pursed lips. Instead, she wrapped herself in even more mourning shawls, stiffening into an obvious frigidity and pretended disdain. To her relatives and friends, she wrote that she loved the life she was leading at Cuernavaca.

Yet this strange remark did escape her: "I follow national politics in the newspapers," which proves that Maximilian no longer told her anything, and that she was not privy to confidential state information. She was aware that on the old Continent, people were saying it was only out of vanity and ambition that she was holding onto what had become the impossible dream of an empire. That was untrue, she protested in a letter to the countess of Hulste. She was no dupe of vainglory. As for ambition, was she supposed to hop on the next boat for Europe the minute a few dark clouds appeared on the horizon? No, she would never turn back: "Put yourself in my place and wonder if a life at Miramar is preferable to a life in Mexico City. No, a hundred times no. And for my part, I prefer a position that offers activity and duties, even difficulties, if you insist, to sitting and staring at the sea until I am seventy years old." She had said it—she would never give up.

At the time, an odd French priest by the name of Father Domenach was living in Mexico. With a penchant for literature, this man also had a remarkable gift for observation. Perhaps he had even acted as Charlotte's confessor. In any case, this military chaplain, who had become the press office chief for Maximilian, was well situated to see and understand what was going on. In his carefully diplomatic way, he defined Charlotte: "An imperial crown may well have seduced her, but it is not blind ambition that pushed her to throwing her august husband into this venture. History must maintain a certain discretion and speak only of public matters, and thus I shall remain silent on the true reasons for her legitimate ambition and for the feverish activity of her noble intelligence and ardent nature, so in need of the outlet afforded by a great undertaking." In simpler terms, Charlotte was unhappy, Charlotte was frustrated; yet she had found her one, irreplaceable means of expression in her crown and the duties it entailed, so she would never give it up. If she lost it, she would waste away.

As if Charlotte needed it, a new misfortune befell her while she was in Mexico City: her beloved grandmother Marie-Amelie died. In her will Marie-Amelie left Charlotte an impressive amount of jewels, paintings, and objets d'art that Charlotte could easily have lived without. Charlotte felt as if it were her mother who had died all over again, especially since it had happened at such a difficult point in her life. Her migraines returned, and she remained bedridden in utter silence. Her condition became so alarming that her entourage sent her off to find solitude in Cuernavaca, to rest and recover a while. Maximilian immediately returned to Chapultepec, and the couple's game of hide-and-seek continued. Locked away in the Borda garden's little paradise, Charlotte concentrated her attention on things of no consequence: a bird that flew over her, a rare butterfly that passed by, the national habanera that she was trying to learn to play on her mandolin. But what horrible thoughts were torturing the brain of this woman sitting quietly in her garden, what inner storm was swirling in her mind as she gently leaned over to sniff a tea rose?

In truth, Cuernavaca had become intolerable to Charlotte ever since she began suspecting her husband of infidelity. As soon as she felt a little better, she rushed back to the city. Her coach was pulled by twelve snow-white mules with blue harnesses. The coachman and the squires in their embroidered and silver-encrusted uniforms wore huge gray sombreros. Inside her coach was everything she needed to write and snack on. During the trip, as always, Indians from the towns and countryside that lined the court procession's path came to behold the magical spectacle. Charlotte did not even see them. She decided against Chapultepec, her favorite residence, setting herself up instead in the immense old palace in the center of the capital.

Naturally, barely had Charlotte returned to Mexico City when Maximilian left again for Cuernavaca. "My sincerest thanks for your charming letter of yesterday, which brought me great joy and consolation," he wrote her. "How sorry I am to hear that you are melancholy. To remedy that condition, which is generally caused by an ailing stomach or liver, you must walk and work a lot. I also miss your presence. It is much less pleasant and fun than the other times. Moreover, just now I have a great deal of work. . . ." Where was the fiery longing and passion he had expressed all the other times they had been apart? From now on, the coolness would be palpable—an unspoken indifference that may well have betrayed the effects of both artificial paradises and petite Indian women. In his selfishness, Maximilian did not want to witness Charlotte's melancholy, since he was the one to blame for it. He did not realize that he was the reason she no longer had anything left to do. No more ministers' councils, no more audiences, no more laws or constitutions.

Charlotte wandered idly from room to room, chewing furiously at her handkerchief, tearing at the monogram, silent and wounded. When she sank to her lowest points, she could not even offer herself rides around town in her convertible coach, for she would come across the stares of the curious, and they would see through her. Instead, she would go down the steps (still today called "the Empress's staircase"), leave the place as the sun set behind the canal left over from Aztec times, board a long boat, and set out for Chalco lake, one of several near the capital. She would drift away from the shoreline, watching the gentle wake her boat left in the calm waters. She would go where no one could follow her, wholly given over to her misery, far from others and their eyes. Each time she went out farther, until the shore disappeared into the rays of the dying day.

Holed up amidst the flowers and birds of Cuernavaca, with its country walks and more secret pastimes, Maximilian was ready for bad news. The first of it came from his childhood friend, Bombelles. Maximilian had sent him to Vienna, where Bombelles, who had been raised at the Austrian court, knew everyone. Maximilian had first ordered him to reassure his family, Archduchess Sophie in particular. Indeed, the alarming reports on Mexico and the constant newspaper articles foretelling the empire's end had deeply panicked the imperial family. "Everything is fine, don't worry" was the message that Bombelles repeated, and that was only half believed. Next, Bombelles sounded out the emperor for the possibility of increasing military aid to Mexico: since the French troops were withdrawing, why should Austrians not replace them? Impossible, Francis-Joseph replied. The third mission was to see if it might be possible to consider toning down the renunciation Maximilian had been forced to sign. Bombelles told Francis-Joseph that Max had proclaimed with all due conviction that he would never leave Mexico, but just in the case, in the event that one day he might be forced to, he was fully aware that he would be nothing anymore in Austria. True to form, Francis-Joseph refused even to entertain the request. Bombelles had nothing left to do but return to Maximilian and deliver his report of a triple failure.

On the heels of this series of disappointments came Eloin's equally pessimistic report. Eloin had been on a mission to Belgium, where he had expected to be welcomed with open arms. But King Leopold II had not even deigned to receive him, thus insulting both Charlotte and Maximilian.

The third messenger, Loysel, came back from Paris, where he had met with Napoleon III and Empress Eugenie. Both of them truly felt for Maximilian and Charlotte. With all their hearts, they would have loved to help their friends, but their government, parliament, and public opinion prevented them from doing so. Whatever his personal feelings, Loysel was first and foremost a French officer—he would not criticize France in front of Maximilian.

Already weighed down by all the bad news, Maximilian could not help but suspect that Loysel had betrayed his confidence. When the recall of French troops was announced, Maximilian's first reaction had been to take Napoleon III violently at his word. Since then, prudence, if not his counselors, had convinced him to try to delay the troops' withdrawal as long as possible, and by whatever means necessary. For this last-ditch mission, Maximilian chose a man who had been faithful since the beginning: Almonte, whom he immediately expedited to Paris.

Meanwhile, Maximilian continued to reign, and thus to act. He founded a new national theater, gathered archeological collections in a museum, and acquired portraits of his predecessors, the viceroys and presidents. He expanded Alameda, the city's meeting point; planted trees on the Zocalo; and finished "el Paseo de la emperatriz," the wide avenue connecting Chapultepec to the capital, opening it to the public. During the few free moments he enjoyed, he fine-tuned his plans for Miramar: each courier going to Europe bore instructions for the architects to furnish such and such a room, or for the gardeners to change the flowers in this garden or that. Taking care of his beloved residence, which in principle he was never supposed to see again, gave Maximilian a few moments of healthy escape.

Charlotte tried to find something to occupy her time within the tight limits her husband had set for her. She had been put in charge of gathering objects to represent Mexico in the following year's Worlds Fair in Paris. Without rhyme or reason, she chose a few religious paintings, a collection of laws published by the empire, an album of photographs showing the different provinces, folkloric dress, some fruit, a model of the ruins at Uxmal she herself had visited, bottles of mescal, Cordoba coffee, Orizaba tobacco, cigarettes from the Yucatán, the complete works of Mexican poets, native ebony furniture and bookshelves, a full collection of coins bearing Maximilian's image, court almanacs, and finally, marble busts of herself and Maximilian.

Their respective activities did not require the empress and emperor to meet, and with Maximilian at his refuge in Cuernavaca while Charlotte was cloistered at the Mexico City palace, they no longer appeared in public. Moreover, in order to combat the financial crisis, they had to cut court spending drastically. Gone were the great spectacles where the monarchy paraded in sumptuous procession, the flocks of ladies-in-waiting, the gentlemen's embroidered uniforms. The only thing left was the exciting life of the capital. The theaters were sold out, horse racing went on every day, as did the concerts and military orchestras on Alameda, the romantic meetings of beautiful people, and the coach rides on the new Empress Boulevard.

Due to the lack of money, the soldiers were no longer paid, and they were hungry. They were forbidden to leave their camps or they would be considered deserters. To the south, Oaxaca still held out, but its garrison was under siege by the same flamboyant rebel chief, Porfirio Diaz, who had once lost the city to Bazaine. To the north, Juárez brilliantly resumed the offensive with the help of barely hidden American funds, American weapons smuggled to him, and "volunteers" sent by Washington to bolster his troops. He made a triumphant entrance into the large city of Chihuahua, from which the loyalist troops had chased him several months before. Between Chihuahua and Mexico City, the important city of Matamoros fell easily to dissident troops. Maximilian received both bits of miserable news on the same day.

He had so much work that he spent the whole day in Mexico City, only returning to Chapultepec in time for dinner. He barely took the time to write to Charlotte, who was staying at Cuernavaca since he was in Mexico City: "My dear angel, I thank you from the bottom of my heart for your two adorable letters. I am glad that Cuernavaca is doing such wonders for you and that you are enjoying yourself there. . . ." In one day, he gave an audience to the Spanish minister, held a ministers' council, and drafted a law on the taxation of noncultivated lands.

Then there was more bad news. The dissidents had taken the town of Hermosillo, killing thirty-seven French soldiers in the process.

For the upcoming solemn Feast of Corpus Christi, there was to be no street procession. The ceremony was to take place "solely in the palace, on the second floor, in the galleries of the great patio," Maximilian wrote Charlotte. "It's the best and only solution. That way, we won't have to put up with the sun and the mud, and the priests will see that we know how to celebrate the feast with dignity. You will therefore have the kindness to come back to Mexico

City in the next few days in order to attend the procession. On this occasion, you will wear as many jewels as possible so that no one will think you have sent them off to England for safekeeping. . . ."

Once the feast was over, Charlotte remained in Mexico City, and Maximilian hastened to his Cuernavaca paradise. That was where an aide handed him a thick envelope that had just arrived from Paris—Almonte's report on the negotiations under way with the French government. Maximilian could not fully grasp its meaning, because he did not know that, from Washington, Seward had increased his demands: he had already obtained France's agreement to withdraw her troops from Mexico, and now he wanted them withdrawn immediately.

Once again, Napoleon III had yielded to the pressure and the implied threat from the United States. It was at that very moment that Almonte arrived in Paris. Thus, when Almonte begged the emperor of the French to delay the evacuation, he learned that instead it was to be pushed up. Just for good measure, Napoleon III reminded Almonte that the Mexican empire still owed him most of its debt, and as a guarantee, he asked for half the profits from Mexican customs taxes.

Upon reading the report, for the first time, Maximilian gave in to discouragement. He was overwhelmed by fatigue. Sadly, he looked around him at the trees, the flowers, the fountains. Then he sighed, "There is nothing left to do. I abdicate."

This declaration flew to Mexico City, and to Charlotte. The terrible word "abdicate," far from crushing her, galvanized her immediately. The perspective of finding herself again with Max at Miramar, "staring at the sea until I am seventy years old," made her forget her stupor, and in a flash, she found all her energy restored. First, her childhood memories came flooding back to urge her on.

As a child, she had learned of her grandfather Louis-Philippe's abdication from her parents' mouths. Before his, there had been Charles X's, and before Charles X, several others. By abdicating, each had signed his own condemnation. She had learned from their example, and now she refused to follow it. Charlotte found her arguments, planned her rhetoric, and addressed her plea to Maximilian. Abdication was nothing more than suicide, an admission of one's own incompetence. It was acceptable only from old men or the feebleminded; it was not the act of a thirty-four-year-old prince, full of life and promise. Emperors did not give up—one did not abandon the throne as one left an assembly surrounded by the police. One did not leave one's post in the face of the enemy. In the Middle Ages, kings waited for someone to wrest their lands away from them before they surrendered. Abdication was invented the day the kings forgot how to jump on their horses and defend themselves. It was just a tiny step between being pathetic and being ridiculous. To set out as the champion of civilization, the great liberator, only to pull out with the pretext that there was nothing left to civilize or liberate, was the biggest absurdity that could be done on Earth. If they had lost all their credit and money, there would always be a way to find more, but it was essential not to lose hope in oneself. Her conclusion: the only way to save Mexico was to continue the empire. Everything had to be done to preserve it, for they had sworn an oath, and no excuse could undo that sacred bond. The empire had to go on.

Her words struck Maximilian like the lashes of a whip. But far from putting up a fight, he asked for more. Maybe deep down he liked whiplashes, and Charlotte was more than willing to dole them out. She continued her withering diatribe until Maximilian, as if waking from a bad dream, cried out, "I don't abdicate, I'll stay, I'll go on!"

The surprising thing is that Charlotte never spoke these words aloud. She did not see Maximilian in person to deliver her speech, but instead she wrote it down, and just reading it was enough to rouse Maximilian from his depression.

After so many weeks spent fleeing Charlotte, Maximilian arrived from Cuernavaca, Charlotte from Mexico City, and at last they found themselves face-to-face in Chapultepec, their creation.

Maximilian had perhaps made a brave decision, but how could he put it into practice without the French? Charlotte revolted: the French had to stay, no matter what the cost. Without them, the empire would not last. Carried on by her momentum, she took the initiative. She announced to Maximilian that she herself would go to France to request an extension of the troops' stay in Mexico. Where underlings like Eloin, Loysel, and Almonte had failed, the empress would succeed. Once again, she was sure of the power of reason and of her own feminine abilities to persuade. They had nothing left to lose — why should she not try? She alone could make Napoleon III see the true situation in Mexico and the full impor-tance of the French presence.

Maximilian accepted. Charlotte would go to France and plead their cause. The same man who, just a few months before, had de-nied his wife any power whatsoever now bowed before her initia-tive, for he was decidedly still under her yoke.

Charlotte's decision could not have long remained a secret, for already the rumors abounded: the empress was going to leave, the empress would never come back, the emperor would soon leave after her, the empire was over, they were giving up.

For Maximilian's name day, which at the time fell on the sixth of July, Charlotte decided that in order to silence the gossip, the *Te Deum* would be conducted with particular splendor. She was getting dressed when news reached her that in Europe, Prussia had at-tacked Austria. War had begun.

Maximilian immediately decided he would not take part in the *Te Deum* to be given in his honor. Charlotte put on her imperial outfit, the embroidered white gown and the long gold and red coat of which her grandmother Marie-Amelie so disapproved. She was wearing her most precious jewels. The palace guards were resplendent in their newly polished silver breastplates, the pages were dressed in their gleaming livery, and the chamberlains in their dress uniforms. The ladies-in-waiting, in the latest fashion, had taken out their best family jewels. The procession started off with Charlotte enthroned alone in the enormous rococo coach brought from Vienna. The sun was shining, the flags snapped in the wind, the military orchestras played the national anthem, the crowds cheered — everything was going beautifully.

At the cathedral doors, the archbishop and his clergy were waiting in their gala finest. A throne had been installed in the usual place, behind a gold prie-dieu. Charlotte kneeled and lost herself in prayer. She remained with her face in her hands for a long time, as if the crowd and the officials were of no importance. Then she emerged from meditation and returned to the world.

As usual, at the end of the ceremony, a reception was scheduled at the Imperial Palace. Charlotte received the authorities' respects and gave an elegant little speech. Then, after a low curtsy to the people, she retired, followed by her ladies, into an adjacent room. Now that the chore was through, it was time for relaxation. The noble Mexican women in their silk and crinoline primped and preened in a flutter around the empress who was glittering with diamonds. Suddenly, one of them, Madam Panceco, approached the idol. "May I kiss Your Majesty?"

In her surprise, Charlotte held out her cheek. The lady kissed it, then burst into tears. "What is wrong, Madam Panceco?"

"Ah, milady, I am wondering if this is not the last time we will be accompanying Your Majesty."

The other women froze in their tracks. Charlotte stared at them one by one, detecting the same anxiety in their eyes as in Madam Panceco's. She went around and silently kissed each one in turn. Some maintained control of themselves, others let themselves cry. Then, her eyes red, barely holding back the tears, Charlotte left for her private suite after a last wave to the assembled company. In her room, she removed the diadem, the necklaces, the earrings, and then she left for Chapultepec, where no cheering multitudes, no arches of triumph, decorations, or fireworks awaited her. She found herself in the silence of the vast castle, alone with a weakened, depressed, and feverish Maximilian.

They remained alone together behind closed doors for two full days, seeing almost no one. On the evening of July 8, 1866, Madam Bazaine was dozing in her elegant Mexico City residence, where she was recovering from giving birth to a son, when her bedroom door suddenly flew open to reveal Empress Charlotte. "I am leaving tomorrow for Europe, and I have come to say good-bye. Pray to God for the success of my mission and for me to return soon."

Despite her astonishment, Pepita was truly moved. She saw tears glistening in Charlotte's eyes. The empress leaned over and embraced her. "I will be the one to safeguard the emperor's crown," she said.

Then Charlotte returned as quickly as possible to Chapultepec. As night finally fell, the candles were lit and gas lamps appeared from nowhere. Charlotte and Maximilian disappeared into a room, locking the door behind them. There would be no maudlin sentiment; it would be politics before everything. They discussed what she would have to do, and how she would have to do it, and Charlotte, like the good wife, listened to Maximilian's instructions as if they were gospel. They parted early.

The departure was scheduled for four o'clock the next morning, on July 9, 1866. Those who would stay and those who would go had assembled in the palace courtyard. Bombelles, Maximilian's faithful childhood friend, would be going, since Maximilian had asked him to watch over his wife; and with him, two ministers, several members of Charlotte's household, the grand chamberlain, Count del Valle, and the Barrio family. Charlotte had long known Madam del Barrio, the daughter of Gutierrez d'Estrada, one of the empire's first supporters, and granddaughter of Countess Lutzoff, the one who had inspired Maximilian's candidacy in the first place. The treasurer Kuhacsevich and his wife would also be accompanying her. Maximilian had described them as perfectly acclimated to Mexico, but the truth was that they were dying to return to Europe, for they did not like Mexico very much. There were also the servants, the baggage piled high on wagons, the coaches the travelers were boarding, the mules that were being yoked, and the cavalry officers that would be escorting the empress.

Maximilian had left his sickbed to ride out from the capital with Charlotte. The empress looked out one last time at the spectacular view over the plain, where the dawn's light was growing brighter with each passing minute. The couple rode out together to the little village of Ajotlan, just outside of Mexico City, where the convoy came to a halt. They descended from their coach and Maximilian took Charlotte in his arms. She kept her self-discipline, but Maximilian, weakened by his illness, burst into tears. He sobbed uncontrollably in front of everyone. His aides rushed up to support him and led him back to his own coach, which took the road to Chapultepec. Charlotte felt the tears welling up in her eyes, but bravely fought them back. Just as she felt she was about to faint, she regained her composure, and managed to look away from the coach that whisked her husband from her, and climbed back up into hers.

✤   ✤   ✤

The first stop was at Rio Frio, where the poor Baron of Huart had
been killed. The accommodations were questionable at best. Charlotte showed no irritation, and instead maintained a placidity and
tranquility that astounded her entourage. She thought solely of
Maximilian, and she wrote him to relieve the pain of their separation, but also to breathe some of her own strength into him: "Swear
that you will not give up. . . . My heart would be broken if I were
to learn that you had given up. . . . Luckily, I know you well enough
not to believe that of you, and that will console me, though an ocean
separates us." She knew that her husband was in despair. "How
much it hurts me to be apart from you, I cannot tell you," he wrote
her back. "To know that my companion, the star of my life, is so
far away, just as Europe is aflame, that is very hard. These months
during which the ocean will keep us apart will be the hardest challenge of my life, but when striving toward a great goal, one must
know how to make great sacrifices. . . ." To take Maximilian's mind
off that, Charlotte told him of her voyage.

At Puebla, the authorities welcomed her in accordance with
protocol, but she also heard hostile shouts as she passed by. Esteva,
the imperial representative to the city, was not there. Perhaps he
did not wish to publicly greet the sovereign of an empire without
much chance of survival. He was replaced by Madam Esteva and
her palace ladies, and after the official dinner, Charlotte asked to
be brought to the woman's house, since she had heard so much
about it and would like to see it. It was but a minor whim, but one
that, later on, blown out of proportion and twisted, took on enormous significance.

The welcome at Orizaba was palpably warmer. Hundreds of
horsemen came out to meet her. An old doctor whom she had decorated the year before with the medal of civil merit shouted out,
"Long live our august sovereign Carlottita, little Charlotte!"

At Cordoba, she was greeted icily. The miserable weather, with its torrential rain, thunder and lightning, and the *vomito negro* must have been to blame, she thought. The storm was so violent and the roads so bad that the wagon bearing the luggage tipped over. Soon, an axle of the empress's gentlemen's carriage broke, and the whole vehicle overturned. Charlotte went through the trouble of detailing all the repairs that needed to be done to the roads, and suddenly transformed into a transportation engineer, she sang the praises of pavement.

As the storm grew even more violent, floods and mudslides broke out everywhere. When night fell, the baggage wagon overturned again, and this time, she did not have the patience to wait for it to be repaired. She left her luggage in the mud and pressed on to the locality known as Paso del Macho, where she spent the night.

The next day, she arrived at Veracruz, where she was received by the municipal council and...the French navy. No one else, no cheering crowds or even a single curious onlooker. Charlotte admitted that the scene was fairly sad. Perhaps the people misunderstood and thought she was leaving for good, and Charlotte understood their cold reaction. Moreover, the sticky heat could not inspire anyone to come outside.

The authorities accompanied her to the dock where the French steamer that would bring her to Europe, the *Empress Eugenie*, was moored. Noticing that only the French flag fluttered above the tall mast, Charlotte declared that the empress of Mexico would not board it until the Mexican flag was also hoisted on the ship meant to transport her. Only when the captain executed her wish did she agree to step into the rowboat, after taking her leave of the authorities. "In three months time, I will be back," she promised them in a clear voice.

Greeted onboard by the captain, she immediately went down to her cabin and locked herself in. She would not come on deck for the ship's departure, nor would she watch the coast of Mexico slowly disappear against the horizon. In her memory, she recalled the song that her adversaries had composed against her and whose ironic lyrics, sung to the tune of "La Paloma," she heard during the course of her wearing trip:

Adiós mamá Carlotta
Adiós mi tierno amor
Se fueron los Franceses
Se va el emperador.

Farewell mama Charlotte
Farewell my tender love
The French are gone
The emperor is going.

10

The coast of Mexico had long since disappeared; the ship was sailing in the open sea. Like most of the other passengers, Charlotte kept a travel log. A spacious, comfortable, first-class cabin. The food, excellent if not imaginative, gave no cause for complaint. But in the Gulf of Mexico, summer was a season of high winds, even of hurricanes. The ship pitched and rocked. Never one for the sea, Charlotte was suffering from seasickness. Her cabin was situated astern, above the engines, whose awful smell and noise prevented her from getting any sleep. And the infinite blue expanse extending in every direction around the ship, without so much as an island to break the monotony, filled her, she admitted, with anguish.

After three days of sailing, the ship arrived at Cuba, still a Spanish colony at the time, and anchored off Havana. Charlotte looked at the beautiful yellow houses with their green shutters. She remarked that the population must not have had anyone of African extraction, since she spotted only Spanish tropical types: pale, lanky, and very tall. Though at first she was nervous about the sort of welcome that awaited her, she was soon reassured. The flagship of the Spanish fleet fired off a twenty-one-gun salute in her honor, and the authorities, led by the *correjidor* and the archbishop, came aboard the *Empress Eugenie* to pay their respects. Charlotte would not go ashore, and instead limited herself to a rowboat ride around the bay. She enjoyed the incessant movement of small and big ships on the background of lush vegetation; the picturesque poetry of old Spain mixed with the opulence of worldly wealth under an enchanting sky reminded her of the beauties of the Mediterranean, though in colors much richer and more beautiful. In the local paper, she noticed an ad for a slave auction. Five hundred pesos for a cook, two hundred for a coachman, a hundred for a nanny, half price for a sick slave . . .

The ship now undertook the long crossing of the Atlantic; three and a half weeks without interruption. Every day at noon, the captain knocked at Charlotte's door to show her the ship's position. The empress leaned over her maps, and before he could even open his mouth, she pointed out the spot where according to her calculations, the ship must be. Much to the captain's surprise, she was always right.

Most of the time, she remained locked in her cabin to think, analyze, and prepare for her mission, but she did not live the life of a recluse by any stretch of the imagination. Once she learned that there was a sculptor named Garbeille aboard, she decided to try her hand at sculpting. Garbeille was summoned to give her lessons, and her cabin was transformed into a workshop. She picked it up so quickly that within a few days, she was able to sculpt the cameo profile of her lady-in-waiting, Madam del Barrio. She also came up on deck, despite the anguish she felt at the sight of the infinite expanse of water, and the passengers, keeping a respectful distance, saw her laughing with Bombelles, Kuhacsevich, and other members of her entourage. Then she went astern and leaned against the rail, staring motionless for hours in the direction of Mexico. She would return in only three months, and already she could not wait.

Her wedding anniversary fell during the crossing. From Chapultepec, on July 27, 1866, Maximilian wrote her the most moving testimony of his love: "On this day, the anniversary of my happiness, I cannot fail to write you, my angel and the star of my life. For nine years now, I have owed you the solace and happiness in my life. Anything good or beautiful that I have ever felt has always come from you. How terrible it is to be separated by the sea on this sublime day. These days are the most bitter of my life. Never have I felt so unhappy and depressed, and only my duty and my love for you, my life, keep me going."

On August 8, 1866, the *Empress Eugenie* anchored off Saint-Nazaire. Charlotte scanned the brand-new city, pride of the French empire's shipbuilding docks. Having always preferred the beauty of old cities, she saw little more than deserted stretches, and ugly, sad rows of houses and apartment buildings. She was expecting twenty-one-gun salutes and visits from the local authorities, but unlike the welcome she received in Havana, this time no one showed up. A rowboat was launched from the deserted pier. It bore the Mexican empire's representative to Paris, General Almonte, and his wife, who sheepishly held out a bouquet of wilted roses to Charlotte. Immediately after them, in another rowboat, the mayor arrived and stuttered out an awkward, rehearsed compliment. By the force of her upbringing, Charlotte responded with a few kind words, but she was still stunned: there was no prefect, no troops for a salute, no official reception. Where was everyone? Not knowing what to answer, the mayor flailed about a little more, then proposed a visit of the city, some refreshments, and a stop in one of the excellent hotels that had just been opened. "I want to leave immediately for Paris," Charlotte firmly replied. There was no train available, so they would have to spend the night in Saint-Nazaire. "Where are the carriages to bring us to the hotel?" There were none. They hailed a coach. Charlotte climbed up into it with her lady-in-waiting; the rest would have to follow on foot.

Charlotte had the honesty to admit that the hotel was rather comfortable. She took advantage of the wasted day to telegraph Napoleon III: "I have arrived at Saint-Nazaire, under orders from the emperor to discuss with Your Majesty various matters concerning Mexico. I ask you to transmit my best wishes to the empress and to believe me when I tell you of the great happiness I will feel to see Your Majesties again." The emperor of the French's response came quickly and brutally: "I have just received Your Majesty's telegram. Having returned ill from Vichy and being now forced to remain bedridden, I cannot come to meet you. If, as I expect, Your Majesty first goes to Belgium, that will give me the time to recuperate." In simpler terms, I do not want to see you, especially not now, so first go to your family and we will advise later. Charlotte blanched under the affront. Already the reception, or rather lack thereof, was an insult. And now the one for whom she left her husband and crossed the Atlantic, the one who represented her final hope, was shunning her. He had already made her waste an entire day in a city devoid of interest, in an ordinary hotel, with nothing to do but worry.

To top it off, as a welcome, Almonte told her that a few days before, in Bohemia, Austria was attacked by Prussia and suffered a crushing defeat at Sadowa. Beaten and humiliated, Austria had been forced to sue for peace. Charlotte's thoughts flew to Maximilian and to the sorrow he would feel when he learned the news. Even more importantly, this lightning bolt in the European sky would not make her task any easier. She realized that she had arrived at the worst possible moment.

The whole morning of the next day was spent in forced idleness. The sun was shining, it was warm, but Charlotte was in no mood to go out. Her blood was boiling. In the middle of the afternoon, she was finally able to board a train.

In several hours, she reached Montparnasse station in Paris. A few Mexicans, including Gutierrez d'Estrada, old Lutzoff's son-in-law, were there to meet her, but there was no sign of an envoy from Napoleon III, not a single coach from the court. As she climbed down from the train, Charlotte felt the earth give way beneath her and clutched onto one of the members of the rather meager welcoming committee. "Bring me your carriage." Since no invitation had come for her, she would not be staying at the palace, as she had hoped, as protocol had directed, and as friendship had demanded. The Mexicans had reserved her some rooms at the Grand-Hotel. Ever sensitive to the nuances of protocol, Charlotte was wounded to her core by the treatment she had received—she, a reigning sovereign. The poor welcome only amplified the humiliation she felt at her role as beggar and her worries about the success of her mission.

The coach slowed down on the Boulevard des Capucines, passed through the triple-arched portico, and entered the ceremonial courtyard of the Grand-Hotel. Charlotte descended from the coach amid the normal hustle and bustle of carriages, travelers, luggage, and porters. Pale, purse-lipped, and silent, she barely responded to the nervous greetings of the director who brought her up to the suite reserved for her.

She entered her room. Twin beds under a canopy, red drapes, a marble fireplace, the omnipresent mirror—a far cry from the luxury of the Tuileries. From her window, she could see the new neighborhoods being built around the Boulevard des Capucines, in particular the immense construction site that would become the new Paris opera house.

Soon Napoleon III's aide, General de Genlis, arrived, red-faced and embarrassed. He had indeed been ordered to welcome Charlotte at the station with carriages from the court. The only problem was that he had gotten the station wrong, and had been waiting for her at Orleans station. Charlotte calmed down slightly. Genlis gave her a message from Eugenie: "At what time tomorrow would Your Majesty like to receive Her Majesty?" "Anytime she likes," Charlotte answered. After apologizing once again, Genlis took his leave. The ordeal had shaken Charlotte. She asked for tea, then went to lie down.

The next morning, she remained in her room. Where would she go in a city that welcomed her so meanly, in a Paris that she had known since her childhood but that now seemed so hostile?

It was not yet two o'clock when she went downstairs to the ground floor. From the last step, she heard the carriages and saw the agitation in the street at the approach of the French empress's procession. As Eugenie entered, Charlotte went forward to meet her. The two "sisters" kissed. Charlotte greeted Eugenie's entourage as Eugenie greeted hers. The Mexican women curtsied to the French empress, the French women curtsied to the empress of Mexico.

They went upstairs to a small salon, a white and gold room, with a purple marble fireplace decorated with an overly ornate clock placed between two oriental vases. The armchairs covered in faux cashmere were vast and comfortable. The two empresses congratulated each other under the crystal chandelier. As they exchanged news, they sized each other up.

Charlotte noticed that the empress had lost some of her youth, and some of her energy. She no longer had that drive and airy grace that had once so characterized her. Still wonderfully elegant in her Worth crinoline, she nonetheless showed her years, and Charlotte could not help thinking that "in France, the throne quickly ages those who occupy it." Eugenie noticed Charlotte's wrinkled and dusty clothes, and the paleness, the uptight feeling she exuded, the fiery glimmer in her dark eyes, the square chin that denoted determination, the briskness of her gestures.

Eugenie overwhelmed Charlotte with questions about Mexico, just as one friend would ask another who has just come back from a sightseeing tour. Charlotte answered politely, but with fewer and fewer words. Finally they broached the subject of the political problem. Charlotte gave an astounding report on the situation of the empire and on the need for French aid. In reply, Eugenie could only hesitatingly offer banal and unconnected observations that betrayed her total ignorance of the question. "My word," Charlotte told herself, "she knows less about our country than she does about China, even though our country is the biggest undertaking of Napoleon III's reign." But she was not discouraged. She resumed the logical progression of her arguments, which she had also written down, and she finished up by presenting Eugenie with a long memorandum for her husband.

Eugenie kept changing the subject in an attempt to avoid at all costs the question she knew Charlotte was dying to ask, so much so that Charlotte eventually blurted it out: "When may I return the favor of the visit that Your Majesty has given me today?"

"The day after tomorrow, if that is convenient to Your Majesty."

"And may I see the emperor as well?"

"The emperor is very ill."

"The day after tomorrow is Sunday. I wish to see him tomorrow . . . otherwise I will burst my way into Saint-Cloud." For fear of Charlotte, and perhaps also out of regret for the poor treatment she had given her, Eugenie gave in. Until tomorrow, then.

Charlotte spent that whole night and the next morning, August 11, 1866, rereading Maximilian's instructions, memorizing the facts, numbers, and statistics, reorganizing her plea. She knew that the imminent interview would decide the empire's fate, as well as Maximilian's and hers. Would Napoleon give in? She did not even ask the question. Bracing herself with her sense of duty, she would do what she had to; the rest was in God's hands.

She got dressed with her chambermaids' help, choosing to wear a black dress, which, though ironed, still showed the effects of a month-long trip at sea. She had sent Madam del Barrio to buy her a white hat in one of the boutiques on Rue Saint Honoré. She was ready to go much too early, and paced back and forth with nervousness, constantly running to the window to see whether the court coaches had arrived.

Exactly at noon, the coaches came to a halt before the hotel. Charlotte got in, accompanied by her ladies-in-waiting. Having learned of the empress's arrival in the newspapers, the curious recognized her as the procession passed by and applauded her. No matter how lost in thought she was, she responded to their cheers graciously out of habit. They passed through the Bois de Boulogne, crossed the bridge, and entered the magnificent park of Saint-Cloud. At the top of the slope, the coaches rode into the courtyard of the vast palace built by Charlotte's own ancestors, the Orleans, a palace so splendid that it had aroused even the jealousy of Louis XIV. The soldiers jumped to attention, the drums beat, the trumpets sounded, the officers tilted their sabers; the entire court had come together to welcome the empress of Mexico. It was now, for the first time since she arrived in Paris, that Charlotte found herself back in her element, the pomp of monarchy. The bright August sun brought out the gold of the uniforms, the colors of the crinolines, feathers, and diamonds. Among the courtiers, the inveterate gossip Prosper Mérimée remarked that Charlotte's ladies-in-waiting, whom everyone had believed to be languid beauties, actually had skin the color of gingerbread and looked rather like orangutans! On the other hand, he made this comment of Charlotte, which out of his mouth was a compliment: "She is a masterful woman who looks just like Louis-Philippe."

The young imperial prince, whom Charlotte had seen two years before when she had come to see her relatives, helped her down from her coach. He was wearing the Mexican decoration that Maximilian had sent him. Eugenie, who was waiting on the staircase, rushed forward to Charlotte and embraced her. Then she led her to Napoleon III's office. Napoleon III greeted the empress with his legendary courtesy, and also with the kind of tenderness and admiration that a ladies' man always brought to bear on a beautiful specimen of womanhood. As they exchanged a few compliments, Charlotte looked around her, struck by the room's austerity. Everywhere there were only maps, filing cabinets, and files—so many files piled up on the tables. There was one large portrait of Eugenie, and a smaller one of the imperial prince. But Charlotte was more interested in Napoleon III. He had changed so much in two years that she could barely recognize him. Not only had he aged, but he seemed a broken man. His kidney stones had taken their toll on his health, and the cures, even the waters he had just taken at Vichy, were to no avail.

His worries were also affecting his health. After Prussia's defeat of Austria, he was finally seeing the extent of the mistake he had made by giving Bismarck free reign. Who would be the next victim? Perhaps France. Lastly, American pressure over Mexico was increasing. From the perspective of the Washington representative in Paris, Charlotte was not even the empress of Mexico anymore.

Charlotte began her plea, following step by step the instructions Maximilian had laid out for her: "You, the French, you say that we have failed in Mexico and that there is no use in going on. First, we have not failed. Of course there are difficulties, but we will surmount them with your help. But if there are delays to the success, it is not because of us, but rather because of you, the French." Then she switched to a merciless list of the French commander in chief's shortcomings. During three years of war, and after spending phenomenal sums of money, Bazaine had not managed to bring the majority of the country under control, neither had he helped the empire raise an army of its own to one day replace the French. The Mexican empire was Napoleon III's own project and desire. To abandon it would mean endangering his own dynasty.

Napoleon III did not answer. Charlotte was horrified to see him come undone before her eyes. His hands trembled; his head bowed lower and lower; he looked exhausted and sick. Tears rolled down his cheeks. Unable to speak, he seemed completely lost, and continuously looked to Eugenie as if he needed help, someone to whisper an answer in his ear. Finally, he managed to mumble that if the choice were up to him, he would do something, but the decision was in other hands. Charlotte exploded. "What? A sovereign ruling over more than thirty million people, the unmatched leader in Europe, with unlimited capital and credit available from anywhere on Earth, with victorious armies always at the ready—that sovereign can do nothing for Mexico where France and he himself have so many interests to protect?"

She had much more to say, but she was suddenly interrupted. A butler in imperial green and gold livery came into the room, presenting a glass of orangeade on a silver platter. Eugenie, herself surprised by this interruption, did not know what to do with the glass, and handed it to Charlotte. Still involved in her argumentation, Charlotte made a gesture to refuse it, then caught herself and found her politeness reflex. She took the glass from Empress Eugenie's hand and drank its contents. She put the glass back down

on the silver platter and the butler disappeared. This minor incident would become a key event in the tale people would later weave
around Charlotte's life.

Distracted by the interruption, Charlotte remained silent for a
few moments. She remembered where she was and started off again,
even more strongly than before. Her arguments were so well set up,
her demonstration so well documented, and her intelligence so well
prepared that Napoleon was left powerless, so he dodged the issue.
He promised Charlotte that he would discuss the question one last
time with his ministers and then give Charlotte his definitive response.
He had turned a shade of green; he could barely stand and seemed
about to faint. Eugenie led Charlotte out to the next room where the
ladies-in-waiting and chamberlains were expecting them. "Of course,
Your Majesty will remain for lunch." No, Charlotte would not remain for lunch. At the risk of offending Eugenie, she asked to be
brought back immediately to her hotel. But lunch was ready, orders
had been given, the coachmen had already gone for their meals. They
would have to wait until the coachmen could be found and the
coaches could be hitched up again.

The minutes passed, minutes that seemed like centuries. Ladies-
in-waiting and chamberlains hugged the walls, hoping to disappear.
Charlotte, with a terrible expression on her face, paced back and
forth in the room in silence, tearing at her embroidered handkerchief. She was suffering as she had never suffered before. After such
a horrible disappointment, she had only one desire: to go back home,
to lock herself in, to be alone, to no longer see those faces turned
toward her, to no longer see those eyes. But she had to wait, and
wait some more.

Finally it was announced that the coaches had arrived, and to
everyone's relief, Charlotte and her entourage took their leave.
Charlotte did not return to her room until the end of the afternoon.
She tore the pins from her hair, threw off her hat, locked the door,

and collapsed into a chair. The golden sunlight of the late afternoon poured in, but she barely noticed it. She thought over the day's events, analyzed Napoleon's words, his looks, his expressions, in an attempt to guess what he was going to do. She was tired, so infinitely tired.

In order to be rid of Charlotte, Napoleon III ended up advising her to meet with his ministers to try and convince them herself. She happily jumped on the opportunity. Starting the very next day, she received them: Drouyn de Lhuys, Marshal Randon, and especially Achille Fould, one of the great promoters of (and profiters from) the Mexican project. She even saw the Austrian ambassador, Napoleon III and Eugenie's close friend Prince Metternich, son of the illustrious chancellor. The ministers proved much tougher than their master; they did not have the slightest amount of pity. But Charlotte was so intelligent and persuasive that for a moment they let themselves be swayed by her plea. Eloin was stunned by it, good loyal Eloin who had arrived in Paris soon after his empress. In an enthusiastic report to Maximilian, he described the talent and "virility" with which Charlotte was going about such a disagreeable task, so much so that even those least predisposed to helping the Mexican empire listened despite themselves. Though he had come to lend her his help and advice, Eloin found that she did not need them, and that it was much better just to let her faith, ardor, and lucidity take their own course without outside interference.

On the thirteenth of August, two days after the first interview with Napoleon III, Charlotte returned to Saint-Cloud. This time, the welcoming ceremony was reduced to a modicum. Charlotte had no intention of bringing out statistics, analyses, and plans, for she had a much more formidable weapon in her arsenal: memory, particularly Napoleon III's letters to archduke Maximilian when it was a still a question of founding the Mexican empire: "You can be sure that you will have my full support in accomplishing your task." She continued with page after page of dialogue and promises, all of which followed the same line of thought. What could he say of this sentence, written when Maximilian was thinking of giving up: "What would you think of me if, with your imperial Highness already set up in Mexico, I suddenly told you that I cannot uphold the conditions that I signed?" In conclusion, she quoted from memory the articles of the Miramar Treaty which guaranteed that the Foreign Legion would remain in Mexico for at least six years. The only answer she got was Eugenie and Napoleon III's tears, much more abundant than the first time. "How old we have gotten," Charlotte thought as she watched the bent, sobbing couple who looked so pathetic and childish to her.

With his back to the wall, Napoleon III decided to admit the truth, which, perhaps from pride, he had hidden from Maximilian and Charlotte until then: the United States was exerting a great deal of pressure on him; the United States was threatening him. He could not do anything for Mexico because Washington was preventing him from doing so. Charlotte shrugged her shoulders. United States or not, Napoleon III had compromised himself with Mexico, and to abandon Mexico now would only compromise him further. Napoleon III lowered his head and mumbled that Charlotte should not expect anything further of him. Before she could answer, Eugenie pulled her as quickly as possible out of her husband's office.

Minister Achille Fould was waiting for Charlotte in Eugenie's office. He would be happy to discuss the subject with the empress of Mexico. Knowing full well that she had fired all the weapons in her arsenal, Charlotte accepted the debate.

With Achille Fould, there could be no discussion of memories; it was purely about money. First, he demanded that the loan be reimbursed. Answering immediately, Charlotte responded that it would be instructive to compare the amount of the loan with the amount that actually reached Mexico. It would be seen that a large part of the millions mysteriously disappeared en route, probably even before they left France. The interview ended; Charlotte had not made any headway, but she also had not backed down at all.

As she analyzed the facts, Charlotte began to realize that she was coming up against quite a bit of bad faith. The "high spheres," as she called them, had abandoned the Mexican empire, but she had the sneaking suspicion that surprises could still occur. She felt that the public had some sympathy for the Mexican cause, for each time she went out, the curious onlookers increased in number, and the applause grew stronger. Even people whom she had tried in vain to get interested in the Mexican economy seemed to be coming around—even Napoleon III and Eugenie, despite their weakness.

Over the next few days, Charlotte thus insisted on receiving and gathering information, and on spreading it. There would be no high life, no theater or expositions, no shopping. Paris was not a pretext for frivolity, but a place to stand and fight. Among the people she spoke with, there was one visitor she could have lived without, but whom her entourage urged her to see: Doña Alicia Iturbide, the mother of the little Augustin adopted by Maximilian, was announced. To welcome her, Charlotte had put on her most haughty face. Standing very straight, majestic in the center of her little drawing room, she stared at the ravishing American without making a single gesture in her direction. But Alicia did not seem intimidated. She made a half-hearted curtsy, then immediately got to the heart of the matter, which she summed up in one sentence: "Give me back my son."

Charlotte responded with a frown of disdain. Fine, she could have her son back, but let Doña Alicia also give back the money they had paid her to take the child. Doña Alicia shivered. That was not what she wanted to hear. When she spoke of the cruelty of her forced separation from her son, Charlotte shrugged her shoulders. Her child was not unhappy, he had been made a prince — his mother should be happy with that promotion. What an idea! "My son is the grandson of an emperor; he was born a prince, even if he did not bear the title."

Shocked by the American woman's gall, Charlotte raised the tone of her voice. "What advantage does your son give me? The emperor and I are young; we can have children of our own." This was quite a declaration. Was Charlotte sincere, which would imply that her relations with Maximilian would leave her the glimmer of a hope, or did she simply want to bluff the exasperating Doña Alicia in the heat of the argument?

But the American did not give up. To be rid of her, Charlotte advised her to write directly to Maximilian. "I have done that twenty times, but he has never answered."

"Well then, try again." With a quick bow of the head, Charlotte signaled that the audience was over. As she left the room, full of rage, Doña Alicia's curtsy must have been poorly executed indeed.

After this interlude, the parade of political visitors resumed. Charlotte received Rouher, the omnipotent minister nicknamed "the vice-emperor." He repeated Fould's argument: give the money back first. Charlotte let him understand that she was growing weary of hanging around Paris. Napoleon III was hardly proving very courteous: she had already visited him twice, and not once had he deigned to show up at the Grand-Hotel. One way or the other, it had to come to an end.

Napoleon III and Eugenie completely agreed. They could not continue to have the stubborn empress in France, especially since she was a living reminder of their remorse. Napoleon III would thus give her the visit that protocol demanded, and which Charlotte expected at the Grand-Hotel.

On August 19, 1866, the policemen with their moustaches and top hats had taken up position all along the Boulevard des Capucines. Charlotte, at the height of her nervousness and anxiety, was waiting in the Grand-Hotel's ceremonial courtyard. The din of horse hooves and coach wheels heralded the convoy's arrival. The butlers opened the doors, the aides rushed in, and Napoleon III entered the hotel. He was in civilian clothes: a black waistcoat and gray slacks. He was rather short and stocky, and his hair, moustache, and goatee had already turned gray. He no longer had the nimble gait he used to, and he approached the tall, stiff and immobile woman with small steps. As he greeted her, his eyes were at once provocative and admiring. Charlotte was unaffected by the doddering Don Juan's attempts at charming her. She immediately led him to her suite's little sitting room, which she reserved for very intimate audiences, and the discussion heated up right away. Once again, Napoleon III said that he could not act against the wishes of both public opinion and the parliament. That was neither here nor there, Charlotte countered; he had to dissolve the chamber and hold new elections, which he might be able to push "in the right direction." After all, Napoleon III was no stranger to coups d'état now, was he? That was how he came to power in the first place. The only problem was, of course, that the withered, exhausted emperor no longer had anything in common with the adventurous man he had been in 1852. Charlotte's forced reminder of the long-lost good old days annoyed Napoleon III enough to give him the strength to say what he had come to say: France would no longer be helping Mexico. Charlotte sank brutally into despair. "All we can do then is abdicate," she mumbled. In front of her, the man once responsible for her existence then abandoned her to her fate. He was so tired of everything, most of all of Mexico and Charlotte, that he agreed: "So abdicate, then." Refusing to continue, he quickly fled.

Despair was not part of Charlotte's personality, and she soon recovered her courage. She now hated Napoleon III, and let off some of her fury in her report to Maximilian: "I have the satisfaction of having destroyed all his arguments, of having cleared away the false pretexts, and of having thus given you a moral victory, but in a word, Napoleon does not want to help, and anger is of no use because he has the devil behind him, while I do not. . . . He wants to commit this heinous deed he has been concocting for so long not out of coward-ice, discouragement, or any other reason, but simply because he rep-resents the power of evil in this world. . . . You can be assured of it, as far as I am concerned: he is the devil himself. During our last in-terview, yesterday, he had such an expression on his face, his hair was standing on end, he was hideous. . . . From the beginning to the end, he never loved you. He fascinated you like the serpent would; his tears were as false as his words. His actions are all lies. . . . You will think perhaps that I am exaggerating, but it reminds me of the Apocalypse. . . . Seeing the devil so close up could convince atheists to believe in God. Bazaine is insane, they are merely satellites and have satellites of their own. . . . Please don't think that I begged these people, all I did was shake them up a bit. I made them lower their masks, but without being impolite. Certainly, nothing so painful has happened to them since they have been on this Earth. . . . You must chase out Napoleon's fiscal agents or gain control over them, and you must take military affairs out of French hands, or else you will be ruined. . . ." The spurned woman took comfort in saying that at least she made "them" tremble. In short, the proud princess was convinced that Napoleon would have to have been the devil himself to have been able to resist her.

Once she had spewed forth her anger, Charlotte also rediscovered her usual realism, and telegraphed Maximilian a summary
of her long, strenuous days of negotiations with a single sentence
in Spanish: *"Todo es inútil."* "Everything is futile."

What should she do now, the empress asked herself. First,
leave Paris as soon as possible, because she could no longer stand
it. But to go where? To Austria, as some people were advising her?
Maximilian's family might give her the help her ex-friend Napoleon III had refused. But Austria was just emerging from a disastrous war that had destroyed its finances, and everything there was
in ruins. The imperial family had never much liked her, no more
than they liked Maximilian; Francis-Joseph, most of all, had proven
time and time again how indifferent and cold he was toward his
brother. He would not be the one to help them.

Belgium, then? After all, that was her own family, her own
country. Moreover, her brother Philippe had told her he was shocked
and hurt that she did not come to see them first. Charlotte replied
that it was very difficult to find a date that suited everyone, and
that she had no intention of making the trip there only to find no
one around. Also, though Philippe was pushing her to come, her
brother King Leopold had sent no invitation.

On her list of priorities, however, Rome took precedence. As
soon as she had landed at Saint-Nazaire, Charlotte had begun forming the plan: after Paris, go see the pope. The second half of her
mission would be to negotiate with the Vatican for an accord that
would reestablish peace among the government, the clergy, and the
conservatives, a goal that had become all the more pressing due to
the failure of her negotiations with Napoleon III. She had to gain
the Holy Father's blessing at all costs, for that would win much of
the Mexican population over to the side of the empire. Lastly, with
his moral power, the pope might be able to persuade Napoleon III
to give them his financial and military aid. The only problem was

that a visit to the Holy See could not be arranged in a day. In the meantime, she decided to go to the only safe haven that came to her mind: Miramar.

Charlotte left Paris on August 23, 1866. Though he had refused her everything else, Napoleon had put a special train at her disposal. She crossed Burgundy, the province of Lyon, the Alps, Turin, and Milan, and stopped for a few days of rest at Lake Como to visit one of Maximilian's uncles, Archduke Rainier, in his beautiful Villa d'Este. Everything there urged her toward relaxation: the weather was beautiful, the Alps were ablaze in the sun, the sumptuous homes had gardens spilling down to the lake's pale water, and the people were kind—beautiful singing could be heard from the neighboring village. Maximilian loved the area, and Charlotte could not stop thinking of him. In her room, her hosts had had the delicate attention to hang a portrait of her husband from the times when he was the viceroy of Lombardy-Venetia. Everything spoke to Charlotte of peace and love. Why were there so many problems and threats elsewhere? Why did she have to be alone, so far away from the man she loved?

After this stop, the train headed off along Lake Garda, which formed the border with the Austrian empire. Soldiers shot off salutes, and Austrian officers sent by the emperor came to greet his sister-in-law. On the train, they met Italian officers sent by the king of Italy, and got on well with them, even though two of them, formerly Garibaldi's men, had been wounded during the war with Austria. Charlotte was received everywhere with the highest honors. Where her "brother" Napoleon III had greeted her as an intruder, her former enemies, Victor-Emmanuel and Garibaldi's men, treated her as a sovereign and a friend. The king of Italy even went so far as to meet her train at Padua station. Other kings had always loved to laugh at the bearded roughneck Victor-Emmanuel, whose love affairs had always been splashed across the newspapers, and whose vulgarity of gesture and expression had always been scandalous. But he made a good impression on Charlotte. Even if he rolled his eyes, which made Charlotte laugh as it did the rest of Europe, he showed her a cordiality and a kindness that touched her deeply. Above all, he expressed his admiration for Maximilian and for his ideals.

After this reenergizing interview, the train passed through Mestre, then Venice, and soon came to the small private station at Miramar.

Charlotte welcomed her home and refuge with relief. At Miramar, there would be no more intrusions, no more humiliations. The summer was shining, the sea seemed made of gold, the intense heat was softened by a gentle wind from the north. The garden was exploding with flowers. The trees had grown over the couple's two years of absence. The house had also grown: the second floor now ended in halls heavily decorated with allusions to the glory of the Mexican empire.

Retreating into herself, Charlotte did not want to see anyone. She dined alone with Madam del Barrio in the ground-floor dining room, whose windows opened out onto the Adriatic. She accepted service only from her maid, Mathilde Doblinger. This newcomer was probably already part of her household in Mexico, but Charlotte had never paid her much mind. From now on, however, Charlotte could bear no one but this precise, silent, and efficient Teuton who inspired her full confidence.

The young woman reflected on Europe, this "sickening and depressing old world," and particularly the Austrian empire Max was so proud of. What remained of it after Sadowa? A second-rate power. Charlotte felt lucky that she and Max had been able to distance themselves from it in time.

Though locked in her somber thoughts, Charlotte still noticed first one, then two, then a whole series of Austrian ships coming into view. The Austrian fleet had entered the bay of Trieste for maneuvers. At the beginning of his career, Maximilian had been in charge of forming the fleet, and had made an excellent war machine of it; indeed, the navy had been the only military branch to have remained unbeaten during the recent, humiliating defeat. The sight brought Max to Charlotte's mind, and she wrote him a long and somewhat overblown letter. *"Morituri te salutant,* that is the navy's last salute, then it will leave Trieste and perhaps history. The navy cast the first rays of light on your future power, on the independence you so dearly won. It saved the coast you loved so much, and now it will abandon Austria and your brother to their fate. Its mission is complete, and yours is as well. The honor of the House of Austria has crossed the Atlantic with the name of one of its last victories, *Novara.* It disappears here with the sun, only to resurrect over there, *plus ultra* (the motto of Charles V). Here is the call of your forefathers: Charles V was showing the way; you followed it; do not regret it. God was behind him."

Finally she received a telegram from Max in return: "The morale situation is good, the military situation is horrendous." Tampico was lost, just like Monterrey and so many other cities. The "dissidents," as he called them, were besieging Veracruz and the important town of Jalapa. Why? Because of Bazaine's cowardice. Instead of acting, all Bazaine had thought to do was retreat. The circle was closing; they needed help now, but from where? France had already given its answer. As for Austria, their natural ally, Charlotte had just learned that Francis-Joseph had canceled the official visit he was going to make to Trieste, for the sole reason that he did not want under any circumstances to meet his sister-in-law, "Her Mexican Majesty," as he contemptuously called her. Yet another snub, this time from her closest family. And why? Because Francis-

Joseph was blamed for Austria's shameful defeat. When he returned to Vienna, the streets resounded with the cry "Long live Maximilian!" He was told constantly of his people's laments, asking where in such desperate times had his younger brother gone, the only one able to save the empire.

In Mexico, Maximilian bewailed his country's defeat, saying to anyone who would listen, "I said that that would happen. I foresaw that catastrophe, I warned everyone, I am not at all surprised. I just would have expected a little more dignity, a little less incompetence." Eloin, who was crisscrossing Europe, confided to Maximilian in a top-secret report that Emperor Francis-Joseph had lost heart, and that the people were demanding his abdication. On the other hand, Eloin added, Maximilian's reputation had never been so good — the entire empire adored him. . . . But the top-secret report did not stay secret for long. The entire report, together with Maximilian's criticism, soon got back to Francis-Joseph, warped, blown out of proportion, and exaggerated by courtiers always happy to widen the breach between the two brothers. The elder's mistrust, which had never really gone away, returned immediately to its full strength: "Maximilian is a traitor, he wants my crown, especially now that things in Mexico are going so poorly." It is no wonder, then, that he would not see his brother's wife.

At this very moment, Charlotte was losing a precious source of moral support. She had recently been very happy to send the medal of the Order of San Carlos to her former governess, the countess of Hulste, with whom she had always remained in contact through letters. In her response, the countess of Hulste did not only refuse the medal in an almost insulting way, but she also sent her former pupil a merciless diatribe: "I told you so, I told you that you should not accept the crown of Mexico. You accepted it, and now look at the price you are so rightfully paying. Do not tempt Providence any further: get out of that deadly undertaking now, while you still have your honor and there is not too much danger. Stew in your bitterness, and think on this proverb that is as old as the hills: 'Woe to the vanquished'—especially when the vanquished have gone of their own free will to expose themselves to defeat, and this without even being able to say that they have accomplished their duty." This was followed by countless paragraphs of the same thing, each of which pierced Charlotte to her core.

She locked herself in her boudoir to think, and refused to come out. Situated on the ground floor of the corner tower, it was a pentagonal room with pale blue damask drapes. Arabesques of dark wood meandering through the light wood décor added to the ornamentation. There were landscapes and watercolors on the walls. Four big windows opened out onto the sea. Charlotte paced back and forth. From time to time, she cast a glance outside and saw only the water, the sky, and the light. Everything was blue and gold, except when the excessive heat turned the colors pale.

The countess of Hulste, the dear governess who had hurt Charlotte so, was wrong. Providence was Mexico—it had always been Mexico and would always be. Charlotte had gone to France to ask for the French troops to stay. She failed. Well, then, not only would they make do without the French troops, but they would also be happy to see them go, and thus clear up the situation.

Charlotte sat down at her precious wooden desk and began a letter to Max in her slanted handwriting: "I consider the abandonment of French protection as a stroke of luck so great that it will compensate for the lack of material and financial aid." Once Mexico was rid of foreign interference, she said, the United States would naturally accept the Mexican empire. As for the political parties, the liberals were already behind Maximilian, and the conservatives would not fail to come over to him once he completely personified the nation. Which left the "dissidents," or rather, the rebels: the departure of the French had robbed them of any reason to keep fighting, and they too would come around. For all these reasons, Charlotte strongly urged Maximilian to stand firm: "You have the flag; you are the nation; you are the *sobrano*," as Juárez used to say — with the slight difference that, when Juárez said it, he meant the sovereign was the people, from which he had sprung. "You must tell everyone 'I am the emperor, not the president.' Before you, they must bow their heads, for the republic is as poor a mother as Protestantism, and the monarchy is humanity's salvation."

To show that the Empire lived on at Miramar as well, Charlotte decided to celebrate the Mexican national holiday, September 16, with all due pomp and circumstance. The people of Trieste were woken at dawn by gun salutes shot off by the Austrian fleet. Like all the royal parks at a time when heads of state were not yet trembling for their safety, Miramar's park was still open to the public. The people of Trieste hurried there to see the beautifully maintained gardens brimming with flowers, to hear the Austrian orchestra playing national anthems interspersed with waltzes, and, if possible, to catch a glimpse of the empress of Mexico.

She had dressed with the sumptuousness she reserved for ceremony, in an embroidered dress, a diamond diadem, and a diamond and pearl necklace, just as if she were in Mexico City. The archbishop of Trieste said high mass in the castle's chapel. With her long train and court mantle, the tiny sanctuary with its neo-Gothic vaults and images of saints was barely big enough to hold more than Charlotte. The few Mexicans and Austrian authorities in attendance were crowded into the adjoining room, named the Compass Card, after the One who adorned the ceiling. Sliding doors allowed it to be an extension of the chapel, just as Maximilian and

Charlotte had planned, so that the domestic servants would be able to follow the masses from there.

That evening, the empress presided over a banquet with her usual grace and courtesy. No one suspected how tired she was. It was only later, when at last she found herself alone in her dressing room, that her features collapsed and the lines on her face revealed the toll the ordeal was taking on her.

The next morning, she set out for Rome. Arrangements for her interview with the pope had been made, and Charlotte was quite anxious to see him. But cholera was raging in Trieste. The epidemic was not very serious, but still, travelers from Trieste were quarantined for a few days in Venice. Charlotte could not wait that long, so she had to go around Venetia, which was easier said than done. Rather than traveling toward the southwest, first she went in the opposite direction, toward the north. With her entourage, she took the express train to Marburg in Austria, where she changed trains to go east to Villach in Carinthia. The train could not go any farther, so she took a stagecoach to cross the Alps through a series of small valleys. She reentered Italy and stopped at the relay station of Brigsen, now known as Bressanone. All around her, the flanks of the snow-capped mountains were covered with pine forests. A stream snaked its way through prairies alive with wildflowers.

An advance party had already been sent on to Mantua to prepare for the continuation of Charlotte's trip when suddenly she decided to backtrack. The telegram left for Mantua immediately: "Turn around, come back now." Then she changed her mind, and decided that she would continue on as originally planned. A second telegram canceled the first. They boarded their coach again.

That evening, they arrived at Botzen, now called Bolzano. Charlotte stared out of the coach's window, soaking up the scenes of street life. The music of an organ attracted her attention, but not so much as the organ grinder who was turning its handle. "But look!

It's the commander of the Mexican Guard!" she exclaimed. Her entourage was stunned: "Your Majesty is mistaken." Charlotte insisted, "No, it is, it is he, it's the commander of the guard of Mexico City!" They arrived at the inn where they were to spend the night. As they went in, Charlotte suddenly flew at a member of her entourage, the naval officer Radonetz, one of Maximilian's right-hand men who had stayed at Trieste to watch over his affairs there. She shouted: "You are nothing but a thief, and you are robbing me! You're not only robbing me, you are betraying me!"

Radonetz stared at her in fear, wondering what he could have done to deserve these accusations. "Thief, traitor!," Charlotte repeated, and then she wiped her face with her hand as if she were wakening from a dream. Her entourage stared agape, petrified as she went up the stairs to her room. No one saw her that night except for her trusted maid, Mathilde Doblinger, who of course had come along for the trip.

The next morning, at the time they were to set off, everyone was waiting for Charlotte at the door. She came down, carefully dressed and made-up, completely calm, completely natural. She greeted each person individually, stopping for a moment in front of her grand chamberlain, Count del Valle: "I was ill. If it comes over me again, say the word 'Botzen' to me to make me come to my senses."

They boarded first a coach, then a train. At Mantua, military dignitaries came to welcome Charlotte and her entourage. That evening, the town was ablaze with lights lights for her, and a military parade passed beneath the windows of her inn. From Mantua, they took a stagecoach to Bologna; then yet another special train, which passed through Ancona into the Papal States and headed toward Rome. At Foligno, north of the capital, a luncheon awaited the empress in the park. Charlotte did not show up. She remained in the train. She had taken ill — her heart was galloping in her chest.

Finally, on September 25, 1866, Charlotte arrived at the train station of Rome. Once again, the Italians, led by the papal authorities, put on a grand display. A delegation of cardinals awaited her beside the track, surrounded by members of the Roman aristocracy and noble guards in sparkling breastplates. The pope's police were lined up to hold back the immense crowd, for the Mexican affair had filled the newspapers, and Charlotte's visit, announced everywhere, aroused curiosity. It was raining torrentially, though the weather had been steadily beautiful until the day before. Countless torches illuminated the scene, sparkling off the unsheathed sabers, deepening the cardinals' purple, and bringing out the livery's gold. Charlotte was led with great pomp to the Albergo di Roma, where an entire floor had been reserved for her. It was situated on the Corso, the most animated boulevard in the city, which cut across from the Piazza del Popolo to the Piazza Venezia. From her window, Charlotte could see the baroque façade of the church dedicated to Charles Borromée. Nearby, she found the Tomb of Augustus and the Piazza di Spagna, from which the steps of the Holy Trinity led away. Charlotte knew Rome well, since she had visited it thoroughly in the past.

The next morning, she could not resist the urge to wander a bit through the streets. The pope had sent an honor guard to the hotel, composed of his own soldiers as well as French troops, who were still occupying Rome to safeguard his throne. The fanfares sounded, and the national anthems played several times a day. Charlotte was offered escorts and guides, but she would have none of them. She took only Madam del Barrio with her and set out like any sightseer, happy for the freedom. She walked the full length of the Corso, went into a few sanctuaries, admired the Caravaggios in the Church of Saint Louis of the French, pressed on to the Piazza del Popolo, visited its twin churches, then went up the high steps to see the Pincio garden, shaded by magnificent pines. There, she leaned against the guardrail of the terrace, which was decorated with flower-filled marble pots, and looked out over the spectacle of the city stretched out beneath her. In the distance, she could discern the top of the Castel Sant'Angelo, and behind that, the enormous dome of Saint Peter's and the roofs of the Vatican, where Pius IX awaited her.

In the beginning of the afternoon, a beautiful coach stopped in front of the Albergo di Roma. The sentries jumped to attention, the valets lowered the step, and Cardinal Antonelli—the secretary of state, which was equivalent to a prime minister of the Vatican— appeared. He was the most magnificent, the most traditional, and the most representative of the pontifical prelates, the heir to a glorious past. Yards and yards of red silk trailed along behind him, for he was wearing his *capa magna*. An enormous stone sparkled on his finger; it was whispered that he owned a collection of rings unique in the world, and that he put on a different one every day. The onlookers knelt to receive his blessing.

As protocol required, Charlotte awaited Cardinal Antonelli at the bottom of the stairs, flanked by two servants in livery holding torches, who then led her and the cardinal upstairs to the drawing room.

The discussion began, not directly and clearly as it had with the French, but in nuances, innuendoes, allusions, and slippery subtleties. An agreement with the Mexican empire? Of course, we must sign an agreement, but why has Emperor Maximilian not returned the clergy's property? Why the proclamation of religious tolerance, which opened the way to all sorts of heresy? As a diversion, Charlotte told him of her visit to Paris and of her disappointment that Napoleon III failed to keep his word. The cardinal was careful not to respond. He had no desire to voice the slightest criticism against the emperor of the French, who was protecting Rome. The interview went on, with Antonelli couching his refusals in so much rhetorical decoration that Charlotte did not suspect how bleak her prospects were.

Her audience with the pope was scheduled for September twenty-seventh at eleven o'clock. According to custom, Charlotte had dressed in black, covering her hair in a veil of the same color, and for jewelry, she was wearing only pearls. Surrounded by the pomp that was her due, she took the coach to Piazza Bernini. The admirable décor was somewhat obscured by an unending rain. The coach stopped to the right of Saint Peter's Basilica, at the entrance to the Vatican palaces. In the colonnaded vestibule, Charlotte's grand chamberlain, Count del Valle, was waiting with the members of the premier Roman families who, by tradition, held the highest ranks in the Vatican: Prince Chigi, Marquis Sachetti, and Princes Orsini and Colonna, all wearing outfits from the time of Philippe II, with puffy shorts and millstone ruff collars. The Swiss Guard, in the blue, red, and yellow uniforms designed by Michelangelo, lined every step of the Nobles' Staircase.

Though glorious in her dark clothing, Charlotte was nervous and tense. As the great nobles kissed her hand, she responded with a tight smile. Slowly, she climbed the steps to the second floor, preceded by the grand master of the Holy Hospice, the grand squire, the assistants to the throne, and the marshal of the Holy Church, and entered into the Throne Room. Under a canopy emblazoned with his coat of arms, Pope Pius IX awaited her, seated on a gold and red throne. His cardinals surrounded him, together with other members of his court; the noble guards stood in an ordered row against the walls, the many historical tapestries behind them. The pope rose. He was a tall and corpulent man, with a kind smile, dressed in a cassock and a fine white cape made of wool. Charlotte knelt to kiss his train, but he stopped her and held out his ring. As she leaned toward him, she whispered, "Holy Father, save me, I have been poisoned."

The pope pretended not to have heard her. She rose and introduced the Mexicans in her entourage, who rushed forward to kiss the red velvet slipper embroidered in golden thread with the pontifical coat of arms. Pope Pius IX then led Charlotte into an adjoining smaller hall next door. Valets in red damask dress shut the tall gold and white doors behind them. The Holy Father and the empress remained alone, sitting next to each other in armchairs.

Charlotte took out the draft of an accord that she and Maximilian had worked out. Without reading it, the pope declared that he must first consult the Mexican bishops. Charlotte offered the arguments that she had saved up. The pope did not change his mind. Knowing that she was playing her last card, Charlotte became even more persuasive, stooping low enough to beg, which she had never done with anyone else, not even Napoleon III. The pope took refuge in diversions and double-talk, and would not give an inch. For now, there would be no accord. The interview lasted an hour and a half, and left Charlotte exhausted. The pope rose; her audience was over.

She left amid the same pomp. The noble guards flanked her with their cadenced gait. Her coach rode off before knights holding their bared sabers aloft.

At the Albergo di Roma, the Mexicans who had accompanied Charlotte followed her to her suite's drawing room, burning with curiosity and anxious to know how the interview turned out. Charlotte did not snap out of her dark mood. Since leaving the Vatican, she had not unclenched her teeth.

"What happened, Your Majesty? How did the pope receive the accord? Was Your Majesty satisfied?"

Charlotte raised her smoldering eyes. "You may leave now. Ah, yes! Have my lunch brought to my room. Doblinger shall bring it to me." She turned her back, slammed the door, and locked it behind her.

The next day, it was the pope's turn to visit Charlotte. Custom suggested that he come, but it did not oblige him. That he did visit her can therefore be seen as a particular act of respect to the empress of Mexico. Once again dressed in black, with the same pearls and veil that she had worn the day before, Charlotte waited for him in the vestibule and brought him to her little drawing room. The interview lasted only a few minutes, since it was merely a formality. Then the doors flew open, and she beckoned to the Mexicans of her entourage to come in and receive the pontiff's blessing. With his kind smile, Pius IX took the time to bless each one individually, as Charlotte stared at her countrymen with an increasingly contemptuous frown. She accompanied the pope back to his carriage, then returned haughtily and silently to her suite.

That night, however, she agreed to preside over her entourage's dinner. The Albergo di Roma had prepared a menu of no fewer than twenty courses, but Charlotte did not touch them. She asked for nuts and oranges instead, checking that they had not been cracked or peeled, then opening them with her own hands before tasting them. "Would Your Majesty care for a little wine or water?" Charlotte refused. She did not touch liquids, even water, and in her bedroom, the crystal carafe remained full.

The next day, she did not leave her suite, eating the same nuts and oranges without a drop of water.

11

The following day, the thirtieth of September, Charlotte burst out of her suite at eight o'clock in the morning. She called for Madam del Barrio, who was luckily already awake and dressed, dragged her downstairs, had her order a coach, and jumped into it with her. "To the Trevi Fountain!" she cried. The coach stopped in front of one of Rome's most beautiful monuments, but Charlotte had no eyes for the Neptunes, Tritons, and other ancient figures. She knelt before the fountain, scooped up water in her hands, and drank greedily. Then she stood up and climbed back into the coach with an ever more distraught Madam del Barrio. "To the Vatican!" she cried. The coach rode along the early morning's empty streets to the entranceway, where Charlotte had been met with such pomp three days earlier. The Swiss guards recognized her and let her through. On the second floor, she ran into a few courtiers. The butlers in red damask had taken their stations before the doors, and one or two cardinals were on their way to their offices. All of them stared at Charlotte in stupefaction, but no one thought to question her. She approached a dignitary: "I want to see His Holiness right away."

"That is impossible, Your Majesty. His Holiness is having his breakfast."

"I don't care, tell him I am here."

The dignitary did not dare refuse, and slipped through the emblazoned door. Soon he returned, and silently led Charlotte into the office where Pius IX was indeed having his frugal meal. Charlotte barely greeted him, and instead rushed at the steaming cup of chocolate he had just sipped. She stuck her fingers into it and sucked them, whispering, "I am so hungry, but I don't dare eat—they are all trying to poison me."

The pope maintained enough self-control not to show his surprise. He rang and another cup was brought, which he himself filled with chocolate. "No, I only want to drink out of Your Holiness's cup; if they know it is for me, they will put poison in it."

The pope let her finish his cup. On the desk, she spotted a silver goblet and grabbed it. "Give it to me, most Holy Father, so I can drink from it without being poisoned."

With a gesture, Pius IX acquiesced. Then she began a speech that left the pope flabbergasted. Everyone was trying to get her, she said. They were all on Napoleon III's payroll, and "they" wanted to poison her. "Protect me, most Holy Father, I am only safe here."

The pontiff was at a loss. Alone in a room with a lunatic, it was not fear that he felt, but rather deep pity and unbearable embarrassment. He meekly offered to show Charlotte around the library. Charlotte accepted. Passing through a series of halls decorated with frescoes and tapestries, they came to the private library. The cardinals waiting in the antechamber followed them. The pope opened a cabinet and took out a manuscript dating from the high Middle Ages. "Please, Your Majesty, take a look at these beautiful illuminations."

Charlotte leaned over them in fascination. The pope took advantage of her distraction to step back, walk away, and disappear through a side door. Charlotte did not even notice. She was turning the pages slowly and contemplating the illuminations.

One or two cardinals and a few dignitaries had stayed in the room, and Madam del Barrio soon joined the group.

They proposed a visit to the Vatican gardens, and the empress accepted. They descended a small staircase, and reached the sunny gardens. Charlotte ran to the first fountain she saw, took the pope's goblet out of her pocket, dipped it in the water, and drank with gusto.

"I want to have a ride around town," she demanded. The prelates and nobles sighed with relief while Madam del Barrio turned green. They led Charlotte back to the Vatican palaces' entranceway. The coach that had brought them was still there. As it moved down the wide avenues, she distractedly watched the monuments slide by until suddenly she snapped to attention: "Stop!" She opened the door, ran to a fountain, and once again drank from the pope's goblet. "Ride on!" she ordered, stepping back into the coach. From stop to stop, the coach slowly made its way back to the Albergo di Roma, and came to a halt before its doors. Charlotte calmly stepped out and climbed the stairs to her apartment. Night was falling, the lamps had already been lit, and Madam del Barrio was at her wits' end, beyond horror.

Messages from the Vatican had already arrived at the hotel to warn the Mexicans accompanying Charlotte of her condition, and of her suspicions that they were trying to poison her. Under no circumstances were they to let her see them. Once she was at the door of her suite, Charlotte noticed that the key had been taken out in order to prevent her from locking herself in. She turned to her lady-in-waiting: "We are leaving for the Vatican again."

Madam del Barrio felt the Earth opening up beneath her feet, but what could she do? She could not abandon the empress. With her heart sinking, she followed her out.

Once again, they ordered a coach and left for the Vatican. The Swiss guards, who by now were used to seeing Charlotte, let her through. On the second floor, she found everyone getting ready for bed. This time the pope was careful not to receive her, so she turned to the cardinals and dignitaries, telling all of them that she wanted to sleep at the Vatican, the only place she felt safe. A woman sleeping at the Vatican! Even the popes' mistresses during the Renaissance did not sleep in the shadow of Saint Peter's. Now almost hysterical, Charlotte screamed that she would not leave. They could not treat an empress like any ordinary lunatic. They could not use force — it never crossed anyone's mind — for they were all feeling that terrified awe that insanity inspires.

Once he was informed, the pope raised his hands to the sky. "All we needed was to have a woman go insane in the Vatican," he said. But he also thought that the only solution was to pacify her. He thus agreed to offer her hospitality for a night. Charlotte was hungry, and demanded her dinner. The pope hastily had the leftovers from his meal arranged nicely for her. But Charlotte refused to eat unless the pope himself fed it to her. Pius IX had no choice, and the dignitaries watched him spoon-feed the empress of Mexico as if she were a child. He himself then walked the empress to his library, where he had had two copper beds brought up for her and Madam del Barrio, together with a solid silver dressing table and beautiful candlesticks. Charlotte seemed much calmer.

The Holy Father and his aides shut the library doors on the two women, and could finally breathe again.

An exhausted Madam del Barrio stretched out on her bed, and Charlotte did the same. The candles burned slowly; silence descended on the room and on the palace, disturbed only by the cries of the Swiss Guard. An hour passed, then another, and suddenly Charlotte, still dressed, jumped out of her bed and woke Madam del Barrio. "I want to see Cardinal Antonelli right away."

Madam del Barrio summoned the secretary of state. The butler returned and said, "His Eminence is in bed and cannot be disturbed." The door closed. Madam del Barrio lay back down. Charlotte paced back and forth, mumbling incomprehensibly. She threw herself on her bed, dozed off, then got up again to pace through the library. Only at dawn did she fall into a half sleep, which did not last very long.

When she woke up, Madam del Barrio noticed that she was much calmer. The empress poured water from the ewer into the large silver basin, washed herself, and scrubbed her face and hands. She had always taken good care of herself. She fixed her hair meticulously and brushed off her dress. Then she exited the library and wandered from room to room, opening doors without anyone stopping her. She thought out loud: since I have been poisoned and I am going to die, I must resign myself to it and write out my will.

She asked for paper and a writing set, which were immediately brought to her. She sat on the first armchair she found, most likely one of the tall Renaissance cathedras made of gilded wood and red velvet, emblazoned with the pontifical coat of arms. She wrote a note, stopped, got up to wander again, then sat down and wrote again:

"Rome, October 1, 1866.

"I do not wish my body to be laid out after my death, nor do I want an autopsy. I want to be buried simply in the church of

Saint Peter, dressed in the habit of the Clarissian nuns, as close as possible to the Holy Apostle's tomb, unless the emperor decides otherwise."

"Rome, October 1, 1866.
My beloved treasure, I bid you farewell. The Lord is calling me back to him; I thank you for the happiness you gave me. May God bless you and grant you everlasting peace.
Your faithful Charlotte."

"Rome, October 1, 1866.
To the Holiest Father Pius IX,
Holiest Father, I am going to die, as I announced to Your Holiness the other day. I ask Him for His blessing, and I am your Holiness's affectionate daughter, Charlotte."

"Rome, October 1, 1866.
To the Holiest Father Pius IX,
I ask Your Holiness to immediately send me a priest to give me confession and bring me the holy Eucharist."
Finally, she wrote out her will, in which she left Maximilian her fortune and jewels, with instructions to distribute a few jewels as souvenirs to her two brothers. She ended by forgiving all those who had contributed to her death. Now that her duty was complete, all she had left to do was wait for the end to come. At last, she agreed to return to the hotel. Prelates and courtiers breathed a sigh of relief, but fearing that she might decide to come back, the pope gave her an escort and one of his chamberlains to accompany her . . . and prevent her from turning around.

The coach set off, surrounded by pontifical guards. In the middle of the Piazza del Pilota, Count Linanche, commander of the guards, heard the word "Stop!" Charlotte jumped out of the coach and ran to the fountain, this time using not the pope's goblet but the cup attached to a chain that all the tourists used. She drank greedily before climbing back onboard. Seated next to her, the pope's chamberlain, Egidio Dati, did not know where to look.

When the coach came to a halt outside the Albergo di Roma, Charlotte turned to him and said, "I am hungry. Go buy me some roasted chestnuts, but make sure not to remove the peels. My wish is your command." In his rich uniform, the chamberlain had to walk up and down the street to find a vendor selling what Charlotte had demanded. In the hotel vestibule, Charlotte tore at the paper cone containing the hot chestnuts, ripped off their peels and threw them on the floor, and devoured the nuts voraciously. Then she went up to her suite, followed by Madam del Barrio, whose legs were giving way beneath her, and by Mathilde Doblinger. Charlotte left her lady-in-waiting in the sitting room, went into her bedroom with her maid, and turned the key that had been put back into the lock. The Mexicans showed up to question Madam del Barrio mercilessly, but she barely had enough voice left to tell them of the horrible night.

Suddenly the bedroom door opened. Mathilde Doblinger announced that Her Majesty wished to see Madame Kuhacsevich, the treasurer's wife, immediately. After a search, the woman was found, and they shoved her into the bedroom. Charlotte slammed the door behind her before yelling, "Never would I have thought that someone like you, whom I have known for so many years, whom I have showered with acts of kindness, to whom I have given my love and my confidence, could sell herself to Napoleon III's agents to poison me."

Indignant, the woman protested, "How can Your Majesty accuse me of such crimes? How unfair it is. My husband and I have given the emperor and Your Majesty so much proof of our devotion."

"Get out, Madame. Get out and tell your accomplices that their plot has been exposed, and that I know who the traitors are. Tell Count del Valle, your husband, and the doctor that they should run if they do not want to be put in prison immediately, and you run too. I do not even want to hear your name."

Madame Kuhacsevich burst into tears and stumbled out of the room.

Charlotte came out immediately afterward with an empty pitcher in her hand. She summoned Madam del Barrio, now more dead than alive, who saw that the nightmare was starting all over again. Charlotte dragged her downstairs, went out onto the sidewalk, and hailed a coach. "Find me a fountain," she yelled at the coachman, "and stop there!" The coachman obeyed. Charlotte got out, filled the pitcher, and returned to the hotel. She went into her room where the faithful Mathilde Doblinger was waiting, and locked the door. Madam del Barrio was finally able to have some rest. It was the evening of October 1, 1866. Charlotte remained locked in her room for five days.

Understanding that the empress trusted only her, and that she believed she had been poisoned, Mathilde Doblinger had had the foresight to buy a few chickens, a coal oven, and a basket of eggs, which she had stored in the bedroom.

It was a big and comfortable, if ordinary, room, with windows opening out onto the Corso. Mathilde offered the empress other food, but she refused: toxic chemicals could easily be injected under the skins of fruit or into bread crust, she said. She would only accept food prepared by Mathilde in her presence. The maid took a chicken out of the cage and chopped off its head in front of the empress. Blood gushed onto the carpet. The feathers Mathilde tore off flew onto couches, armchairs, and tables. She gutted the chicken, throwing its entrails into a basket. Charlotte never took her eyes off her. The maid lit the little stove she had set up on a round marble table and cooked the poultry in a pot. Charlotte waited impatiently for it to cook to medium, then devoured the wing that Mathilde held out to her. After she devoured the entire chicken, she was thirsty. She grabbed the empty pitcher, dragged Mathilde out onto the street, ran to the first fountain she saw, filled the pitcher, and ran back to her suite.

Night fell and Mathilde closed the shutters and drew the curtains. She left the window open to let some air in on the suffocating heat. The sounds of the Roman night penetrated the room. Charlotte refused to be undressed and threw herself on her bed, only to rise moments later and pace back and forth. She didn't stop pacing the whole night. Mathilde couldn't get any sleep. God only knew what would have happened if she had left the empress unattended. She tried in vain to convince Charlotte to lie down. Only at dawn, as the gray light slowly replaced the room's darkness, did Charlotte sit down in a chair, still dressed, and doze off for a couple of minutes.

A few days of this drove Mathilde to distraction. The endless sleepless nights, the massacres of chickens on the carpets of the Albergo di Roma, and especially Charlotte's interminable talking were exhausting her. The empress's confessions and revelations at once astounded and terrified the maid.

Charlotte herself realized that things could not go on this way, but who could she trust, if not her favorite brother Philippe? She wrote a telegram to him: "I am surrounded by traitors and assassins. Come save me as soon as you can." She dispatched Mathilde to send it, but the family had already been warned. The tale of the scenes with the pope and the news that Charlotte was losing her mind had spread like wildfire. Rome was talking of nothing else. Each day, the press made ever less discreet allusions to it, and the Vatican itself was moved to action. Antonelli had sent a long encrypted telegram to the nuncio in Belgium so that he might discreetly inform the royal family. In any case, all the brothers had to do was read the Belgian newspapers to hear of their sister's fate in much less guarded terms. Leopold II had no intention of cutting his vacation in Ostende short. "Fat Philippe" would have to be the one to leave for Rome, especially since he was the one his sister had chosen to call on for help.

One morning, Charlotte broke her isolation and appeared in her drawing room, where her entourage had been waiting for five days. She spotted Madam del Barrio and asked, "Is Blasio still in Rome?" Maximilian's Mexican butler had come with the empress to Rome on the emperor's instructions. Charlotte had him summoned. The valet, who was staying in a different hotel, was located and came immediately. He was pushed into Charlotte's bedroom, that mysterious temple in which the enigmatic liturgy of insanity went on far from probing eyes, and upon which the thoughts of the Mexicans, the Vatican, and the Romans dwelled. Blasio expected to find a disheveled lunatic, but instead he saw a beautifully dressed and groomed woman, covered from head to toe in black as if in great mourning.

She welcomed him as graciously as always, with a charming smile, and spoke to him in a sad and gentle voice: "You have already seen many things in Rome. If you would like to visit other cities in Europe, you may do so. But first, I want to dictate to you the following decrees. Sit down and write."

Blasio took a seat at a little table, straightened the paper, and picked up his quill. Charlotte began: "We, Charlotte, empress of Mexico, seeing that Count del Valle . . ." What followed was the proper and customary formulation of a decree of destitution for her chamberlain, whom she relieved of all titles and duties, with the order to leave the court and never again appear there under any circumstances — ". . . our present disposition will be submitted to

His Majesty the emperor Maximilian for his signature . . . made in Rome, this the seventh of October, 1866.

"Read it back to me!"

Blasio obeyed. "Is Her Majesty satisfied?"

"Perfectly. Now write similar decrees for Mr. del Barrio, the treasurer Kuhacsevich, the doctor . . ." and the empress listed several others.

As he scratched the paper, Blasio cast furtive glances at Charlotte, who was walking back and forth, and took advantage of the fact that she was paying no attention to him to observe her. The extent to which, in the space of a few days, her appearance had changed astounded him. She was completely different from the woman he had known just a few days before. Her face had thinned out and grown tense, her cheekbones stuck out of her flushed face, and her dilated pupils shone with a bizarre light. She rarely looked at one thing for any length of time, and she wandered around distraughtly as if she were looking for an absent person or distant landscapes. Blasio also noticed that her bed, with its silken canopy, did not seem to have been unmade for days, and he was sure no one had slept in it. On the nightstand, there was a single, half-burned candle, and a beautiful little gold pocket watch. At the foot of the bed, he saw the armchair where he knew Charlotte collapsed at the end of the night for a half sleep. In this room that was exciting the curiosity of the entire city, Blasio noticed a wardrobe, a dressing table covered with silver objets d'art, a few chairs, and a marble-topped table, upon which Mathilde had set up the charcoal stove to cook Charlotte's chickens and eggs. Tied with a rope to the leg of the table were the few chickens that still survived. There was no trace of blood or feathers — Mathilde had washed everything — but the contrast between the palace's luxury and this barnyard with chicken manure on newspaper, the little stove, and the last meal's pathetic leftovers made such an impression on Blasio that he was hypnotized.

Once the writing session was through, Charlotte thanked him graciously, and handed him a telegram to take to the post office for her brother Philippe, who had announced his arrival for that very evening. "Empress Charlotte to the count of Flanders at Foligno. I hope you are well. Don't eat too much on the train, I will come pick you up at the station. Charlotte."

That afternoon, as she received Bombelles, who had arrived in Rome the day before, Charlotte appeared perfectly in control of her senses. She spoke to him of her stay, and of the Italians' wonderfully kind reception; she mentioned Mexico, her crossing of the Atlantic, and other subjects. Not a single gesture or word could lead him to believe that she had just lost her mind.

After dinner, when night had completely fallen, Charlotte left for the train station. She was waiting by the tracks when Philippe stepped down from his compartment. They embraced. Once in the coach, she advised him to be very careful about what he ate, but besides that little detail, he noticed nothing out of the ordinary. He had come to see his sister with great apprehension, but there was not the slightest hint of the insanity he had so feared to see. They wished each other a good night before entering their respective suites.

The next morning, when Philippe joined Charlotte, she was perfectly dressed, powdered, and calm. She took him for a ride through Rome. The coach brought them from monument to monument, and Charlotte surprised him not only by her self-control, but also by her astounding knowledge of architecture, art, and history. He took advantage of the situation to mention the objective of his mission. "Perhaps it would be better not to stay in Rome, am I not right, Charlotte? You could await the results of your negotiations with the pope at Miramar. It is pointless to wait here; you would feel so much better at home."

He anxiously expected a refusal or a scene, but she meekly and immediately acquiesced. He returned to the hotel with her with a sense of infinite relief. They had lunch with the empress's entourage and his aide. Gone were the chickens butchered and eaten in her bedroom. The brother and sister sat facing each other at the heads of the table.

As the dishes were passed around, each of which Charlotte refused, she scratched out little notes in a legible, if distorted, handwriting, and had them brought to him. "You can eat that. Philippe, I beg you to eat as little as possible, because I think the dose is rather strong."

Philippe read them, blushed, and did not know how to respond. He was hungry and wanted to eat, but feared that if he did so, Charlotte would make a scene. He smiled at her from across the table and nibbled as she watched him. At the end of the luncheon, which was interminable for Philippe, the signal to rise was finally given, and Charlotte dragged her brother into her bedroom. "I'll tell you everything, my chubby boy," she said. She counted all the ways she had been poisoned: in her coffee, in her chocolate, in fruit, meat, and bread. From her table, she picked up a little knife covered with dried ink. "You see, that is strychnine." Frozen in horror, he let her go on. "And it is not just me, my chubby boy. None of them died a natural death. Father, mother, Lord Palmerston, Victoria's husband, Prince Albert, and so many others—all of them, you hear, all of them were poisoned by the Antichrist Napoleon III." Yes, she was truly insane, Philippe saw, and in his disgust and fear, he now expected the worst.

But nothing happened. That afternoon, Charlotte had planned to bid a royal farewell to the king and queen of Naples: Francis II, the last monarch of the realm from which Garibaldi had chased him, and his wife, the beautiful Queen Sophie, sister of Empress Elisabeth of Austria. They lived in the magnificent Farnese Palace, which was their personal property. Charlotte announced her visit for five o'clock, but she arrived at three. The king was out, and the queen, who was getting dressed, hurried to welcome her visitor. Well aware, like the rest of Rome, of Charlotte's condition, she tried to limit herself to banalities. Charlotte spoke to her a little strangely, but Sophie later admitted that if she had not been warned, she would never have suspected there was anything wrong with her. Soon the king joined them, and refreshments were offered. Francis II, who still had the scene at the Vatican fresh in his mind, was anxious to reassure Charlotte, and committed a faux pas: "Eat them and don't be afraid, there is no danger here."

"You are the one who should be paying close attention to what you eat, if you do not want to be poisoned," Charlotte responded.

The king hung his head, and the queen avoided Charlotte's eyes and sank into the bleakest thoughts. It was said that insanity ran in her own family, the Wittelsbach. Would she one day wind up in the same condition as Charlotte? Luckily the empress did not stay too long. They bade farewell with the greatest cordiality before they took their leave of one another.

Philippe had decided to spend the night in his sister's room. He removed his waistcoat, unbuttoned his vest, and sat in an armchair. Charlotte lay down on her bed as he urged her to, but she did not stay there for long. She got back up to speak with him about the palaces she was planning to have built in Mexico. The magical word "Mexico" unleashed a flood of memories and images. She told him of the scenery and landscapes, and digressed into political analyses. He tried to put her back in bed. She tamely let him do it, only to jump up again and pace back and forth. Then she stopped in front of the armchair where he was beginning to drift off. "I have been poisoned, they have poisoned me, all of them, del Barrio, Kuhacsevich, del Valle. I will tell you how they poisoned me . . ." And the dramatic litany began again.

Philippe rose, and gently helped Charlotte lie down on her bed. She closed her eyes and dreamed, speaking out loud of Mexico, of memories, and of poison. Exhausted, Philippe returned to his arm-chair, but he did not manage to close his eyes. Though he knew all the trouble that Mathilde Doblinger had withstood, he still wished she were in his place, and he in his bed. Never could he have imag-ined that the ordeal would be so rough. This lunatic was his Char-lotte, his sister, so much stronger, so much smarter than he, the one he had idolized and revered, and who was now losing herself in delirium. He was almost angry with her for it.

The rising sun freed him. Mathilde Doblinger came in with breakfast and he took the chance to run home to his suite. After resting for a little while, he wrote three telegrams: to the Rothschilds in Paris, the Rothschilds in Vienna, and Cuza Bank in London. On his own authority, he instructed these establishments, which held much of Charlotte's great fortune, to ignore any request from his sister unless countersigned by Radonetz, Maximilian's right-hand man. Charlotte had to be prevented from destroying her capital in her insanity.

He then made preparations to take the special train he had ordered. Charlotte was already prepared to go. At the station, there were numerous officials, but not a single member of the Mexican entourage. No one had wanted to arouse Charlotte's fury by sub-jecting her to seeing the people she had accused of poisoning her. Unfortunately, imperial pride got the better of insanity's disillusions, and Charlotte became indignant that none of the Mexicans had seen fit to come see her off. Philippe had to gently explain to her that they had been detained, some of them even indisposed. Charlotte accepted these excuses, bade farewell to the dignitaries, foreign ministers, and to the cardinal Pius IX had sent to present her with a written message. The cardinal also handed her an envelope con-taining the outline of the accord that she and Maximilian had drafted, which she had left at the Vatican. The pope gave it back to her without so much as a comment.

What use would the accord be now anyway? She energetically and gracefully boarded the train, followed by Philippe. During the trip, the landscape slid by as brother and sister chatted normally for hours. Calm also reigned over lunch, but as soon as the meal was through, Charlotte came to sit beside Philippe and took his hand. "What have I done to you to make you want to poison me too? If it's my money you want, I'll give it to you right now, but my life is my own." Philippe not only protested, but he grew indignant. Charlotte turned her back on him and refused to say another word. This allusion to money was also curious, coming only hours after Philippe had given the bankers orders to ignore Charlotte's wishes.

The afternoon continued with the same tense and heavy atmosphere, though Charlotte remained silent and calm. The train stopped at Ancona, where the travelers boarded a specially chartered Lloyds steamship. During dinner aboard ship, Charlotte did not speak to Philippe. It was instead toward Bombelles that she turned. "You know, I have been poisoned. My husband was the one who poisoned me, it was Max. He had me poisoned during my trip to the Yucatán, that is why he sent me there."

Bombelles respectfully protested. Charlotte did not insist; she said not another word on the subject. The night passed fairly calmly. The next morning, Charlotte got off the train at Miramar's private station, from which, two years before, she had set out for Mexico. The estate's gates, normally open, had been shut. The park was closed to the public. The fairy-tale castle, built as a love nest, had become an asylum.

Charlotte was locked into the lovely ground-floor apartments, but no one had thought of the many windows, balconies, and verandas. The empress escaped and ran through the garden, furious that they dared lock her up. At the height of the incident was the fact that she left without a hat or gloves, which was unthinkable for a woman of her position, and which would prove her insanity, as if any further proof were needed.

Philippe ran after her. He found her wandering through the lawns and flower patches. Though he tried to reason with her and convince her to come back to the castle, she would not listen to him. She wanted to go to Trieste, to Vienna, to Brussels, she wanted to go far away, and without delay.

It took her brother four hours to persuade her to voluntarily come back with him to the house. He himself was surprised by his patience and calmness, but he had become disgusted with his role: "It is a vile affair to watch over the insane." At twenty-seven, his sister, in the full flower of her youth and beauty, had lost her mind, and was condemned to life imprisonment. Philippe could not yet accept this horrid reality.

Maximilian's faithful doctor, Jilek, who had remained in Europe, and Professor Reidel, the famous Viennese alienist, put everyone at ease with their diagnosis: "Her Majesty the empress of Mexico is indeed suffering from insanity, with a persecution complex produced by a mental disease more serious than we could at first believe. . . . The prognosis is poor, due to her growing agitation, but it is not completely without hope in light of the symptoms' accentuation. . . ."

An indiscretion on the part of one of the servants informed Philippe that the next night, Charlotte was preparing to take advantage of the darkness to escape from her Miramar prison and run away. The doctors judged the castle to be too easy to break out of. On the other hand, there was the Castelleto, the modest villa Maximilian had had built to resemble a Gothic pseudo-castle while he kept an eye over the big castle's construction. Its very smallness and its tight, barred windows offered better chances of controlling her. The decision was made at six o'clock in the evening: Charlotte would be brought to the Castelleto.

But she would hear none of it. The doctors begged Philippe to go away for a while. He heard Charlotte's pleas and screams as they used force on her, and finally they brought her down and carried her like a parcel across the park, which was lit by the rays of the setting sun. She was fighting furiously. They arrived at the Castelleto and pushed her into her bedroom, where the windows were defended by thick bars, and they locked her in. Then the doctors asked Philippe to go in and calm her. He resigned himself to his duty and found her bruised by her ordeal. She begged him to let her out, "Save me, Maximilian is trying to poison me!" At the same time, she was making the sign of the cross and mumbling prayers.

She grabbed Philippe's arm and would not let go. He called for help and the doctors came in, tearing her violently off her brother. She screamed and pleaded; Philippe ran out, unable to bear his sister's shrieks any longer. "What a horror to be restrained like that," he sighed.

Still trembling from the scene he had just witnessed, Philippe wrote a long report to his elder brother Leopold II on October 10, 1866. He told him of the first symptoms of their sister's insanity according to the information he had gathered: her signs of delirium, her accusations against Radonetz during their trip from Miramar to Rome. He spoke at length of her outburst of insanity at the Vatican. He told him what he saw with his own eyes, an experience that had crushed all hope in him: "The doctors believe they can cure such things, but I do not." Like everyone around him, he wondered what could have caused this inexplicable illness.

According to the alienist Reidel, it came about due to the climate and conditions in Mexico, and to the painful failure of Charlotte's negotiations with Napoleon III, which may have caused an irrepa-

rable shock. But Philippe knew more about it than did the doctors, and he had his own explanation: "I believe that her husband's
recognized and notorious impotence played a large role in it. If she
had had children, her imagination would have been busy with other
things besides politics, and her blood would have taken a different
turn. It is said that Maximilian has never even touched her."

As Charlotte's brother, Philippe was in a good position to know
what other people did not talk about. Finally the truth had come
out: Maximilian and Charlotte had never had physical relations.

Luckily, the next day, Charlotte seemed to have calmed down
enough for Philippe to be allowed to come visit her in the Castelleto.
She confided in him that she was not quite well, that perhaps she
was sick and needed help. Infinitely relieved, Philippe now wanted
to leave Miramar as soon as possible. The doctors and guards, led
by Bombelles, came together to support him and to disperse any
twinges of conscience he might be feeling. In fact, all they wanted
to do was to get rid of this member of her family in order to treat
her as they saw fit, far from prying eyes.

They thus persuaded Philippe that not only was his presence
useless, but it might even be harmful, since it put Charlotte in an
alarming state of agitation that could lead to a breakdown. The
sooner he left, the better it would be for his sister's health. Terror-
ized by the spectacle of his imprisoned sister, Philippe needed no
more convincing. He left by train on the night of October 14, 1867.
From now on, locked away in the Castelleto, Charlotte was cut off
from the world.

Gossip about the empress's insanity exploded throughout Europe. At
her relatives' imperial and royal palaces, in the press, among the
people, it was the only topic of conversation, fed by the most
fantastical of rumors. As always, the ones most willing to talk were

the ones who should have remained the most silent: the members of Charlotte's entourage, Mexicans as well as Austrians. Besieged by questions on all sides, they embellished the truth for effect. They had known about the empress's insanity for some time, since signs of it had appeared long before the fateful day in Rome.

It had all started during the trip to the Yucatán, in November. There, the empress had acted bizarrely several times, saying all sorts of strange things. Then, while she was heading toward Veracruz, there was that innocent overnight stay at the Esteva household at Puebla when the prefect was not there. The truth was even stranger. It was a sort of fixation of the empress's, and even though it had been explained to her several times that the masters of the house were absent, she had gone to their residence in the middle of the night and woken up the night guards. The empress had wandered at length throughout the house, and no one could understand why.

Later, during the journey back to Mexico City, an axle in her convoy broke, and they had to take refuge in an inn filled with travelers, including many republicans; she had heard the song that had been composed against her, "*Adiós mamá Carlotta,*" sung a hundred times that night. Suddenly, she began to see enemies everywhere, she was afraid for her life, and everyone had to leave in the middle of the night. During the long sea voyage to Europe, she remained locked away in her cabin and would not come out for any reason, refusing to speak except to utter incomprehensible sentences. But the worst was yet to come. In Paris, during her visit to Saint-Cloud, someone offered her a glass of orangeade, and she pushed it away screaming, "Murderer, do not let me take your poisoned drink, run away!"

During the second interview, when Napoleon III refused to give her the help she wanted, she lost her temper and insulted him: "How could I have forgotten who I am and who you are? I should have remembered that the blood of the Bourbons flows in my veins. I should never have dishonored my race and my person by humiliating myself before a Bonaparte, and by dealing with a usurper." She had fainted not once, but three times. Eugenie had had to unbutton her corset, take off her stockings and shoes with her own hands, and moisten her temples, feet, and hands with cologne. What a scandal!

This information came from Madam del Barrio, the gentle and patient lady-in-waiting, and from Blasio, the faithful butler, the ones who loved their monarch so much.

As the conversations and confidences about Charlotte's illness blossomed, new details and episodes formerly unknown slowly came to light. On the day Charlotte had not wanted to leave the Vatican, the only way they had been able to put an end to such indecency was to ask her to inspect an orphanage. She had accepted, and the visit had started off well, when all of a sudden, in the kitchen, she had thrown herself to the floor, thanking God for saving her from certain death. Then, spotting a stew simmering on the oven, she had jumped up so fast that no one could stop her, and had plunged her hand into the boiling liquid. Screaming and horribly burned, she had pulled out a hunk of meat and devoured it on the spot, like a hungry cannibal. But the pain had been so excruciating that she had fainted, which had given them the chance to bring her back to the hotel.

Once again, it was Madam del Barrio who told this story, adding to her lies. Perhaps she was looking for a way to avenge the treatment she had received from Charlotte. But in her, just as in Blasio and the other members of her entourage who invented more and more stories, we may detect a classic reaction. The announcement of the empress of Mexico's insanity had plunged Europe into astonishment. Her intimates found nothing better to do than to claim that they had known the truth for a long time, and had only kept their mouths shut out of discretion. Picking through their memories, they began to unearth the most banal anecdotes and transform them into harbingers of insanity in order to explain the incomprehensible to themselves as well as to the public. Even when she was sane, when she was suffering in silence, Charlotte had wrapped herself in her position. She had confided in no one. The more her heart bled, the more closed, haughty, and unfeeling she appeared, unlike Maximilian, who always remained the personification of charm and kindness. Loners like Charlotte are never truly popular, while seducers like Maximilian are always loved. Thus, butlers and ladies-in-waiting had come to prefer the emperor to the empress. Perhaps they even held a grudge against her, which would explain the vicious stories about her condition.

There had been no known case of insanity among Charlotte's ancestors. The Saxe-Coburgs were a sane and balanced people, and Leopold I's neurosis was not enough to explain his daughter's condition. As for the Orleans, there was not even the hint of insanity among the lot of them. At the time she was succumbing to madness, Charlotte was a deeply unhappy and frustrated woman, largely due to the husband whom she loved and who loved her. Added to this was the horrible ordeal of the trip to France and Rome, which brought her to despair. In her introversion, she said nothing and showed nothing. But the lava was boiling slowly within her, building up each day, until the pressure was too strong and the volcano erupted. If it is true that "in each of us sleeps a lunatic," then the lunatic awoke in Charlotte and made its presence known in the most brutal of ways.

Charlotte was already locked up at Miramar when on October 18, 1866, Maximilian received two telegrams. The first was from his ambassador to Rome, announcing that Charlotte had been stricken by cerebral congestion; the second was from Bombelles, stating that the empress had arrived at Miramar, that her condition was serious, but that all the proper dispositions had been made and that Professor Reidel had been summoned from Vienna. In his anguish, the last detail caught Maximilian's attention, and he had a feeling that something was very wrong. He asked his private doctor, Basch, "Do you know a Professor Reidel from Vienna?"

"Yes, sire, he is the director of the asylum."

Finally, Maximilian understood the full extent of the truth in all its horror. His reaction was immediate—he was leaving for Europe. Too bad for Mexico. Besides, everyone wanted him to abdicate: the French, Bazaine first of all, and several of his advisors, who never stopped singing the same tune. So he would abdicate now to rush to Charlotte's bedside, and that is what he announced to his brother-in-law Philippe: "We will surround our dear Charlotte with so much care and affection that God in his immense goodness will have pity on our sorrow and give back our love her poor ailing faculties." If Charlotte was to recover, he wanted it to be thanks to him; he knew that it would be thanks to him, and that was worth the sacrifice of a crown. Charlotte was sick, Charlotte was in danger, and he loved her more now than he had ever loved her before.

That very evening, he gave instructions to Hertzfeld, an advisor he had recently summoned from Austria, to prepare his departure with all due discretion. Messengers were sent to Veracruz to charter an Austrian corvette, the *Dandelot,* to bring the emperor to Europe.

But first, he had to put his affairs in order. He simply annulled the infamous decrees of October 1865 that had inaugurated a reign of terror and aroused universal disapproval. He dissolved the legions of Belgian and Austrian volunteers. He sent his heir, the little Iturbide, back to his family, since his mother, Doña Alicia, was so stridently demanding him back. "*Qué pasa?*" the boy asked, surprised at having to leave his adoptive father, and panicked by the sudden commotion all around him. "Nothing, my child, we are just saving you from a misfortune," Maximilian answered.

The emperor wasted no time. Two days after he learned of Charlotte's insanity, preparations for his departure were already under way. The reason for his departure was not announced, but everyone knew it anyway. He had not abdicated, but he was expected to do so at any moment. Though he had given instructions to Hertzfeld, it was Father Fischer who took care of everything, since he was particularly worried about the emperor's failing health, still undermined by dysentery and by the new depression caused by his wife's plight. They were anxious not to push him too much, so it took a week to cover the distance from Mexico City to Orizaba, twice the normal time, which exasperated the French soldiers escorting Maximilian — the countryside was so unsafe that they expected an attack at any moment. The "dissidents" were lurking around Mexico City itself and around Veracruz. The only way the emperor was able to leave the capital at all was under the protection of the occupying army.

At Orizaba, Father Fischer had organized a reception, which he hoped would raise the emperor's spirits. Maximilian had expected to be booed, but suddenly his aides announced enthusiastic crowds. He now assumed he no longer needed his French escort. He could not tolerate them anymore anyway, so he hastened to send them back without so much as a thank-you, anxious to make his triumphant entrance into Orizaba.

The trunks containing his effects were forwarded on to Veracruz to be loaded onto the *Dandelot*. Hertzfeld was sent on ahead to prepare for his arrival. But Maximilian no longer seemed to be in a hurry. Once he was set up in the luxurious Jalapilla hacienda, he came back to life and enjoyed the beautiful natural setting. He had no choice but to recall the French troops to protect his little paradise, but he enjoyed tricking them, eluding their surveillance and going off riding in the thick forests.

In the isolation and silence of the lush vegetation, he thought about his future. He imagined his family's welcome, and the coldness of Francis-Joseph, who would make sure not to offer him the smallest position as consolation. He would no longer have his place among the imperial family. He could already hear the *we told you so*'s. With such a steady diet of humiliation, he would have no choice but to flee to Miramar. Of course, he would like to see Charlotte and help her, but what if she did not recover? At thirty-four years of age, he would be forced to retire and live out the rest of his life caring for a lunatic.

"And after all, this departure is the same thing as running away."

"What do you mean, running away?"

"Of course it is running away, sire," Fischer whispered again in Maximilian's ear. He was now the only intimate with the emperor, and he took ample advantage of the situation. This adventurer with a murky past, this massive, graying Teuton with thick features and squinting eyes, was able to apply almost Byzantine subtlety to twist the emperor around his finger. Maximilian replied that whether it was running away or not, he could not logically stay in Mexico.

"On the contrary, sire, it is now or never."

"But the French are about to leave."

"That is exactly what will save the empire."

"You have taken leave of your senses, Father Fischer."

"Not at all, sire. The French soldiers are unpopular in Mexico, so much so that their very presence has become a liability to the empire. Once they leave, a movement of unheard-of enthusiasm will sweep across the Mexicans, who are finally rid of their occupiers, and Your Majesty will easily be able to raise ten, twenty, even thirty thousand men. With them, without the help of foreigners, it will be simple to crush the rebellion and establish the empire on much a sturdier base."

But on what political party should he rely? On the natural supporters of the throne: the conservatives, of course, Father Fischer's silent partners. Maximilian took note of the argument, but he made no decision. The preparations for his voyage continued, but he himself remained where he was. The days passed and still he did not emerge from his indecision. He learned that Juárez's best general, Porfirio Diaz, had taken back Oaxaca from the imperialists. This bad news should have nudged him one step closer toward Veracruz, but then he received a letter from his mother. Archduchess Sophie had learned of his intention to abdicate, and strongly disapproved. The honor of the Habsburgs forbade Maximilian from leaving his post just because the French army was pulling out. Let him stay in Mexico at least until the cause of the empire played out one way or the other. Reading this letter, the emperor of Mexico acted just like he did when he was a little boy: he obeyed whatever his mother said.

In Washington, everyone was so sure that Maximilian would leave Mexico that for them, he had ceased to exist. The only person who mattered was Juárez; the American administration dispatched a delegation that included the famous General Sherman to make arrangements with the new leader of Mexico. The French were also certain of Maximilian's abdication. They were in a hurry, and were only waiting for Maximilian to leave before they permanently withdrew themselves. But he was taking a little bit too long. Respectfully but firmly, they worked up the courage to tell him so. Maximilian took offense. The French could not understand. Had not the emperor informed them of his decision to abdicate? Of course, but he could not formally do so without first having heard the opinions of his ministers and advisors still in Mexico. So he gathered them together at Orizaba.

The French had little choice but to agree to his wishes, just as Fischer, the puppeteer in this affair, had foreseen. The highest dignitaries in the empire thus left Mexico City to meet at the Jalapilla hacienda on November 28. Maximilian left them alone to discuss the matter. He did not attend the meeting, and instead went out on a butterfly hunt, though not without first writing thank-you notes to the faithful who had served him so well during his reign. For he had already decided: he would be leaving after the council. But when the council ended, the members, organized behind the scenes by Fischer, voted overwhelmingly to maintain the empire. Maximilian must not abdicate.

"Fine," the emperor announced, "I will not abdicate."

The French watched in shock as Father Fischer sipped champagne with his accomplices, the conservative ministers. At last, Maximilian had obeyed the directive Charlotte wrote him in each of her letters until she reached the verge of insanity: never give up. By obeying her, he decided, he was giving her the best proof of his love.

At the same time, the American frigate *Susquehannah* had entered the Veracruz bay, bearing the American delegates who were to enter into talks with Benito Juárez. They heard the church bells ringing throughout the city, and learned that the emperor had decided to stay, that he was not going to abdicate, that the empire would go on. There was nothing the Americans could do but turn around and go home. Maximilian set off on the road back to Mexico City. This time, he wasted no time. In a few days, he passed Puebla. He rang in the New Year not far from Mexico City. "I have spent a melancholy New Year's longing for you," he wrote Charlotte. "On such days, the ocean feels doubly as wide, but with God's help, every-

thing will work out. I squeeze you against my heart . . ." He hoped
she would be able to understand his message, but it was the last
letter he sent her.

At Buenavista, Maximilian came across Colonel Van der Smissen, the commander of the now defunct Belgian legion, going in
the other direction. Maximilian received the colonel coldly, since
he had never gotten along with him. Van der Smissen started out
speaking in French; Maximilian answered him in Spanish. Van
der Smissen begged the emperor to reconsider his decision and
abdicate, in order to spare the country, and especially himself, the
emperor; otherwise, he said, it would be a catastrophe of epic proportions. Refusing to hear him out, Maximilian cut the interview
short. Van der Smissen set out again on the road that would lead
him back to Europe, and Maximilian watched the doors of destiny
shut behind him.

The happy racket of *cohetes,* Mexican firecrackers, cannon
salutes, and church bells welcomed him to Mexico City. Chapultepec
brought back too many memories, and in any case, the castle had
mostly been evacuated and emptied, since Maximilian had never
meant to return. He set himself up next door, in the Teja hacienda,
a poor excuse for an imperial palace, but one that suited its occu-
pant's present state only too well.

Barely had Charlotte been declared mentally incompetent when the Saxe-
Coburgs and the Habsburgs both started sniffing around her immense fortune, made up of funds, stocks, and investments placed
in banks in many different countries. The Austrian imperial family
announced that since she was married to Maximilian, her fortune
should be administered by the head of the House of Austria, the
Emperor Francis-Joseph. Leopold II responded that since Charlotte's fortune came from the royal family of Belgium, the Habs-

burgs had no right to touch it. Discussions went on discreetly, but ferociously. The Austrians proposed to administer Maximilian's fortune as well as the part that would rightfully fall to Charlotte, while returning to the Belgians their former princess's dowry. Understanding that this would allow Francis-Joseph to annul the marriage contract and avoid paying Charlotte her rightful portion of Maximilian's estate should he die, Leopold II cried foul against what he considered an act of "deep-seated dishonesty."

As for the proprietress of these millions, they all said there was no need to worry about her: the doctors were taking good care of her, and it was not worth the trouble to go see her, since in any case, the doctors had forbidden all visits for her own good. But Charlotte still had a few faithful friends left. The Belgian Eloin made the trip to Miramar. He was not allowed to see Charlotte, but he kept his eyes open and registered quite a few details. The Mexican entourage had dispersed. Some were now living in Trieste, while others had left for Paris. Only the grand chamberlain, Count del Valle, remained at Miramar, and he had no access to Charlotte either. She remained in the Castelleto. Bombelles was in charge of everything: he had set up Doctor Jilek and the other doctors assigned to Charlotte on the ground floor of the Castelleto; he had had Charlotte's bedroom windows nailed shut, and the door that opened out directly onto the main entranceway sealed. Charlotte could leave only through the bedroom, where her maids were stationed around the clock, keeping an eye on her even at night after the shutters were closed. Only Mathilde Doblinger tried to humanize the incarceration, and Charlotte continued to rely on her alone.

Bombelles informed Eloin of the patient's routine. Wake-up between seven and eight after a calm night; for breakfast, coffee with milk, and bread and butter; then a bath in warm water; next, music and drawing. Each morning, the doctors and the chaplain visited her. Weather permitting, she might walk under escort through the park, but in this windy, rainy autumn, she was rarely allowed outside, which did not improve the patient's mood. Lunch was at one-thirty. Charlotte decided on the menu herself, with the help of the chaplain and one of the doctors, who tried to serve her only healthy and light meals. During the afternoon: news and conversation, a stroll, and in good weather, a boat ride. During the evening, conversation and cards until eight-thirty. By nine, Charlotte was in bed. Her physical health was excellent. The principle of the alienists' treatment consisted of constantly distracting her to keep her attention off the fixations that were poisoning her mind.

Eloin was surprised to find out that Charlotte, who had always written volumes of letters, had become rather lazy in that regard. She only remembered birthdays and anniversaries, telegraphing her wishes to her relatives, for example to Queen Victoria's eldest daughter, who cordially sent a response. Other relatives, such as her sister-in-law, Empress Elisabeth, sent her carefully worded letters. Charlotte said she was too tired to write back. On the other hand, she took great pleasure in writing her mother-in-law Archduchess Sophie a perfectly normal letter limited to pure banalities. She proved more frank with her brother Leopold II, telling him in a letter that she had not read the newspaper in a month, probably because she was forbidden to, and that she would very much like to know what was going on in the world. She would so much have liked to go to Naples, "but I was brought back here, I suppose it will have to be for another time . . . in any case, in this little world known as Miramar, the *bora* [a terrible northern wind that is said to adversely affect the mind] is starting to blow, though it is still moderated by the natural gentleness of the climate."

Eloin carefully questioned Charlotte's doctors in order to make the most complete report possible to Maximilian. The practitioners still had sincere hopes, but they refused to commit themselves to an exact date for her cure. Eloin was a sincere and sensitive man. The doctors' reassuring words did not at all change his surprise at what he had seen and intuited: "Courage fails me as I write His Majesty, but I do have faith that she will be cured."

November fourth was Charlotte's name day. She took great pleasure in reading and answering all the congratulatory telegrams. She was even allowed to have a few visitors, including the castle's architect, her former lady-in-waiting, Princess Auersberg, and even Bombelles who, though controlling everything, had kept himself out of sight ever since she had accused him of trying to poison her as she had accused the others. But today, far from reproaching him, she welcomed him graciously, reminding him that Saint Charles' Day was also his name day, and wishing him the best. Encouraged by this attitude, the doctors permitted her to stroll in the park. As Charlotte had asked for music for her name day, four violinists had come, and started playing a quartet the moment they saw her appear. Suddenly, Charlotte began to tremble. "They are here to kill me!" she cried. They led her back as quickly as possible to the Castelleto. As they were walking, she saw the castle's governor. "He's a spy!" she shouted. "They are all spies!" she repeated, pointing at the workmen repairing the roof and the washerwomen carrying their large baskets toward the washhouse.

For the next few days, she fell into a sort of apathy, but the obsession remained: everyone was trying to kill her. Doctor Jilek and Mathilde Doblinger accompanied her daily to the little pond in the center of the lawn to gather the only water that she would drink. The same alienists, who just a few weeks before were reassuring Eloin, now tinged their reports to Maximilian and the Belgian royal family with a new pessimism. Instead of getting closer, Charlotte's cure seemed to be slipping ever further away.

Still, she continued to be interested in what was going on around her. She learned that the head of her kitchen had just had a child, a boy. She wanted to see him at all costs. They brought her the baby; she took him in her arms and called him Augustin, just like little Iturbide, Maximilian's adoptive son. She squeezed him so violently against her that her entourage jumped—they rushed to her and tore the baby out of her arms. In the space of a second, all the frustration of a woman who had never been able to be a mother had flared up to the surface.

From her bedroom window, which she could not open, Charlotte stared out at the sea. Every day, she spent hours looking out at the horizon, waiting to see the boat that would bring her husband back to her. She did this with the stubbornness, but also the instinct of the insane. She was sure that Maximilian would come back, and yet she did not know that a telegram had just arrived at Miramar announcing his departure for Europe.

As soon as he received the telegram, Bombelles set out for Gibraltar to greet his childhood friend. Charlotte's family prepared to receive Maximilian. "Finally we are at the end of this deplorable adventure, which it would have been so much better never to have undertaken," Philippe remarked.

Unfortunately, he was mistaken; the "deplorable adventure" was far from over. Maximilian would not arrive at Gibraltar, since he had remained in Mexico. He received the blessings of his mother Archduchess Sophie, who, in a new letter, congratulated him on having resisted his legitimate urge to see Charlotte. But the emperor was seized by nostalgia as he read his mother's description of the family's Christmas. For the first time, she and his father had gathered all their descendants together, and mountains of presents were piled up beneath the tree. Gisele and her brother, the young heir Rudolph, opened their gifts in a frenzy. Francis-Joseph cradled the baby Otto, his younger brother Archduke Charles-Louis's new son. Otto's older brother, young Francis Ferdinand, preferred to sit with his aunt Sissi, Empress Elisabeth. As the imperial family celebrated the Savior's birthday, the musical clock on the mantelpiece began to chime. Archduchess Sophie felt tears coming to her eyes, since the clock had been a gift from Max. How much more she would have cried if she had known that her grandson Rudolph would one day be the sad protagonist of the Mayerling tragedy, that her other grandson Francis Ferdinand would be assassinated in Sarajevo, that her daughter-in-law Elisabeth, even though she did not like her, would be stabbed on a pier in Switzerland, and that the baby Otto would be the father of the last emperor of Austria. As for her dear Max . . .

On February 5, 1867, a great commotion shook Mexico City at dawn. The inhabitants ran out of their homes to find out what was happening. This was the day that the French were leaving; pouring out of every barracks in the city, the soldiers made up an endless procession. Marshal Bazaine in his dress uniform and his officers glimmering with decorations, medals, and feathers paraded one last time through the streets of the capital, lined with curious onlookers who kept a reverential silence. The soldiers passed in front of the imperial palaces, all the shutters of which had remained closed by command from on high. The enormous building seemed deserted, but it was not, for behind the blinds of a window stood a single, solitary man. Emperor Maximilian waited in absolute stillness until the last soldier disappeared around the corner, and then he mumbled, "At last, I am free."

"Finally, we are free," his subjects answered in their silence, thrilled as they were to see an end to the reign of the foreigners who, claiming to have brought peace, had acted like conquistadors, and who, in their opinion, were leaving the country poorer and more miserable than they had found it.

By a tacit agreement with Benito Juárez, the French were able to reach Veracruz without being attacked or otherwise harassed. Bazaine headed toward the sea without wasting any more time, but without haste either. At every halt, he expected Maximilian to join them. The emperor had refused to see him before his departure, but Bazaine had hoped that, at the last moment, he would come to his senses and come with them. As he climbed up into the ship that would bring them to Europe, Bazaine turned around to scan the road from Mexico City. He waited a long time to spot a cloud of dust heralding Maximilian's arrival, but no dust cloud ever came.

When his ship had sailed from the Mexican coast, Bazaine mumbled, "I should have dragged him away by force."

Father Fischer and the conservatives told Maximilian endlessly that now that the French were gone, he was finally the true emperor of Mexico. In case he might have doubted that this assertion was subject to certain conditions, a bit of news soon came to remind him of the truth: the terrible defeat of the loyalist troops at San Jacinto by the hands of the dissidents, who had executed no less than one hundred and one prisoners. "Too bad for them," Father Fischer whispered to Maximilian. "For each defeat we take, we will have a hundred victories, but since after his victory at Oaxaca, Porfirio Diaz controls the south, in order to crush him, Your Majesty must leave Mexico City for the time being and go join the main loyalist army at Queretaro. From there, we will be able to act much more efficiently to end this rebellion once and for all." Dominated by the strange priest, Maximilian acquiesced.

On February 13, 1867, he quietly left the capital at dawn and headed for the town about one hundred and twenty miles to the north. Among his rather meager staff, the handsome Colonel Lopez, the same one who had been with Maximilian when he had first taken power, rode by his side. Other favorites had eclipsed him since then, but one after the other, they had all disappeared, while Lopez alone had stayed with his emperor for better or for worse. Maximilian had not wished to bring any foreigners with him; the army of Mexico should be made up of nothing but Mexicans.

The only exception he had made was for a strange couple. The man, the prince of Salm, was a German noble, quite the adventurer. He had found his perfect mate in a young and beautiful female squire of French origin, just as much a daredevil as he, whom he had married. Maximilian had met them recently, had not been able to resist the pleasure of speaking his mother tongue, and had now brought them along for the ride.

As usual, the conservatives, urged on by Father Fischer, had taken things well in hand, and Queretaro had prepared a grandiose reception for its monarch. An immense crowd, with cheers and applause, troops presenting arms, triumphant orations, a *Te Deum* — nothing was missing. Maximilian felt his confidence double.

Queretaro was a wide and rich city, dotted with magnificent churches and opulent convents, spread out on a wide plain. The rebels soon occupied the low, rocky hills around it. At the beginning, they were just a thin line of men, easy to break through, but the loyalist troops went about it poorly. Skirmishes continued to occur, but each time, the loyalists lost more and more men, while the rebels only gained new recruits. By the end of March, Queretaro was completely surrounded by the rebels, though they kept carefully to the hills.

Having learned that Juárez's flamboyant general, Porfirio Diaz, had taken Puebla and was now threatening Mexico City, Maximilian called a war council, during which General Marquez proposed moving part of the troops gathered at Queretaro to go help the capital. Although this contradicted the very reason Maximilian had concentrated his forces at Queretaro in the first place, he agreed to divide his troops.

Thus, Marquez left Queretaro with a portion of the troops, but the rebels did not make a move. He went to fight the triumphant Porfirio Diaz, was soundly beaten, ran away without further ado to take refuge in Mexico City, and immediately surrendered the city the moment Diaz began to besiege it.

Benito Juárez then sent Maximilian an offer: he could leave Queretaro now, with all the honors due to his rank, and board a ship without trouble for Europe.

Maximilian refused haughtily. By the end of April, Queretaro was surrounded. For Maximilian, there would be no escape.

12

On an April morning in 1867, several ships flying French flags docked at the port of Trieste, bringing back the survivors of the Austrian legion that had gone to fight in Mexico. As they watched them come ashore, the people of Trieste were horrified to see what had become of the soldiers, now so haggard and emaciated, their clothes in tatters. Not only had they not received any pay in months, but their equipment trains had also been attacked and burned by dissidents on the road from Veracruz. Archduke Albert, dispatched by his cousin Emperor Francis-Joseph, had come to officially greet the veterans. He was careful not to make a detour through Miramar, for he had no desire to see the person the imperial family now considered a leper: the lunatic.

Charlotte was not such a lunatic as before, the newspapers announced. In fact, the press said that the empress of Mexico was on the way to a complete recovery, so much so that she was now once again able to deal with Mexican affairs. The Spanish consul to Trieste, Don Joaquim Garcia Miranda, was a witness of choice. He must have had spies at Miramar, for his reports contained extraordinary details otherwise unknown. "Do not believe the papers. They are lying," he wrote his minister. It was true that the empress was calmer, but her obsessions and phobias had not gone away.

Consequently, the total isolation that the press had announced as being lifted was to continue, even though the patient enjoyed long periods of lucidity during which she recovered her intelligence and wrote quite normally to her friends and family. Her letter to her old friend, the countess of Grunne, was the very model of clarity, vivacity, and alertness: she wrote that since she did not understand the turn that modern history was taking, she preferred to study ancient history. She was reading *Holy History* by Victor Duruy, and she was beginning a history of Greece. She was devouring a recent biography of the Swedish king Gustave III, whose tragic death inspired Verdi's *Un Ballo in Maschera*. She was also reading Tocqueville's *Democracy in America*. She confided to her brother Philippe that she was still painting fans, and that she had finished one for her mother-in-law Archduchess Sophie, and another for her aunt Clementine. She also enjoyed making collages out of butterflies, identifying each one brought to her by its scientific name. She wrote to her elder brother Leopold II to congratulate him on the speech he gave at the opening of the Belgian parliament, described to him how work on Miramar castle, which had never stopped, was progressing, and proudly told him that the second-floor imperial hall was at last complete. She kept abreast of family events and its members' comings and goings, and was enchanted by the engagement between her brother Philippe and Princess Marie von

Hohenzollern. She already loved this new sister-in-law, whom she would very much like to meet. Of course, she was not invited to the wedding, but she made no comment on being ostracized. As a wedding present, she designed a bracelet for the bride and had it made by a jeweler in Trieste.

She was happy that Philippe and his young bride had been invited to attend the World's Fair opening in Paris, the same one for which she had drawn up a list of items to represent the Mexican empire. She thought about all the people they would see there: Napoleon III and Eugenie, their English cousins, Bertie, Vicky, and so many others. She complained about the laconic way her brother described the fair that she would have liked so much to see in person.

To judge from the empress's letters, one might have imagined her walking through the gardens and picking flowers, reading newspapers and the latest books, going about her voluminous correspondence, practicing different arts as a talented amateur — in a word, freely living the existence of a noblewoman in her fairy-tale domain. Between the lines, however, one noticed that she spoke a great deal of others and very little of herself, while the doctors' reports and the information given by Bombelles to the Belgian royal family grew a little thinner every day. It was known that Charlotte asked her entourage about Maximilian on a daily basis. "Is there any news of him? What is becoming of him? Where is he?" Each time, she got the same answer: since the civil war was continuing in Mexico, the emperor was so busy defeating the dissidents that unfortunately he did not have the time to send news to his wife. As for Charlotte's family, they no longer knew anything about her condition, or even about her existence. No one saw her because she did not receive anyone, by her doctors' orders. As the weeks passed, the vise tightened and her incarceration grew more severe.

✿ ✿ ✿

And yet, strange news filtered out through the bars at Miramar, though Charlotte's family was unable to check its veracity. The faithful maid, Mathilde Doblinger, had a Viennese assistant, Amalia Stöger, a thirty-three-year-old beauty with magnificent eyes and a sumptuous head of hair. Though divorced from her husband, she remained deeply religious. But on the morning of June 2, 1867, she was found dead in her room on the second floor of the castle, hanging from the chandelier. She had unhooked a silk cord that had been used to hold back the drapes, rolled it eight times around her neck, and killed herself. The Spanish consul to Trieste, Garcia Miranda, always informed, had at first thought that it was Charlotte's Belgian lady-in-waiting, but there were no ladies-in-waiting at Miramar anymore. Then he found out that it was a Viennese maid who was said to be deeply in love with Maximilian. Reflecting on the elements of this tragedy, he let his eyes wander, until they came to rest on the front page of a local paper, *L'Osservatore Triestino.* The headlines of the paper had caught his attention: they stated in big letters that in Queretaro, Emperor Maximilian had unconditionally surrendered to Benito Juárez's troops.

In the heat of the Mexican summer, Maximilian and his army had held out for days, even weeks, under terrible conditions. Water had been cut off; food was running out; soldiers and townsfolk were forced to eat the corpses of horses and dogs. The only bread they had was cooked by a nun, who used the flour meant for communion wafers. The only thing Maximilian ate anymore was canned fish. Bit by bit, everyone was losing confidence. Desertions were growing more frequent, and, to top it off, a typhoid epidemic had broken out in Queretaro. The situation was desperate. Then Maximilian's last

favorite, the handsome Colonel Lopez, intervened. One night, slipping through the lines of loyalist soldiers, he reached the republican
camp, where he came across an old friend, Manuel Ricon-Gallardo.
This man had a father who was a monarchist and a sister who had
been one of Charlotte's ladies-in-waiting; he and his brother were
serving under Juárez, for in the noble Mexican families, the two
sides often lived right next to each other.

Lopez sat down at a table with him, asked for a glass, and raised
it to toast the republic. Ricon-Gallardo threw his own wine in
Lopez's face with the words, "I don't drink with traitors," but he
agreed to bring Lopez to General Escobedo, commander of the
republican troops besieging Queretaro. Lopez offered to hand the
city over to him, on the condition that Maximilian and his men could
leave without trouble and board a ship for Europe. Escobedo accepted the proposal. He put his men on alert and followed Lopez.
But Ricon-Gallardo, who suspected a trap, took out his revolver
and pressed it against his old friend's temple: "One false move and
we both die. In the meantime, show us what you can do."

This took place during the night of May 14, 1867. Maximilian,
horribly ill with dysentery, had to take tranquilizers, and was resting in a stupor in his headquarters, the convent of Santa Cruz.
Suddenly, Lopez ran into the room shouting, "Hurry, save the
emperor, the enemy is here!" Despite his weakness, Maximilian
jumped up and got dressed. Followed by Blasio and a few other
faithful supporters, he managed to leave the convent and go out onto
the street. Sentries from the republican army were everywhere. The
convent and the city were already in the hands of Juárez's troops.
As a soldier came to block Maximilian's way, an officer intervened:
"Let them pass, they are peasants." A strange outfit for peasants,
perhaps, those embroidered uniforms covered with medals.

At the convent's exit, Blasio clearly recognized Manuel Ricon-
Gallardo, who looked away and let Maximilian pass. Obviously,

the republicans were purposefully letting him escape. Maximilian made his way into the night on foot.

Colonel Lopez caught up to him. "This way, sire, I will hide you so that we can get you out later."

"Hide me? Never."

Maximilian would let himself be saved, but not without trying everything else first. He would abdicate, he would go back to Europe, he had said so, but only after a heroic resistance that would wash away the shame and humiliation of returning like that. He thus continued walking, while Lopez slipped off into the shadows toward Cerro Las Campanas, a rocky hill just outside the city where the one hundred soldiers he had left had regrouped. Barely had he reached them when tens of thousands of republican soldiers surrounded the hill. The guns blasted nonstop during this last-ditch fight which, surprisingly enough, did not claim a single casualty. As the gunshots grew more numerous on every side, Maximilian realized that it was useless to go on. At that moment, Maximilian no longer had any desire to be saved; he would much rather have been done with it right then and there. He would have liked to die in combat by throwing himself in front of a bullet that would free him forever from this nightmare. But it was not to be.

The order had probably been given to spare his life at all costs. So he raised the white flag and surrendered to General Escobedo. As he crossed the city in his enemies' hands, he heard thousands of the victorious soldiers singing ironically as he passed by, "*Adiós mamá Carlotta.*" Tears welled up in his eyes. Finally, he was incarcerated at the very Santa Cruz convent where he had been living since he had arrived at Queretaro.

At Miramar, the ravishing Amalia Stöger had hanged herself when she found out her handsome emperor was being held prisoner. The news of Maximilian's fate was kept from Charlotte, and she was thus the only one who did not know what the rest of Europe was talking about. Soon it was learned that Benito Juárez intended to put Maximilian on trial, and everyone feared the worst. Agnes de Salm, the former squire and wife of the German prince who had accompanied Maximilian, decided to play their last card: she was going to help Maximilian escape. To this end, she offered millions, and even, it is said, her body to Juárez's soldiers so that they would take part in her undertaking. To no avail; now that Juárez had Maximilian, despite his promises, he intended to make an example of him that would crush all desire for a monarchy among the Mexicans, and all urge to interfere among the Europeans.

In his prison, the emperor read *The Life and Death by the Axe of King Charles I of England* with one hand, and with the other, signed decrees awarding the Order of Guadalupe that he himself had founded. At the same time, the thick book *Protocolo de la Corte Imperial* finally came off the printing press, as if nothing had changed. Maximilian lost his courage and confidence only when one of his fellow captives told him that Charlotte had died. Without completely believing the news, he mumbled, "One less bond holding me to life."

His trial began without him, for he was too ill with dysentery to appear in the courtroom. The trial was short, as was usual with kangaroo courts. Two days were more than enough for the judges to reach the verdict of a death sentence.

Europe was moved. Victor Hugo, and even Garibaldi, who was above any suspicion of royalism, joined their signatures to those of people from all walks of life in petitions asking for the sentence to be commuted. The Italian, Belgian, and Prussian representatives tried everything they could to convince Benito Juárez, but the Indian remained unswayed. The ambassadors on duty in Washington begged Seward, the eternal secretary of state, to intervene, for they knew that without Washington's approval, Juárez would never dare execute the brother of the emperor of Austria. Seward pretended not to take the business seriously. "Don't worry, Maximilian is in no danger. His life is as safe as mine," he said.

At Hofburg, Francis-Joseph, harassed by his near-hysterical mother, decided to act. With a solemn decree, he began to return to his brother the very titles and honors he had extorted from him at the renunciation. Perhaps Juárez would think twice before executing someone who was once again an archduke of Austria and a royal prince of Hungary and Bohemia. At the same time, the Austrian ambassador to Washington went back on the attack and demanded that Seward prevent Juárez from executing Maximilian. Seward promised to take action, and telegraphed Campbell, the United States representative to Juárez, to formally request that the death sentence be commuted.

But Campbell, who found the climate in Mexico, with its civil war and unrest, distinctly unhealthy, was in New Orleans, and refused to set foot any further south. When he received Seward's instructions, instead of setting out, he chose to play for time, and sent him a response that delayed action even further. Several days later, he received a perfunctory telegram from the secretary of state ordering him to drop all other affairs and head to San Luis Potosí, where Juárez was stationed, and get Maximilian pardoned. He answered that he was too ill to travel, and quit his job. Seward gave up. Maximilian's last chance for salvation disappeared, while Seward, along with the entire American administration, kept his hands clean. The only thing left unsure was whether or not Juárez would dare execute an archduke of Austria, who was related to all the crowned heads of Europe, without the tacit permission of his masters in Washington.

Maximilian knew all hope was lost. He wrote a last letter to his mother, Archduchess Sophie. It was a very revealing text, written just hours before his execution, when he was terribly weakened by illness. He began by justifying himself: he had succumbed, he said, but with honor, to the enemy's superiority and to treason. He and his troops had put up a valiant and noble resistance for seventy-two days in a poorly defended city against an enemy seven times greater than they. And yet, only "betrayal under cover of the night delivered us into their hands." As his last hour approached, his thoughts flew back to Europe and to his family. He did not believe that Charlotte was dead. He did not know what her condition was, since for months he had received no word directly from her. He consequently abstained from writing to her, but this did not stop him from thinking incessantly about her. He sent his love to his brothers, his family, and his friends. He sent two souvenirs: his wedding ring for his "poor beloved Charlotte," and another ring that he bequeathed to his mother, one that had never left his finger, containing a lock of hair from Maria Amelia of Bragance, his first fiancée.

As his last request, Maximilian asked to hear "La Paloma," not with the insulting lyrics "*Adiós mamá Carlotta*," but with the poem that originally went with the romantic melody. His captors found a singer and brought her into his cell. As she sang the famous song, a thin smile spread across Maximilian's lips.

On June 13, 1867, Maximilian was awakened at three o'clock in the morning. He dressed in black and hung the small Golden Fleece pendant on his collar. His confessor, Father Soria, was upset by the fact that the emperor handed him his bottle of smelling salts. Maximilian was also the one to console his tearful butlers Blasio and Grill: "Be calm, you see that I am." At six-thirty, the soldiers came for him. He left in a coach for Cerro Las Campanas, the very spot where he had surrendered. As he got out of the coach, he handed his gold watch to his confessor, saying, "Send this as a souvenir to my dear wife. Tell her that my eyes will close with her image before them, and that I will bring it with me to heaven."

With the two generals also condemned to death standing next to him, Maximilian took his place before the soldiers of the firing squad. All of different heights and sizes, the soldiers seemed a motley crew in their ill-fitting uniforms. Though they tried to assume a martial air, they held their rifles awkwardly. There was nothing military, or even vengeful, about them. To each of them, Maximilian gave a gold coin, and then told them in a loud voice, "I forgive all of you, may all of you forgive me. May my blood that is about to flow be shed for the good of the country. Long live Mexico! Long live independence!"

The soldiers took aim. The officer gave the command. The shots rang out in the pure air of the early morning. "Poor Charlotte," Maximilian whispered as he slid to the ground.

The victors decided to embalm Maximilian, and handed his body over to Doctor Liera, who tried to assuage his years as a monarchist and conservative by treating the body with almost indescribable savagery. He did such a poor job that the corpse soon began to rot, and when at last it was time to deliver the body to representatives of the imperial family, it was no longer presentable. Other doctors took over the job and tried to repair the damage, but it was beyond their abilities to replace the now liquefied eyes — those magnificent blue eyes that had given Maximilian all his charm. At a loss, the only solution they could think of was to go into the nearest church and tear out the black glass eyes from a statue of the Virgin, and shove them into the dead emperor's empty sockets.

On June 30, 1867, at dawn, the telegraph officer on duty at the Tuileries palace received the news: Maximilian had been executed. He rushed to hand the information to Napoleon III, who burst into tears. Empress Eugenie was getting dressed when she

heard the news. She blanched and nearly fainted. The prize ceremony for the winners of the World's Fair was supposed to take place
a few hours later. Napoleon and Eugenie hesitated for a long time
over what to do, but finally decided not to cancel the ceremony.
Before attending it, Eugenie, dressed completely in black and accompanied by a single lady-in-waiting, went to Saint Roche church
near the palace, and prayed, crying, at the foot of the altar.

Upon returning to the palace, she changed into a white gown,
covered herself in diamonds, and appeared graceful and smiling
before the representatives of all Europe. The ceremony began, and
as Eugenie awarded the gold and silver medals, she noticed two
empty chairs in the honor gallery: those belonging to the count and
countess of Flanders. Since the news had already been announced
in Brussels, Philippe and his wife had abstained from appearing at
the ceremony that Charlotte would have so liked them to describe
to her.

Throughout Europe, once the events were known, there was
a wave of indignation. Queen Victoria proposed that all diplomatic
ties be cut off with the American continent, and solemnly put on
mourning clothes.

By way of mourning, for his part, Seward made an official visit to
Mexico in order to reap the benefits of the United States' tenacious
support. Thanks to their protégé Juárez, Mexico was now an
American colony in all but name, or at least that was what Seward
thought.

On the very morning of his execution, after writing the letter
to his mother, Maximilian had dictated to Blasio another letter to
his murderer, Benito Juárez, in which he asked that the blood he
was about to shed, his own, be the last spilled in that unfortunate
land. "I lose my life gladly if my sacrifice can contribute to the peace

and prosperity of my new homeland." Then, with a firm hand, he had signed his name with a magnificent flourish. This letter, the expression of a patriot, gentleman, and man of honor, had been brought to Juárez, but he refused to accept it. "I never had contact with this man during his life, I will not start now after his death," he declared.

Maximilian had had the time to specify the treason that had befallen him in his letter to his mother. Baron de Lago, Austrian minister to Mexico, had been allowed to visit him in his cell. "You have seen Lopez's betrayal," the emperor told him, "but the one that hurts me most is General Marquez's. I can forgive Lopez, but Marquez, never." In fact, by taking half of the troops stationed at Queretaro, by being beaten by Porfirio Diaz, and by handing over Mexico City without a fight, Marquez well deserved all suspicions about his loyalty. Lopez had betrayed the emperor, but Marquez had betrayed the empire.

Maximilian probably did not know of the other, less visible traitors. Perhaps he did not want to ask any questions about Father Fischer. And yet Father Fischer had indeed engaged in some strange affairs. It had been he who had suggested little Augustin Iturbide's adoption, who had insisted on the bloody decrees of October 1865, and who had prevented Maximilian from following the wisest course of action and sailing for Europe. He had also been the one to send Maximilian to indefensible Queretaro, a situation that he had wisely foregone getting into himself. Who was pulling Father Fischer's strings? It was hardly in the interests of the conservatives, his most plausible accomplices, to push Maximilian into fatal error. But before he had come to Mexico, of course, Fischer had lived at length in the United States.

Following the emperor's execution, a veritable manhunt raged throughout Mexico for his supporters and servants. None was so visible, and thus so wanted, as Fischer, yet not only was he left alone, but he was also allowed to keep the considerable fortune he had amassed.

Maximilian's faithful supporters, however, particularly the Mexican butler Blasio and the Austrian butler Grill, who had been serving Maximilian since Miramar, were not so lucky. Fully aware of the threat hanging over their heads, they were anxious to leave Queretaro, so full of bad memories and of danger, but they knew they could be arrested at any moment. Even if the republicans spared them, the bandits infesting the countryside would finish them off on the roads. So the two butlers disguised themselves as ranchers and joined the first regiment of republicans leaving Queretaro for Mexico City to prepare for Benito Juárez's triumphant entrance. They were neither recognized nor arrested, and managed to escape under the protection of the republican troops. Together, they could not stop talking about their secret, which they obviously could tell no one. Under their breath, they continued to sing the praises of the emperor and empress who had showered them with kindness. The relations between that man and woman still intrigued them. Blasio could still not understand why they slept apart. Had they ever been in love?

"Yes," answered Grill. "At Miramar, I always saw them together and in love, but then there was a certain trip the emperor took to Vienna, and something shattered their bond. Ever since then, they remained loving and tender in front of others, but in private, they lost all trust and tenderness. That was when I started noticing they slept apart."

Blasio went one step further: "I have known since the beginning that an infidelity on the part of the emperor had reached the empress's ears, and that, wounded as a woman and as a sovereign, she pushed aside scandal and had proposed observing this rule of conduct with her husband that she never broke during her whole stay in Mexico—namely to sleep apart from him and refuse his advances. It is easy to imagine that for her, but I knew the emperor in the fullness of his youth and virility; is it possible to think for a single moment that he would have lived in complete chastity during the whole time he stayed in Mexico, while his simple presence fascinated, even hypnotized, the most beautiful women? And yet, during the whole time I served him, I did not catch the slightest hint of an affair. What about you, Grill?"

"Maybe you did not see anything, but I saw a lot. In his bedroom, the emperor very often received visits from the most elegant ladies in the court. How many of those women, whose reputations remained unblemished, yielded to the emperor's desires?"

"Please, Grill, give me a name or two."

"No, my dear Blasio, I promised to keep them secret."

"In the Mexico City palace, it would have been easy to keep up the mystery, to sneak the ladies out at dawn, but what about Chapultepec? Or Cuernavaca?"

"As far as Chapultepec is concerned, I can assure you that no woman ever entered the emperor's suite. At Cuernavaca, there were the bodyguards on the first patio who could not have missed a woman coming in or going out, but did you never observe, dear Blasio, in the garden wall, the little door so small that a person could barely squeeze through? Well, if that little door could talk, it would expose very curious revelations on the people who used it."

Who could claim that Maximilian was impotent, when he had a string of mistresses from all social classes, from the grand ladies of his wife's court to the frisky Indian women of Cuernavaca? The name Guadalupe Martinez was bandied about, a beauty barely of age, the daughter of a government worker singled out by Maximilian at the first ball thrown in his honor at Cuernavaca. There was also mention of a certain Lola Ermoscillo, an Emilia Blanco, and others. Lastly, there was the most beautiful, the most notorious, Concepcion Sedano, the daughter of the Borda gardener. He loved this last one so much that he bought the pretty Acapazingo farm to serve as their love nest, and to house her there, he built the house known as El Olvido. Impotent Maximilian! So many little Indian bastards proved the opposite. To judge from what the modern-day inhabitants of Cuernavaca say, half the village is made up of Maximilian's illegitimate descendants.

From this mass of information and speculation, what arose most often was a series of contradictions. Rumors portrayed Charlotte as a woman spurned, perhaps stricken with syphilis, but Maximilian was the one who pushed her away. He was supposed to have had a great number of mistresses, but no one but a single butler noticed them, in a country like Mexico where news spread like wildfire. As for the pretty Indian women whose names were known, such as Concepcion Sedano and Guadalupe Martinez, they existed only on paper, in works based on the memories of contemporaries. But strangely enough, there was no information on them, no description of what they looked like. They had no existence either before or after the short spring of 1866, when they filled the pages dedicated to Maximilian. There was not a word on what happened to them afterward, on their families or possible descendants. Could it all simply have been camouflage invented by the emperor's friends to cover up his impotence? The mystery remains.

"Why is the emperor late for dinner?" Charlotte asked, taking her seat at the tiny Castelleto dining room, the very evening that the news of his execution struck all of Europe like a bombshell. Doctor Jilek, who lived with her, had given very precise orders: she must under no circumstances find out the truth. No one must wear mourning clothes, and friends such as Bombelles must swallow their sorrow in Charlotte's presence. But Maximilian's heartbroken childhood friend had come to hate this woman who had pushed Maximilian

into accepting the Mexican crown, and thus into a hopeless adventure. In his mind, she was indirectly responsible for Maximilian's death. Where he was dead, she had somehow managed to pull through. Yes, she was insane, but she had fled Mexico and abandoned Maximilian, and now she was in no danger. Whether he realized it or not, Bombelles was becoming more and more petty, even cruel, with the patient. Fully aware that his masters, the emperor of Austria and his family, hated Charlotte, he felt completely unhindered. At the same time, the need for utter secrecy, since no word of the shameful sickness of insanity could be allowed to filter out, allowed him to tighten Charlotte's incarceration however he saw fit.

Charlotte revolted, sometimes violently, against her situation. In those cases, her guards had no qualms about using force. Her doctors, and most of all Doctor Jilek, knew that they were in no danger of having their methods questioned, and they sensed Bombelles' hatred for their patient, so they did not hesitate to use the straitjacket and other harsh treatments. The few people who might have complained—Charlotte's friends—had all been sent away. The only affection Charlotte received was what her cats gave her. They were allowed to roam throughout the Castelleto, all the doors of which were equipped with cat flaps, and since she had no one else to speak with, Charlotte spoke with them. Mathilde Doblinger, the Viennese maid, the only person Charlotte trusted, disappeared. People said she died suddenly. One morning, she was struck with violent pains and died in the space of a few hours. Even though an impenetrable barrier had been set up around Miramar, snatches of news still filtered out to Brussels. No one had seen Charlotte in weeks, and the doctors had stopped sending reports. They heard Charlotte was chained up and inflicted with the most savage cruelties. And the faithful maid who knew too much died too quickly not to arouse suspicion.

❖   ❖   ❖

The Belgian royal family, judging that enough was enough, decided to pull Charlotte out of her prison.

Who would take care of the prickly mission? King Leopold was out, since his duties and position disqualified him. The best choice was the younger brother, the count of Flanders, Charlotte's favorite. When asked, he refused, since he disapproved of the idea. The best thing, he said, was to leave Charlotte where she was. "If my wife went insane, I would quite simply have her locked up," he declared grumpily, as his wife blushed and wept. They explained to him that the Belgians would not understand how the royal family could sit by and do nothing to save Charlotte. Philippe agreed, but he would not be the one to go to Miramar; his encounter with Charlotte's insanity had left such a mark on him that he would not deal with it again for anything in the world. The family had reached an impasse.

"I will go," Queen Marie-Henriette, Leopold II's wife, decided. Dismissed until then as unimportant, suddenly she took center stage. She was not very graceful, and people had always said she acted like a tomboy and was interested only in horses, which she rode extremely well. Her in-laws had not treated her very nicely. It had taken years before her father-in-law, Leopold I, started to like her. Her husband cheated on her fairly openly with many mistresses. As for Charlotte, when young Marie-Henriette had arrived in Belgium, all Charlotte had shown her was scorn, complaining endlessly about her awkwardness and lack of tact. She was not just an outsider to the Belgian royal family; she had also been born an archduchess of Austria. And yet, it was this courageous woman who volunteered to go tear the sister-in-law—who had only treated her with contempt—from the clutches of her own family, the Habsburgs.

Under her direction, Leopold II started by writing to Charlotte to announce his wife's visit, as she would be in the neighborhood.

Charlotte answered that she was deeply touched by Marie-Henriette's desire to see her, but that "the castle is not very big, and I am living in quite cramped quarters"; the apartments had barely been finished, and there were no accommodations suited to the queen of Belgium. "I am therefore forced, very regretfully, to forgo the sincere and, I assure you, heartfelt pleasure that a visit from Marie would have given me. I hope that later, on another occasion, I will be able to embrace her. . . ." Charlotte's excuses did not ring true. Did she really not want to see her sister-in-law again, or had the response been dictated to her, even forced upon her, by her jailers? Marie-Henriette's determination did not change in the least.

To help his wife, Leopold II thought of a good man, Baron Goffinet. Coming from a very traditional family of the Belgian aristocracy, this insightful, intelligent, and discreet man was unshakably solid under any conditions. He was able to twist confidences out of witnesses; he did not listen to gossip; and he only affirmed what he truly believed. He was also an extremely loyal servant of the Belgian dynasty and a strong defender of Charlotte.

The king summoned him to the royal palace in Brussels to give him instructions. The queen and he would first have to discover exactly what Charlotte's health was like, how she was being treated, and lastly, if possible, they could bring her back to Belgium. Leopold II did not hide the fact that Francis-Joseph disapproved of his cousin Marie-Henriette's undertaking. Goffinet quickly understood that the Austrians would greatly complicate the Belgian mission. Then he asked the question at the heart of the matter: did the king truly wish them to bring his sister-in-law back to Belgium? He wanted to know how far he could go to carry out his sovereign's command. Leopold took his time to reflect, then stated his response with a firm voice: "Yes, assuredly, my dear Goffinet, it is desirable that my sister return."

❋   ❋   ❋

On July 5, 1867, Goffinet found himself at Brussels' North train station. The queen arrived, accompanied by the king and her brother-in-law, Philippe. Besides Goffinet, she would be bringing along two ladies-in-waiting, an aide, twenty thousand gold francs for traveling expenses, and an unlimited letter of credit issued by the Rothschilds of Vienna.

Once they arrived at Köln the next day at five o'clock in the morning, the queen got off the train to hear mass; then she sent a telegram to the emperor of Austria, asking him where she could meet him. The next evening, the convoy reached Augsburg, where Marie-Henriette and her entourage spent the night at the Hotel of the Three Negroes. There she found a telegram from Francis-Joseph informing her that he was expecting her in Vienna.

On the evening of July 8, as the train pulled into the East train station, Francis-Joseph was waiting to welcome his cousin with a huge following of aides, generals, and chamberlains. The emperor of Austria received the queen of Belgium with great pomp. He whisked her off to Hofburg, and brought her to the suite he had reserved for her. Once the doors were shut, he immediately began speaking of Charlotte's fate. Marie-Henriette remained on her guard—wrongly so, for to her great surprise, Francis-Joseph immediately informed her that Charlotte could not decently be allowed to stay on at Miramar. Marie-Henriette suggested that she might go back, however temporarily, to her family in Belgium. To that, Francis-Joseph responded by offering what the Belgian royal family had been asking for nonstop for months: a medical consultation with an alienist of the queen's choice. Marie-Henriette proposed the name of a prominent Belgian specialist, Doctor Bolkens. Francis-Joseph agreed, saying: "This is a question of affection, my dear cousin, that we must work out in the family. I am happy that the king has sent you, for that simplifies everything." Marie-Henriette could not believe her ears, since she had imagined she would have to fight tooth and nail to accomplish her mission.

Barely had the emperor left her room when Marie-Henriette summoned Goffinet to tell him of the happy outcome of the interview. Goffinet immediately set about hammering out plans for Charlotte's evacuation. They could rent a boat, but how would they find one? They would put seals on Charlotte's possessions to prevent the Austrian emperor from using them. But above all, they had to summon the Belgian alienist agreed upon by Francis-Joseph, Doctor Bolkens, who unfortunately could not be located.

The next day, the queen was bombarded with requests for audiences from Bombelles; from Doctor Reidel, the alienist in charge of Charlotte; and from Commander Radonetz, prefect of Miramar castle, as if all Miramar had rushed to Vienna to sound out the queen's intentions and evaluate her determination. In her report to her husband, the queen did not hide the fact that she disliked Bombelles, especially "his airs and embarrassment." He declared that a guardian must, at all costs, be chosen for Charlotte from among the members of the imperial house. Outraged, Marie-Henriette replied that this demand contradicted what the emperor himself had told her just the day before.

Meanwhile, Doctor Reidel showed up. "He looks like a lunatic himself, and like quite the sneak," Marie-Henriette reported. In his opinion, Charlotte could be transported, but it would probably be necessary to use force. He also spoke of the need for a guardian.

When Marie-Henriette saw Francis-Joseph the next day, he remained just as encouraging as before, and even urged her to leave as soon as possible for Miramar. But his tone had changed ever so slightly, and she attributed the new reserve to Bombelles' despicable influence. She also received several others of her cousins, archdukes, and the princes of Wurtemberg. All of them begged her to rush to Miramar and free Charlotte "whatever it takes," as if the empress of Mexico was held there by unknown tyrants, and not by Francis-Joseph's command.

On the day before Marie-Henriette's departure, she received a new visit from Francis-Joseph, who this time was horribly embarrassed. He announced to her that he was obliged to give in to repeated demands made of him to choose a guardian for Charlotte, and that he had named his brother, Archduke Charles-Louis, to the position. But, he added under his cousin's furious glare, it was merely a formality that would not in the least hinder the queen's action. This initiative nonetheless contradicted the emperor's initially conciliatory attitude, and Goffinet, summoned by Marie-Henriette, also saw in it a desire not to let Charlotte go. And who other than Bombelles, Reidel, and the other members of their group had any interest in keeping her at Miramar? Theirs were the "repeated demands" Francis-Joseph mentioned. Goffinet admitted in the journal he updated every day that "this last-minute nomination worries me a great deal. For me, it only spells trouble." Francis-Joseph did not seem to be free in his decisions as far as Charlotte was concerned, which meant that her Miramar jailers had something over him.

Wisely, instead of openly contradicting Bombelles and Reidel, Marie-Henriette went about smoothing their ruffled feathers. She took them along in her train, and during the trip, acted as graciously as possible. Reidel would not cause any problems, since she understood that he no longer wanted to stay at Miramar. Bombelles, on the other hand, had some hidden motives, clearly beyond his control. Goffinet shared the queen's opinion, and tried to get on the enigmatic Bombelles's good side, treating him almost like a friend. The train arrived at Trieste on the evening of July 12. The queen and her entourage set themselves up in the best hotel.

The next day, to officiate their mission, they attended a requiem mass in memory of Emperor Maximilian. The archbishop officiated, and all the authorities were present. Marie-Henriette was determined to see Charlotte as soon as possible. Bombelles showed up at her hotel just after the mass: "He arrives trembling and then starts to cry, a most ridiculous scene, speaking of his attachment for the poor woman that my visit just might kill. I made it clear to him that since the empress is our sister, it is probable that my affection for her might equal his own."

Goffinet went to see Bombelles, with the intention of enacting a little blackmail. The Belgian giant leaned over the short Austrian and whispered to him that if he tried to prevent the queen from seeing her sister-in-law, the queen had decided to set herself up in person at Miramar to keep a better eye on the situation. Now hysterical, Bombelles blurted out protestations, oaths, tears, and excuses, all in a jumble. The massive Belgian could only wonder what was driving this neurotic.

The next morning, Bombelles once again showed up and handed the queen a letter from Charlotte, in which she insistently begged her sister-in-law not to come to Miramar. "This goes too far," cried Goffinet. "It must have been that horrid Bombelles who forced the empress to write this letter."

"What?" shouted the queen. "I gave specific instructions that no one should speak of my arrival to the empress. My request was completely ignored. Since that is the case, I am leaving immediately for Miramar. Bring my coaches up." When he heard this threat, Bombelles almost had a stroke, much to Goffinet's joy, but he could not oppose the queen's wishes. And so they left.

At the gates, the guards did not dare bar the way to the queen of the Belgians. In a panic, Bombelles had no other choice but to bring Marie-Henriette to the Castelleto. With deep sadness, the queen discovered her sister-in-law's prison. In a single motion, she crossed through the vestibule and the maids' room, knocked on the door, and without waiting for a response, went into the little

room. Though she had great self-control and courage, she was still
extremely apprehensive. Charlotte threw herself into her arms and
showed her the greatest affection. "The ice is broken," Goffinet noted.
To Marie-Henriette's surprise, Charlotte was not only friendly, but
she seemed perfectly normal, even if Marie-Henriette could barely
recognize her. Frightfully thin, with yellow, taut skin, she looked less
like an insane person than like someone who had met death a thousand times. Marie-Henriette suspected that she had been subjected
to stupid maids, dull-witted subordinates, insensitive masters, and
tyrannical and cruel doctors. The summer sun of the Mediterranean
summer poured into the room. Through the bars, the magnificent
park extended outward, and between the pine trunks, there was the
glimmer of the sea. Outside, there was light and freedom, so close
and yet so far from the terrible prison. Marie-Henriette remained with
Charlotte for an hour and fifteen minutes.

What most upset her about the interview was how calm and loving
she found her sister-in-law to be. Her emotions affected Goffinet
and came out in his journal: "The sadness of this day. The family's
interest, the desires of Belgium demand that the empress leave, but
that goes against everyone at Miramar who has a job to protect,
all of them foreigners ruled by their own personal ambitions. Yet
Emperor Francis-Joseph has given his consent for her to leave—
he even wants it. If she were to fall seriously ill, could the family
abandon Charlotte here? What would they do? Who will answer
for this poor woman, who is also a princess? Will we have to make
off with her by the sea, tell her lies to convince her, invent a false
command from Emperor Maximilian?"

Goffinet's determination was palpable. Without knowing her
well, he had come to feel a great affection for Charlotte, dictated
by pity. Yes, Charlotte felt she had been poisoned by everyone, but

she had no intention of killing herself. She was afraid of being assassinated simply because she wanted to go on living. Goffinet implied that, in fearing an assassination attempt, the empress was perhaps not entirely wrong. To judge from the way she was being treated, anything was possible.

But before they could take her out of her prison, they had first to obtain the definitive consent of the emperor of Austria, and to this end, first present him with the alienists' decision. They also had to overcome the obstacles that Bombelles and his lackeys would set up, since they would see their well run dry when Charlotte left. Lastly, they had to convince the patient of the importance of leaving, for whatever the alienists said, using force was out of the question.

The next day, the royal family's choice alienist, Doctor Bolkens, finally arrived. Goffinet cursed him for his delay, when days and even hours counted. Goffinet was convinced that they had to hurry, before "the Miramar court" or the imperial family could react. He took Bolkens aside and dictated to him precisely what he was to do and say. Doctor or not, diagnosis or not, the alienist had to conclude what Goffinet wanted him to. Then he let Bolkens get down to work. This was the first time since the beginning of Charlotte's insanity that an impartial doctor would examine her, since until then only Jilek and Reidel had done so. The truth, perhaps hidden until then, would finally see the light of day. "This lethargic and tedious Fleming," as a lady-in-waiting described Bolkens, truly irked Charlotte, since he began by brutally tearing out of her hand the key to her room that she had been trying to hide. Then, once his patient had been tamed, and was probably terrified, he listened to her heartbeat and observed her. The Spanish consul, Garcia Miranda, learned within the hour that when he left the room, the alienist declared that Charlotte's insanity could not possibly have been completely natural in origin. A poison had been administered to the empress, probably before she left Mexico.

Everyone was stupefied. Charlotte had become insane not on her own, but because of a criminal act.

The explosive discovery was still being discussed at Miramar when, in France, a long article appeared in the *Figaro*, written by a certain D. G. d'Auvergne. He had made an inquiry, and had gathered eyewitness accounts from Mexico. It was certain that Charlotte had been poisoned. At Veracruz, he wrote, she even received a note informing her of it. She was given "voodoo poison." This was not to be confused with *tolguache*, or *Datura straumonium*, which was used by witches to break others' will. According to d'Auvergne, *tolguache* had a viscous consistency and a bitter taste, which, even if mixed with another liquid, would still not fail to be noticed. The poison used on Charlotte, however, would have to have been undetectable by taste. He cited a few victims of this unnamed poison, such as a European man living in Matamoros engaged to a Mexican woman; after breaking off the engagement, he had been struck by the exact same symptoms as Charlotte's.

Father Domenach, the strange French chaplain who had been the head of Maximilian's press office, could not remain indifferent to these rumors. Without explicitly confirming that Charlotte had been poisoned, he simply listed and described cases of poisoning involving the same symptoms as Charlotte's.

The *tolguache* theory, however, gained momentum. In the Yucatán, everyone was talking about it, affirming that Charlotte had been poisoned on the day of her visit to Uxmal. Certain members of the Austrian legion in Mexico said that the *tolguache* had been administered by Napoleon III himself during the infamous Saint-Cloud interview, and that the poison had been hidden in the glass of orangeade Eugenie offered her.

But the best evidence was Charlotte's. The insane often possess extraordinary insight, and from the outset, she had claimed that she was poisoned, even on the very day she returned from the

Yucatán. But by whom and for what reason? Someone might have wanted to get rid of her by sending her to the next world, which would be quite plausible in Mexico's political climate. But a poison meant to drive her insane could have been administered only by someone filled with hatred and lusting for revenge. Consul Garcia Miranda had heard that Amalia Stöger, the maid who had been found hanged at Miramar, had killed herself out of remorse. Could she have been the one? She could have committed the crime because she was in love with the husband and wanted to get rid of the wife. Similarly, suspicions would arise later that one of the Indian women Maximilian was cavorting with at Cuernavaca had used a local recipe out of jealousy.

This was a fairly implausible hypothesis. If there had indeed been poison, it had not been administered to drive Charlotte insane: the intention behind the act was completely different.

As he wallowed in the languor of Cuernavaca, Maximilian had perhaps tasted aphrodisiacs and Indian women, but that did not address his fundamental problem—conceiving an heir. He had to impregnate Charlotte, and he knew that he could do it, now that his copper-skinned mistresses had proven his abilities. But Charlotte, frustrated for years, and perhaps since her very wedding night, had grown frigid. The intensity of her intellectual and political activity proved it all the more. Though she was in love with Maximilian, she was not ready for the physical act, which it was quite possible she had never known. Could the idea have arisen then to administer to her the same aphrodisiacs that had been so effective on her husband? Unbeknownst to her, of course. Who would have been asked to pour the drug into her chocolate? Certainly an intimate, just as she had accused her entourage of doing during her periods of insanity.

Abusing aphrodisiacs can cause serious psychological problems. Except for a deep loosening of his entire being, Maximilian
held up well under their effects. But they would have been disastrous on Charlotte's fragile and exhausted mind, especially under
the stress of her European voyage.

As everyone was speculating on Charlotte's condition, the Belgians at
Miramar, belabored by a series of obstacles, secrets, and lies, were
trying to find out what had really happened. Queen Marie-Henriette
received Maximilian and Charlotte's familiars one at a time, listening as they talked, generally against each other. She questioned
Madame Kuhacsevich, the treasurer's wife, with particular attention. Maximilian had believed she had completely adapted to
Mexico and that she loved living there, but in truth, she had detested the country. Marie-Henriette noticed that the embittered
woman was very intelligent and observant. But she also smelled
fear in the woman—fear for the future, fear of what others would
say she had done. Under all the trappings of kindness, the queen
knew how to be tenacious and persuasive, and it wasn't long before Madame Kuhacsevich started talking. She complained about
Charlotte, whom she found cold and heartless, but especially about
Bombelles, whom she could not stand. Her revelations were of
such importance that Marie-Henriette wrote her husband Leopold
II that same night:

"I cannot help but think that terrible things took place around
the poor empress, and that Count Bombelles' terror is due in large
part to his fear that I will discover his complicity in them. To judge
from my interview with Madame Kuhacsevich, the poor empress
was terrified of her husband and of Bombelles long before she
showed the slightest sign of insanity.

"The relations she had with the emperor were not the normal ones between a wife and her husband. She acted as his political advisor and especially as his secretary. In private, he was thoroughly indifferent to her, and often offended her with his lack of regard. One of the chamberlains was courting the empress, but Madame Kuhacsevich does not believe that the empress shared his feelings. In other words, she says that she was a deeply unhappy woman. Kuhacsevich was the only person to whom she spoke openly. Otherwise, she kept it bottled up inside. No wonder she became sick. . . ."

But Madame Kuhacsevich did not fully understand the subtleties of Maximilian and Charlotte's relationship. She did not see that beneath the strangeness of their marriage, there had lived a great passion. What Marie-Henriette could not understand was Charlotte's fear of Maximilian and Bombelles. Could sweet, gentle, lovable Maximilian have had another face, hidden from everyone? And why would Charlotte fear noble, courteous, faithful Bombelles? What bonds could have united Maximilian and Bombelles for them to be able to terrorize such a brave and strong woman? What was the secret that Bombelles so feared would reach Marie-Henriette's ears? Finally, there was that chamberlain who had been in love with Charlotte. Could he have been the mysterious person who accompanied her as she touched the depths of despair on her solitary excursions to the Chalco lake? In any case, according to Madame Kuhacsevich, who had no particular love for Charlotte, the empress had always remained unmoved by his love.

Once informed by the queen of Madame Kuhacsevich's revelations, Goffinet began his own inquiries. On July 17, 1867, he noted in his journal: "Madame Kuhacsevich was received by the queen. The woman also told Bolkens that the empress did not love her husband, or rather only loved the emperor in him—that she did not like anyone, neither her entourage, nor her brothers." This image of a Charlotte totally unable to love showed what a poor psychologist Madame Kuhacsevich was, but it also showed that the shy and introverted Charlotte hid her suffering so well that she had appeared absolutely indifferent.

The next day, Goffinet wrote down an even more interesting tidbit: "The empress does not seem to have been happy with her husband. The emperor never wanted to be alone with her. Madame Kuhacsevich doubts that there had ever been physical relations between them. Whenever her husband came to her room, the empress would feel as if she were suffocating. I hear that the emperor was a man of bad morals." In the terms of the time, Goffinet had said it: the emperor may have been a homosexual.

In this murky ambiance of intrigue and gossip, brimming with backstabbers and frightened tyrants, Goffinet was coming to truly hate Miramar. The horrendous heat, more than ninety degrees in the shade, exasperated the Belgian. Even the location was beginning to seem abominable to him: a bare rock, waterless, uneven, and steep. To think that the place cost more than ten million francs! That masterpiece was nothing other than the absurd expression of a capricious mind trying to be grand and poetic, but managing only to be unbalanced. "Miramar is a sad curiosity, a gingerbread house useless as a permanent residence. I have gone through the castle and gardens twice, and that was one time too many. It would be a cruelty to leave the sister of our king here."

The Belgians had been at Miramar a week when on July 20, Bolkens suddenly burst into Goffinet's room: "Victory, my dear friend, victory!" They fell into each other's arms. The victory was Bolkens's diagnosis: if Charlotte stayed at Miramar, she would die. By bringing her back to Belgium, they would be saving her life.

With constant pressure, Bolkens had been able to convince Jilek and Reidel to agree.

They telegraphed Emperor Francis-Joseph for his permission for Charlotte to leave. He immediately agreed. Goffinet decided that the voyage would not be by sea, which would take too much time, but by train. There was not a minute to lose: certain indiscreet persons had informed Goffinet that Bombelles was telling everyone he would do whatever it took to stop Charlotte from leaving Miramar. Goffinet told Bolkens to keep his eye on Charlotte's entourage, and in particular on the inhabitants of the domain, since the "Miramar court" apparently needed Charlotte to stay so much that they would stop at nothing. Goffinet tried to find a special train, but the difficult logistics, especially of crossing the mountains, soon revealed the problem to be insurmountable.

Another worry for Goffinet was Charlotte's luggage: she did not want to leave anything behind for fear of never seeing it again. He had to personally oversee the packing of the jewels, the toiletries, and the trinkets, each of which was carefully inventoried. Goffinet himself negotiated an agreement with the Austrians on Charlotte's belongings, without which Francis-Joseph would never have given permission for her to leave. King Leopold would get Charlotte's fortune, but would have to take care of her upkeep. He renounced all the rights ceded to Charlotte in her marriage contract, and handed back over to the Austrians all the estates she owned within the Austro-Hungarian borders, including Lacroma and especially Miramar. This was a bit rich for the Belgians, but they had to take it or leave it if they wanted to have Charlotte. As he took care of everything, Goffinet showed not only his fatigue for the affair, but also his admiration for Queen Marie-Henriette, who never got discouraged, tired, or afraid, and whose bravery far surpassed that of the men's.

But everything was soon thrown into chaos by the sudden arrival of Charles-Louis, whom Francis-Joseph had named Charlotte's guardian. When he showed up at Miramar, Marie-Henriette received him graciously; he was her cousin, after all. If it had been up to him, he declared, he would never have taken the job, but public opinion was accusing the imperial family of abandoning the empress to her fate, and Francis-Joseph had dispatched him just to have someone on the scene.

Goffinet held his breath before this new prospective obstacle, for despite Francis-Joseph's assurances to the contrary, the guardian could very well have taken his role seriously and tried to change the plans, or even tried to prevent Charlotte from leaving. When the archduke asked to see the patient, Doctor Bolkens brought him to the Castelleto. They found Charlotte's room locked. Through the door, Bolkens asked Charlotte to let the archduke in. She refused vigorously. When Bolkens persisted, Charlotte became obstinate: "I am a monarch, and I do not wish to receive the archduke." Bolkens noticed that Charles-Louis would have sold his soul to the devil if it meant not having to be there. Charles-Louis did not insist, and simply made note of his failure.

The next day, the archduke sent a letter to Charlotte, asking her to receive him. She responded with a charming letter of her own, in which she bade him a bon voyage. Vexed by her mockery, the archduke took his revenge; as Goffinet wrote down, "The archduke told Bolkens that it seemed his sister-in-law was too tight for coitus, and that the marriage had never been consummated."

At the suggestion that Charlotte had a vaginal deformity, Goffinet became indignant and set the record straight: "That is strange, because I heard the archduke was impotent and never had a woman in his life."

Put back in his place and feeling more and more ill at ease, Charles-Louis decided to leave that very evening. Goffinet accompanied him to the train station, out of politeness, but also to make sure they were truly rid of him. It was with a glad heart that he wished His Imperial Highness bon voyage on Marie-Henriette's behalf.

Now came the main problem: how to convince Charlotte to go to Belgium. Bolkens had already broached the subject with her, with all the gentleness he was so proud of and which made her so happy to see him. So happy to see him, in fact, that she vigorously refused his proposal. But Goffinet found the solution: he knew that Jilek had always used Maximilian's name to bend Charlotte to his will. Every time she resisted what he wanted, he would tell her that her husband had ordered it, and she would bow to his wishes. So Goffinet invented a telegram from Maximilian to Charlotte, supposedly from Veracruz, announcing his departure for Europe, and that he would meet her in Brussels. Doctor Bolkens brought the telegram up to the Castelleto. Charlotte glanced at it and threw it on the floor. She did not believe for a second that it was from her husband. "They are impossible!" she said, referring to forgers.

Not to be discouraged, Goffinet invented a second telegram, this time from King Leopold to his wife, announcing Maximilian's imminent arrival in Belgium, and asking Marie-Henriette to bring Charlotte back. "Emperor Maximilian is asking for her." Marie-Henriette went to the Castelleto and had Charlotte read the telegram. "So Charlotte, will you come with me?"

"No, Marie-Henriette, I'm staying."

"I'm leaving tomorrow evening; be ready for the trip."

"I'm not leaving, I tell you."

"Yes, you are," Marie-Henriette concluded, firmly, but without raising her voice. When she left the room, she heard Charlotte summoning her maids, "Pack up my things, but I don't think I'll be leaving."

Exhausted, Marie-Henriette was still eating dinner at her hotel when her servants announced the arrival of Archduke Charles-Louis, who had returned to Trieste on Francis-Joseph's orders. The trouble continues, she thought to herself. It was ten-thirty at night by the time she received her cousin in her drawing room. Bombelles was with him, and he was beaming, which immediately put Marie-Henriette on her guard. The archduke handed her a letter from the emperor of Austria, forbidding the Belgian queen to use any force to make Charlotte leave. As head of the House of Austria, he could not permit an archduchess to be abused, and preferred, if necessary, to put off or even cancel Charlotte's departure.

His eyes glowing with excitement, barely containing his joy, Bombelles observed Marie-Henriette as she read. When she finished it, she threw the letter on the table and burst into laughter. "This letter is nothing to me. I saw His Majesty the emperor, and he was in complete agreement with me. I have his consent for my sister-in-law's departure. This document does not come from the emperor, who has a good heart . . . though he sometimes comes under outside influences. In any case, sirs, I am leaving tomorrow with the empress."

"But the emperor opposes violence."

"And do you think I would agree to use violence?"

Marie-Henriette knew her element well. During the last few days, ferocious discussions had broken out between Goffinet and the Austrians over Charlotte's private possessions, especially over her impressive collection of jewelry. With contempt, the queen addressed her two visitors: "If this is about the jewels, I will have them returned to you. Thank God that in the family I belong to now, it is never a question of monetary gain." She had managed to intimidate them. Bombelles kept quiet while the archduke apologized over and over before taking his leave.

The next day, the appointed day of their departure, Queen Marie-Henriette was up and dressed before six o'clock in the morning, and sent a messenger to Miramar to warn Doctor Bolkens that the "guardian" had returned to Trieste and would probably soon show up at Miramar. During the morning, she learned that the archduke had indeed gone to the castle, where, for three hours, he was in a conference with Bombelles; with Radonetz, the castle's governor; with Charlotte's confessor; with Treasurer Kuhacsevich; and with the other Austrians, but she was unable to find out what the subject of the conference was.

Late in the morning, Bombelles showed up at Goffinet's hotel room. He announced that everything was ready for their departure, that Charlotte had decided to go, and that she would not make any trouble. By way of proof, she had ordered all her toiletries to be packed. Goffinet pretended to play along with Bombelles, congratulating him on his success, and asking him to tell Queen Marie-Henriette the good news in person, so that any bad blood between them could be cleared up. Invited to lunch at the queen's table, Bombelles repeated his words, then apologized for any difficulties he might have caused, with the wish that her trip would be crowned by success. Marie-Henriette found him "unctuous and brimming with repentance." On his way out, Bombelles gave his word of honor that he would not be present at Miramar when Charlotte left. But Goffinet found out that, just the day before, during a dinner among friends, Bombelles had sworn once again that he would stop Charlotte from leaving. The guardian's sudden return only confirmed the Belgians' fears.

As if all obstacles had disappeared, Marie-Henriette telegraphed Francis-Joseph to inform him that she would be leaving that very evening. "I am happy to tell you this good news. Signed: the queen of the Belgians." A few hours later, she received a most gracious response from the emperor.

As for Goffinet, he was so determined to save Charlotte that he declared himself prepared, if necessary, to carry the empress to the train in his own arms.

Departure was scheduled for ten o'clock in the evening. Marie-Henriette dined early and lightly at the hotel, then her procession of coaches set out, slowly climbing the coast road, until it arrived at Miramar. The torches that the butlers bore aloft in a straight line cast an eerie and magnificent light on the décor. The entire Miramar court was assembled in front of the castle, with the exception of Bombelles, who, as he had sworn, was not present. Marie-Henriette greeted each person individually. Then, accompanied only by Bolkens, she went to pick up Charlotte at the Castelleto. The paved pathway was lit by little gaslights, but as they approached the Castelleto, the shadows seemed to thicken. The house's bizarre silhouette stood out against the starry sky. It seemed uninhabited, except for the few dim lights that filtered through the blinds. Marie-Henriette and the alienist went around the building to the entrance, which was located in the back. A large lantern illuminated the porch. Queen Marie-Henriette had arrived early; the coach that was supposed to bring her and Charlotte to the train station had not yet been brought up. Anxious not to disturb the empress ahead of schedule, the queen went to a small antechamber on the ground floor that had been used as a waiting room. To her surprise, an Austrian chambermaid whom Bolkens had quickly fired during his first visit was standing in front of the door. What was she doing at that time of night at the Castelleto, especially when she had been let go? Marie-Henriette asked her to move aside, but the maid did not move, and said cheekily to the queen, "It's locked here."

"Who locked it? Where is the key?"

"The room is empty. The key is in the castle."

"Go get it." The maid did not move. "Well?"

"The key is not in the castle. It is inside."

"Well, then someone is inside as well."

Suddenly, the maid lost all her insolence and threw herself at Marie-Henriette's knees, grabbing at her gown and bursting into tears. "Majesty, I did not say anything."

"Come on, what is this nonsense. Get up and tell me who is in there."

"The count."

"What count?"

"Count Bombelles."

Now Marie-Henriette's anger truly exploded. She forced the maid to her feet, dug her fingers into her arm, and ordered her to go immediately and sound the alert at the castle. "Count Bombelles!" she shouted through the door. Nothing. "Count Bombelles!" Not a sound. "Open this door!" Still nothing. She called Bolkens, who was waiting outside. "Knock down this door!" Bolkens obeyed. The poorly bolted door gave way on the first try. The waiting room was completely dark, but the light coming from the antechamber enabled her to see Bombelles, who was squatting behind the door, watching her through the cat flap. He had been hit full in the face by the door. Marie-Henriette glowered at him. "I ask you to leave here immediately."

"I cannot, Your Majesty." Bombelles was haggard and pale, and he was trembling from head to foot.

"I ask you to leave here immediately."

"I am here on the orders of the emperor of Austria. I must give him a report on the departure, and ensure that no violence is done the empress."

"I doubt that the emperor would wish to insult me by ordering such surveillance. Leave."

"I cannot. I have an order from the emperor."

"Show it to me."

"I do not have it here, but I give you my word of honor."

"That is unfortunate for you, for I have in my pocket a telegram from my cousin the emperor approving the departure. As for your word of honor, you seem to forget that you have already broken it once today. Leave, I command you, or I will be forced to call one of the men of my entourage."

Bombelles did not move. Pointing at Charlotte's room, he mumbled, "That poor woman can hear us. I am in a terrible position."

"She can hear us. Even though she is sick, I am beginning to think she has good reason to think what she does of the people around her. Doctor, call Baron Goffinet."

Marie-Henriette left the Castelleto, followed by Bombelles, who tried to reason with her. Marie-Henriette quickened her pace. On the garden path, she met Goffinet, who was rushing to her side. Her relief upon seeing his familiar and reassuring face was so great that her entire body began to shake—though she had held up throughout the entire scene, now she nearly fainted, and Goffinet had to hold her up. She mumbled to him, "Goffinet, make sure this man does not attend our departure." Goffinet was hoping she would give that order. With unspeakable happiness, he grabbed Bombelles, lifted him like a rag doll, and dragged him away violently. Finally the coach meant to bring the two monarchs to the train station arrived. It was time to go get Charlotte. She had certainly heard everything, and was certain to be in a horrible state.

Bolkens, who was frightened, hesitated. Once again, Marie-Henriette found the courage to face the situation. With a sturdy step, she went to the door, opened it, and entered Charlotte's room. The room was sparsely lit by a single oil lamp. At first, Marie-Henriette could not make out the empress, who was rolled up in the fetal position in a corner. Charlotte lifted her head at the noise and recognized her sister-in-law: "Oh, it's you, my dear."

"Me and the coach."

"Yes, I heard the coach, but who is it for?"

"It's for us. Did I not tell you yesterday that we were leaving for Belgium?"

"Leaving? No, I'm staying, you can leave if you want."

"Not without you. Come on, let's go."

"No, no."

Marie-Henriette turned to Bolkens, who had followed her on the tips of his toes. "Give me her shawl and her hat." Bolkens obeyed. Marie-Henriette went to Charlotte and tried to dress her. Charlotte threw the clothes in her face.

"No, I am not leaving, absolutely not."

"We'll see about that."

This time, Charlotte let Marie-Henriette put on her hat, and she even took Marie-Henriette's arm; then she grabbed a leg of the table with the other hand and pretended to faint. Marie-Henriette held her up by her waist. At last, giving up all resistance, Charlotte let herself calmly be escorted out. The two women climbed aboard the coach. During the short trip from the Castelleto to the private Miramar train station, Charlotte talked incessantly. She told Marie-Henriette of the way she was first locked up in the Castelleto. She remembered the horrible day in full detail. "Please, Marie-Henriette, don't let me ever be separated from you again."

At the end of the shadowy path, they reached the tiny, brightly lit station. The steam engine of the special train Goffinet had finally been able to charter was blasting clouds of white smoke. The Belgian entourage was lined up waiting along the platform. As she regained the sense of her imperial status, Charlotte asked Marie-Henriette to present them to her. She recognized all of them, from the ladies-in-waiting to Baron Goffinet. She addressed each one with a kind word, as if she were on an official visit. Marie-Henriette invited her to take her place in the compartment. Charlotte smiled at her graciously. "After you, Marie-Henriette. Here you are at my home." The Belgians boarded the train and it slowly moved off.

That very morning, while the maneuvers meant to delay her departure were going on, Charlotte had asked to take a final stroll in the Miramar park. She had stopped in the Belvedere, Maximilian's favorite place, where a telescope had been installed. She had looked out for a long time over the sea, along the distant coast; then she uttered a prophetic sentence loudly and clearly for everyone to hear: "I'll be waiting for him for sixty years."

13

After being locked up for ten months, Charlotte was finally free. The train had barely left Miramar when she calmed down completely. She let herself be undressed, but asked Marie-Henriette to have their beds set up side by side. The next day, she was still calm; she ate very little but talked incessantly. Suddenly, she understood that the train was heading toward Vienna, and she took fright. Marie-Henriette reassured her that the train would merely bypass the Austrian capital. "I know," Charlotte replied, "we are not going to Belgium, but straight to Hertzendorf." Located just outside Vienna, Hertzendorf was a sinister castle in the Habsburgs' history. One archduchess who died in it was burned alive; another was locked up there when she went insane. Charlotte said over and over, "We're going to Hertzendorf—that's where they lock up sick archduch-esses." Marie-Henriette had a hard time convincing her otherwise.

When Charlotte saw she was mistaken, she could finally breathe, and as they crossed the border into Belgium, her relief was visible. From the window, she joyfully saw the villages and landscape slide past, the peasants who looked up from their work to watch the train go by.

Near Brussels, the train went through the Forêt de Soignes, and then came to a halt at the little Groenendaal station. Char-lotte put on her hat herself, and without any help, jumped down onto the platform, happy and light. Court coaches were waiting; she recognized the coachman and the groom, and the procession set off.

Suddenly, she panicked: "They are going to kill me, please don't leave me, I don't want to be separated from you." She took Marie-Henriette in her arms, squeezed her tightly, and began to cry. The queen managed to calm her down. They arrived at Ter-vuren Castle, where the royal family had decided to put Charlotte up. As she got down from the coach, she recognized the grand marshal of the court and greeted him with a few kind words. As per the instructions the queen had telegraphed ahead, the ladies-in-waiting had taken off the mourning clothes they had been wear-ing for Maximilian and put on bright outfits. Marie-Henriette led Charlotte to her suite. Soon, the door opened, revealing Leopold II. Charlotte hugged him. The king did not stay very long, and left to let his wife take care of Charlotte. "Marie-Henriette, may I take the keys out of the doors?" Charlotte asked her.

"No, Charlotte, but I promise you, no one will lock you in."

"Please, I beg you, stay with me, sleep in my room with me."

Marie-Henriette managed to sidestep the request: "I cannot, Charlotte."

After dinner, when the empress was brought back to her room, she refused to lie down on the bed. She sat down in a chair instead and decided to spend the night there.

Goffinet had remained with his traveling companions, and was gathering their impressions. That was how he learned that Doctor Bolkens had tried to rape Miss Frisch, Charlotte's chambermaid, on the train. Charlotte had already insisted that the alienist had behaved badly with her, and said that she never wanted to see him again. But who listened to someone with a persecution complex? Still, faced with this beautiful twenty-seven-year-old woman, it was not wholly impossible that the doctor might have had a moment of weakness, which was perhaps the worst treatment he could have found to cure his patient.

Charlotte rediscovered Tervuren Castle, where her mother had brought her when she had had whooping cough as a child. She recognized perfectly the thick, square building built on a hill, with its colonnaded pediment. The view from the long paths that cut through the forest stretched out as far as the eye could see. Long unoccupied, the house was not very well-furnished, and comforts were few. But when the royal family had had to find a home for Charlotte on such short notice, they thought that the peaceful castle in the middle of a magnificent park would do the job.

Since they also wanted Charlotte to be treated not just as a human being, but as a monarch, they appointed a house for her under the direction of the indispensable Goffinet. She had nearly forty servants at her command, and protocol was strictly observed.

Charlotte loved to visit the immense park. She went around the pond in her coach and stopped in her favorite place, the chapel where Saint Hubert had built the famous apparition of a stag bearing the cross between its antlers. She headed off toward the beech trees that shaded the brick sanctuary, and she climbed up what remained of the splendid castle of the Infanta Isabella, the daughter of Philip II of Spain, who had also governed the Netherlands. She pressed on to the stables of Prince Charles of Lorraine, another governor. She walked to the edge of the water and watched the birds frolicking in the pond.

Everyone agreed that Charlotte's insanity was rather mild. She grew delirious from time to time, but she also had periods of intelligence and lucidity. And she always remained docile and easy to direct.

The entire royal family and all of Charlotte's friends unanimously declared themselves horrified by the condition in which her interment at Miramar had left her. All of their accounts sadly agreed. "What a barbarous and despicable entourage we had to tear poor Charlotte away from," Marie-Henriette decried. "I do not think that in all of history there has been an example of a young woman so abandoned as the poor empress."

Leopold II confided, "My sister came to us in a horrible state — she was skin and bones. The treatment and isolation at Miramar did her great harm; my poor sister was living in a perpetual trance, abandoned by her entire family."

Minister Jules Devaux lamented, "The poor empress; what a ruin, a wan ghost, skinny, faded, without beauty or expression, like some poor creature that has been beaten half to death."

And perhaps she had been beaten half to death. Everyone vowed never to hand her back over to the Austrians, and to take care of her with all the love, tenderness, and care she needed.

The most resolved in this was Queen Marie-Henriette, who had discovered her true calling through Charlotte's tragedy: that of a loving nurse and gentle woman. . . . Everyone praised her firm patience, her intelligent kindness, her concern, and the lavishness

with which she devoted her time to Charlotte. She spent nearly
every day at Tervuren. She pulled Charlotte by the arm whenever
she dragged her feet; when Charlotte refused to go to bed, Marie-
Henriette brought her up to her room and undressed her herself.
She distracted Charlotte by showing her the illustrations in a book,
or by sitting her down with her at the loom. She reassured her when
she was frightened by noises in the hallway; she got her to eat when
she was afraid of being poisoned. She accompanied her to Sunday
mass, at which, much to her surprise, Charlotte appeared beautifully groomed and dressed in a blue gown.

Certain confidences the empress let slip stunned her. One
evening, when she was being difficult, Marie-Henriette managed
to get her into bed and then sat down beside her. "What a good
bed," Charlotte exclaimed. "Are you sure no one will come? I see
someone at the door." Charlotte's whole body was trembling. "I am
so afraid. Tell me, are they going to come to tie my hands and feet?"
She burst into tears and squeezed Marie-Henriette against her.
"Swear to me that no one will come for me, that no one will tie me
to the bed like they did to me that day over there." Marie-Henriette
once again glimpsed how daily life must have been at the Castelleto.
She barely dared to imagine what awful treatment her sister-in-law
was forced to undergo. She was bursting with rage for the torturers
at the same time that her tenderness was growing for the innocent
woman so attached to her.

Yet Charlotte's condition was improving every day. The change
of diet suited her: she was getting color back in her face, her cheeks
were filling out again, and most important, she had found calm. The
moments of delirium were growing further and further apart.

Winter was approaching, announced by the fog drifting up from the
pond, the misty, chilling rain, and the biting wind. Marie-Henriette

decided that the poorly heated Tervuren Castle would no longer do. Reassured by Charlotte's condition, she resolved to bring her to her home at Laeken.

On October 9, 1867, Charlotte finally saw the castle where she had spent her childhood. Just outside of Brussels, it was a large structure built at the end of the eighteenth century, situated halfway up a hill in the center of a green and hilly park. A dome and a colonnade lent it a rather cold elegance. Napoleon had given it to his Josephine, and since then, the Belgian royal family had made it their favorite residence. There, Charlotte joyfully rediscovered images and memories from the past, such as her father's dog. She recognized the butlers, foot servants, and maids. Marie-Henriette set her up on the second floor in her brothers' old rooms, a suite she rediscovered with obvious pleasure. The queen herself had overseen the decoration of the little drawing room and private dining room, formerly a billiards room.

Charlotte's condition had so improved that she was now able to live a more or less normal life. From then on, her brother Leopold II was the one who took her out for strolls through the park. They had family music hour, they went for sleigh rides, they went out to see the skaters on the lake. They took excursions to the Ardennes mountains, and to Ciernon Castle, their father's once inviolable retreat; they picnicked in the woods of La Cambre, and had lunch in country inns.

Charlotte had become a full member of the family again. Besides Leopold and Marie-Henriette, she often saw Philippe and his wife. She played with her nephews and nieces: the heir, little Leopold, and his sisters Louise and Stephanie. The countess of Bassompierre, whom the queen had named Charlotte's lady-in-waiting, curiously observed the woman whom all of Belgium could not stop discussing. Her features had grown a little heavy, but she was still a great beauty, with the waistline and suppleness of a young woman. She took great care of her person, and was meticulous with her clothing. She never wore crinoline anymore, only elegant dresses, especially her favorite, which was cut from gray material and decked out with amaranthine laces. Each time the countess talked with Charlotte, her intelligence, the breadth of her knowledge, and the precision of her memory left her stunned. She remembered, discussed, and judged everything with astoundingly rigorous logic. Occasionally, she would blossom, unclenching her severe features and abandoning her intense expression to joke and laugh, which gave Marie-Henriette hope: "Without being able to pinpoint exactly why, I have a great deal of hope for my beloved sister's recovery."

But Mexico remained a taboo subject, never to be discussed in front of Charlotte. She was allowed to read the Brussels newspaper *The Belgian Star*, but if ever there was an article on Mexico, they did not give it to her. Charlotte had noticed the newspaper's irregular delivery, and it gave her an idea for a new name for the paper: *The Shooting Star*. Whenever she asked a question about Maximilian, they told her that the civil war was dragging out, that he had no time to send news, but that he would soon, very soon.

But how long could they keep hiding the truth from her? Benito Juárez had decided to hand his enemy's corpse over to Austria. One night, he went to contemplate the poorly embalmed emperor; then he closed the coffin, which was shipped off to Veracruz and loaded aboard the *Novara*, the same frigate that had brought the young archduke to Mexico in the first place. The ship was therefore crossing the Atlantic at that very moment in time. The lie had to be changed. The family began by suggesting that if they had received no news from Maximilian for such a long time, something bad must have happened. They allowed Charlotte to meditate on this possibility while they sought out someone who could announce her husband's death to her.

They decided on the former Father Deschamps, Charlotte's first spiritual advisor who, since then, had completed his religious instruction and become the archbishop of Malines. He was summoned to Laeken. Marie-Henriette bowed out, and went to pray that God help Charlotte withstand the horrible shock she was about to receive. Once he was announced, the prelate came into Charlotte's drawing room, and she knelt to kiss his ring. Monsignor Deschamps helped her to her feet and took her hand, just as he had done when she was a teenager. "Madam, I have very bad news. Emperor Maximilian is dead. The Mexicans assassinated him; they shot him just as they did Emperor Iturbide."

"Is this true?"

"Yes, Madam, it is confirmed."

Charlotte began to weep gently. Monsignor Deschamps offered her words of consolation and called the queen from her chapel. Marie-Henriette appeared, ready as always to deal with difficult situations. Charlotte threw herself into her arms and continued to cry, but without excess, saying, "Ah, if only I could make my peace with heaven and confess." Marie-Henriette and the prelate looked at each other in wonder. As she had done in Mexico, Charlotte continued to go to Sunday mass, but she had inherited her grandfather Louis-Philippe's deep-seated impiety, and she practiced her religion more to satisfy the demands of her position and of society than from a true belief. Heaven had finally granted Marie-Henriette's ardent prayers, using the miserable situation to restore Charlotte to her faith.

In the middle of the night, a maid came to wake Marie-Henriette. Charlotte could not sleep and asked that she come. Marie-Henriette quickly complied. Charlotte cried calmly, without agitation, on her sister-in-law's shoulder. "I don't have the courage, Marie-Henriette.

I prefer not to go to confession." Marie-Henriette held her tight, kissed her, and proposed that they kneel and pray together.

The next morning, Charlotte went to confession, then asked to be informed of all the details of Maximilian's death. Marie-Henriette was sure that her husband's glorious death would be a consolation for her. They brought her the articles that had been written that described all his heroism with admiration without sparing the details.

Of course, Charlotte had put on mourning clothes, covering herself with black wool and crêpe. For her husband's funeral booklet, she had picked out the Bible quotation that, according to custom, would be printed on it—she had decided on Psalm 3: "The memory of the just man will live on forever and never fear the ill men will say." A curious quotation and a curious choice, for actually, nothing ill was said of Maximilian any longer.

At last, family and friends were allowed to send Charlotte their condolences. She received a particularly touching note from Empress Elisabeth of Austria. Charlotte responded to all of them with dignity and sorrow, in French, German, English, and Spanish. She asked Leopold II to decorate the Austrians, Belgians, and French who had so loyally served Maximilian. This request was completely normal and her arguments were fine, but its careful style differed markedly from that of her other letters. Moreover, the names that she proposed contained a few surprises. She wanted Bombelles, her cruel jailor at Miramar, to be decorated, and also Loysel—the French officer with whom she had perhaps had a platonic tryst now reappeared in her thoughts for the first time, just after she learned of Maximilian's death.

Despite her mourning, Charlotte wished to continue her visits into town, but she wanted to wear certain jewels that she particularly liked. The horrible scene, terrifying crisis, and endless despair that everyone was expecting never came.

The *Novara* finally arrived at Trieste. A special train brought Maximilian's coffin to Vienna. It arrived on a freezing winter day after night had fallen. Despite the late hour and the cold, a huge crowd was waiting in the streets of the capital, for the Viennese had never forgotten their beloved Max. An endless procession followed his coffin up to the palace. The snow kept falling, dimming the torches and blanketing both living and dead in white.

The coffin was installed in the Hofburg chapel, draped entirely in black by the newly appointed court decorator — none other than the widower of Amalia Stöger, the maid who had hanged herself at Miramar. During the entire night, an old woman with nearly white hair, crying inconsolably, would keep watch over Maximilian's body: it was his mother, Archduchess Sophie. When she entered the chapel, she ran to the coffin to see her son through the small glass window, but the poorly embalmed corpse's grotesque face and black glass eyes made her jump back with horror.

The next morning, the burial took place at the Capuchin church, the Habsburgs' pantheon. Maximilian was laid to rest in the crypt next to the duke of Reichstadt, Napoleon I's son, who had been so tender with his mother, and who had died the same day he was born.

While the emperor was being buried in Vienna, in Brussels the main concern was with the empress's fortune. Between the various shares deposited in England with Coutts, the funds administered by the Rothschilds of Paris and Vienna, her inheritance from Leopold I, the real estate held jointly with Leopold II, and the jewels, the sum of Charlotte's fortune totalled more than eleven million Belgian francs, an enormous amount for the time. Charlotte herself was far from uninterested in her little nest egg — during the darkest times of her Miramar incarceration, she had summoned the viscount of

Conway, the Belgian royal family's financial administrator. He had declined under one pretext or another. Since then, by the terms of his agreement with the House of Austria, Leopold II had been responsible for Charlotte's upkeep, but by the same token, he had also been in charge of managing her money. Now, since the time of Charlotte's marriage, Leopold II had never accepted the idea that a part of the family fortune should go to the Austrians as Charlotte's dowry. He therefore decided to pool his entire family's money together into an inalienable fund, from which the pensions insuring each family member's lifestyle would be drawn, but from which not a penny could ever disappear from the country in the form of a dowry. In this way, he preserved the royal fortune, but he also put Charlotte's money exclusively at his own disposal. With such a huge amount of money, he waxed lyrical: "If God grants me life and if I keep my present position, I will be at once very rich, and the creator of great things."

Summer came. Charlotte's letters continued to depict a peaceful and pleasant life. Her brother Philippe had moved into a new home, "a superb palace dripping with gold." Laeken Park had been remodeled in a more modern style. As for Charlotte's former suite, it had now been passed on to her brother Leopold II, and it was there that "political inspirations abounded." Charlotte saw Monsignor Deschamps often. She practiced tapestry-weaving and read voraciously, more about the lives of saints than histories. She was upset with her greyhound: "Iona has fallen from grace and I have banished her from my room because of her increasingly unbearable odor."

These reassuring descriptions were belied by the discordant notes appearing in the writings of one of Charlotte's correspondents, the countess of Grunne. The patient's condition was not always so good the countess said. She almost had a crisis a few days after the first anniversary of Maximilian's death. July was much calmer, and

Charlotte rediscovered the serenity she had enjoyed during the winter. And yet the tics and little manias continued to reappear, so much so that the countess of Grunne lost hope of ever seeing Charlotte lead a normal life. The improvement, in her opinion, was only temporary.

Nor was Charlotte the only ill person at the palace. In her letters, she often spoke of the poor health of her nephew, little Leopold, Leopold II's only son and the apple of his eye. He was now nine years old, and a lung infection made him cough constantly. The family believed he had become sick when he fell into the park's pond. Though the illness was not getting any worse, it was not getting better either. "The boy's condition is unchanged," Charlotte wrote. "For my part, I still believe that a full recovery is possible, and I do not believe that his health should decline. May God let me be right."

But as he progressed from attack to attack, the heir to the throne was growing weaker, and even the doses of opium he was given no longer had any effect. He dragged on in that condition a few weeks longer, but died on January 22, 1869. Belgium went into mourning and all of Brussels descended into the streets to watch the funeral procession go by. Julie Doyen, Queen Marie-Henriette's faithful chambermaid who had now been assigned to Charlotte, asked for a few hours off so she could join the hundreds of thousands of other Belgians in mourning. Charlotte forbade her: "One does not go to see such sad things."

Throughout her heartbroken sorrow, Marie-Henriette found great consolation in her deep faith, and her strength of character did not leave her for a moment. Leopold II, on the other hand, was a broken man, and would probably remain so forever. For him, his son was the symbol of hope for the future, and he had centered all his plans around the boy. He soon conceived another child with Marie-Henriette, in the hope that it would be a son. It was a girl,

Clementine, the last child they had together. Leopold never touched his wife again. Never a very demonstrative man, he shut himself up in harshness and cynicism, as if building a rampart against his grief.

Through the routine of her daily life, Charlotte felt a dissatisfaction growing within her, and it appeared in a lucid and clear letter she wrote the countess of Hulste: "I live day by day in my solitude, reading and knitting, writing and strolling through the park. You ask me to pray for you, my dear countess, but the roles are reversed, and now I ask for your prayers with the sincere fervor of a daughter." In contrast to this gentle melancholy, Charlotte's disturbed personality was suddenly struck by extreme agitation. On the night of December 10, 1868, she had a dream that changed her convictions forever. Her husband Maximilian appeared to her and told her that he was not dead—it was not his corpse that had been sent to Europe, but rather a wooden likeness. He was still alive. Charlotte threw off her mourning.

During the course of this winter of 1868–1869, Charlotte's sanity tottered precariously. She suffered not so much from attacks of violence as from lapses of reason, manias, and incoherent speech: in short, she was delirious. Since her physical health remained excellent and she was surrounded by enlightened care and affection, those around her wondered what the cause of this aggravation could be. Was it little Leopold's sickness and death? Charlotte was of course hurt by it, but she never lost her serenity. Was it the first anniversary of Maximilian's death? But Charlotte had controlled her grief when she had learned of his execution. There was only one other explanation. Charlotte continued to complain that she was being poisoned. The Mexican drugs were a thing of the past; she was now being treated with many different medicines, tranquilizers, and the like. What concoction were they forcing her to swallow to calm her frequent stomachaches? "They give me coffee with milk that is saturated with morphine," she complained. "It blocks up my intestines, turns my skin pale, puts rings around my eyes, and whitens my tongue. They put all their meals containing the most violent poisons under my nose and I look them over—I know them well enough not to miss them, I sniff them, I refuse them, that is my right—but I have to keep up my body with something other than morphine. And I know why they give it to me. That is what upsets me: it does not produce a feeling of peace, it stupefies; it slows the heartbeat and undermines the will. That is what offends me. . . ."

Besides these reasonable arguments, there was the crisis Charlotte suffered from February until June of 1869, one that manifested itself in an unexpected though familiar way—through writing. Ever since her incarceration at Miramar, she had slowed the pace of her correspondence considerably. But one winter day, she sat down at her writing table in the little drawing room of her suite at Laeken palace. She started writing and could not stop, blackening thousands of pages in the course of several months. Her penmanship at first remained beautiful and legible, but slowly it changed. It lost its former ease and became tighter, shrinking into tiny scratches. Its regularity did not betray any mental disorder, but the pages and pages of insanity slowly piled up. The last sheets were wrinkled, often torn, and stained. They have been poorly treated, often by Charlotte herself, which makes it difficult to decipher them.

The first one, dated February 16, 1869, was addressed to Loysel. Charlotte had learned of his marriage and asked him to accept a bracelet she would like him to give his new wife—a completely normal sentiment.

On February 28, she invited Loysel to come to Laeken with his wife, whom she said she would be very happy to meet. On March 3, she sent him a picture of Our Lady of Victories.

On March 14, she plunged into insanity. The next day, she told Loysel she had to go to Brussels to see a friend, Madame Moreau, at her house. She asked him to meet her there—to escort her to Paris. She had decided to run away. Loysel was to reserve seats on the train and rooms at the Louvre Hotel in Paris. "I will have three napoleons in my pocket, and 180 francs; I don't have any more than that lying around."

During the next few weeks, the idea of escape persisted, lurking beneath everything Charlotte said. She sent Loysel a map of the castle with its exits and guard posts; she listed the sentries; she plotted the course he should take through the park and into the castle to her room. Soon, Loysel was not her only accomplice. She sometimes included Van der Smissen, the former commander of the legion of Belgian volunteers, but always in a secondary role. He was to transmit messages, and was dispatched to lay the groundwork. Charlotte kept him at arm's length, and once or twice even voiced the contempt she held him in.

Another recurring motif in her writing was the dream, which she described with a beauty and poetry that the sane of mind can rarely muster: "If earlier I said the word 'dream,' it is not to be understood in its common meaning, but rather as the light that is cast on the future during sleep, blessed by reason and enrapturing the entire soul. I have had two, the first about the my beloved husband the emperor on December 10, and I rediscovered my taste for life, the second last night, about you, and my hope was restored. . . ."

Sometimes, the paths of insanity do not much differ from those of revelation. Like a mystic, Charlotte spoke with invisible people, and she told of "the mysterious voices being used to teach me everything."

In the long letter, she went off on a series of historical, political, and religious divagations. Her encyclopedic knowledge of the

Bible, of history, and of genealogy explained how Charlotte was able to mix the Trinity with Napoleon, her ancestors the kings of France, and Jesus Christ. Several notions continuously appeared in this jumble: Maximilian was the Messiah, he was Jesus. "You were at the foot of the cross, you were there in Mexico City, and the apostle Judas was at Queretaro. . . ." For Charlotte, there was only France, her French ancestors, the present emperor of the French, and her obsession with Napoleon I. Strangely, her political lucidity never failed her. In this, the beginning of 1869, she clearly perceived the danger Prussia represented to the French empire. She listed the weaknesses of the reign of Napoleon III, to whom she had written several times. Her only goal was to defend France, which she knew was threatened. She asked to be named division general so that she could go and fight. She was the daughter of Napoleon III, she declared in her letter of April first.

Carried away by her plan to rush, sword in hand, to France's defense, Charlotte nitpicked as much as an old general. She wrote page after page of details about uniforms, decorations, honors, hierarchies, and nominations. The army was made up of little toy soldiers that she fiddled with endlessly.

On April 5, 1869, she forgot Loysel for a moment and wrote her younger brother: "Dear Philippe, I have gone without food for twenty-four hours. I took a long walk this afternoon, but I cannot eat, it makes me cough and suffer pain for hours. I almost feel like I did in Rome. Would you like to play the part of the pope and put me up for a night at your house? I will not be any trouble at all to you, and I will sleep anywhere. Please come get me as soon as you receive this note, I will wait until nine o'clock. Your tender sister Charlotte."

None of these letters was ever sent—her entourage snatched them up and submitted them to the alienists. The note to Philippe in particular raised alarm that she might resume the same horrible scenes as had occurred in Rome. She could no longer stay with the royal family at Laeken, and she was thus sent off to Tervuren Castle, once again habitable now that the winter was ending and spring was near.

The move did not sweeten Charlotte's attitude toward her family. A few months before, in one of her letters to Loysel, she had worried over what was becoming of her fortune, which "my brother has put under his own name." She complained of "this supervision, which is nothing but the forced continuation of the violence I have already suffered."

She was losing her affection for Belgium. "I have nothing, now that I have been treacherously brought here — nothing but baseness, shame, sorrow, and humiliation." In fact, the bad treatment she had suffered all started, according to her, on October 11, 1866, the day she left Rome and her brother brought her to Miramar. Since then, she had been her brothers' victim and prisoner. Even generous Marie-Henriette did not escape her revenge: "I invite you to kill yourself with me," she wrote her, "since I would like to leave the captivity to which you have so unjustly subjected me."

Barely had she returned to Tervuren when her delirium intensified, especially in her obsession with Loysel, to whom she addressed the majority of her letters: "May God bless you, enlighten you, strengthen and guide you. . . . I can already see you appearing like a ray of sunshine."

At the same time, her biblical babblings intensified: "Then will be heard the voice that will speak onto me and the emperor, reunited in that instant, and say 'Here is my beloved son in whom I have instilled all my kindness.' This voice will be that of Napoleon III, your father and mine." She inserted Loysel into her mysticism: "I learned today that you are the second Messiah, that Emperor Maximilian, you, and I make up the Trinity of Messiahs." Then she mixed up their genders: "You must marry Emperor Maximilian in my place."

On April 12, the motif of longed-for death made its appearance: "If you do not want to save me from this den of infamy and sorrow, then shoot me, well-aimed through the heart. That would be the last act of love I would ask of my beloved France."

Her memories were remarkably precise. She remembered the scene when Loysel gave a negative report on his mission to France and Maximilian accused him of betrayal: "I seized this word as it flew through the air and pulverized it, I defended you as I would have defended myself, and once I deflected it from you, the word landed on Lopez's head. It was that broken word that turned Lopez into a traitor. . . . On that day, I saved your future; I understood that and I saw it in your eyes. Later I was to save your life, but that day, I saved your honor."

On April 16, her delirium showed a marked escalation: "Can you come bring me the two swords I so desire? I walk in the park every evening from six-thirty to seven o'clock. You would find me with a lady-in-waiting and a foot servant, but we would go fight them with our swords in whatever place you choose." The same day, as often, she wrote a second letter to Loysel: "We will plunge our swords again and again into each other as much as we can, until they are soaked red in blood up to the hilts."

A few days later, she went off the deep end. "From today on, I will no longer sign my name Charlotte, but rather Charles, and that is what you may call me. Everyone else must call me Charles as well. . . . As for my person, do not expect to find me as you knew me in Mexico:, there are already three quarters of a man in me."

Then, abandoning the impossible idea of a duel, she proposed another solution: "Since it seems that Emperor Napoleon has forbidden you to fight me in a duel, I think that the best thing for us to do is meet each other anyway and whip each other excessively with riding crops." She seemed to love this idea: "Come with two thick riding crops of equal size. You will take off your pants, and I will whip you with one of them. Then you will put all your clothes back on, and I will remove my skirt and pants, I will tie my shirt above my waist, and you will whip me just as I have whipped you, for ten minutes."

Once this punishment united them in blood, the only thing Charlotte and Loysel would have left to do was to get married. "Before all of heaven and Earth, I choose you as my husband." But was it Charlotte or Charles who would marry Loysel? Neither; Loysel would be marrying Loysel, for the next day, she signed her name "Loysel" for the first time, on a letter beginning with the words "My dear Loysel."

Then she imagined a series of meetings between them, filled with long sessions of undressing and violent whippings, the events of which she described in detail, and which intensified her feelings for him a little more each time: "I think I have made you see that the love I have for you is to the death, and that mine is as great for you as yours for me, and I know that it is superlative in you as it is in me.

"It is clear that we must whip each other on the skin; I will first remove all my woman's clothes; I will stand naked before you."

On May 12, she decided for the first time to punish herself: "I whipped myself today, Loysel, so hard that my legs were still all red an hour later. . . . I whipped too hard in your name and in mine. . . ."

Finally having found her path, she proceeded down it with gusto: "I whip myself as I would whip a horse, harder even, on my naked thighs; it gives me such great pleasure, it is a true ecstasy that I have discovered. . . . I am overcome by a raging desire to be whipped. I take off my pants and shove them into a closet, I lie flat on the couch, I take the riding crop in my right hand and whip so hard that it hums in the air and raises welts."

❈   ❈   ❈

Her Imperial Majesty, Princess Charlotte of Belgium, empress of Mexico, woke at eight o'clock. After she had her breakfast, her maids helped her fix her hair and get dressed. Her bedroom doors flew open and she entered the salon. Her ladies-in-waiting rose and made low curtsies. She said a few kind words to each one, and then, accompanied by one or two of them, made her way to the porch, where her carriage was waiting. Coachmen and squires bowed respectfully and helped her climb in. She was leaving for a ride through the park. On the way, she chatted with the ladies. On her command, the carriage came to a halt; she climbed down and headed to the edge of the water to watch the swans. Perhaps she also picked a few wildflowers. Once she returned to the castle, she left her entourage and locked herself in her office. Family portraits and photographs covered the damask-draped walls and end tables. Vases of flowers and precious trinkets cluttered the chests of drawers.

She sat down on a gilded chair at her emblazoned desk, took out a sheet of letterhead stamped with her crowned monogram, dipped her quill in the gilded stone inkwell, and in her neat, slanted penmanship, began to cover page after page with her sadomasochistic delirium. She had just transformed herself into "Charles Loysel, first staff colonel."

During the last week of May, delirium and desire escalated violently. Henceforth, she began her letters with the words, "Beloved and charming Loysel." She suddenly remembered that her correspondent was a married man. "I propose that we kill all the animals, starting with Mrs. Loysel. . . ."

Her last letters were revealing. "I no longer wish to be called 'Majesty' — a simple 'you' will suffice. It will be difficult for me though, because of habit." She had abdicated; she no longer wanted anything to remind her of her royal and imperial past.

Suddenly, the letters stopped. There was a series of short, meaningless notes addressed to another man, General Douay, Bazaine's aide in Mexico whom both Maximilian and Charlotte particularly esteemed. Now her manias were pulling her in different directions. "General Douay, Hotel Mangele, Royal Street, Brussels. The devil was seen here with a squirrel's tail. . . .

"Sword of Belgium, Van der Smissen, for it is through him that I will get my brother's sword. . . .

"I propose that Judas sell me to Saint Peter to save the Church and the papers of the House of Croy, which were almost swallowed up in the flood when the dove was carrying the olive branch. . . ."

How could Charlotte, in the middle of her delirium, have remembered that the illustrious house of the princes of Croy possessed a painting from the Renaissance depicting the Great Flood, in which a crow carried the following words, written in Gothic letters within a bubble: "Save the archives of the House of Croy"? She had seen the painting, as had so many others, but the mystery of insanity dictated that the memory resurface at that precise moment. The incoherence went on, still addressed to General Douay: "I was pregnant for nine months with the devil's redemption—nine months of the Church—and now I am pregnant with the army. Have me give birth in October." And finally, this last note which was not insane at all: "I am the Pen of the world, for all I do is write."

These were the last things Charlotte ever wrote. Except for a few, very short notes written in pencil and asking for one thing or another, she never expressed herself again. The eruption of insanity was over, but how revealing it was, how many secrets and mysteries it evoked in all those letters.

"The marriage I had left me in the state I was," she wrote to Loysel on May 5, 1869. "Never did I refuse children to Emperor

Maximilian. . . . My marriage was consecrated in appearance, the
emperor had me believe it, but it really was not, not by my fault,
for I always obey him, but because it is impossible, or I would not
have remained what I am," which was a virgin.

Four months of feverish letter-writing had left Charlotte exhausted; she had nothing left to write in her seething conscious and
unconscious. Free at last, there was nothing left for her to do but
close in on herself, defenseless against the insanity into which she
would sink forever.

Around her, the members of her entourage watched her with
concern; faced with an illness that inspired as much awe in them as
it did pity, they tried to help her: the ladies chosen by Queen Marie-
Henriette, Charlotte's best friend Madame Moreau, Muzer, de la
Fontaine, Mockel, the alienists, the castle's administrators, not to
forget the most humble, most important, and most devoted—the
maids who took turns caring for Charlotte twenty-four hours a day.
They were headed by Julie Doyen, who had served the queen for
a long time before she was reassigned to Charlotte. Last was Baron
Goffinet, chief of the empress's household, who did not reside at
Tervuren because he had other responsibilities, but who remained
in charge of this little society, settling their arguments and making
the important decisions. The opinion was unanimous: the gates of
hope had closed; the empress would never recover. To make matters worse, her physical health had never been better, and she was
resplendent with beauty, much more so than she had been before
she went insane.

The Austrians, who never gave up, sent a spy to Brussels, where all
doors were opened to her. The spy was a notorious gossip and in-
triguer, Charlotte's aunt Princess Clementine of Orleans, the wife

of a Saxe-Coburg prince who was living in Vienna and was loyal to Francis-Joseph. She demanded to see her niece the moment she arrived in Brussels. Marie-Henriette could not refuse the interview, but she sent Goffinet a long list of precautions to take. She knew full well that Aunt Clementine was hostile toward the Belgian royal family, whom she, with the Habsburgs, had accused of cruelly incarcerating Charlotte. The risk was that Aunt Clementine would offer Charlotte the option of returning with her to Austria. Marie-Henriette recommended revealing as little as possible, since Aunt Clementine was dangerously curious and knew how to make people talk. She almost hoped that Charlotte would have a crisis during Aunt Clementine's visit, just to prove her condition: "The king said that if there were a scene in her presence, it would be good for all of us, and it would be better still if the aunt could get a nice dressing-down from our dear, august sister." Unfortunately for Marie-Henriette, there would be neither a scene nor a dressing-down—the visit went off without incident.

But Marie-Henriette's affection and concern never flagged. Not only did the queen frequently come to visit her sister-in-law, but she also had word sent to her of Charlotte's condition on a daily basis. For example, she learned that Charlotte was being obstinate, refusing to be dressed or have her hair fixed by the chambermaids, and demanding instead that butlers do the job. It was a horrible scandal when she forced men to put her to bed. But the alienists said that if they stood in the way of her wishes, the empress would not go to bed at all, and would walk through the castle all night, barefoot and in a nightgown, which could have given her a pulmonary infection. If they tried to force her into bed, she might have a "cerebral congestion," perhaps even "a hastened end": "We are dealing with the daughter of a king and the sister of a king and queen." So, the alienists concluded, let's give her the butlers if she wants them so much.

❊   ❊   ❊

During these years, Europe was violently shaken. In Spain, Queen
Isabella II was overthrown by General Prim, the same man who
had commanded the Spanish squadron in Mexico just before Maximilian's arrival, and who had written that most lucid and pessimistic
report on Maximilian's chances. Finding a replacement for the de-
posed queen created a crisis throughout Europe. As Charlotte had
foreseen in her insane ramblings, France was in great danger, since
the candidacy of a German prince had brought about the Franco-
Prussian War. France was defeated, the empire was overthrown,
Napoleon III was the Prussians' prisoner, and Empress Eugenie was
on the run. Soon Paris fell into the hands of the Commune.

During the clashes, a patrol of armed men from the Commune
came across a frightened banker: "Who are you?"

"I am Swiss, my name is Jecker."

It was the same banker who, twenty years before, had issued
the bonds covering the Mexican loan, and who had involved the
French in the affair and brought about their intervention. One of
the men from the Commune knew about him. "You're the one to
blame for all the bad things that happened!" he said, and Jecker
was thrown up against the wall and shot.

Once the Prussians freed him, Napoleon III joined Eugenie
in exile in England, but he soon died painfully. The only one left
was his only son, the imperial prince, his mother's pride and joy,
whom Charlotte had known as a boy. A few years later, he was killed
by Zulu spears in South Africa. Napoleon III and Eugenie had
brought down misfortune on Charlotte and Maximilian, and now
misfortune had come to them.

The fall of the second empire brought the Orleans back to France with
their fortune restored, and the hope of seeing the monarchy rees-

tablished. In the midst of all these changes, they did not forget their niece Charlotte, and frequently inquired after her health. In November 1870, Leopold II admitted to them that Charlotte would not speak to anyone anymore, that she let no one into her room, and that she did her morning routine, made her bed, and cleaned her room on her own now. Whatever objects she might need had to be left outside her door.

She was suffering from "a certain indisposition, a problem" that was worsening her mood. The doctors prescribed a tartar cream to slip into her jam so that she would not detect it and once again scream that she had been poisoned. During the violent attacks that seized her, some of the fantasies she wrote about in her letters to Loysel actually came true. She struggled with the alienists and the domestics, revealing a physical strength no one had imagined in her: "I have received enough kicks and punches from the empress," one of them admitted, "and I have held her down often enough to feel how strong she is and not be afraid of it, but what I am afraid of is getting her angry, because that has an effect on her brain, and shows as a decrease of intelligence, which tends to worsen over time."

One morning, servants cleaning out the ashes from the salon's heater found two desk trimmings among them, one of bronze and malachite, the other of gilded bronze studded with garnets and turquoise, as well as a frame that had contained a miniature of Maximilian. In a fit of rage, Charlotte had broken them.

As these crises continued, her entourage's pessimism deepened. Charlotte's favorite lady-in-waiting, Marie Moreau, was convinced that the sad illness would not only never go into remission, but would also "follow its course toward a fateful end." At the same time, her staff did notice certain improvements: "Her Majesty is forgetting herself a lot less often, and is returning to the modesty it was so painful to see her neglect." If the nights were generally good, despite the bouts of insomnia interspersed with incoherent talk and shouting, Charlotte took advantage of the darkness to perform "acts that may be qualified as unsuitable," and the alienists underscored that they must at all costs help the empress cease "these morbid manifestations before they degenerate into a habit essentially harmful to the august patient's health."

Despite the insanity's inevitable progression, the decision was made to forgo certain precautions that had been taken at the beginning of her stay. The alienists had had a padded room set up at Tervuren, where they could lock the patient up in case of an attack of violence. Marie Moreau took joy in announcing to Marie-Henriette that the room was to be dismantled; she was so enthusiastic that she asked the queen for permission to use the stuffing from the padding to make mattresses for the poor.

Ten years passed in this way. Charlotte was moved to Tervuren in the spring of 1869; it was now the end of the winter of 1879. She was thirty-nine years old. Once a glamorous celebrity whose lifestyle was the envy of Europe and Mexico, Charlotte now watched the years go by in the dull grayness of an endless routine punctuated only by the same small events occurring with merciless repetition.

14

On March 5, 1879, Marie Moreau's maid had woken up early. It was barely five o'clock in the morning, and outside, the sky was pitch black. She went to the window and, as always, looked up to her mistress's apartments. Smoke was pouring out of a ground-floor window. She immediately sounded the alert. It turned out that the laundresses had stayed until late the night before, and had forgotten to put out the oven when they had left. It had burned all night long against a thick beam, and fire had broken out just beneath Charlotte's suite. The servants woke Madame Moreau, who threw on a raincoat over her nightgown and ran to Charlotte's rooms. The drawing room was already filled with smoke. She woke the empress, who refused to budge. "Madame, please, come."

The empress saw the smoke through the doorway. "That should not be, that should not be," she repeated over and over. Madame Moreau tried to convince Charlotte to escape. She wanted to dress her, but the clothes she took off the night before had all burned in the finery room. There was no time to look for anything else. One of the maids ran into her own bedroom next door and grabbed her own clothes, which they nearly had to force Charlotte into. Doctor Hart and Madame Moreau helped Charlotte down the stairs. The doctor handed her over to one of the women on call, Miss Muzer, and said, "Take her to my house in the village."

Miss Muzer led Charlotte, who was half dressed and wearing slippers, through the park. It was cold, but luckily there was no fog or rain. The village was at least a half hour's walk away. All the villagers had been alerted and were awake. Miss Muzer brought the empress into the doctor's little house, but Charlotte did not want to miss the spectacle. She went back onto the street and headed toward the medieval gate. The tall trees were blocking the view; she could not see a thing. She turned to Miss Muzer and declared, "The fire is over—let's go back to the castle." Miss Muzer had no choice but to obey.

Suddenly, a small coach pulled by a single galloping pony pulled up. Queen Marie-Henriette, informed by Baron Goffinet, had grabbed a butler, jumped in the first vehicle she had found, and flown to her sister-in-law's rescue. "You can't stay here, Charlotte, come with me," she ordered. Charlotte complied, but before she got into the coach, she turned around and took a long look at the castle, now ravaged by fire. "It is serious, very serious, but it is beautiful," she said several times. Just then, the entire roof collapsed into the blaze, and huge flames, now liberated, flew into the sky. Charlotte moved back. "Let's go," she said with a trembling voice. The only problem was that the little coach could not fit three people. The butler climbed down and Marie-Henriette took the reins herself.

Marie-Henriette was afraid that Charlotte would fall out of the light coach during the trip, so under the pretext of protecting her from the cold, she wrapped her in a shawl that she tied to the iron body of the coach. The queen of Belgium and the empress of Mexico headed off alone toward Laeken in the first light of dawn. When they arrived, Charlotte refused to rest even for a minute. She left immediately for a walk in the park, and as she looked around, she mumbled, "Yes, here are a few old memories."

When morning came, all that was left of Tervuren was four blackened walls. The castle would have to be razed. The members of Charlotte's household came later that day to move into Laeken; the rest of the royal family, meanwhile, prudently stayed at the royal palace in Brussels.

The simple fact of being back in the familiar surroundings of her childhood markedly improved Charlotte's condition. She took walks in the park and read more and more. As she became increasingly active, she began making bandages for the wounded. Miss Muzer was teaching her to play the piano, and far from fleeing society, Charlotte now went out of her way to see people. She even agreed to have her meals with her ladies and her doctors, which she had always refused to do at Tervuren. Her nieces, King Leopold's daughters, came to play with her in the park. The youngest one in particular, little Clementine, so struck her with her beauty that she nicknamed her Jewel.

Yet the fire at Tervuren had affected Charlotte, to the point that, as they were reciting the "Our Father" together, Marie Moreau noticed that instead of "and deliver us from evil," Charlotte said, "and deliver us from fire."

Nonetheless, despite her improvement, the royal family did not think it wise for the incurably ill woman to stay too long in their home. They very quickly found a castle near Laeken, called Bouchout, which just happened to be for sale. Leopold II soon bought the castle from its owner, Count Beaufort, and added to it the adjoining property of Meysse that another aristocrat sold him.

On April 5, 1879, after a little more than a month's stay at Laeken, a procession of court coaches brought Charlotte and her household to Bouchout Castle, where she was to reside from then on. In its beginnings, Bouchout Castle had been an imposing medieval fortress. A part of it had since been knocked down, and the entire property had been restored and redesigned in the nineteenth century, so that it had lost its forbidding atmosphere and taken on the feel of Sleeping Beauty's castle, just perfect for Charlotte. Big towers surrounded a graveled courtyard, where in springtime, laurels and palm trees were planted in neat rows. The castle looked as if it stood on the water of a pond, an illusion which at first had been a means of defense. The pond had since become a habitat for all sorts of different birds. Near the entrance, prairies dotted with centuries-old trees rose up toward the beautiful commons, and, further on, toward the hothouses. On the other side, an English garden stretched out, crisscrossed by paths meandering around the groves. As one wandered through the park, one would find little bridges spanning brooks, sudden views of the castle, and cheerfully dipping branches. Right at the gates of Brussels, Bouchout seemed a place forgotten by time, an enchanted domain no one would ever want to leave—provided it was not her prison.

During the 1830s, the former landlords had decorated the interior entirely in the Troubadour and neo-Gothic styles. Everywhere was a mass confusion of ribbed arches, escutcheons, coats of arms, mullioned windows, and suits of armor, with here and there a few authentic leftovers from the Middle Ages. Almost none of this typical décor has survived until today, but there is still enough of it left to reveal one curious detail. The successive landlords of Bouchout all left their marks in endlessly repeated coats of arms, but not a single monogram, not a single imperial crown or emblem serves to remind the visitor of Maximilian or Charlotte. Her presence left no trace . . . except for her often-sighted ghost.

Though it is heavy with the tragic spirit of the empress of Mexico, the castle has nothing sinister about it. Rather, it is welcoming and warm, as if Charlotte had wanted the modern visitor to feel at home there.

Before Charlotte moved in, Marie-Henriette and Goffinet had come several times to the castle to make sure every detail was in order. They wanted Charlotte to live there in comfort, and also to make sure that there could never be the sort of fire there that had annihilated Tervuren Castle. Goffinet had written endless reports on the conditions of the fireplaces, the heating system, the risks of fire, and the measures to be taken to avoid them.

Charlotte's existence continued to follow the same unchanging schedule as it had in Tervuren. As the alienists had dictated, she woke early and went to bed early. The amusement—reading, weaving, piano, and strolls—never varied. As one of her ladies-in-waiting told it, "Monday: there is a torrential rain, impossible to go out. Her Majesty takes a bit long getting dressed. She is unhappy because we tell her so. After lunch, Her Majesty looks at engravings with the colonel while I sing. We organize the flower arrangements. Her Majesty is interested in what we are doing. She is thrilled to have new plants for her gardens. A long walk after dinner, her mood is gentle and good. . . ."

In this monotony, the slightest occurrence became a great event. One day, for example, someone brought a gramophone to Bouchout and put a record on. Struck dumb with astonishment, Charlotte came closer and examined the machine at length. She observed the head butler as he wound the handle. When the record stopped, she shouted, "More, more!" From then on, she wanted to hear the gramophone every day. Whenever she was nervous, all anyone had to do was put on a record to see a smile widen and relax her features.

Similarly, the annual cleaning of the castle, featuring the novelty of a vacuum cleaner, was a fascinating spectacle, at least until Charlotte became upset with the workmen's slowness. She would look askance at them and snip, "I think that will be all now."

Charlotte continued to love everything that was beautiful and refined, demanding and obtaining only the best quality. Her clothes were of finely cut, pale silks, her lingerie decorated with the most delicate lace. She liked the inlaid furniture and brocade drapes that proclaimed her as the descendent of great patrons of the arts.

Because she broke an inordinate number of plates, someone had the brilliant idea to replace her gold-rimmed, monogrammed porcelain with ordinary white dishes. The day that Charlotte sat down to eat and noticed the new service, her royal blood boiled: "These white dishes, we will have none of it." She immediately smashed the offensive plate against the wall.

Despite her long periods of calm, Charlotte still fell victim to these attacks of violence, during which she eviscerated books, tore her skirts and trousers with her teeth, and broke whatever she found. One day, she stopped playing piano for a moment, ripped the score to shreds, and finished playing the piece flawlessly. Her faithful lady-in-waiting, Madame Moreau, sadly remarked in these crises "a tendency to cruelty that bursts out at the slightest provocation."

Often, around the dinner table, the empress struck, slapped, or scratched her guests, and she did not spare herself, as she banged her fists against her head or tore clumps of hair out of her scalp. Then she would calm down, take the ladle out of the soup, and as it dripped on her clothes, cradle it as if it were a baby.

❊   ❊   ❊

Time had no hold over Bouchout; it remained forever out of touch with the outside world. In 1888, there was no way for Charlotte to know that the parish priest of a Mexican village had died: his name was Father Fischer. This strange priest and dangerous adventurer, after pushing Maximilian on toward his tragic end, had "miraculously" escaped the anti-monarchist repression and returned to Europe. In Paris, he had found a job as a tutor for a noble Mexican family in exile. Then he had disappeared from all records until his humble death.

Soon afterward, one of the other major players in Maximilian's fate also died: Colonel Lopez. The word "traitor" had followed him his entire life. Strangely, the more republican and Juarist the Mexicans had become, the more they had accused Lopez of betraying the emperor. He had published his memoirs in an attempt to justify himself, but in vain, since no one believed him. Just as futilely, General Escobedo, who had only been able to capture the emperor with Lopez's help, revealed that Lopez had only acted on the express orders of the emperor himself. Whenever Lopez went into a tavern, everyone else got up and left. If he sat down in a theater, those around him would immediately rise. His sons had not been accepted into any boarding schools. One day, a little dog he particularly liked bit him. It had rabies, and he died of it, killed by the one he loved best.

Faithful Eloin, who had been imprisoned and released after his master's death, had come back to Europe, and had hastened to challenge Van der Smissen, also back in Belgium, to a duel. The combat had taken place without anyone getting hurt. Van der Smissen had continued his career in the Belgian military, eventually retiring with the rank of lieutenant general. Five years later, he inexplicably committed suicide. A month after that, the brother he had been living with for years did likewise, shooting himself in the head.

Nor did Benito Juárez take his victory with him to heaven. Although suspicions of poisoning surrounded his end, he seemed to have died of natural causes, and just in time, as his former general Porfirio Diaz was preparing to overthrow him. Diaz, who may as well have offered Mexico to Juárez on a silver platter, continued scheming and plotting throughout a career marked by aborted coups d'état and exiles. Though his fortunes fluctuated madly over the years, he eventually grabbed power in Mexico in 1876, and did not relinquish it until his death in 1872.

Of even greater consequence was the death of the heir to the empire of Austria-Hungary, Archduke Rudolph, Maximilian's nephew, who had married Charlotte's niece, Stephanie of Belgium, one of Leopold II's daughters. His death remains mysterious in its tragedy: his corpse was found with that of his mistress of the time, Marie Vetsera, in the Mayerling hunting lodge. As there was never any clue how the heir met his end, the most diverse and extravagant theories were bandied about. In his will, the archduke asked the man he most trusted to destroy his personal papers, which must have been revelatory: the man he chose for the job was none other than Bombelles, Maximilian's childhood friend and Charlotte's jailer.

Though he had been relieved of his position as Charlotte's guard for reasons of incompetence and cruelty, and after he had given the Belgians all sorts of evidence of his worthlessness, Emperor Francis-Joseph had named Bombelles governor of his only son and heir, Archduke Rudolph, then nineteen years old. The results of this decision were not long in coming. Bombelles had initiated, or at least encouraged, the young man along the path of debauchery. Rudolph's relatives, though they had grown disenchanted with Bombelles, had nonetheless kept him on in his position. He had even been named grand master of the archduke's court. He had also been the one to receive Rudolph and Stephanie at

Laxenburg Castle, where they had gone for their wedding night of a marriage that would soon prove disastrous. He was one of the few people in the world who knew the secret of Rudolph and Marie Vetsera's relationship, and thus he was the only one to possess the key to the Mayerling mystery.

In thanks for his role in the tragedy, suspicious at best, Bombelles was named admiral. How can it be explained that a man with such a shady past was able to climb the ladder so well, winning every honor in the process? The same question that hovered above the Miramar incident now returned with a vengeance: why would Francis-Joseph never dare touch Bombelles?

Six months after the Mayerling tragedy, Bombelles died of a heart attack during an orgy with two prostitutes. In his will, he bequeathed his entire fortune to one of them.

One day toward the end of the century, Leopold II and Marie-Henriette brought their daughter Stephanie, Rudolph's widow, to see Charlotte. Though her aunt had so impressed her with her intelligence and beauty when she was a little girl, Stephanie had not seen Charlotte in years. A coach brought the three from Laeken to Bouchout. When they arrived, they found the empress's household lined up in the courtyard to greet them. The ladies-in-waiting led the visitors up to the second floor, where Charlotte was expecting them in her suite. Stephanie was surprised by her aunt's looks. Though frighteningly pale, Charlotte had retained all her beauty. Her features were still just as delicate and fine, with a gentle melancholy hardened by innate authority.

Stephanie rushed forward to kiss her hand, and Charlotte lifted her to her feet and kissed her. They took their seats in the little drawing room, and Charlotte began to speak in an uninterrupted flood of words and incoherent sentences. Suddenly she turned to

Stephanie and stared at her with her dark eyes filled with all the sadness in the world. "So you have just come from Austria, dear child—how is your father-in-law the emperor?"

Without waiting for a reply, she stood up, taking Stephanie by the hand, and led her before a full-length portrait of Maximilian. Charlotte performed a long court curtsy before the painting, and said, "And they killed the other one." Stephanie's eyes welled up with tears.

To get her mind off the painful memories, Marie-Henriette tried to change the subject. "Charlotte, would you mind playing us something? We would so love to hear you at the piano."

Charlotte obeyed, and Stephanie was astounded by the perfection of her skill. Music and painting had always been the empress's favorite pastimes.

After the musical interlude, Charlotte brought her visitors back downstairs to the castle chapel. It was a hollow recess under one of the towers. Delicately ribbed arches met at a point under a decorated keystone in all the colors of the Troubadour style. Charlotte knelt and lost herself in prayer, surrounded by her family.

Stephanie would never forget that beautiful and tragic woman, that aunt who filled her with the fear that the insane alone never fail to inspire.

As time passed, the alienists' reports shrank to the same few words: "Everything is fine, the year was good." Though the reports were always addressed to the king or queen, the bearers of these titles changed. Death came first to Marie-Henriette, who passed on in August 1902 in melancholy and solitude, with Goffinet as her only company. Then it was Philippe's turn, and finally Leopold II's. From then on, the "Majesties" mentioned on the reports' envelopes would be Albert I and Queen Elisabeth, named after her aunt, the empress of Austria.

❖   ❖   ❖

Leopold II's death had raised a shiver of impatient anticipation in his daughters and heirs, all of whom were counting on the windfall of their father's fortune, combined as it was with Charlotte's and her brother's. But for decades, the old king had been investing heavily in the project he held dearest to his heart: namely, the Belgian Congo. Honest collaborators had long ago warned Marie-Henriette in the direst terms: "Madam, the king is going to be ruined. No amount of money could cover what your husband is planning. . . . The king will be ruined, and he will be ruined for good." The king no longer listened to her, and she could do nothing. Africa continued to swallow up millions.

Leopold II's will therefore struck his daughters with horror: "From my mother and father, I inherited fifteen million. I leave this sum to be divided among my children." Fifteen million was nothing compared to what they had expected! The deceased had also tacked on this mysterious sentence: "Due to my position and to the confidence of certain persons, large amounts of money at different times have passed through my hands, though they did not belong to me. . . ." Had he been thinking about Charlotte's sixty million, which he had been able to double? In any case, his own millions had disappeared, and his daughters could find no trace of them, despite intensive inquiries. As for Charlotte's money, no one, especially not her nieces, ever heard a word about it again.

The deaths in the family had been hidden from Charlotte in order not to upset her. And though she never asked for news of her family, somehow she knew everything. Young Albert I had barely begun to reign when she exclaimed, "To think I have a nephew who is still so young, already taking care of a throne . . . and people call him 'king'!" A short time later, on the very day that the newspapers mentioning the death of Philippe's widow, the countess of Flanders, were banned from the castle, Charlotte said, "I will die too someday, *miserere mei, Deus.*"

Mexico never left her thoughts, but her Mexico was the Mexico of the past—it was Maximilian. She did not know that Porfirio Diaz had assumed her husband's old mantle to become emperor of Mexico in all but name, combining Juárez's grim wisdom with Maximilian's panache. For thirty years, Don Porfirio had never once loosened his hold over the country, and slowly but surely, the former peasant had donned ever more ornate and embroidered uniforms, had surrounded himself and his beautiful wife Doña Carmelita with an ever more numerous court, and had ended up moving into Chapultepec, Maximilian and Charlotte's former castle. But the voices accusing him of oppressing the poor in favor of the rich grew louder and louder, and in the 1930s, the leftist painters Diego Rivera and Siqueiros would depict the atrocities of his regime in murals covering hundreds of square feet. He was finally overthrown in 1911; his strong-arm order was replaced by the blood-drenched chaos of Pancho Villa, Zapata, and other bandits whom cinema would transform into heroes. Curiously, Porfirio Diaz had not granted the Mexican oil concession to the Americans, but they were able to obtain it anyway in the chaos that followed his downfall.

At Bouchout, the Feast of the Holy Eucharist was a break in the normal routine. Charlotte's entourage had decided to have the procession pass through the park so that Charlotte could see it. The experiment started off poorly. When the priest placed the Holy Eucharist in the chapel which opened out onto the drawing room, Charlotte ran to the stairwell and hid in her suite. An alienist managed to bring her back down, and she watched the rest of the procession calmly and attentively. It was June 1914.

Two months later, war broke out: the Germans invaded Belgium. Despite a heroic resistance, the sadly courageous little country could not long withstand the savage attack. The Belgian royal family did not leave the country, but retreated to a tiny stretch of beach at La Panne, which the Germans would never manage to capture. The thunder of war swept over Bouchout. Charlotte's people had to deal with requisitions, and were forced to set up a dispensary in the commons; most of all, they had to take measures to defend against the marauders wreaking havoc throughout the countryside.

The first order of business: keep Charlotte away from outside events, do not speak of them to her under any circumstances, and prevent her from seeing any newspapers. As it happened, the empress was having one of her good periods; her personality was charming, her health was excellent, and she was sleeping wonderfully. Several times, however, the others heard her mumble the word "war." Then came this declaration—"everyone is seeing red"—and at last, most explicitly: "The border is black, very black, we must not hand over our prisoners." As usual, she saw everything, despite all precautions.

At the end of August 1914, the war had reached the gates of Bouchout. Battles were raging all around the castle. German soldiers were spreading terror throughout the region, and the wounded were everywhere. The feared Uhlans, as the German soldiers were called, reached the ceremonial gate; the shots they fired at the castle whistled past the governor's ears. He decided to bring Charlotte, along with her ladies-in-waiting and personnel, down into the castle's cellars. They stayed there for two hours. Luckily, the storm headed away, and dinner was held as usual, though the diners could distinctly hear the thunder of cannons in the distance. The Uhlans had cut the telegraph lines, but they had not come into the castle, since the governor had had the presence of mind to hoist the Austrian flag. Whatever the situation may have been, Charlotte was still the wife of an archduke who was the brother of the emperor, who in turn was the kaiser's ally.

The words she mumbled prove that Charlotte was fully aware of the situation, but her mood remained unchanged. Her ladies-in-waiting, her doctors, and her help could not hide the fear they felt for their own families, and the anguish they had for their brutalized country. Sometimes, danger drew near. German troops invaded nearby Meysse Castle, where the governor and certain members of his household lived. They continued to respect Bouchout, but for how long? "The events do not seem to affect the empress in the least," wrote a member of Charlotte's entourage, or at least that is what her entourage would have liked to think. But no one could have explained this prophetic sentence Charlotte uttered: "It will be a final catastrophe, sir, and one that will not come all at once, but little by little."

As the situation in occupied Belgium stabilized, the Germans agreed to take into consideration the fact that a member of the Austrian imperial family was living at Bouchout, and they proposed sending an honor guard from Brussels. Politely but firmly, the governor of Bouchout declined.

The terrible occupiers slowly metamorphosed into vacationing tourists. One day, Charlotte's personnel found a hapless Uhlan in the courtyard. Another day, the duke and duchess of Ratibor showed up at the front gates with their sister-in-law, Princess Oettingen, trying to catch a glimpse of the curiosity Charlotte had become. Finally, Charlotte did not suspect that Emperor Francis-Joseph had sent a special train to Miramar to empty out the castle and bring all its contents back to Vienna. Furniture, baubles, paintings, and books disappeared, but also files that would be swallowed up into the imperial archives once they had been duly censored.

The twentieth century had come up with new inventions that war soon made deadly. That was how Charlotte discovered the existence of airplanes. As they flew over Bouchout, German planes dropped shell after shell on the park, which made quite an impression on the empress. One day, she summoned one of her ladies-in-waiting; when she was a little too long in coming, Charlotte shouted angrily, "Well, let her come in an airplane then."

At dawn one day in October 1917, soldiers were getting ready for an execution in the trenches of Vincennes: Julio Sedano y Leguizano had been born fifty years earlier in Mexico. Without a job or money, he had come to France, where a rich Mexican had offered him his protection. He had gotten married and started his own business, which had soon gone bankrupt. Poverty had forced him to offer his services to the highest bidder. The German spy network had hired him, for he knew Paris well, and had important relations there. For two years, he had handed over the most important French military secrets to the enemy, but counterintelligence had finally discovered the trick of his invisible handwriting, and his letters had been intercepted and deciphered. Just as he was preparing to send off another letter chock full of information, he was arrested at the post office. Despite the flair with which he defended himself in court, he was still sentenced to death. He refused a chair, and listened to the verdict standing. He also refused a blindfold, preferring to see the firing squad when he died—just as bravely as had his father. For, according to him, he was the son of Concepcion, the *India bonita* from Olvido, Maximilian's "mistress" at Cuernavaca. For his entire life, Julio had proclaimed himself Maximilian's illegitimate son, and had never stopped mentioning the resemblance between them.

The end of the First World War went by unnoticed at the castle, just like the death of the Austrian empire and the exile of the Habsburgs, now ruined and hunted down. Trieste had become part of Italy, and Miramar had been passed on to the crown of Italy.

After their triumphant return to their liberated capital, King Albert and Queen Elisabeth could finally visit their aunt Charlotte. The park was being cleared of the debris of war, including German projectiles of the most dangerous sort, containing asphyxiating gas, which luckily had never gone off.

But the war's consequences went on. Just like the Austrian empire, the Russian empire collapsed. The Bolsheviks came to power and began a reign of terror of unheard-of proportions. Just like the predecessors they had murdered, they refused to give up Poland, which, though once a Russian possession, had been scheduled for liberation by the winners of the war. They squeezed the poor country in their bloody clutches. Their former allies reacted quickly: France sent troops, Warsaw was freed in no time, and the rest of Poland was liberated. The world thus learned the name of the French strategic mastermind, Maxime Weygand.

The reporters immediately took interest in him, and his past aroused their curiosity. Weygand was born on January 21, 1867, in Brussels, of an unknown father, but even more strangely, of an unknown mother. As they delved into the subject, the reporters discovered that a Belgian lawyer, acting as the agent of a mysterious third party, had paid for all his studies. Weygand seemed to enjoy some secret protection. Slowly but surely, the investigation led back to the Belgian court. Hypotheses abounded: could Weygand have had an illustrious background? Could he have been an illegitimate son of Leopold II, who produced a whole series of them during his long reign? If he was indeed the bastard son of the Belgian king, then everything fell into place: the mysterious birth, the secret protection, the bond with Belgium. In the autumn of 1920, the press leaked the rumor of Weygand's royal origins for the first time.

But the journalists did not leave the investigation at that; something in their hypothesis did not ring true. Was there not another member of the royal family who could be Weygand's father . . . or mother? There was only one possibility: the empress of Mexico, born Princess Charlotte of Belgium. Weygand had been born at the end of January 1867, which meant that he was conceived in May

1866. At that time, Charlotte was living almost completely separate from Maximilian. He had been frolicking with Indian women in Cuernavaca, while she had been locked up nearly alone in the palace in Mexico City. This was the time during which she had been disappearing on excursions to the Chalco lake. She had not been going alone. Overwhelmed by Maximilian's indifference, discouraged by the poor state of the empire, could she have let herself get carried away, and in her abandon, might she have gotten pregnant? Her ample dresses could easily have hidden a swollen stomach. And the seasickness she suffered during her entire trip across the Atlantic — was that not a sign? It could have been the fear of scandal that touched off her insanity. Her inexplicable internment at Miramar could have been imposed by the necessity of keeping the birth a secret. Weygand was said to have been born in Brussels, but there was no real proof of that. If he had been born at the Castelleto, faithful servants could have immediately brought the dangerous baby abroad.

If Charlotte was the mother, who could have been the father? The reporters dug through all documents relating to Maximilian and Charlotte's reign. One of them came across an old photograph of Van der Smissen, commander of the Belgian legion. He compared it with a photograph of Weygand, and the resemblance was uncanny. With both of them in uniform, it was impossible to tell which one was the father and which one the son. For Weygand's part, he had the honesty to admit his entire life that he knew nothing of his parents: "My birth remains a mystery to me," he said, over and over. But the hypothesis identifying his mother as Charlotte spread, and Weygand did nothing to stop it. Was he perhaps flattered by it?

Famous people believed the theory — among others, General Charles de Gaulle, who mentioned it even though he hated Weygand. The incredible resemblance between Weygand and Van der Smissen was a clue, but was hardly sufficient proof, and if Van der Smissen was indeed Weygand's father, that did not mean that Charlotte was his mother. The only thing that could be affirmed is that General Weygand's birth remained a mystery, and that in one way or another, the Belgian court was involved in it.

The letters and diaries of the royal family of Belgium and of the members of their most intimate circle did not once mention any pregnancy. The theory of Charlotte's poisoning, however, appeared immediately after her first onset of insanity. The rumor making her Weygand's mother only appeared in 1920–1921. As a particularly public, tragic, and childless couple, Maximilian and Charlotte had drawn attention to themselves and left the door open to all sorts of speculation.

Although Charlotte was now over eighty years old, her attacks of dementia remained violent. To cure them, she was given injections of camphor oil that made her horribly sick. The poor woman screamed, "Take them away, take them away, I will try to bear it alone!" Once the crisis had passed, the injections stopped, but not the memory of the injections. At the same hour of the day that the injections had been administered, Charlotte continued to scream, "Take them away, take them away!"

During her moments of lucidity, the empress knew that she was insane. One evening, as she was dawdling, one of her ladies tried to convince her to come to table. Charlotte remarked, "Do not pay any attention, sir, if I grow incoherent." This "sir" she was addressing was herself. And yet Charlotte accepted her insanity; it was her refuge, her true life, her way of escaping from disappointment, dissatisfaction, and the bitterness of reality, and to hide in her own world, where everything was beautiful. "The empress has never loved anyone," Madame Kuhacsevich had once confided in Queen Marie-Henriette, with all the venom of her hatred for Charlotte. But the opposite was true: no one had ever known how to love Charlotte. Insanity had allowed her to invent love in the person of Loysel, and motherhood in the silver ladle she cradled as she walked around the Bouchout dining room. It was in her insanity that she had discovered the desires of what a woman looked for most in the world: a lover and a child.

Insanity left no room in Charlotte for God. The return to religion she had begun upon receiving news of Maximilian's death had not taken root. She had refused to attend mass for months. One Sunday, like so many others, her people had convinced her to come down for the service, only to watch her recoil from the duty she most hated. "Your Majesty, we must hurry, the priest is waiting for us."

"If there is such a rush, the priest can come up here," she answered drily. And yet the problem did worry her; she was heard saying to herself, "You have lost your way, Charlotte, you have forgotten that God is eternal."

Charlotte had been a prisoner of her insanity for over fifty years, but even that was unable to lessen the weight of age anymore. She wanted to believe that she no longer had much time to live, and it was with hope that she announced to herself, "Sir, death is approaching." But the poor woman was mistaken—for death was claiming everyone around her, but it refused to take her. She was condemned to life, locked away in the solitude of madness.

Her family continued to visit her. She always favored her niece Clementine, who had with time become a great, even magnificent woman, married to the heir of the Bonapartes, Prince Napoleon. King Albert and Queen Elisabeth brought along their own children, the future Leopold III, Prince Charles, and Marie-José, who would one day become the queen of Italy. Despite Charlotte's gracious reception, they remained huddled together in a corner, somewhat intimidated, especially when she took a watering can and carefully began to water the flowers stitched into the carpet.

She had them participate in a strange liturgy, perhaps recreating her departure for Mexico. She brought the children to the edge of the pond surrounding the castle. The ritual had them dip one foot in the water and pull it out. Then, she put the children in a boat with her, took the oars, and rowed away from land. The parents let her do as she wished, though not without concern, since on the shore, they had posted lifeguards ready to jump into the water at the slightest alert. Charlotte had looked at them in surprise, saying, "Why are there so many soldiers?"

For her visitors, the insane empress had become a living monument. She had survived everything, both personal and worldwide disasters. Born under Louis-Philippe in 1840, she was now nearing the 1930s. More precisely, it was the end of 1925. Charlotte was barely eating. She shut herself off more and more from the rest of the world, without violence, but gloomily, and she no longer smiled. As her lady-in-waiting wrote, "It is not very much fun." Her silences stretched out ever longer. "Her Majesty wants only one thing—for everyone to leave her alone," it was said, but death continued to elude her. She lamented, "Yes, sir, we are old, we are stupid, we are insane."

Instead of gladdening her entourage, her tame resignation only worried them, for it meant that Charlotte was giving up on life. So close to her final hour, her prodigious past came back to her, and Maximilian appeared, larger than life: "For our husband, we have an eternal longing. We had an eternal affection for him. He is . . . in History."

At the end of 1926, a paralysis of the legs forced Charlotte to take to bed, and deprived her of the strolls in the park she had so enjoyed. She recovered, but not completely. "The empress is not regaining her strength and progress is slow. Her Majesty contents herself with taking a few steps around her suite from time to time, but she needs help getting out of an armchair." The diagnosis was a general weakening of her body and a pulmonary infection. But what was actually happening was that she was willing herself to die. "It is all finished and will come to nothing." That was her farewell, so enigmatic and yet so clear at the same time.

On January 19, 1927, at seven o'clock in the morning, she passed on. The prediction she had made upon leaving Miramar had come true. She had had to wait sixty years to see Maximilian again, sixty years of insanity.

As soon as she was dead, Bouchout Castle, which for so long had been an impenetrable fortress, opened its doors wide, and the people of the vicinity were allowed to pass before Charlotte's deathbed to pay their last respects. Wearing a lace bonnet, she was holding rosary beads in her crossed hands, placed peacefully atop the bedsheet. Her nearly wrinkleless face had maintained its admirable delicacy and perfect bone structure. From her wrist hung a charm bracelet with jeweled medallions. Inside each stone was painted the eye of someone she had loved: her parents, her grandmother Marie-Amelie, her brothers, Maximilian.

The solemn burial took place three days later. A snowstorm began just as the hearse left the castle, led by the guard's cavalry and surrounded by soldiers. The huge apparatus overflowing with black feathers made its way along the path, pulled by six black horses through the thick flakes, leaving black tracks behind it in the virgin snow.

SOURCES

There are several good biographies of Empress Charlotte. The best by far is the one written by Countess Reinach Foussemagne, published during Charlotte's lifetime, and containing many otherwise unpublished and important letters. It is also essential to read the biographies by Count Corti, Mia Kerckvoorde, André Castelot, and Joan Haslip. Finally, Laurence Van Ypersele did a wonderful job in publishing and analyzing some of the letters Charlotte wrote when under the full influence of her insanity. Another portion of her correspondence was published in Spanish by Luis Weckmann. It is just as indispensable to read *Maximiliano Intimo* by José-Luis Blasio, his butler.

Those who participated in the Mexican expedition, soldiers for the most part, published abundant memoirs, which, though not containing essential information on Maximilian and Charlotte, do evoke the atmosphere of the times.

But above all, I had the chance to be granted access to archives of the utmost importance that remain for the most part unpublished. First of all, there are those now located at the University of Texas at Austin, which contain more than three hundred letters from the correspondence between Maximilian and Charlotte that have somehow or other ended up there. The Royal Archives of Belgium at the royal palace contain in particular the writings of Goffinet, which have only now begun to be explored.

Finally, certain members of the royal family still possess essential documents. From these sources, I have quoted numerous excerpts of letters from Charlotte to her father and brothers, reports written by Queen Marie-Henriette, notes from Baron Goffinet, and lastly, letters Charlotte wrote in her insanity.

ACKNOWLEDGMENTS

I deeply thank all those who helped me write this work. Without them, I would never have been able to complete it.

Albert and Paola, Aunt Liliane, Esmeralda, Ella, Micky, Margherita and Crista, Isabelle L., her sister Birky, and Isabelle W.

Olivier Nouvel, Sébastien, Madame de Crépy, Olivier O., Gilles, Alexandra B., Francisco, Thérèse-Marie, and Patrick.

Mr. Gustav Janssens, director of the Royal Archives, M. P. Borremans from the National Garden of Belgium, Joseph Cahoon of the University of Texas at Austin, Thierry de Neuville, Dottoressa Rosella Fabiani, Baron Stackelberg, and Doctor Guérin.

Guillermo Tovar de Teresa, Feodora de Rosethweig-Diaz, Margarita Chavez, Mercedes Iturbe, Patricia Perez Walters, Lizandra Salazar, Señor y Señora Conde, Juan Urquiga, and Olivia Alvila.

And of course, Marina.